Chaos at the Crossroads

CHAOS AT TH

CROSSROADS

CHAOS AT THE CROSSROADS
by Frank McDonald and James Nix

Published by Gandon Books, an imprint of
Gandon Distribution Ltd.

ISBN 0948037 13X hb / 0948037 148 pb

design   John O'Regan (© Gandon, 2005)
production   Nicola Dearey
                              Gunther Berkus
photographs   The Irish Times
           (addit. photographs individually credited)
maps   Irish Times Studio
graphics   Claw Design (www.claw.ie)
               (Ronan McDonnell, Olly O'Neill)
other illustrations   individually credited
printing   Betaprint, Dublin
distribution   Gandon Distribution

GANDON BOOKS
Oysterhaven, Kinsale, Co Cork, Ireland
tel / fax   +353 (0)21–4770830 / 4770755
e-mail   gandon@eircom.net
web-site   www.gandonbooks.com

Gandon is grant-aided by The Arts Council /
An Chomhairle Ealaíon.

frontispiece – The uglification of Ireland: at Muckinish,
on the road to Ballyvaughan, Co Clare, the centuries-old
setting of a medieval castle is despoiled by townhouse-
style holiday homes and industrial sheds

Contents

List of Supporters

The authors and publisher would like to thank the following individuals and companies who have generously supported this publication:

Anon
David Arnold
Bloxham Stockbrokers
Bruce Shaw Partnership
CB Richard Ellis Gunne
Colliers Jackson-Stops
Hooke & MacDonald
Horwath Bastow Charleton
HT Meagher O'Reilly
HWBC Chartered Surveyors
Jones Lang LaSalle
KPMG
John Lally
Lisney
Manor Park Homebuilders Ltd
WK Nowlan & Associates Ltd
Sharon Ó Buachalla,
      Lease Plan (Ireland)
Brian O'Farrell
Sherry FitzGerald Group
Sisk
TileStyle Ltd
Ulster Bank Property Finance

Acknowledgements

A lot of people have helped us put this book together. Some of those who assisted most cannot be named because of the positions they occupy, but we are extremely grateful to them.

We would like to express our gratitude to John O'Regan and Nicola Dearey of Gandon Editions for the speed with which they handled many changes to the text; Geraldine Kennedy, Editor of the *Irish Times*, for allowing us to quote from articles in the newspaper, and Peter Thursfield, the paper's Picture Editor, for supplying many of the photographs. Though not individually credited, they were taken by a superb team of photographers that includes Alan Betson, Cyril Byrne, Brenda Fitzsimons, Matt Kavanagh, Eric Luke, Dara MacDonaill, Frank Miller, Bryan O'Brien and David Sleator. We also want to thank Tony Cerasi, head of the Irish Times Studio, for maps and other illustrations, Martyn Turner for his cartoons, and Francis Bradley, John Cassidy, Conor Goodman, Derek Grant, Siobhán Hargis, Shay Kenny, Mairín McGrath, John Maher, Esther Murnane, Patsey Murphy, Kevin O'Hare, Kevin O'Sullivan, Liam Reid, Paul Scott and Irene Stevenson, all from the *Irish Times*, for the help they provided.

Others we wish to acknowledge include Diarmuid Collins and Patrick Cosgrave of An Bord Pleanála, and Harry Cullen of the National Roads Authority. We are also grateful to a number of architects for their assistance, including Jim Barrett, Brian Brennan, Gerry Cahill, Felim Dunne, John Graby, Paul Keogh, Feargus McGarvey, Alan Mee, John Meagher, Joan O'Connor, Shane O'Toole, Tony Reddy and Derek Tynan.

Many others need to be thanked for their help and/or encouragement: Richard Barrett, Edel Bhreathnach, Trish Brazil, Jude Byrne, Philip Cantwell, Shirley Clerkin, Shane Coleman, Thomas Cooke, Kevin Duff, Graham Egan, Joe Fenwick, Seán Finlay, Martin Fitzpatrick, Bernadette Gallagher, John Gormley, Derrick Hambleton, Richard Hannaford, Eoghan Harris, Jeff Harvey, Paul Hogan, Treacy Hogan, Robert Legg, Kevin Leyden, Ian Lumley, Liam McDonald, Fergal MacCabe, Ruadhan MacEoin, Bernard McHugh, Brenda McNevin, Ryan Meade, Nick Miller, Mike

Milotte, Paul Moley, Dermot Murray, Stephen Neylon, Catherine Nix, John Nix, Lisa Noonan, Stephen O'Farrell, Diarmuid Ó Gráda, Seán Ó Riordáin, Judy Osborne, Dan Pender, Paddy Prendiville, Eamon Ryan, Javier Saez, Mike Shanahan, Beth and Ken Sherrard, Lorna Siggins, Eamonn Slater, John Sweeney, Carolyn Swift, Fergal Tobin and Brian Yore.

Frank McDonald and James Nix
November 2005

Chaos at the Crossroads

1. Introduction

IT WAS LIKE *A TALE OF TWO CITIES*. THE AUDIENCE IN THE OLD SYNOD HALL ON Dublin's Christchurch Place for the Young Environmentalists of the Year Awards in May 2002 could not have been more unlike the gathering in the Fianna Fáil tent at the Galway Races a few months later. Only Taoiseach Bertie Ahern was common to both. The Synod Hall, now trading as Dublinia, was full of enthusiastic, idealistic transition year students from all over Ireland. Smartly dressed in school uniforms, they were anxiously waiting to hear the adjudication results on their projects, all of which aimed to improve the environment. Three months later, the Fianna Fáil tent in Galway was a different animal entirely. Bigger than half a dozen haybarns, it was one of the most impressive structures at Ballybrit racecourse, accounting for nearly a third of its sprawling marquee village. This political mecca became, once again, a vehicle for making money from those who feel that Fianna Fáil is good for Ireland's, and their own, prosperity. For €350 a plate, guests got medallions of beef in a pepper cream sauce, and 'goodie bags' that included titanium golf balls billed as having 'optimum spin for maximum control'. Those who paid for the grub included some of the country's leading business people, notably big building contractors, property developers, auctioneers, estate agents and others with a stake in 'development'. They probably didn't realise that the Taoiseach had told the transition year students that sustainable development and a clean environment were 'fundamental' to his vision of Ireland. And if they had been aware, would it have made any difference?

But could Bertie Ahern's notion of 'sustainable development' be the same as the definition used by the World Commission on Environment and Development (the Brundtland Commission)? According to its 1987 report, *Our Common Future*, 'sustainable development is development that meets the needs of the present without compromising the ability of future generations to meet their own needs.' In other words, a balance must be struck between the resources used by this generation and those placed in reserve for the next. But that's not how the Taoiseach sees it. When

---

→ *Killenard, a rural area in Co Laois, has been swamped by unplanned development since 2000*

↑ *Taoiseach Bertie Ahern is offered money in the Fianna Fáil tent at the Galway Races*

one of the authors of this book put it to Paddy Duffy, his former special adviser, that Ahern's definition of sustainable development was 'development that has to be sustained', he replied: 'Exactly!' In other words, a rip-roaring pace of development was to be maintained at all costs, even at the expense of future generations – the polar opposite of what Brundtland had in mind. Yet in April 1997, before the general election of that year, Fianna Fáil pledged that 'protecting the environment will be the imperative consideration in every economic and planning decision that we make.' Though it had historically been 'the party of development', it now wanted to develop an economy that was 'both competitive and sustainable'. Not only that. There was to be a 'binding plan for sustainable development' from which no sector of the economy would have the right to opt out. The environment would have to be integrated into all areas of policy – not as an afterthought or as 'some form of window dressing'. There would also be a 'root and branch review' of all economic activities impacting on it. But although the party's policy document, *Our Environment – Our Future*, was said to have been produced in consultation with local councillors, it was hard to reconcile its benign approach with some of their activities on the ground – in particular, decisions made in defiance of clearly expressed public opinion.

Seven years on, Fianna Fáil had little to show for its 1997 environmental manifesto apart from the belated introduction, in March 2002, of the 15 cent levy on plastic bags. There was certainly no indication that the environment had been integrated into all areas of policy. The chickens were coming home to roost. In July 2004 the European Commission announced that it was taking another batch of legal actions against the Government for breaching EU directives on environmental protection. Though the Minister for the Environment was quick to point out that our record of 'transposing' EU directives into Irish law had been better than most, the real problem on the environmental front was actually implementing them. So the Commission is taking us to the European Court of Justice in seven cases involving breaches of directives relating to habitats, sewage treatment, water pollution, wildlife, waste management and two of failure to comply with previous rulings in other cases. As Dublin Labour MEP Proinsias De Rossa pointed out in a letter to the *Irish Times*, Ireland has one of the worst records when it comes to respecting EU environmental laws, with no less than 85 'first warnings' issued by the Commission in the five years to 2002. This was more than the number issued against Austria, Denmark, Finland, Luxembourg, the Netherlands and Sweden combined. And though Ireland accounts for just 1% of the EU population, it received twice as many first warnings as France, which has 15 times as many people.

The Commission accused Ireland of failing to protect nature and wild birds, failing to safeguard shellfish in Irish waters, failing to tackle illegal waste dumping, failing to ratify an EU directive on emissions-trading in time, and failing to stop the continued use of ozone-depleting pesticides on crops. The Commission also accused the Government of failing to protect Ireland's 'rich biodiversity' and of failing to deal adequately with 'unlawful, environmentally damaging waste operations, and to properly implement other EU laws aimed at providing Europe's citizens with a healthy environment'. On the issue of illegal dumping, Ireland is facing possible sanction by the European Court over 'unauthorised waste activities' between 1997 and 2001. And though the Commission accepted that some progress had been made in this area, such as setting up the Office of Environmental Enforcement, it said 'serious problems persist'. According to Margöt Wallström, then Environment Commissioner, full implementation of the directives from Brussels would ensure that Ireland protects its 'stunningly beautiful' natural environment. 'Ireland also has to continue to fight against illegal waste operations and clean up the damage they have created to give its citizens the quality of life they have the right to expect', she said.

Environmental consultant Shirley Clerkin, who is also An Taisce's natural environment officer, established that there were no less than 128 legal actions outstanding against Ireland at the end of 2003 for breaches of EU directives on the environment, while a further 85 complaints were still being assessed. In a report published by the Green Party in June 2004, Clerkin noted that proceedings against Ireland for infringing the 1985 Environmental Impact Assessment Directive had been lodged with the European Court, with a daily penalty of €21,600 proposed if the Government loses. In another case, also involving the EIA Directive, the Commission is seeking a daily penalty of €20,000 for continued non-compliance. Altogether, over the previous 10 years, the European Court issued nine judgments in environmental cases relating to breaches of EU directives on impact assessment, animal experiments, habitat nominations, sheep overgrazing, polluted drinking water, major accident hazards, biocidal products, nitrates and persistent pollution of shellfish waters.

July 2004 saw an oral hearing in Luxembourg on a long-running case involving the Tramore dump, in Martin Cullen's Waterford constituency, and whether it is being operated in breach of EU directives on waste management and habitat protection. Located in the mudflats and saltmarsh of Tramore's Backstrand, it was first the subject of an official complaint to the European Commission by Coastwatch Ireland 13 years ago. 'It is deeply shocking and outrageous that illegal landfilling of a Special Protected Area, a proposed Special Area of Conservation, a proposed Natural Heritage Area, and a wetland site protected under the RAMSAR international

↑ *Margöt Wallstrom, former EU Environment Commissioner: directives from Brussels would ensure that Ireland protects its 'stunningly beautiful' natural environment*

↓ *Karin Dubsky, Coastwatch: things would be much worse if we didn't have Europe trying to pull errant authorities into line*

Convention was deemed acceptable by the local authorities and the EPA', said the former Green Party MEP Patricia McKenna. But however slowly the wheels of justice turn in Luxembourg, Coastwatch's Karin Dubsky believes that things would be much worse if we didn't have Europe trying to pull our errant authorities into line. Indeed, the likelihood is that very little would be protected, not even the air we breathe or the water we drink, never mind the birds and the bees.

In April 2005 the European Court of Justice delivered its most damning indictment of Ireland's failure to comply with EU environmental legislation. As Denis Staunton reported, the court found that there had been a persistent flouting of rules on waste disposal, dating as far back as 1977. In particular, illegal dumping had been ignored. 'The Irish authorities have tolerated unauthorised activities in numerous places in Ireland, often over long periods, failing to require that those activities be brought to an end', the court said. 'Such a failure to fulfil obligations is general and persistent in nature.' In its case against Ireland, the European Commission noted that illegal waste sites in several parts of the country – notably Dublin, Louth, Wicklow and Waterford – were not the subject of effective enforcement action. These sites, including the notorious Tramore dump, would need to be cleaned up, and the Government was given three months to outline how it would comply with the court's ruling. If it failed to do so, fines of €20,000 *per day* would be imposed. Not only that, but because successive administrations since 1977 had blithely ignored their obligation to implement EU waste management directives, local authorities were facing a

↑ *A 1992 photograph of the Tramore dump, in Martin Cullen's Waterford constituency, first the subject of an official complaint to the European Commission by Coastwatch Ireland 13 years ago*

potential bill running into hundreds of millions of euro to clean up some 300 old dump sites throughout the country. Environment Minister Dick Roche saw the European Court's judgment as 'a very clear wake-up call that we have to get on with the job of providing waste infrastructure, including thermal treatment' – in other words, incinerators. He also issued the first-ever general policy directive under the 1996 Waste Management Act with a view to ensuring that the cost of cleaning up illegal dumps would be borne by the 'criminals' who created them.

An Taisce had predicted in March 2004 that Ireland would find itself hauled repeatedly before the European Court because of the Government's laissez-faire approach to environmental protection, lately highlighted by the new liberal regime on one-off housing in the countryside, which threatened a free-for-all. 'How can the Government's new rural housing guidelines be squared with sustainable land use and transport, greenhouse gas reduction, habitat protection and waste and water management – all now covered by EU directives?' it asked. The answer is that they can't. The new guidelines were specifically designed to make it much easier for people to build houses in the countryside, ostensibly to overcome an alleged battery of planning restrictions. Yet official figures showed that one-off houses in rural areas accounted for 43% of the 68,819 new homes built in the State in 2003 – up from 36%

Frank McDonald

in 2000. Housing output figures for 2004 were higher again, with nearly 76,954 new homes completed, setting a record for the tenth year in succession. Noel Ahern, Minister of State for Housing and Urban Renewal, hailed this as a 'tremendous achievement', saying it showed that measures to boost the supply of housing were producing results. Incredibly, a third of Ireland's total housing stock was built during the past decade to meet unprecedented levels of demand generated by population and economic growth, as well as changing patterns in migration and household formation. According to Maria Graham, principal officer in the housing section of the Department of the Environment, as Ireland's population grew by about 8% between 1996 and 2002, the real driver of demand was an 18% growth in the key household formation age group of 25-34. At the same time, the impact of population growth and social change, including marital breakdown and more elderly people living alone, means that Irish household sizes have been falling, from an average of 3.28 people per household in 1996 to 2.97 in 2002. Addressing the National Housing Conference in Limerick in May 2003, Graham said the key issue underpinning current housing policy was 'to deliver housing at levels to meet the overall demand and changing needs of a population, and to do this in a sustainable manner'. This is not happening, however. According to a study by the Economic and Social Research Institute, as many as a third of all new homes built since the late 1990s are out of reach of basic services such as shops, schools and sports facilities, except by car.

But anyone with their own home, particularly in Dublin, could luxuriate in the spectacular increase in property values since the mid-1990s. We congratulated ourselves when Ireland's GDP per capita outstripped Britain's for the first time in history, and the 'Irish model' of economic development was held up as an example to the rest of the world. Our new lifestyle, at least among the comfortable middle and upper classes, is characterised by conspicuous consumption of clothes, cars, eating out and holidays abroad. Sales of SUVs (sports utility vehicles) accounted for more than 6% of the market for cars in 2004 – up by a third on the previous year – while sales of people-carriers rose by 44%. According to the April 2005 Household Quarterly Survey by the Central Statistics Office, Irish people took 50% more holidays abroad in 2004 than they did just four years earlier, and even more significantly, the number travelling to holiday homes they own themselves – mainly on Spain's Costa del Sol – trebled between 2000 and 2004. As Kate Holmquist wrote: 'The once-a-year package to Marbella of 20 years ago has evolved into a sophisticated holiday portfolio. This may include visits to second and third homes abroad, in addition to winter weekends at the place "down the country" – a lifestyle unheard of for all but the perma-tanned, jet-setting elite in the 1980s.'

Who talks now about the bad old days? The 1980s saw Ireland teetering on the edge of national bankruptcy, and emigraton was reaching 45,000 a year. With so many people leaving, comparisons were being drawn to the 1950s when, as Dr TK Whitaker put it, there was an 'all-too prevalent mood of despondency about the country's future'. Before anyone knew it, the economy began to pick up. The turning point is hard to pinpoint, but by the mid-1990s things were ticking over nicely, and as the decade closed, they were flying. The key difference was that people were now staying, and even coming back, with the influx mirroring the outflow of a decade earlier. Ireland grew like a country which had been repressed for ages, enthusiastically embracing Parnell's declaration that 'No man has the right to set a boundary to the onward march of a nation. No man has the right to say: "Thus far shalt thou go, and no further".' By 2005 there were 1.9 million people at work – 56% more than in 1990 – while unemployment has been below 5% for years. Nowadays, the debate is largely about the precise rate of economic growth, and it is conducted knowing that our shirt doesn't depend on it. But the type of growth is what's now under the spotlight because this determines whether Ireland will move with a thunderous plod or a lively step as the 21st century rolls on. Most Irish politicians don't seem too bothered either way. For them, it's not about being able to grow sustainably in the future; compared to the next election, the next generation is irrelevant.

With projections that the total number of homes in 2020 could be double the number recorded in 1992, a countryside already blighted by haphazard housing will be annihilated if the proportion of one-offs continues to increase. What's happening on the ground is far from sustainable, not least in terms of water sources being contaminated by pollution from a proliferation of poorly maintained septic tanks. The doctors, lawyers and shopkeepers who were once quite content to live in towns began moving out in the 1960s, as homes in rural areas became more fashionable, even de rigeur, and left a trail of decay behind them. The upper floors of many urban buildings, once alive with families, have been turned over to storage or simply not used at all. Nearly every town in Ireland has its share of derelict buildings and sites crying out for rehabilitation – even in attractive small towns like Newport, Co Mayo, or Ramelton, Co Donegal. Urban decay of this type is the flip-side of Bungalow Blitz. And if this trend is allowed to persist, Irish towns are in danger of losing their most important feature – informal streetscapes formed by an accretion of buildings over time. But all the while, more and more new houses are being added to rural landscapes, gradually turning the countryside into an 'exurb'. Even those who thought they had finally 'got away from it all' or captured the perfect panoramic view will end up looking at other houses if the present rate of construction continues.

'Digger bucket teeth in stock', said a hand-scrawled sign outside a general store in Castlebar, Co Mayo, at the height of the building boom; what it was advertising was the arrival of steel dentures for JCBs whose original teeth had been worn out excavating sites for the Celtic Tiger economy. The sign said a lot about the type of development during the boom. So much new ground was being prepared that the pace of it all even took the digger-bucket stockist by surprise. As for what is being built, John Moriarty, a Kerry-born writer and mystic, once observed that the brashness of so many of these one-off houses suggests that their owners are 'taking revenge on the land' for all the years of foreign overlordship, poverty, dispossession and famine. This helps to explain why the Irish vernacular tradition of housing, particularly thatched cottages, has been so comprehensively rejected in favour of imported idioms derived from Spanish haciendas or the ante-bellum pastiche of Southfork, the

The flip-side of Bungalow Blitz
↑ *a derelict shop and house in Ramelton, Co Donegal*
↓ *a terrace of derelict houses in Newport, Co Mayo*

↑ *The way things were – a traditional farmhouse nestling in the west Cork countryside*
↓ *The way it is now – a 'McMansion' in west Cork, typical of the scale of houses now being built in the Irish countryside*

More 'McMansions'
↑ *on the Ennis-Lahinch road in Co Clare*
↓ *near Burt, Co Donegal*

Ewing home in *Dallas*. The latest phenomenon is what Tony Lowes, US-born founder of Friends of the Irish Environment, has dubbed 'McMansions' – larger and even more ostentatious than what went before, and usually plucked from the luxury end of pattern books like *Bungalow Bliss*. The threat to the landscape simply isn't seen because of a misplaced perception that this country is full of wide-open spaces, there for the taking, as if it was Oklahoma and someone had fired a starting gun. That's what prompted Lowes to declare as his mission to 'save Ireland from the Irish'.

Word is getting out. A highly negative feature in the *Guardian* magazine in December 2004 billed Ireland as 'The Concrete Isle'. According to the lengthy article, if tourists wanted 'a tamed landscape dotted with off-the-shelf mock-Georgian houses, congested with nose-to-tail traffic and suffused by an ugly suburban sprawl, then *céad míle fáilte* – welcome to Ireland ... This is the land of the bulldozer, where tarmac, churned-up mud and shopping malls are as likely to greet the visitor as historic castles and windswept bays. This land has been mauled by the Celtic Tiger ... and what's left is barely recognisable.' The article by Mark Lynas, author of *High Tide: News from a Warming World*, said readers should not be deceived by tourist-brochure images of 'mist-wreathed mountain vistas, wild open bogland and friendly, brightly painted little towns' because today's reality is so different. 'Ireland is used to violent change. Over the centuries scores of armies of conquest, from the Danish hordes to Oliver Cromwell, have left their brutal mark on this soft and beautiful land.' But the current threat was an internal one, 'and too bad if anything gets in the bulldozers' way'. It referred to the Government's programme for new motorways, saying they 'will plough their way without mercy through field and forest, hill and dale, bringing the roar of traffic to parts of the country more used to the chatter of bird-song than the thunder of trucks'. Turning to housing in the countryside, it noted that most of the new houses 'are not Irish cottages in the traditional sense, but much grander buildings with mock-Georgian façades, large conservatories and immaculate driveways'. What it described as a 'Shanghai-style building boom' had also hit Killarney, where the skyline 'is now dominated by cranes ... Five-bedroom McMansions line the road, their American-style clipped lawns and neat, white-painted angles providing an incongruous backdrop to the brooding MacGillicuddy mountains.' Standing on the Hill of Tara, with its setting threatened by the M3, the author pondered on how 'Celtic royal dynasties must have risen and fallen from this very spot', and how 'this magical country, intoxicated by wealth and fixated by "progress", seems fated to wreak a destruction on itself worse than that left by any colonial invader'. Lynas recalled that it was the proposal for Britain's M3 'slicing through Twyford Down' that led to a popular revolt against its road-builders, and he suggested that running the M3 through the Tara landscape may be the spark that sets off a similar movement here. Otherwise, he concluded, 'God help the Hill of Tara. And God help Ireland.'

Greater affluence, including the availability of cars, has made it possible for people to live in a rural setting and commute to work in nearby cities and towns. So, too, has the massive EU-funded road-building programme which has given them easy access to new motorways. The number of people driving to work jumped from 39% to 55% between 1991 and 2002 – a rise of 16 points in just 11 years. Incredibly, Ireland is already among the most car-dependent countries in the world, according to *Transport Investment and Economic Development*, by Banister and Berechman, published in 2000. Figures compiled by its authors showed that the average car here travels 24,400km (15,250 miles) per year, a figure that is 70% higher than France or Germany, 50% higher than Britain, and 30% higher than the US. These statistics reflect our dispersed settlement pattern and the growth in long-distance commuting. Sometime around 2000, Ireland leapfrogged Britain in terms of commuting distance. Census figures show that the average length of trips between home and work increased from 10.8km (6.7 miles) in 1996 to 15.8km (9.8 miles) in 2002, a rise of nearly 50%. Average commuting distance in Britain has seen a more modest increase, up from 13km (8.1 miles) to 13.8km (8.6 miles) over the same period. Clearly, this is something of a trial for the individuals involved, but it has effects on society too. The social effects of long-distance commuting in the US have been well-documented by Robert Putnam in his book *Bowling Alone*, particularly in terms of their negative impact on 'social capital', or traditional community life, involving face-to-face contact with neighbours in local shops, pubs, parks and community groups. Putnam found that long commutes are 'demonstrably bad' because they substantially reduce the amount of time people have to get involved. 'In round numbers, the evidence suggests that each additional 10 minutes in daily commuting time cuts involvement in community affairs by 10%.' Bertie Ahern is said to have *Bowling Alone* on his bedside table and read the book twice; he even flew in the Harvard professor to address a Fianna Fáil parliamentary party gathering at the Slieve Russell Hotel near Ballyconnell, Co Cavan, in September 2005. But Ahern's fascination with Putnam has not translated into a commitment by him or his government to curtail suburban sprawl here.

Clearly, the development of 'sustainable communities' cannot be advanced by allowing Dublin, willy-nilly, to sprawl all over Leinster. Yet that is what has been happening at an accelerated pace since the mid-1990s – largely coinciding with Ahern's period as Taoiseach. The village of Rochfortbridge in Co Westmeath used to be memorable mainly for its Bord na Móna model housing scheme, designed by architect Frank Gibney in the 1930s. What Gibney could never have imagined was that suburban housing estates would appear right across the road to provide dormitories for people commuting 80km (50 miles) to Dublin every weekday. This is a phenomenon that's happening on the outskirts of almost every town and village within the capital's hugely extended commuter belt; in effect, Leinster is being colonised by refugees from Dublin's inflated property prices. Those who choose to buy the cheaper semi-detached houses in Rochfortbridge – or Dunleer, Co Louth, or Virginia, Co Cavan, or any number of other places – are condemning themselves to years of commuting by car. Other than at weekends, they cannot be part of a 'community' in any meaningful sense of the word. According to Prof Kevin Leyden of West Virginia University, exhausted Americans learn what they know about their world and the people in it via television, instead of participating in the world they actually inhabit and talking to the

↑ *The Lakes of Killarney, seen from the Kenmare road: the landscape is threatened because of a misplaced perception that Ireland is full of wide-open spaces*

people in it. And having studied the development of Galway in particular, he had this dire warning for us: 'Car-orientated sprawl will ruin the social fabric of your nation.'

The 2002 census confirmed that attempts by planners to curtail Dublin's sprawl had been unsuccessful. As Tim O'Brien of the *Irish Times* reported in April 2004, growth was happening in precisely the places the 1999 Strategic Planning Guidelines sought to curb it. The census showed that some 70% of the growth of Ratoath and Sallins, neither of which was designated for development, had taken place since 1996, and that a quarter of the total housing stock in Meath and Kildare was built in the same six-year period. The Department of the Environment's *Housing Bulletin* in mid-2001 had already picked up on this trend, showing house completions in Dublin down by 15% while in the rest of Leinster they were up by almost 20%. 'Increasingly, the province is functioning as one giant bedroom for the Dublin metropolitan area', wrote economist Jim O'Leary in the *Sunday Times*. 'The Government's spatial development plan is keenly awaited, but the spatial planning horse has long since bolted from the stable and is grazing away in far-flung pastures.' Census 2002 also confirmed that slavishly following the model of increasing the capacity of radial routes had simply boosted the reach of the Greater Dublin Area. Nothing was done to stem this tide of development mushrooming alongside them, and Martin Cullen, as minister in charge of spatial planning, was entirely blasé about it. In an interview with the *Irish Times* in May 2003, he made it clear that he saw no case for using his powers under the 2000 Planning Act to rein in cowboy councillors in Leinster counties seeking to grab a share of Dublin's growth. Interestingly, observers in Britain have drawn similar conclusions about the south-east of England. According to Anthony Sampson, efforts at maintaining the relative power that Manchester and Newcastle enjoyed in the 19th century were frustrated by 'all kinds of communications which separated the North further from the South. The media were still more controlled from London; the airports in the South-east multiplied; the high speed trains to Paris took preference.' In Ireland, facilitating access to and from Dublin reinforces its role as a primate city that feeds Ireland with its airport, ports, concert venues, stadiums and shopping centres.

The Government attempted to cod the public into believing that its decentralisation plan, which aimed to shift more than 10,000 public servants out of Dublin to 53 locations in 25 counties, would relieve some of the pressure as well as promote better regional balance. Yet it flew in the face of the National Spatial Strategy, published just over a year earlier, under which growth was to be directed to eight regional 'gateways' (apart from Dublin) and nine 'hubs'. It also ran counter to a trend in the corporate sector to gather staff from outlying offices to headquarters, pursued by AIB, among others. And it contradicted the Government's own policy on hospitals – as expressed in the Hanley report – to concentrate facilities in towns with critical mass. As in so many other areas, such as one-off rural housing or the motorway programme, there was a distinct absence of 'evidence-based policy'. Civil servants and employees of State agencies in particular were overwhelmingly opposed to it, as were thoughtful politicians who saw it as misdirected, at best, and a dire recipe for dismantling the Civil Service, at worst. Serious practical issues have also been raised, such as how people will be able to interact with a widely dispersed State bureaucracy, eight of whose departments would be headquartered outside Dublin. Anyone who has lived in Ireland for the last few decades knows that one of our deepest problems is the lack of joined-up thinking in public policy. As Fintan O'Toole wrote: 'The fact that 41 of the 53 new locations are not listed in the National Spatial Strategy as focal points for development is a symptom of the ludicrous inability to co-ordinate policies. The solution? Fragment things even more. Have your civil servants clocking up mileage allowances travelling between BIM in Cavan and the Department of the Marine in Clonakilty, Garda HQ in Thurles and Justice in Dublin, or Bus Éireann in Mitchelstown and the Department of Transport in Dublin. Have eight Ministers and their advisers working many miles away from the Dáil...' As Labour Party leader Pat Rabbitte TD acidly observed, it would mean a whole lot of civil servants 'criss-crossing the country like Keystone Cops'. The difference, Rabbitte might have added, is that there'll be no fun in it for anybody, except those claiming 'the mileage'. Figures released in March 2005 showed that taxpayers were already footing an annual bill of €30 million for travelling expenses, the vast bulk of it paid to public servants using their own cars. The Department of Justice alone accounted for a third of the total, distributed among the Garda (€7.2 million), the Courts Service (€1.3 million) and the Prison Service (€1.2 million).

Yet, when it came to selecting a site for a new prison complex to replace Mountjoy, the Government shelled out nearly €30 million for a relatively remote 150-acre farm at Kilsallaghan, in north Co Dublin. Not only was this site not zoned for development, but it couldn't be served by high-quality public transport to facilitate prisoners' relatives. The Cabinet had approved the closure of Mountjoy in February 2004, and asked the Prison Service to identify a greenfield site in the Dublin area for a replacement prison, to be built within three years. A committee representing the Department of Justice, the Office of Public Works and the Prison Service considered a total of 31 possible locations, ranking them on eight criteria: cost, general location, proximity to public transport, availability of emergency services, access, shape/size of site, availability of services, and impact on the community. After a more suitable site in Finglas fell through, the committee recommended Thornton Hall, in the parish of Kilsallaghan, owned by Richard Lynham; he became an instant multi-millionaire when the Government agreed to buy his land for €29.9 million in January 2005 – even though it only scored high on shape/size. Located not far from the N2 and a planned interchange on the M2, it is nowhere near a railway line. 'A blind man on a galloping horse could see this is not a suitable site', one angry local resident commented. Another resident of the area, Richard Merne, was given leave by the High Court to challenge the selection of site, after arguing that it suffered from inadequate water, sewerage and transport facilities, was archaeologically significant, and should have been subjected to an environmental impact assessment. However, because the €400 million project involves a State security installation, it is exempt from the normal planning process.

The new prison, and the decentralisation programme in general, are planned at a time when transport is the fastest-growing contributor to the greenhouse gases blamed for causing climate change. The emissions from Ireland's transport sector are prodigious, and growing year by year as we rapidly move up to the EU norm of 470 cars for every 1,000 people. Incredibly, between 1993 and 2000 the number of new cars bought annually increased by 370%. A 2002 report by Goodbody Economic Consultants noted Household Budget Surveys reveal that 'average car use does not decline with increasing household car ownership'. Assuming one-fifth of car travel takes place within urban areas, average annual kilometres per car stood at 24,830 in 2001. One might have expected a government confronted with figures like these to rebalance capital expenditure to favour public transport, at least in major urban areas, in an effort to persuade some of our latter-day centurions to leave their chariots at home. But instead ministers committed themselves and their successors to an investment programme that will see much more going to roads than to railways, at a ratio of almost five to one. And with rail freight reduced to a Cinderella role, it can confidently be anticipated that road-freight traffic will also increase year by year. Perhaps the politicians had forgotten what the great economist John Maynard Keynes had to say: 'When the facts change, I change my mind.' This useful little dictum may

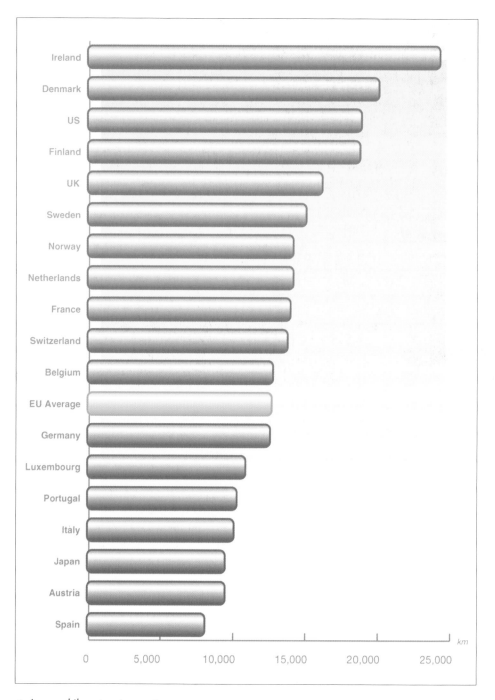

↑ *Average kilometres per car per annum*

As the figure for Greece was not available, the EU average is based on 14 member states. [source: Banister and Berechman, Transport Investment and Economic Development [UCL Press, London, 2000]; the source for Banister and Berechman is the international comparisons section of Transport Statistics Great Britain [UK Dept of Transport, 1997]]

↑ *Early morning traffic heading for Dublin on the Naas dual carriageway. Ireland is already one of the most car-dependent countries in the world.*

well be observed in other countries, but not in Ireland. We have bumbled along.

Appendix 4 on the last page of the National Development Plan 2000-2006 conceded that the possibility of 'some unsustainable patterns of development' emerging within its framework 'cannot be excluded'. Just like chaos theory, it explained that this could arise from 'the pace of current economic development, unforeseen interaction between measures, or unanticipated consequences of particular measures'. Given that the roads programme is such a key element of the NDP, Terence McDonough, economics lecturer at NUI Galway, saw Ireland unwittingly locking itself into car-dependency. Drawing on examples from telecommunications, he argued that this issue of 'lock in' hadn't even been considered when it should have been clear that massive investment in one mode (road) would effectively preclude competition from another (rail). 'The Irish government is supposedly committed to providing both an elaborate motorway system and decent public transport through rail. But the roads are to be built first ... In the face of extensive roadways and an antiquated and inadequate public transportation system, people will choose to rely on their own cars. Housing will be built around the road system, relying on automobiles for transportation. Shopping centres will be built on highways with large parking lots. Employment will be sited on the assumption that employees drive their own cars.' According to McDonough, the opportunity to create an efficient and environmentally sound transport system was being thrown away. However, as Fintan O'Toole observed in March 2004, 'when the Taoiseach loftily dismisses all infidels to the great god of motorways as "swans, snails and people hanging out of trees", he gives voice to a deep contempt for anything that can't be measured in tonnes of concrete and loads of money.'

We had lost the run of ourselves. The money generated during the Celtic Tiger boom did something to our psyche, turning modern Ireland into a 'vulgar fest', according to the Ombudsman, Emily O'Reilly. In a November 2004 address to Céifin, an Ennis-based research institute which promotes discussion of changing values in society, she referred to 'the rampant, unrestrained drunkenness, the brutal, random violence that infects the smallest of our townlands and villages, the incontinent use of foul language with no thought to place or company, the obscene parading of obscene wealth, the debasement of our civic life, the growing disdain of the wealthy towards the poor, the fracturing of our community life, the God-like status given to celebrities...' She went on: 'Drunkenness was supposed to be practised by the marginalised, not the boys and girls with cars and careers and more prospects than their granny could shake a stick at. More cars were supposed to help people get around, not force them to sit in line through the full two hours of a drive-time programme at motorway exits – motorways which, incidentally, were also supposed to help people get around. Bypasses were supposed to relieve bottlenecks, not shuffle them to the next un-bypassed town. Portlaoise was never meant to be a Dublin suburb.'

There have been achievements, of course. Where slums once stood there are now graceful buildings; O'Reilly cited the 'tall skinny-latte front' of the IFSC in Dublin as an example. Items once seen as luxuries are now within the purchasing power of almost everyone; the reality of Irish women's lives has been transformed immeasurably; and 'the stultifying cosh of the Catholic church has been removed and we at least can see ourselves in our new spiritual nakedness.' We have become 'participants at what we would have called, in my teenage years, a free house, but this time on a massive scale. Released from the handcuffs of mass religious obedience, we are Dionysian in our revelry, in our testing of what we call freedom. Hence the staggering drink consumption, the child-like showing off of helicopters and four-wheel drives and private cinemas, the fetishising of handbags and high heels, the inability of some to contribute to charity without a photographer on hand to record it, the supplanting of bog-standard childhood ailments such as measles and whooping cough with fat-induced obesity and diabetes.' The challenge in the short to medium term, O'Reilly suggested, was 'how to accept this newly secular society and inject it with a value system that takes the best of what we have jettisoned and discards the worst'. But whether we're still capable of making that choice is an open question.

At the height of the boom, it seemed as if there was money to burn. Bertie Ahern's obsession with his Sports Campus Ireland project for Abbotstown was an extreme example. Even among madcap schemes, this was probably the most deranged because it would have located an 80,000-seat national stadium on the edge of the M50, not far from the N3 interchange – as if traffic congestion along this stretch wasn't bad enough. Apart from the stadium, there was to be a 15,000-seat indoor arena, a series of multi-purpose sports halls, 30 tennis courts, a golf academy, a velodrome, offices for sports organisations and a sports science and medical centre. Ironically, the only element built so far – an aquatic centre – was added to the list later, at the Government's instigation, to provide a venue for the Special Olympics in June 2003. Three years earlier, Martin Cullen – then Minister of State in charge of the Office of Public Works – headed out to Sydney with senior officials to see Stadium Australia and the other facilities built at Homebush Bay, on the city's western outskirts, for the Olympic Games in September 2000. When it was put to one of the officials that the Abbotstown adventure was very ill-advised, not least in terms of its traffic impact, he said: 'I know. But it's going to happen.' Fortunately, it didn't. Stadium Australia, which had been the model, turned into a huge white elephant, and here at home the penny finally dropped about what the 'Bertie Bowl' would really cost – €1 billion, or more. Meanwhile, the GAA was redeveloping Croke Park as a spectacular stadium with a capacity for 80,000. But that didn't matter. It didn't seem to matter either that Sydney, with a population of three million, couldn't make Stadium Australia pay, or that no other city in Europe, not even London, Paris or Rome, has two stadia of such capacity. 'To hell with the facts, we'll do our own thing', you could almost hear the Taoiseach saying. In the end, sense prevailed, with an agreement reached in January 2004 between the Government, the IRFU and the FAI on the much more realistic option of redeveloping Lansdowne Road at a modest cost to the taxpayer of €191 million.

————

IT IS ONLY WHEN IT COMES TO OUR INTERNATIONAL OBLIGATIONS TO PROTECT THE ENVIronment that we revert to 'poor mouth' mode. As has been widely reported in the media, Ireland is in danger of substantially overshooting its target under the Kyoto Protocol to cap greenhouse gas emissions at no more than 13% above their 1990 levels in the period 2008-12. Despite signing up for this ambitious target in 1998, the Government has done little but produce reports and strategies, while lacking the political will to implement them. Even though Ireland will face multi-million euro penalties a year from 2008 onwards unless emissions are brought down, ministers have dithered over the imposition of carbon taxation, and as the price of oil hit $50 a barrel in New York in August 2004, they came under pressure from IBEC to shelve the tax because it was now 'unnecessary'. Fearing a backlash from motorists, in particular, the Government decided it would be more politically palatable – and perhaps even cheaper – to buy our way out of the problem when the penalties start kicking in. Ministers also reasoned that Ireland is only a small country – as if this was a reason for doing nothing. IBEC's biggest members, the ones with the highest energy bills, had already received CO_2 allowances free of charge (an EU requirement, by the way) in advance of EU-wide emissions-trading in January 2005. But the European

↑ *The proposed national stadium for Abbotstown which will never be built. Bertie Ahern's obsession with the project was an example of how we lost the run of ourselves during the boom.*

Commission's decision to accept Ireland's allocation programme, when it approved a raft of similar 'business-as-usual' plans from other member states, was also a 'severe disappointment for anyone who believes we can no longer dither or dally in the fight against climate change', according to Pat Finnegan of GRIAN, Irish affiliate of the Climate Action Network. But in Ireland, more so than in other EU countries, taxpayers as a whole will foot the Kyoto bill divorced from individual lifestyle choices.

The conflict between environment and development has become more virulent, especially over the issue of housing in the countryside. An Taisce was turned into a sort of national whipping boy for having the cheek to stand in the way of development – and, worse still, for citing public policy as its reason for doing so. Dick Roche, then Minister of State for Europe, conjured up images of Robespierre by branding An Taisce as an unaccountable *directoire*, adding to epithets that already included arrogant, elitist, dictatorial, faceless, undemocratic, secretive, and even Ku Klux Klan. Roche denied that he was staking out the ground for Martin Cullen to strip the trust of its 'prescribed body' status under the planning laws. Cullen had dismantled Dúchas and cowed the Heritage Council, so why wouldn't he go after An Taisce as well? From the end of 2003, he terminated €70,000 a year in government funding, which had enabled the trust to perform its watchdog role, sparking a crisis in the organisation. At an emergency meeting in March 2004, the 50-strong national council of An Taisce unanimously reaffirmed its commitment to soldier on in the planning arena, whatever the odds. Within two months, more than €30,000 was raised from members and supporters to replenish depleted coffers, and the trust began approaching 'high net worth individuals' concerned about Ireland's landscape and overall environment. It was also quite a coup when Eanna Ní Lamhna, well-known to RTÉ radio listeners for her down-to-earth approach on *Mooney Goes Wild*, agreed to become president of An Taisce in July 2004. As she told Kitty Holland, her aim would be to emphasise the good work it does with the Blue Flag and Green Schools programmes so that people would think of An Taisce with a 'warm glowy feeling in their heart'. Though feeling the heat, she had no intention of getting out of the kitchen. As she pointed out, the trust appealed less than 1% of planning decisions in 2003 (248 out of 70,000), and these were all based on 'sound environmental and heritage grounds'. One of the main reasons why it has found itself so much in the firing line is that other prescribed bodies – such as the Arts Council and Fáilte Ireland – had withdrawn from the arena, while another, the National Roads Authority, lodged its first-ever appeal to An Bord Pleanála in March 2004 against a one-off house fronting onto a national primary route.

An Taisce could only be 'nobbled' if the Government took away its statutory watchdog role, which entitles it to be consulted by local authorities on environmentally sensitive planning applications. And if Fianna Fáil and the Progressive Democrats did that, they would be signalling clearly which side they were really on in

↓ *Minister for the Environment Dick Roche branded An Taisce as an unaccountable directoire*

the struggle between sustainable and unsustainable development. Protecting the environment had slipped to the bottom of the Coalition's list of priorities, particularly defending heritage sites from development pressures. This was underlined by its amendment of the National Monuments Acts, which was ostensibly designed to deal with the immediate problem of Carrickmines Castle standing in the way of the last leg of the M50. Whereas previous legislation, going back to 1930, had set out to protect national monuments, this piece of law-making in 2004 gave the Minister for the Environment the power to decide what constituted a monument and what level of protection it might be afforded, if any. In other words, he not only acts as judge and jury, but also as executioner. It seemed as if the Government was determined to roll back the protection that existed for heritage and the environment. For 20 years or more, policy had been generally moving in the right direction. But now, even some of the gains made in those years are being reversed one by one to facilitate unsustainable development right across the board.

The Government is determined to make it even easier for big projects to get the go-ahead, including motorways, waste incinerators, landfills, pipelines, power stations and pylons. New legislation, announced in June 2005, will introduce a 'fast-track' planning regime for *anything* the Government, or even a city or county manager, deems to be of 'strategic importance' – including profit-driven schemes by the private sector. In what Labour Party environment spokesman Eamon Gilmore TD saw as a move designed to 'cut the public out' of decision-making on major projects, none of those covered by the Critical Infrastructure Bill would have to go through the planning process at local level; they would be referred directly to a special division of An Bord Pleanála. And as if taking a High Court action isn't already intimidating, it would become even more so as plaintiffs would have to produce financial guarantees to show they were in a position to cover all costs if they lost a judicial review.

↓ *The harp emblem on Ireland's pavilion at Expo 2005 in Aichi, Japan*

Behind all of this is Bertie Ahern. Visiting China in January 2005 to promote Irish business there, he said he would like to have the powers of Han Zheng, the Mayor of Shanghai – a megalopolis in the throes of spectacular development. 'When he decides he wants to do a highway and if he wants to bypass an area, he just goes straight up and over', Ahern told Mark Hennessy, in his characteristically jumbled language. 'I know that

that is not going to happen at home. I would just like when I am trying to put it on the ground that we can put it through the consultation process as quick as possible.' Referrring to the controversy about the M3 and Tara, he dismissed it as 'a row about who was there 5,000 years ago'. Though he didn't know who inhabited Tara, he was sure they were 'very significant people', but there had to be some finality about what needed to be done 'if we want to be progressive, if we want to be modern' in the present era. Around the same time he was in China, the Irish pavilion at Expo 2005 in Aichi, Japan's industrial heartland, was being fitted out with replica High Crosses. And the Department of the Taoiseach, under whose wing it was prepared, even saw fit to include an image of the Hill of Tara, no less. The pavilion also had a centrally positioned harp motif on its slatted metal façade. 'The harp that once thro' Tara's Hall the soul of music shed / Now hangs as mute on Tara's wall as if that soul were fled...', as the old song goes. The hypocrisy at the heart of the whole presentation would have been lost on most visitors to the Expo; they wouldn't have known that Ireland's heritage was being paraded in Japan by a government hell bent on sacrificing it to 'progress' at home.

———

DO WE HAVE ANY IDEA WHERE WE ARE GOING, ANY IDEA AT ALL ABOUT THE KIND OF Ireland being created during these years of prosperity? Do we care about the indelible imprint we're making on the landscape and the woeful legacy of 'development' we're leaving for future generations to clean up – if they can? That the country is woefully misgoverned emerges clearly from the catalogue of failures and missed opportunities documented in this book. Political and bureaucratic incompetence plays a large part in this shoddy equation, and so does the close collusion between the development-at-any-cost lobby and the short-term thinkers who lead us. The public interest, and what it demands, is too often forgotten in the unseemly willingness to cave in to vested interests or roll out the red carpet, even for madcap schemes like Abbotstown or the current motorway programme.

Ordinary people might imagine that public policy is based on evidence, but this is not the case in dealing with crunch issues in every area. Horror stories abound. Month after month, some community wakes up to plans that will irrevocably alter its environment. Some of the opposition that emerges is driven by NIMBY (Not In My Back Yard) thinking, but there are many cases where cogent arguments, and even alternatives, are put forward in an effort to avert the worst. It is not possible within the covers of a single book to deal with all of the controversies which have erupted since the so-called Celtic Tiger started roaring in the mid-1990s, but the major ones are included. And if, at the end, readers conclude that we are headed down the road to ruin, they might be motivated to do something about it. We cannot simply depend on the likes of Tony Lowes to save us from ourselves.

———

2. Sprawl

DUBLIN IS ALL OVER THE PLACE THESE DAYS. WITH ITS ENTRAILS SPILLING OUT INTO Leinster, the city's commuter belt extends from Dundalk to Gorey and as far inland as Athlone. At the rate things are going, as architect Tony Reddy has forecast, 'Dublin' will soon occupy a land area equivalent to Los Angeles, but with less than a quarter of its population. Some of the most dramatic increases in population recorded by the 2002 census were in Meath (22.1% since 1996), Kildare (21.5%), Westmeath (13.8%), Wicklow (11.7%), Wexford (11.7%), Laois (10.9%), Louth (10.5%) and Carlow (10.2%). Based on what's happening on the ground in all of these counties, there can be little doubt that this trend will be confirmed by the 2006 census. Indeed, the most recent projections by the Central Statistics Office forecast that the Greater Dublin Area will have a population of 2.1 million in 2021, with Meath, Kildare and Wicklow recording the largest increases.

Even the National Spatial Strategy, which has little to say about this phenomenon, concedes that growth is now happening at a faster rate in the counties surrounding the capital than in Dublin itself. The increases in their populations, it notes, 'confirm a widening of the Dublin commuter belt well beyond the Greater Dublin Area (GDA)', which includes Meath, Kildare and Wicklow. Few could doubt that much of this unplanned growth has been generated by Dubliners fleeing exorbitantly high property prices in the city and its immediate environs; the prospect of purchasing a house at relatively affordable prices, even in places they have barely heard of before, has turned them into a new class of refugees... and early risers, too. It is not unusual for many to be up by 6am to face long journeys to work, often leaving home before dawn to beat the worst of the traffic. But no matter how much the roads are improved, they're clogged by commuters in cars, some of them driving 80km (50 miles) or more to workplaces in the city, or strung out along the M50.

Iarnród Éireann has laid on commuter trains to serve Dublin's expanding

→ *Percentage of workers in each Electoral Division who travel 20 miles or more to work*

%	
	< 10
	10 < 20
	20 < 30
	30 +

empire. The 2003 timetable had the earliest of them leaving Athlone at 6.18 am, Longford at 6.23 am, Carlow at 6.30 am, Portlaoise at 6.44am, and Arklow at 6.55am. (Since then, the early Arklow service has been extended to Gorey due to its emergence as a suburb of Dublin.) The number of Dublin-bound passengers using Bus Éireann's commuter services has nearly doubled, from 3,500 in 1999 to 6,500 in 2002 – and it's growing year by year. In 2003 the company scheduled 25 buses from Navan to Dublin during the morning peak to carry 1,200 inbound passengers on that route alone. Buses run every 15 minutes from 7am onwards from places like Navan, Drogheda, and Clane, Co Kildare, and every 30 minutes from outer locations such as Edenderry, Co Offaly. 'We go out as far as Cavan, Mullingar, Tullamore, Portlaoise, Abbeyleix, Tullow and Gorey, which is the latest commuter route within a 60-mile radius of Dublin', Tim Hayes, Bus Éireann's business development manager, told the *Irish Times* in April 2003. The problem is that all of this traffic is one-way. 'We might bring 1,000 passengers in from Ashbourne in the morning, but there's only 15 going out', he explained. And since most of the passengers are travelling to Dublin on discounted tickets, this 'empty bus' syndrome makes commuter services uneconomic. The other problem is that the roads to Dublin are so congested that buses can no longer meet their timetables. 'A bus that leaves Kells at 6am is supposed to be in Dublin at 7.30, in time to return again at 8. Now it doesn't arrive in time to make that return journey, so it has to leave Kells at 5.45am to be ahead of the rush', according to Hayes. Bus Éireann asked the National Roads Authority if buses could use the hard shoulder on some main roads as a de facto bus lane. The NRA first shunned the idea, only to agree to it later. Though the company met its targets under the National Development Plan, increasing its capacity by 50% since 1999, the sprawl of Dublin is clearly a transport operational nightmare because of the huge imbalance between the number of passengers heading for the city and those coming out. Yet the dominant focus of Séamus Brennan during his two years in office as Minister for Transport was to introduce competition – as if that in itself would solve the fundamental problems.

In a city, there is some chance of transport operators getting business in two directions. Establishing the link between land use and transport was one of the major objectives of the Greater Dublin Area Strategic Planning Guidelines (SPGs), published in March 1999. Another principal goal was to consolidate Dublin. Compiled by the GDA's seven local authorities in conjunction with the Department of the Environment, the guidelines were supposed to provide an agreed strategic planning framework for the development plans of the local authorities to cater for rapid population growth up to 2011. Apart from consolidating the existing built-up area of Dublin and its immediate environs (known as the metropolitan area), the SPGs proposed to concentrate development in a limited number of growth centres within its largely rural hinterland – mainly in Meath, Kildare and Wicklow – separated from each other by 'strategic greenbelts'. It was intended that these growth centres in the hinterland area would develop in the longer term as self-sufficient towns with a full range of facilities and only limited commuting to Dublin. The designated centres were Drogheda, Navan, Balbriggan, Naas-Newbridge-Kilcullen and Wicklow, as well as Athy, Arklow and Kildare-Monasterevin. Development outside of these centres was to be strictly limited to 'local needs'. The guidelines expressly recommended that land should not otherwise be zoned for housing in the hinterland area unless it was located within areas identified for development in the strategy and served by adequate public transport, water supply and drainage.

All seven local authorities were instructed to revise their development plans to conform with the SPGs. But though the guidelines were backed by the 2000 Planning Act, they were widely ignored by the same authorities which had supposedly subscribed to them in 1999 – particularly Meath, Kildare and Wicklow. A central weakness in the Act was that local authorities were only required to 'have regard to' the SPGs. As the High Court found in September 2002, in a judicial review case against the Meath county plan, the guidelines barely received a sideways glance while councillors got on with rezoning land for an 'enormous population increase'. Mr Justice Quirke was delivering his judgment in the case brought by Cllr Tony McEvoy, an independent member of Kildare County Council, and Michael Smith, then national chairman of An Taisce, who sought to have the Meath county plan struck down because it failed to have regard to the SPGs. Under revised guidelines published in April 2000, Meath's population was to grow from 109,700 in 1996 to 139,500 in 2006. But the councillors subsequently rezoned so much land for residential development that the population could reach 195,000 by 2006 and 242,000 by 2011 – way above the SPG targets. Minutes of 50 meetings showed that the guidelines were 'rarely if ever discussed or referred to' while councillors were considering submissions to have land rezoned for housing. Instead, the decisions they made 'appear to have been influenced more by pressure and lobbying exerted by interested parties', Mr Justice Quirke found.

Even the overall acreage of land rezoned in Meath is difficult to quantify, as the various maps produced during consideration of the county plan did not have any figures attached. But it was clear from the 2002 census that the county's population had increased by 22% since 1996 to 133,936 – not far short of the revised target figure for 2006. Although Navan was the only town identified in the SPGs for any growth other than to meet 'local needs', Mr Justice Quirke said the councillors had 'decided to zone large amounts of land for residential purposes in dozens of small towns in a manner which appears to be quite inconsistent with the recommendations of the guidelines'. The evidence 'strongly suggests that in a number of respects the Meath plan does not comply with the guidelines, and indeed that in some of its provisions it has substantially departed from the guidelines' policies and objectives ... In many instances, "local interests" appear to have overcome the concept of "local needs".'

In Dunboyne, councillors pressed ahead with the rezoning of nearly 100 acres of land for housing, some of it located in the floodplain of the River Tolka, despite massive opposition from the local community. The 2002 census showed that Dunboyne's population increased by nearly 42% (to 7,755) since 1996. On the same day as the county council was voting through these rezonings – 6th November 2000 – Dunboyne was surrounded by floods on all sides, with many homes under a metre of water. Some of the worst affected had been built in the previous four years on the

↑ *Commuters crowded onto the platform at Tara Street station in Dublin. 'We're not there yet, but we're getting there', according to Iarnród Éireann.*

floodplain of the Castle river. The six local councillors – Mary Bergin (FG), Oliver Brookes (FF), John Fanning (FG), Brian Fitzgerald (Ind, ex-Labour), Nick Killian (FF), and Conor Tormey (FF) – voted for and even sponsored most of the rezonings against the advice of Meath's professional planners, the wishes of residents, and the thrust of the Strategic Planning Guidelines.

In Ratoath the population increased by 82.3% between 1996 and 2002. 'Who are all these people?' Kathy Sheridan asked, in the 'Commuter Counties' series in the *Irish Times*. 'What took them out to a Co Meath village with few amenities, poor lighting, scarce footpaths, horrendous traffic, intermittent public transport and woeful educational facilities? Forget the stereotype of the young, struggling first-time buyer; Ratoath is not a first-time buyer's kind of place. Rampaging developments and building sites may lurk behind every hedge, but it has managed to market itself as a rather exclusive enclave – a step up from Ashbourne, certainly, in the eyes of the marketeers.' Well over half of the residents, it turns out, are migrants from Dublin, some of whom traded-up from ordinary suburban houses in the city to large, detached 'trophy homes' on the outskirts of the village. But with half the population under 16, many people are apprehensive. In eight years, primary school enrolments have quadrupled to nearly 1,000, and there is no secondary school. 'There are no playgrounds, few footpaths and no cycle paths', Sheridan noted. 'Lorries thundering past from Drogheda port, and endless, heedless streams of cars using the tiny, narrow village roads as a rat-run force parents into cars, negating the very reason given by many for moving out of the city – that dream of rural living in which children roam safely and freely.'

Meath councillors could hardly plead ignorance. In November 1999, before embarking on their rezoning spree, they were given a special presentation on the significance of the SPGs by Niall Cussen, a senior planner from the Department of the Environment, who also outlined the obligation to 'have regard to' them. In December 2000, after it became apparent that the Meath plan was at odds with the guidelines, Mary Moylan, assistant secretary in charge of the Department of the Environment's planning division, wrote a detailed letter reminding the county council that it was required to ensure that its plan was in line with the guidelines. But whatever concerns the then Minister (Noel Dempsey) had about the rezoning of so much land for development, they were short-lived. In February 2001, after receiving a response from the council, Moylan wrote back to say it was now the Minister's view that the plan was 'substantially in compliance' with the SPGs.

How could this be true? Clonee is a case in point. Here, right alongside the boundary with Dublin, councillors rezoned 250 acres of land for a 'Gateway to Meath' business park. Not only did this decision severely compromise Navan as the county's principal employment centre – and, therefore, any possibility of it becoming 'self-sufficient' – it also made nonsense of the SPGs' designation of Clonee as part of

↓ *Carol Dougan leaving home in Ratoath, Co Meath, at 6.10am to drive to work in Ballsbridge. Her journey takes 50 minutes. If she left at 8am it would take an hour and 45 minutes.*

↑ *Mary Moylan, assistant secretary at the Department of the Environment, said the Meath development plan was 'substantially in compliance' with the Greater Dublin Area Strategic Planning Guidelines*

the greenbelt. In the High Court, the principal author of the guidelines, Michael Grace of Brady Shipman Martin, endorsed the view of plaintiffs McEvoy and Smith that the elected members and officials of Meath County Council had 'fundamentally misunderstood' the SPGs and the manner in which they should be applied in the context of the county plan. The problem, of course, was that the council was only required to 'have regard to' the guidelines. And as the then Chief Justice, Mr Justice Keane, ruled in another case (Glencar Exploration v Mayo County Council), to 'have regard to' particular policies or objectives does not mean that a planning authority is obliged to implement them. Although Mr Justice Quirke found that the nature and extent of the consideration given by Meath councillors to the SPGs in the zoning of land for housing 'gives rise to concern and, indeed, unease', he was not satisfied that McEvoy and Smith had established that the council had failed to 'have regard to' the guidelines. Or, put another way, to 'have regard to' could mean to have scant regard. However, the judge accepted that the plaintiffs had 'acted solely by way of furtherance of a valid public interest in the environment', and ordered that the county council should pay half their costs. Including its own legal expenses, the council might have to foot a bill of €500,000.

The only way Meath could be compelled to ensure its county plan complied with the SPGs was for the Minister for the Environment to use his power under Section 31 of the 2000 Planning Act. Threatening to seek an order of mandamus to

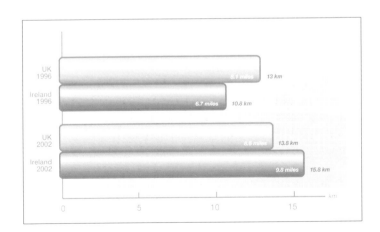

← *Average distance travelled to work in Ireland and the UK*

[source: CSO and Statistics Division of the UK Dept of Transport] compel him to act, McEvoy and Smith said Martin Cullen 'cannot stand idly by while government policy on curtailing the sprawl of Dublin is flouted'. Unless he took action, the National Spatial Strategy and its declared aim of achieving balanced regional development would become meaningless. (In the event, McEvoy and Smith did not pursue this course of action. Noting Mr Justice Quirke's finding that the rezonings in Co Meath were not done pursuant to the public interest, they said the Planning Tribunal should investigate 'these improper decisions'.)

What happened in Co Meath was a free-for-all, yet nothing was done to halt this rezoning spree by the then Minister for the Environment, Noel Dempsey, or his successor, Martin Cullen. Apart from letters to Meath, Kildare and Wicklow county councils expressing concern about what was happening, no action was taken to ensure that their development plans actually complied with the SPGs. Neither was any attempt made to restrain rogue councillors in Louth, Westmeath, Laois, Carlow and Wexford from rezoning large tracts of land for housing quite shamelessly targeted at Dublin commuters. Yet this too had been happening in defiance of official government policy, as expressed in the SPGs, to contain Dublin's growth within the GDA. In an interview with the *Irish Times* in May 2003, Cullen could hardly have displayed a more limp attitude, making it clear that he had no intention of using his powers under the 2000 Planning Act to curb Dublin's sprawl. He did not believe that planning policy should be 'dictated' by him or by his Department; some 'flexibility' was needed because the situation was 'not as black and white as it might be'. Though he was prepared to examine Wexford County Council's local area plan for Gorey, which rezoned enough land to cater for a population of at least 20,000, he would not be 'trying to dictate [policy on] specific rezonings'. Planning was 'not an exact science', he said. People were making choices. Some were prepared to live in higher-density apartments in Dublin, but others wanted a house 'down the country a bit' with a garden back and front. Asked if he had sympathy for commuters getting into their cars at 6am to drive to work in Dublin from new housing estates 80km (50 miles) from the city, Cullen said: 'I do, but unfortunately it is a feature of modern living everywhere.'

Clearly, he hadn't been keeping an eye on our runaway travel distances to work. Gorey is one of those places pushing Ireland's figure up, thanks largely to improvements to the N11 such as the Arklow bypass and the controversial Glen of the Downs scheme. A planned market town dating from the 17th century, Gorey is being swamped by new housing to cater for 'the demand for starter homes from newly weds who have been pushed out of the Dublin region property market', as Wexford County Council's local area plan put it. Although Enniscorthy, New Ross and Wexford all registered marginal falls in population in the 2002 census, the number of people living in Gorey soared has nearly 44% since 1996. Even its rural hinterland showed a population increase of almost 20% in the same period. The local area plan, adopted in 2002, concedes that 'as much as 70%' of the town's new residents commute to Dublin on a daily basis, mostly by car. Development pressures are expected to increase following completion of Gorey's own bypass. The plan anticipates that the population of the town and its environs will double to 11,000 by 2007, turning Gorey

↑ *Gorey's sprawl: Priory Court apartments under construction, with the Hazelwood housing estate rising up the hill. Up to 70% of new homeowners in the town are Dublin commuters.*

into the largest urban area in Co Wexford. But it is riddled with contradictions. With massive over-zoning of land for residential development and almost none for employment, there is virtually no chance that the 'vision' of developing Gorey as 'a self-sufficient centre capable of social and economic interaction with the Dublin region' will be realised. Instead, its role as a 'dormitory or satellite settlement' is likely to be reinforced – whatever the written statement says.

Until the local councillors got their hands on the draft plan prepared by the National Building Agency in 2000, Gorey already had sufficient land available for housing within its development boundary. Zoned residential land amounted to 136 acres, with a further 99 acres available for long-term development. Taking into account planning permissions already granted, the town's population would increase by 3,440, bringing it to 7,380. But that would have fallen short of Wexford County Council's 'pro-active view' towards development in Gorey, so the local area plan aimed for a 'design population' of 11,000. That, at least, is what its written statement says. In fact, so much land was subsequently rezoned for housing that, if all of it was developed, the town would end up with 6,000 new homes (or maybe as many as 10,000, if built at higher densities). And that would give it a population of between 17,600 and 28,900. With no less than 744 acres of land around Gorey zoned for housing – much of it against planning advice, the plan lamely declares: 'While it would appear that there are excess provisions made in terms of zoning allocations, there needs to be adequate lands available to provide an element of choice in the market.' Given the plethora of zoned land, way in excess of what would be required to cater for the 11,000 'design population', developers can pick and choose what sites to build on. So much for the plan's aspiration to consolidate Gorey and achieve a 'balanced growth pattern around the town in all directions'.

Wexford councillors would surely have been aware of the consequences of haphazard development. Under the Seaside Resort Renewal Scheme, at least 1,200 holiday homes were shovelled into nearby Courtown and environs before a sewerage plant had even been built. Although a significant portion of Gorey's development has been happening outside its official boundary, the plan says it is the county council's policy to adopt a 'clear boundary to development' to ensure that Gorey grows in a planned fashion, and lay down a 'clear demarcation line' to prevent it merging with Courtown. How, then, can it explain or justify a decision to rezone 47 acres of land at Raheenagurran, on the Courtown road, outside the development boundary, for 'commercial and mixed land uses'? Or the decision to extend the boundary northwards to incorporate another parcel of land at Ballyloughan on the N11? Of these 47 acres, 37 were owned by Cllr Lorcan Allen's elderly mother, who died not long afterwards. Allen, who rose to become a Minister of State during the Haughey era, chaired the council's four-member Gorey district committee which decided to rezone it, but absented himself when the decision was taken. 'No stroke-pulling' was involved, he said. The other members of the committee were Michael D'Arcy TD (FG), Deirdre Bolger (FG) and Joe Murphy (FF). They would have been well aware that the Allen land was close to an interchange on the future Gorey bypass, and it was a specific objective of the area plan that sites along the bypass be reserved for strategic development. In July 2004 Allen admitted that he was 'totally guilty' of forging Bertie Ahern's signature on a circular letter to some 2,000 constituents in the Gorey area, urging them to vote No.1 for what it described as a 'patriotic and honest' county councillor. The hoax worked; Allen was elected and his running mate wasn't. His only penalty was suspension from the Fianna Fáil National Executive for 12 months.

↓ *Cllr Lorcan Allen (FF): there was 'no stroke-pulling' when his late mother's land adjoining the Gorey bypass was rezoned for commercial development*

The 2002 decision to rezone his mother's holding caused outrage locally as it was made without any public consultation. Neither the lands at Raheenagurran nor Ballyloughan had been proposed for zoning when the draft plan was put on public exhibition in late 2001. They were simply added to the plan and ratified by the full council without going back on public display. 'It's crazy that something like this, which has such a long-term impact for the town, can take place without people knowing', said Malcolm Byrne, then a young Fianna Fáil member of Gorey Town Council. What worried the local chamber of commerce is that the Raheenagurran site could now be developed for a major out-of-town shopping centre. Only public outrage prevented the councillors rezoning an 11-acre site (used as playing fields) given to the people of Gorey by the Land Commission in 1937. Both Allen and D'Arcy were behind the attempt, denying that there was any conflict of interest between their roles as councillors and trustees for the site. Deirdre Bolger had earlier declared an interest when the committee decided to rezone land at Ramstown, on the south side of Gorey, in response to a submission from her husband's firm, J Bolger & Co. However, the minutes do not record that she left the meeting before this decision was taken by her colleagues.

The massive over-zoning in the plan is grist to the mill of landowners and developers. Agricultural land in the Gorey area was selling for about €10,000 an acre, but one afternoon's meeting of the county council's area committee could bring the value up to €125,000 an acre. Little wonder then that a lot of land has been changing hands in recent times. Meanwhile, Gorey Community School is 'experiencing severe overcrowding problems and will have little spare capacity over the plan period', as the local town plan itself concedes. (It is the largest secondary school in the State, with nearly 1,600 students.) And though there are plans to expand the Loreto Abbey and CBS, an additional primary school may now have to be built in Gorey to cater for its explosive population growth.

It was a similar pattern elsewhere in Leinster. Much of Westmeath's growth over the next decade is likely to be focussed on a necklace of villages strung out along the future M6 motorway. In Rochfortbridge, which has already seen housing estates springing up to cater for the overspill from Dublin, indigenous residents are fearful of it 'becoming a mini-Tallaght or Blanchardstown'. Kinnegad is going the same way, and a similar fate lies in store for Delvin, Kilbeggan and Milltownpass. Kinnegad's population more than doubled from 652 to 1,425 between 1996 and 2002. Rochfortbridge, seven miles further west, grew by only 0.4% between 1991 and 1996, but has since soared by 53% (to 1,537), a result of increasing pressure for housing in the area from Dublin commuters.

Under the local plan for Rochfortbridge, adopted in November 2002, 168 acres on the outskirts of the village were zoned residential, much of which has either been developed or carries planning permission for housing. Westmeath County Council conceded that the need for a local plan arose 'because of the unprecedented demand for residential development land in the Rochfortbridge area and the need to properly plan for future expansion of the village in a co-ordinated and sustainable manner'.

The sewage treatment plant, which had a capacity for 1,500, is being expanded to cater for a population equivalent of 5,000 – including any industry which might be attracted by its 'highly strategic location'. Though the local plan – drafted by consultants DTZ Pieda – describes Rochfortbridge as 'an ideal location for industrial and commercial growth', it zoned only 12 acres of land for industrial use. There is no bus service to the nearest employment centre, Mullingar, nine miles to the north. In response to local fears that the village was turning into another dormitory for Dublin, the amount of land zoned for residential development was slightly reduced – an unusual occurrence in itself. But it seems unlikely that the housing estates yet to be built will be any less car-dependent than what's already there. Though the county council's planners favour a more 'village-type' design, the councillors couldn't care less. Traffic is a huge concern, as Kathy Sheridan reported. 'Homicidal commuters racing three abreast on the narrow, winding Kinnegad road at 6.30am "and never a cop in sight"; massive trucks speeding through the village, the anarchic situation around the village schools twice a day when 1,200 pupils, their parents and cars are milling around a tiny area, is, many believe, a tragedy in waiting.'

Much of the running on Westmeath's rezonings was made by a group of local Westmeath councillors known as the Three Wise Men – Donie Cassidy TD (FF), Frank McDermott (FG) and PJ O'Shaughnessy (FF). The latter has become one of the direct beneficiaries. In October 2002 a parcel of 60 acres of land outside the village of Delvin owned by O'Shaughnessy and by Pat Cogan, McDermott's former election agent, was rezoned for residential development against the advice of county manager Ann McGuinness. She pointed out that planning permissions granted in Delvin would nearby double its population to 600. Already 163 acres were zoned residential, and set to cater for an extra 1,400 people. The two parcels now being added were also remote from the village and could impede its development. Fears were expressed by local residents that the rezonings would turn Delvin into 'another Rochfortbridge', with a population exceeding 4,000 – more than seven times the current figure. Cassidy responded with a claim that the village was 'dying on its feet', and new houses had to be built to ensure it didn't become 'a wilderness'. According to him, Delvin's population had fallen by 11% in the previous five years while the rest of Westmeath was 'booming'. In fact, the village – chiefly known as the birthplace of Brinsley MacNamara, author of *The Valley of the Squinting Windows* – recorded a 6.5% increase in the 2002 census. Asked why greenfield sites one kilometre away from

↓ *Donie Cassidy TD (FF), one of the 'Three Wise Men' behind contentious rezonings in Delvin, Co Westmeath*

the village should be rezoned, Cassidy said the intermediate land was not available because its owners 'don't want to sell'. He acknowledged that one of his business activities was house-building, but said he wasn't interested in building in Delvin.

Minutes of meetings of the Coole electoral area committee, which includes Delvin, show that O'Shaughnessy himself was the first person to suggest that lands on the Mullingar road, including his own, be rezoned. When this was rejected by the planners at committee stage, his two council colleagues voted for it. That decision, made in August 2002, was subsequently confirmed by the full council. O'Shaughnessy, a former council chairman, declared his interest in the land and abstained in votes on the matter. He said he was only one of three or four landowners whose property had been rezoned. However, the parcels of land owned by O'Shaughnessy on the Mullingar road, and Cogan on the Castlepollard road, were the only ones rezoned after the local area plan had been publicly exhibited. Many local people were incensed by what they saw as public representatives abusing their position. A public meeting had voted against the rezoning, but the councillors claim they were unaware of this. What also galled some of those at a second public meeting in November 2002 was the fact that the green light had been given for whole housing estates in an area where people had been refused planning permission for single houses.

The two very selective rezonings of land to the north and south of Delvin for suburban housing make a mockery of the local area plan's commitment to 'sustainable development', with the emphasis on spreading outwards from the centre in an orderly way. The organic character of the village will be destroyed. Yet despite its growth feeding off Dublin in opposition to strategic planning, the Department of the Environment has pledged almost €1 million to upgrade Delvin's sewerage system. This represents 40% of the cost; the rest will have to be funded by developers buying up the freshly rezoned land. As for employment opportunities, Delvin hasn't managed to attract industry or retailing. A cluster of small industrial units is being developed, but there's no great optimism that they will be filled. Only housing is on offer; jobs will be somewhere else.

The rezonings around Delvin, Castlepollard, Kilbeggan, Kinnegad and Rochfortbridge also threaten to undermine the National Spatial Strategy's goal of turning Athlone, Mullingar and Tullamore into a growth 'gateway'. This will be compounded if the same pattern is repeated in other Co Westmeath villages. And while the population of Athlone and Mullingar has grown in recent years, especially at their edges, the rate of increase is lower than some of the villages in the east of the county. If they are to attain the critical mass needed to become a gateway, development will have to be targeted in their direction. Regional planning guidelines adopted in April 2004 by the Midlands Regional Authority, which covers Longford, Westmeath, Laois and Offaly, noted that urban areas account for only 37% of the region's population, compared to 57% in the mid-east (Meath, Kildare and Wicklow), and that more than 60% of its recent 20,000 increase was due to an influx of Dublin commuters. Such a scenario, the plan warned, would create 'image' problems for the region. 'A laissez-faire or "do-nothing" approach will not provide the necessary focus and consequential critical mass among the principal towns and increasingly dispersed development', the Authority noted.

Local plans for towns were meant to provide a framework for orderly development at a more micro level than broad-brush county plans. Instead, many have been used as tools to rezone land at the behest of those who stand to gain from it. The village of Dunleer (pop. 1,100) offers an object lesson in how the common good can be swept aside in the rush to profit from Dublin's sprawl. Yet the process of drawing up its local plan started out so innocently. In the autumn of 1998, An Taisce and the UCD School of Architecture initiated work on a plan for Dunleer, with help from the Heritage Council and Louth County Council. Subsequently, the local community formed the Dunleer Steering Committee, which commissioned New Ground planning consultants to prepare a strategic community development plan, presented to Louth County Council in June 2000. Three months later, a further step was taken when the county council appointed architects and urban planners Murray Ó Laoire to compile draft local area plans for three of Co Louth's most historic villages – Carlingford, Omeath and Dunleer. In Dunleer alone, developers were already doing their best to gain approval for suburban housing estates as well as a 'retail outlet village'. Katsar Properties Ltd, a Dublin-based company, had an interest in building 125 houses on the outskirts of Dunleer, but this plan was turned down by the county council. An Bord Pleanála also refused permission for this housing scheme on appeal. Government minister and local Fianna Fáil TD Dermot Ahern made representations on Katsar's behalf, enclosing a letter from the company in which senior county council officials were accused of being 'very opposed to any significant development in Dunleer'. In November 2000, while the draft local plan was being prepared, An Bord Pleanála shocked local community activists when it approved plans by Austin Developments Ltd for a suburban estate of 270 houses on a 31-acre site on the Dublin side of the village. This scheme alone would nearly double the size of Dunleer, making it part of Commuterland. The village of some 322 houses, like so many other settlements within an 80km radius of Dublin, was now in danger of being swamped by haphazard expansion.

Murray Ó Laoire's local plan for Dunleer was intended to provide a framework for orderly development. Though it would have more than doubled the population in six years, this was to be done on a phased basis, with the emphasis on consolidating the village. There had been extensive consultation with local people and councillors throughout the preparation of the plan, and one of the few criticisms was that it didn't propose reopening Dunleer's old railway station. The draft was put on public exhibition in January 2002. Immediately after that, it emerged that the five county councillors representing mid-Louth, which includes Dunleer, had commissioned an alternative plan of their own, in association with a very active development lobby. These councillors had initially approached Gerry Duffy, Louth County Council's senior planner, with a map showing a red line drawn around the village, rezoning enough land to accommodate 40,000-50,000 people. Duffy told them that there was no way he could have 'endorsed a red line on a map as a plan'. So the five councillors hired planning consultant Stephen Ward, an ex-council staff member, to prepare their own plan. Its thrust was to extend Dunleer's development boundary way beyond the Murray Ó Laoire draft. The main proponent, Cllr Tommy Reilly (FF), then council chairman, said the aim was 'to get the zoning done first and then we will be going back to copper-fasten it'. Their intervention was described as unprecedented by a former Dunleer councillor, Hugh Conlon, who attacked the five for focusing on land rezoning while ignoring more important issues such as water supply, lack of recreational facilities and transport.

The motivation of the five councillors in commissioning their own plan was also questioned by Michael Bell TD (Labour), who pointed out that the county council already had a plan for Dunleer in which there had been full public participation. Bell called for an inquiry. One of the councillors, Thomas Clare (FF), the only one actually living in Dunleer, later broke ranks with his colleagues because there had been no public consultation on their 'substitute' plan. He even characterised it as a complete sham. 'If we can sit here and pass a plan which is totally different to the one the public have been consulted on for the past 18 months, there is something seriously wrong', Cllr Clare said. 'What is a local area plan if it is not done in conjunction with the local people?' The other four pressed on and put their plan to a vote by the council at its monthly meeting in May 2002 – ignoring a warning from the county manager, John Quinlivan, that it would be open to legal challenge because they were both proposing the plan and voting on it. After a lengthy and often heated debate, nine councillors voted for it and nine against, with both Fianna Fáil and Fine Gael evenly split on the issue. It was then carried on the casting vote of the chairman, Cllr Reilly, who had played a leading role in putting it together. Gerry Crilly, chairman of the community-based Dunleer Steering Committee, described the conduct of those who voted for the plan as 'most improper'. It showed that some public representatives were 'unable to work on behalf of the community as a whole'. But the developers were delighted. Donal Kinsella, chairman of Fianna Fáil in Louth, saw it as improving the chances of his proposed 'retail outlet village' going ahead because the 57-acre site at Woodland – his family farm – would now be included within the new boundary.

↓ *Donal Kinsella, chairman of Fianna Fáil in Louth, whose family farm in Dunleer was rezoned for a 'retail outlet village'*

There was a glitch, however. As the *Mid-Louth Independent* reported, the councillors' 'Plan B' would be open to legal challenge because it dealt only with zoning, to the exclusion of phasing or infrastructural issues, so it would have to go back to public consultation. The outcome was 'Plan C', which essentially incorporates what the four councillors were seeking, giving Dunleer a population of about 6,000 – five times more than it has at present. Writing in the *Dundalk Democrat* on 1st February 2003, former councillor Hugh Conlon said the community was being 'force-fed a plan which was born out of greed and the short term benefit of a few rather than what is best for the people who live in the community'. Seán Ó Laoire, of Murray Ó Laoire, disassociated himself from the latest plan, saying he was 'saddened that our best endeavours on behalf of Louth County Council and the people of Dunleer have been disregarded'. This could only compound public cynicism of planning, he said. A despairing Gerry Crilly noted that the plan's cover 'tells the whole sorry story in one picture – a view looking north down main street with a big dark black sky over Dunleer'. Crilly later stood as a Fine Gael candidate for Louth County Council, but did not get elected.

Developer-led 'planning' has also become commonplace in Co Laois. Most shocking is the case of Killenard, a small village near Portarlington which has been seriously mauled by the Celtic Tiger. Until 2001, all it had was two 19th-century churches, a national school dating from 1962, a community centre, a pub called The Thatch, and 43 houses – all of them relatively modest bungalows built during the previous 30 years. But the view from the railway bridge coming into Killenard today is radically different. Spread out before you are serried ranks of cream-coloured suburban houses that rise up to a modern-day citadel – the Heritage Hotel & Country Club. New housing estates are strung out along a narrow road with no footpaths, not even outside the school where up to 200 parents deliver and collect children daily by car. There was no plan, no 'village design statement' and no zoning. And because none of the land was actually zoned for residential development, there was no legal requirement to provide any 'social and affordable' housing. In essence, what happened was that developers moved in, bought up land, and turned fields into housing estates, with Laois County Council's approval.

The running was made by Corrigeen Construction Ltd, controlled by Portlaoise developer Tommy Kane. In 2001 the company got planning permission for an 18-hole golf course (designed by Seve Ballesteros and Jeff Howes), a restaurant and a road layout for future development. One of the factors that influenced this fateful decision was that Corrigeen pledged to provide a pumping station and sewerage main linking Killenard with the treatment works in Portarlington – at no expense to the county council. Another was that Laois didn't have many tourist attractions and here was an opportunity to provide a major 'draw' that would also create jobs. But one thing lead to another and the initial plan was followed by separate schemes for 82 suburban houses, a golf clubhouse, a leisure centre, a golf academy and driving range, an indoor bowls arena, 18 'golf villas' – one of them built for Ballesteros – a par 3 golf course and a five-star hotel. Next door, another estate of 55 detached houses, in mock-Georgian style, has been developed by Tipperary-based Surestone Construction Ltd; the houses here had to be protected from the driving range by a 30ft-high fence. Killenard Lodge, an estate of 28 houses, appeared on the other side of the road, and Portarlington-based Liam McMahon, who got permission for it in

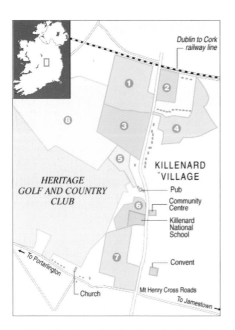

↑ *Map showing what has been built and what is planned for Killenard, Co Laois*

→ *Cattle grazing in a field in Killenard, with suburban houses and the Heritage Hotel on rising ground to the rear*

↓ *Billboard advertising 'exclusive homes' for sale in the village*

2001, later acquired a nearby field on which he hoped to get approval for a further 110 houses. Another developer, Terry Behan, wants to build 89 houses across the road while Corrigeen had no problem getting the council's approval for 86 more houses at the southern end of the village. This decision was overturned on appeal by An Bord Pleanála, which characterised the scheme as an 'unsympathetic, unco-ordinated, haphazard and non-plan-led extension to Killenard village'. Undeterred, Corrigeen came back in April 2005 looking for permission to build 106 houses in the same field.

The brochure for the Heritage

Country Club (www.theheritage.com) describes it as 'a world-class resort, nestled in the charming village of Killenard', and goes on: 'Accommodation at the Heritage Hotel begins with a liberating sense of space. Designed to inspire, its beauty connects you with the beautiful surroundings of the Laois countryside, while ensuring your comfort and convenience at this luxury lifestyle resort.' In fact, the resort complex is approached through a maze of housing. Many of the rooms in the lavishly decorated hotel, which opened in June 2005, overlook the rear ends and boundary walls of the houses built by Corrigeen itself. The golf clubhouse, described in the brochure as 'Ireland's largest and most inspiring', is three storeys high, topped by an octagonal lantern and clocktower. In front is a bronze statue of Seve Ballesteros, in full swing; the resort's golf academy uses his 'natural' method. The golf course, which needed a lot of earthmoving to create 98 bunkers and five lakes, is surrounded by a four-mile walking track, floodlit at night. Some 30,000 trees have also been planted. Michael Cobbe, a long-time resident of Killenard and retired county council engineer, welcomes some of the new amenities, but blames his former employers for what has happened to the village. 'They hadn't the courage to come in and design a new town.

They just allowed speculators to rule.' Michael Starrett, chief executive of the Heritage Council, agrees. At a June 2005 symposium in Durrow, Co Laois, on the future of Irish villages, he said that 'anyone who wants a definition of 'over-development' should go to Killenard', because what's been happening there is 'developer-led' and driven by its relative proximity to Dublin.

Even the tiny, unspoiled canalside village of Vicarstown, Co Laois (population: 168) was targeted for commuter-belt housing without a local area plan that might provide for its orderly development, starting with land closest to the village centre. In March 2000 Laois County Council granted permission to Corrigeen Construction for a scheme of 26 suburban houses and a sports hall at the edge of the village. With the support of a majority of local residents, An Taisce lodged an appeal, saying it would set a precedent for further housing schemes aimed at Dublin commuters – not just in Vicarstown, but on the outskirts of other villages too. Objectors noted that the village had no local industry apart from tourism, and lacked roads, shops, public transport and sewerage. It was not even on the county council's list for a sewage treatment plant. Nobody locally felt they could object to the proposed sports hall, which included indoor football and basketball facilities, even though its promoters had said at least 70 to 100 new houses would need to be built in Vicarstown to make this new facility commercially viable. Apart from one small council housing estate, the village has remained untouched for at least 100 years. 'For Vicarstown to retain its authentic features, which are so distinctive and unique, it is important that the future of the village is planned with great sensitivity', the local heritage group said. Otherwise, 'visitors and tourists will not want to come here'.

An Bord Pleanála agreed, overturning Laois County Council's decision to approve the housing scheme. But less than two years later, the council granted permission for a revised plan by Corrigeen Construction for 20 houses, with their own sewage treatment plant. This decision was again appealed by An Taisce, with the support of local residents, on the basis that suburban housing was 'completely inappropriate for such a tiny village and is typical of a developer-led plan which is designed to maximise profit for a select few'. In November 2002, for the second time in two years, An Bord Pleanála overturned the county council's decision, saying the proposed development failed to respect the design and character of the village. The sewage treatment system proposed was also unsatisfactory. Breda Keena, a local resident and member of An Taisce, said opponents of the scheme had come under pressure from councillors and others who 'fiercely' backed it. They were even barred from using the new sports hall, built with a €120,000 National Lottery grant. Noting that the earlier plan by Corrigeen Construction for 26 houses had been turned down by An Bord Pleanála in November 2000, she said it was 'unfair to local communities when they are under constant threat of having their built and natural environment destroyed'. According to Keena, the local development lobby simply wanted to cash in on Vicarstown's location 50 miles from Dublin by targeting new homes at people commuting to the capital by car. 'The traffic is so bad now that the journey can take up to three hours', she said. For their efforts to protect the essential qualities of

Vicarstown, An Taisce and the local objectors were denounced at meetings of Laois County Council in the aftermath of An Bord Pleanála's two rulings. So was the *Irish Times*, merely for highlighting the case. An Taisce called on the county council to sit down immediately with the residents of Vicarstown to agree on a sustainable development plan for the village, along the lines of a document they had drawn up two years earlier which the council had so far declined to discuss with them.

Martin Riordan, the Laois county manager, agreed that local area plans or 'design statements' needed to be prepared for new housing in villages such as Vicarstown, with the aim of providing a viable alternative to suburbanising the countryside. He was impressed by Kilminchy Village, an estate of 1,000 Dutch-style houses and apartments off the Dublin road, two miles from Portlaoise. Apart from a good mix of housing, it has a pub, a chemist, a convenience store, some small offices and a nursing home. But the colonisation of Portlaoise's periphery by commuter-belt housing estates resulted in a 41% increase in population between 1996 and 2002 while the town itself recorded a marginal decrease – a classic example of the 'doughnut effect'. As Kathy Sheridan noted, many people seem to have ended up in Portlaoise by default: 'We kept looking, going further and further down the road ... you begin looking in the outer suburbs [of Dublin], then you're in Kildare, and suddenly you're thinking, "sure Portlaoise is only down the road and that's a lovely, airy house in a safe estate, and we can afford it".' But local sewerage capacity is a significant issue. The Southern Regional Fisheries Board, which has responsibility for the Barrow, has taken appeals against a number of housing schemes, particularly in the Portlaoise area, arguing that they could threaten water quality. An 'interim upgrade' of the town's sewage treatment plant is planned in the short-term, with developers being levied €500 per house to help finance it. The county manager also sees 'major potential' for new development on sites near Portlaoise's railway station. Mountmellick, Portarlington and Stradbally are also being targeted for commuter housing. In Portarlington, which has a good train service to Dublin, dormer bungalows have been built right next to the railway station – further evidence of wasteful land use. As for what might happen in the future, a strategic study of population projections for Co Laois by Brady Shipman Martin painted a number of different scenarios. The most likely would involve continued 'in-migration' by Dubliners commuting by car, bus or train to the capital.

This trend looked likely to be accelerated by the county council's decision in February 2005 to rezone land around 29 villages and smaller towns, allowing for the construction of thousands of new homes that might otherwise have been built in major centres. There is no provision in the Midlands Regional Planning Guidelines, adopted in April 2004, for such large-scale residential development around the villages of Co Laois. The guidelines focus on building up the region's urban structure based on a 'hierarchy' of towns, with villages way down the list. However, if development started from the bottom of this hierarchy, it is obvious the places that really need to be built up would lose out, and the settlement pattern would become even more chaotic. Unusually, Fianna Fáil councillors voted en bloc against the plan, which had the support of Fine Gael, the Progressive Democrats, Sinn Féin and independent members. Cllr John Bonham (FG) described the move as a 'holistic approach' to planning. 'People want to live and be able to afford housing in local areas, go to local schools, support local businesses – this gives them that opportunity', he told Tim O'Brien, of the *Irish Times*. But Cllr Michael Moloney (FF) feared the rezonings would conjure up a 'Rochfortbridge scenario', saying plans for each village should have been drawn up in consultation with local communities. The only conceivable justification for zoning land around villages is that it would, as An Taisce has argued, provide a viable alternative to indiscriminate one-off housing in the countryside.

Carlow is also struggling with haphazard suburban housing development targeting Dublin commuters. In 2001 the ESRI identified it as an 'emerging large commuter town'; at the same time, an ambitious master plan was being prepared proposing that it should be developed as a 'model town for sustainable living' in the 21st century. The contradiction between that laudable objective and the depressing sprawl of car-dependant suburban housing on its outskirts remains a key problem for Carlow – especially with its ancient rival, Kilkenny, attaining 'hub' status under the National Spatial Strategy. But neither Carlow Town Council nor Carlow County Council has complete control over what happens. The town boundary incorporates only a small part of Graiguecullen, just across the River Barrow, and the rest of it comes under the jurisdiction of Laois County Council. This suburb of Carlow, within walking distance of the town centre, has become one of the fastest-growing areas in Co Laois. Its population rose by nearly 21% between 1996 and 2002, and further

↓ *Karen and Michael Blackburn put their children in the car before dropping them off at a playschool in Portlaoise and driving to work in Dublin*

growth seems likely based on the number of planning permissions granted. There is regular contact between the three local authorities, but no agreed agenda on what should happen in Graiguecullen. Changing the boundary to make it legally part of Carlow would be as politically sensitive as, say, ceding a chunk of south-east Clare to Limerick or a strip of south Kilkenny to Waterford.

This unchecked pace of development took residents of Graiguecullen by surprise. One scheme alone involved nearly 700 new homes, on top of three housing estates already approved by Laois County Council. Their complaint, so familiar in other development 'hot-spots', was that its population was set to double without a corresponding increase in support facilities; just one road – known locally as the Numbers Road – would have to take the extra traffic from all the new housing. The council's response was that this additional pressure on the local road network, caused by the new housing schemes it was approving in Graiguecullen, would in itself make a case for the National Roads Authority to expedite approval for a Carlow northern relief route. The Carlow 800 master plan – so-called because it marked the 800th anniversary of the town's royal charter – conceded that the scale of suburban housing development on its outskirts would tend to intensify long-distance commuting to Dublin, just 50 miles north via the N9. Apart from Castledermot, Co Kildare, every town on the route has now been bypassed, making Carlow more accessible to the capital. Road improvements have also encouraged commuting from rural locations in the county. The proposed M9 from Dublin to Waterford, as envisaged in the National Development Plan, will extend the radius of the commuter belt. As for public transport, there is only one Dublin-bound train per day of any use to commuters, and it leaves Carlow at 6.30am. It's certainly of no use to Dublin-born Barry Wall, who lives in Carlow with his wife Michelle. After a 90-minute journey to Heuston, he would need to get two buses – a No.90 to the city centre and then a No.11 from there to the IT company he works for in Clonskeagh, and this would add another 45 minutes to his journey time. Getting back to Heuston for the train home would be even more of a problem. So he gets up at 5.30am to join the 'convoy of cars' heading for Dublin, to make it to work by 7am.

According to the Carlow 800 plan, compiled by Murray Ó Laoire, commuting from Carlow is likely to rise in absolute numbers until it is constrained by such factors as increasing traffic congestion and a slowdown in job creation in the Dublin area. In the meantime, local movers-and-shakers such as John McLoughlin, the owner of a hotel, pub and disco in Carlow town, are dusting down plans for landbanks they have assembled on its outskirts. One site off the Tullow road is targeted for up to 1,200 houses and apartments. Brownfield sites have been slower to take off, even though encouraging more 'in-town living' was one of the central planks of Carlow 800. While the master plan and civic vision for the town won two certificates of merit in the Irish Planning Institute's annual awards in 2002 – mainly for the extensive exercise in public consultation that lay behind it – putting it into practice is another matter. 'The aim should be to establish Carlow as a domiciliary town, rather than a dormitory town', one well-placed source said. 'The ambitions are good, at least on paper. But the key question about the master plan is whether there's a will to see it through on the part of everyone involved.' The Carlow Environs plan, adopted in 2002, did show some restraint in not rezoning more land for housing on the outskirts. As senior planner Liam McGree explained, this was in the interests of consolidating the urban area and encouraging the development of sites already zoned but still lying fallow. Carlow Town Council's latest development plan also emphasises the need for consolidation, as well as mixed-use schemes, to generate more employment. The latter is intended to overcome the town's 'poor performance in economic terms', as the Murray Ó Laoire plan put it. The urban area accounts for more than a third of Co Carlow's population of 45,845, according to the 2002 census. The county showed a 10% rate of growth since 1996 – not quite so spectacular as some of the growth rates recorded in other counties closer to Dublin.

Co Kildare is growing faster than any other county in the Republic with the single exception of Meath. The 2002 census showed that it was just five people short of the target of 164,000 for 2006, set by the 1999 Strategic Planning Guidelines, having recorded a 21.5% increase in population since 1996 – mainly in areas close to Dublin. The population of Naas, the county town, rose by 30% to 18,312. Newbridge grew slightly faster (by 32%) to 8,686, while Kildare town went up by 29% to 6,893, and Kilcock by more than 45% to 3,251. Athy, more remote from Dublin, rose by 18% to 5,270. All the signs are that it will continue growing haphazardly in defiance of the planning guidelines. As if further evidence was needed, the 2002 census confirmed that villages never intended for development, other than to meet local needs, had become entangled in the Dublin commuter belt. Clane's population went up by nearly 30% to 5,192, and Kill's by 37.5%, while Bodenstown, known more as a place of pilgrimage for Wolfe Tone commemorations, grew by a staggering 120% to 3,206. Growth rates in Leixlip and Maynooth, both in the Dublin metropolitan area and actually earmarked for development, were much more modest.

Other designated growth centres that recorded population increases substantially less than the county average include Kilcullen (up 5.8% to 1,780) and Monasterevin (up 12% to 3,158). Celbridge, where the SPGs sought more controlled development, saw its figure rise by 28% to 14,251. Kildare County Council must shoulder the blame. Even as it was denying that there was any conflict between its own plan and the SPGs, the council was not only targeting Maynooth and Kilcock – both designated for development under the guidelines – but also Clane, Castledermot and Kill, which were not. Like other villages in Co Kildare, these are located in the 'strategic greenbelt' of Dublin's hinterland, according to the SPGs. The draft local area plan for Kill, published in March 2001, even noted this greenbelt designation and the restriction of growth to 'local needs only'; it then proceeded to propose doubling its population. In the case of Castledermot, the local area plan also quoted the SPGs' prohibition on development other than that required for local needs. But it, too, went on to suggest a 200% increase in population by 2006. More than 500 new homes would be needed to accommodate this dramatic increase. Conceding that most of the demand arises from Dublin's overspill, the council's housing strategy estimates the number of households in the county will increase by more than 26% to 65,159 by 2006 and says that improved roads, sewerage, electricity and telecom services will be needed to cater for this growth. As elsewhere, developers tend to get what they want in Co Kildare. Fianna Fáil and Fine Gael councillors unanimously support land rezoning on area committees, and their decisions are then rubber-stamped by the full council. It's another free-for-all, of course, but with chaotic consequences.

Not everyone in Co Kildare is as gung-ho about development as the council-lors. There was fierce resistance in Clane to what local people saw as an unseemly rush by councillors to rezone large tracts of land for housing on the outskirts of a vil-lage that lacked the facilities even to cater for its existing population. A massive cam-paign was waged against these rezonings in 1996, prompting the then minister for the environment, Labour's Brendan Howlin, to intervene. He refused to approve an early draft of the county development plan on the basis that it was being put together in a piecemeal fashion, with no overall strategy. His successor, Noel Dempsey, sent back a revised draft in 1997 because he saw its population targets as excessive, and the county council then engaged planning consultants Jonathan Blackwell Associates to draw up a new strategy. This provided the foundations for the revised county plan, which was finally adopted in May 1999. Though the local area plans for Clane and Kill were quashed by the High Court, on the grounds that they were being adopted out of time, the county council later proceeded to designate Clane as a 'primary growth centre' in defiance of the SPGs, and set a population target of 6,300 for the village, to be achieved by 2006. But Cllr Tony McEvoy (Ind), who unsuccessfully chal-lenged the Meath county plan in the High Court, maintains that if all of the zoned land in the area is developed – some 140 acres in total – Clane's population could soar to 10,000, or almost double the figure recorded in 2002.

Since the present county plan was adopted, a number of other towns and vil-lages have been the subject of local area plans, all characterised by the over-zoning of land. These include Rathangan and even little-known Derrinturn, barely more than a crossroads, which could end up with a population exceeding 3,000. In Sallins the population has soared since 1996, provoking a schools crisis. There were 120 appli-cants for 60 places in junior infants in September 2003, Kathy Sheridan reported in the *Irish Times*, and a house-to-house survey showed that with 500 children under the age of 4, and another 500 aged 4 to 13, 'no less than 130 new applicants will be clam-ouring for places for each of the next four years. And that assumes no further devel-opment will take place.' The local curate, Fr Colum Swan, is performing four bap-tisms a week, compared to 30 a year in the past. 'All of a sudden, Sallins is inundat-ed, almost drowning in new people', he said in May 2003. 'We need schools, foot-paths, lighting, roads, shops, ramps, a community centre, a playground. There is no green space, yet another 50 houses are due to come on stream in a few weeks.' When individual targets for all the towns and villages with local area plans are added to a growing rural population, the Kildare county plan would facilitate a total population of 197,000 by 2006 – 22% more than the target set by the SPGs. Thus, there is no way the county council can claim to be in compliance. The county plan assumed that the

↑ *Sallins, Co Kildare: the pleasant canalside village has seen its population grow by 70% between 1996 and 2002, even though it's not designated for development*

population of rural Kildare would remain constant, at around 36,000. It hasn't, under the tenure of county manager Niall Bradley. In 2001 alone, 900 'one-off' houses were built in the countryside, typically against planning advice.

In recent years, An Taisce lodged at least 60 appeals against schemes in Co Kildare, many of them cases where refusals were recommended by the planners because they breached policy. Of 40 consecutive cases determined by An Bord Pleanála, the county council lost every single one. In one case where a Dublin-based solicitor built a large two-storey house without planning permission in Ballycaghan, near Kilcock, Charlie McCreevy made representations on the developer's behalf in 2002, using Department of Finance headed notepaper. The solicitor involved, Donal Quinn, was prosecuted in the Circuit Court for carrying out an unauthorised development, but the council subsequently granted planning permission, and even consented in writing to the house being sold, unencumbered by its tainted planning history; it is believed to have fetched well over a million euro in July 2005. It was also McCreevy, then Minister for Finance and local Fianna Fáil TD, who allocated £2.5 million (€3.2 million) for the reopening of Monasterevin station in 2001. This was based on projections by the town's railway action committee that 95% of its 270 Dublin-bound commuters would use it – a figure disputed by Iarnród Éireann. There has been a pathetically low return on this public investment, which included a 50-space car park and hydraulic lifts for wheelchair access. Though the town is now served by five mainline trains travelling to and from Dublin, average daily boardings amount to about 50. The only hope is that this will grow with Monasterevin.

The pace of development in Co Wicklow has not been quite as frenetic as in Kildare and Meath. But within 12 months of the Strategic Planning Guidelines being published in April 1999, Wicklow County Council was considering several major housing schemes that would, if approved, treble the population of Newtown-mountkennedy. But Newtown, as it is known locally, had not been designated as a growth centre by the guidelines, to which the county council appended its name. The two-pub village was to be part of a 'strategic greenbelt', with expansion confined to meeting local needs. Under the SPGs, only Bray and Greystones were included in the Dublin Metropolitan Area, while the rest of Co Wicklow was clearly identified as part as the capital's hinterland, with just Wicklow town and Arklow designated for development as significant growth centres. However, this did not deter major Dublin housebuilders such as Dwyer Nolan and Gannon Homes assembling land banks around Newtown. Along with other developers (Springmount, Swanoaks and Garden Village), they put forward plans to build more than 2,200 new homes in the area. The county council responded by drawing up a local area plan for Newtown on the basis that it had already been designated as a 'local growth centre' in the county development plan. One senior official, Bryan Doyle, noted that it was only 20 miles from Dublin and had 'excellent access' to the N11. There was pressure for housing in the area, and the only thing that had held Newtown back was the absence of sewerage facilities. 'It has – or it will have – water and sewage', he said. In any case, 'more houses have to be built' to meet the demand for new homes in the Greater Dublin Area.

It didn't seem to matter that Newtown had no community centre, no health centre, no cinema, no Garda station, no buses to Dublin, not even a feeder service to the DART at Greystones, as local GP Dr Craig Bishop pointed out. And there was only one secondary school between Bray and Wicklow town. Along with other members of the local action group, he complained that the plans had been prepared in the offices of property developers or their agents. Kiaran O'Malley, a very experienced planning consultant engaged by the county council to advise on the Newtown area plan, told his clients the SPGs 'appear opposed to anything other than planning for local needs' and that the indigenous demand for housing was 'extremely modest'. Michael Grace, of Brady Shipman Martin, the consultants who advised on drafting the guidelines, said he believed it would be 'very difficult' to justify Wicklow County Council's plans for Newtown – as well as Kilcoole, Ashford, Newcastle and other villages – in the light of their recommendations. The effect of targeting such villages as 'local growth centres' would be to create a development corridor down the N11, deep into Co Wicklow, peppered with low-density housing estates catering for commuters. This would extend Dublin's sprawl in precisely the way the SPGs sought to avoid. While the plans were being considered, the Dublin Transportation Office lodged a written objection with the county council pointing out that excessive housing development along the N11 would impair the strategic importance of the route to Rosslare by clogging the corridor with commuter traffic.

North Wicklow's ever-expanding commuter belt already accounts for a substantial proportion of the traffic using the N11. It was largely for the benefit of commuters that a dual carriageway was driven through the Glen of the Downs at the staggering cost of €85 million. In March 2001, two months after the SPGs were given statutory standing, the Department of the Environment wrote to the county council querying its plans for large-scale rezoning of greenbelt land in Newtown and Kilcoole, saying this represented 'a very significant divergence' from the guidelines. Noting that the Minister, Noel Dempsey, had requested that each local authority in the Greater Dublin Area 'should ensure that its development plan is in line with the strategy set out in the guidelines', the Department said it was its 'strong view that the proposed town plans should not be adopted'. Wicklow County Council carried on regardless, blithely ignoring a veiled ministerial threat to invoke Section 31 of the 2000 Planning Act with a view to enforcing compliance with the SPGs. Dempsey failed to follow through on his threat, and the council proceeded to adopt the controversial local plans without sanction.

Despite fierce opposition, enough land was zoned around Newtown to double its population in five years, with developers clubbing together to fund a new sewage mains. Commenting on the 'houses before social facilities' scenario, Cllr George Jones (FG) said: 'Show me anywhere it has happened the other way around.' But Dick Roche TD (FF), then Minister of State for European Affairs, said the council was merely licensing land for house-building – 'you couldn't call it planning' – while Cllr Deirdre de Burca (Green Party) called for Wicklow's planning procedures to be independently investigated. If all of the land now zoned for development is built on, Co Wicklow's population will soar over the next five years. This would produce a massive suburban sprawl encompassing all of north-east Wicklow, with no detailed plans for schools and other facilities. In 2003 the people of Arklow, one of the county's designated growth centres, had to rely on tankers for their drinking water after the fluoridation plant broke down. And though hundreds of new houses are being built there, the town still had no sewage treatment plant at the time of writing, and raw sewage was pouring into the Avoca river, already the most polluted in Ireland.

The Wicklow county manager, Eddie Sheehy, emphatically denied in May 2003 that the council had ignored the Strategic Planning Guidelines. What actually happened, he said, was that there had been 'extensive and detailed discussions' with senior officials of the Department of the Environment, following which Sheehy made a report to the county councillors detailing amendments to the draft plan for Newtown to ensure that it would comply with the guidelines. The councillors accepted this report, and the Department said, by letter in July 2001, that it would 'raise no further objections' to the zonings. 'All subsequent town plans were drafted on a similar basis in order to ensure compliance with the Strategic Planning Guidelines and neither the Minister nor his officials raised any objections', Sheehy insisted. But Judy Osborne, of the Wicklow Planning Alliance, said it was obvious that the multiple growth centres identified in the county plan conflict with the SPGs, which would have limited development to Bray-Greystones, Wicklow town and Arklow. The fact that the Department had accepted this plan 'could only have been because the Minister, Noel Dempsey, did not have the political will to enforce those guidelines', she said. It quickly became clear that his successor, Martin Cullen, had no intention of enforcing the regional strategy either. 'Thus, a plan which might have brought a semblance of order to the growth of Dublin and its hinterland has been abandoned in the interest of accommodating the development lobby.'

Like Newtown, the historic village of Blessington in west Wicklow was never meant to become a growth centre under the Strategic Planning Guidelines. Yet it too is on a cusp, as Kathy Sheridan wrote in May 2003. 'The result is that the population, already doubled, is set to double again ... Disastrous water quality in some estates, massive illegal dumping, the quarrying threat to Glen Ding wood, the bursting schools population, the slow, infrequent bus service, a sense of virtually unstoppable, unsustainable development – all conspire to mar the idyllic image of rural life. Many are forced to buy all their water or keep containers in the car boot for filling on visits to obliging friends and relatives. One mother, fresh from a town where the school had 25 children to a class, found 48 in her daughter's class in Blessington. The resource teacher is forced to give her sensitive, one-to-one tuition in a narrow corridor. GAA and soccer coaching facilities are stretched to breaking point. On Saturdays, buses to Tallaght and the city centre are packed with teenagers seeking diversions unavailable near home, while adults head for Naas to do the weekly shopping.' But Frank Corcoran, national chairman of An Taisce and resident of Blessington, pointed out that significant concessions have been wrung from housing developers, including a 200-seat theatre, a pitch-and-putt course, tennis and bowling greens, a 40-acre public park, some underground parking and a commitment that development would be phased.

However, anyone who thought that a new batch of councillors would bring wayward planning in Wicklow under control had their hopes dashed in August 2004 when Liam Reid revealed that the newly elected council had been hoodwinked into voting in favour of a major rezoning at Ballyhenry, two miles from Ashford. Seeking to cash in on the new Ashford-Rathnew bypass, landowner Joe O'Connell applied to have his 172-acre farm rezoned for commercial use, including a 'centre of sporting excellence'. In a formal written submission to the council on behalf of O'Connell, Tim Rowe of Rowe McGill Architects said the 'studios at Ardmore are now not satisfactory and require relocation'. He went on to warn that Ardmore had been approached to relocate to Co Kildare, and that 'if action is not taken by Co Wicklow ... the benefits of this industry will be lost to another county'. On the strength of this spurious claim, as it turned out, 15 of the 24 councillors ignored the county manager's advice and voted in favour of a rezoning motion tabled by Cllr Fachtna Whittle (FF); they included a majority in both Fianna Fáil and Fine Gael as well as a number of Labour and independent members. If the decision was confirmed, the Ballyhenry land might be worth up to €150,000 an acre – or seven times its agricultural value.

↑ *New housing estates are built on the edge of Blessington, Co Wicklow, even though it was not identified as a growth centre under the Greater Dublin Area Strategic Planning Guidelines*

But there was a problem: not one of the councillors had bothered to pick up a phone and check with Ardmore Studios. When its managing director, Kevin Moriarty, later made it clear that Ardmore had no intention of moving from Bray, O'Connell admitted that the claim made by his architect was incorrect, but said it had been made 'inadvertently'. Dick Roche, later Minister for the Environment, was 'absolutely flabbergasted' by the circumstances surrounding the decision. It was just one of a number of 'highly questionable' amendments to the draft county plan made during a 'chaotic' 18-hour meeting on 12th July 2004, which brought the entire planning process 'into disrepute'. Five Fine Gael councillors who had voted for the rezoning based on the Ardmore Studios claim said they would be re-examining their position. At the same marathon meting, Whittle proposed a rezoning motion for an unauthorised quarry at Ballylusk, near Ashford, to legitimise and extend its operations. It later emerged that the newly elected councillor, who is a solicitor, had defended the quarry owners in a legal action by the council to have it closed down. He had not declared this before proposing or voting on the motion, which was adopted by 10 votes to 9, maintaining that there was no conflict of interest. An internal investigation concluded that Whittle was 'unwise' to have acted as he did, though it found no evidence that he had any 'beneficial or other pecuniary interest' in the quarry.

Another controversial rezoning was of a 12-acre field at Leamore, near Newcastle, for the development of a medical centre and nursing home, even though it's located on a small country road beside a bird sanctuary.

Ironically, it was in Greystones, one of the areas designated for growth under the SPGs because of its good transport links and social facilities, that local politicians have opposed higher-density residential development. They include Cllr Derek Mitchell (FG), who campaigned for the DART to be extended there. Though the guidelines emphasise the importance of locating new development close to public transport corridors, he was appalled by An Bord Pleanála's 2003 decision to approve plans for 1,446 houses and apartments on a 108-acre site at Charlesland, immediately south of the town's Surrey-like Burnaby Estate. The scheme is next to a proposed industrial park so huge that there are suggestions to relocate Greystones railway station to serve it. In line with the Wicklow county plan, the scheme provides for a southern relief road which would also serve as a bypass for the expanding village of Delgany. Together with IDA Ireland, the developers, headed by Ballymore Homes Ltd, offered to finance a new €10 million interchange on the N11 at Kilpedder and a new link road costing €13 million. On other issues, Mitchell has been sharper. In August 2004 he warned that a relaxation of planning rules on one-off housing had the potential to damage the environment, especially in green belt areas. 'The northern parts of the county are already under considerable pressure from encroachment from Dublin. It's very serious because this new rule could see most rural roads in north Wicklow being covered with rows of bungalows', he said. Previously, applications from people who were brought up in a particular townland would be entertained, and, in all cases, a visual impact assessment would be required. However, the definition of 'immediate vicinity' was changed, against professional planning advice, to a radius of 8km. This would mean that thousands of residents of large towns in Wicklow, including Bray and Greystones, would be eligible to build in the countryside, Mitchell told Liam Reid of the *Irish Times*. The revised guidelines, adopted in July 2004 by newly elected councillors against the advice of their professional planners, limited visual impact assessment to 20 listed areas of outstanding natural beauty. According to Judy Osborne, these changes will have a much more widespread impact than many of the bizarre rezonings because effectively they would mean that everything was open for consideration in rural areas, including the uplands. 'I've never seen so many "for sale" signs going up', she commented.

Back in 1999, the first set of Strategic Planning Guidelines made it clear that widely strung-out development generates significant levels of car commuting, and is neither environmentally nor economically sustainable. But the authors had nothing to say about 'Dublin' leapfrogging over the Greater Dublin Area's boundaries, even though this was already happening when the SPGs were being compiled. It had never been envisaged that counties in outer Leinster would grab shares in the capital's unprecedented growth, so the issue was never really addressed. Those in charge of implementing the guidelines – to the extent that they are being implemented at all – take the complacent view that housing in the outer commuter belt will become less attractive as the penny drops about the consequences of spending long hours behind the wheel of a car.

It is quite clear also that the central objective of the original guidelines – to consolidate the metropolitan area and restrict growth to designated centres in its hinterland – has not been achieved. The latest set of regional planning guidelines, prepared by WS Atkins, concede 'an imbalance' in the growth of the GDA, with much of it taking place in Meath, Kildare and Wicklow rather than in and around Dublin. There is a migration of population in search of affordable housing, while most of the jobs remain concentrated in the metropolitan area. The result is a huge increase in long-distance commuting by car. If current trends continue, as the guidelines' authors acknowledge, jobs will continue to be predominantly located in and around Dublin while the population of the hinterland area will grow, increasing the amount of commuting and congestion. In its nightmare scenario for 2016, some of the GDA's countryside will resemble an ultra-low-density suburb; designated urban areas will not be as fully developed as planned; and there will be difficulties in managing 'increasingly polluted' water resources. In effect, Dublin would become an 'edge city'. As the authors say, 'if current trends continue ... then the area will fail, perhaps quite badly' to meet the goals and objectives set out in 1999.

The aim of stemming Dublin's dispersal is based on an assumption that the new regional planning guidelines and the National Spatial Strategy will actually be implemented. There is no indication that this will happen. Though the guidelines identify an underground link between Heuston and the city centre as a 'vital project', they concede that transport investment 'will need to be reviewed in the light of ... current and projected budgetary and economic conditions'. In other words, it may not happen at all. There is a similar caveat regarding the proposal floated in the 1999 guidelines that the old Navan railway line should be reopened. With the National Roads Authority committed to proceeding with an M3 between Clonee and Kells, at an estimated cost of €680 million, the new guidelines say the rail-link proposal would have to take into account the impact which the motorway is likely to have on potential rail patronage levels.

In attempting to put some shape on things, the guidelines set out a blueprint to develop the GDA as a sustainable, European-style polycentric city region – or 'bunch of grapes', as it's known – where the hinterland towns around Dublin would expand on the back of their location on new or improved national primary routes, turning east Leinster into a region similar to the Delta Metropolis in the Netherlands or the Rhine-Ruhr Valley area of Germany. With the M50 clogged with traffic, one of the guidelines' key recommendations is an outer orbital route linking Navan, Naas and Kildare – possibly even extending eastwards to Wicklow town, with potentially devastating impacts on the county's mountain landscape. There is also talk of a further 'outer-outer orbital' which would link up Dundalk, Mullingar, Carlow and Enniscorthy, drawing them into the GDA's 'bunch of grapes'. According to the Green Party's transport spokesman, Eamon Ryan TD, 'the remarkable difference between these new guidelines and the earlier version from 1999 is that even the pretence of pre-

↑ *Boyne Hall, one of the suburban housing estates that have mushroomed in the fields around Drogheda in recent years*

ferring public transport to the continued growth in the use of the private car has been dropped.' The first recommendation of the 1999 Strategic Planning Guidelines stated that 'public transport and other sustainable modes should be given precedence over the requirements of the private car in all relevant policy and decisions.' In reviewing that recommendation, the new regional planning guidelines state: 'It is necessary to find a balance between the use of different modes, appropriate to the journey being made. Progress has been made in prioritising walking, cycling and bus. The car also has a role to play in providing balance in the transport system.' The result, in other words, will be even more car-dependency.

One by-product of the development feeding off Dublin is cultural dislocation. Certainly, there is something poignant about the sight of so many Dublin flags flying from houses in Rochfortbridge in Co Westmeath on the day Dublin were playing in an All-Ireland football semi-final in Croke Park. Teenagers who have no choice in the matter are the worst affected by relocation from Dublin to a new home in Commuterland. When Jim Kinsella and his wife Cora moved from Donaghmede to Termon Abbey, a new housing estate on the outskirts of Drogheda in September 2002, it was their youngest daughter Catherine (15) who was most upset. She didn't think it would be so far out, so far away from everything, as Kathy Sheridan reported. 'For a teenager who once lived two minutes from the nearest DART station and two minutes to a vast shopping centre, and had buses at the door every 10 minutes, Termon Abbey – a 20-minute walk from Drogheda town, on the wrong side of the railway station – might as well be on the moon.' In Rochfortbridge, which has much fewer amenities than Drogheda, Sheridan heard 'tales of pining older children who go back to the city every weekend. The youth club, the GAA (to which there is no day-time access due to vandalism) and overstretched scouts can only do so much. To have no car is to be trapped.' And with no direct bus from Rochfortbridge to Mullingar, children can be seen standing on the edge of the road 'with their thumbs out'.

Then there are the costs borne by society as a whole. With so many bits of 'Dublin' popping up on the outskirts of Leinster towns and villages, the Department of Education is faced with the task of providing new schools in areas of unplanned growth. Two new schools are to be built in Navan, and one each in Clonee, Co Meath, Rush and Lusk, in north Co Dublin, and Wicklow town. 'Unfortunately, there's no scientific formula that if you build 1,500 houses, you're going to have ready-made families with X number of kids', one of the Department's officials told the *Irish Times*. 'In some areas, it's not going to impact all at once, but rather evolve over a period of 10 years, while in others new housing may redress dropping enrolments.' Provision will also be required to build new sewage treatment plants and upgrade existing ones, to provide piped water, electricity and phone lines for all the new housing, and more road space to cater for extra traffic, not to mention new Garda stations, playing fields, post offices and health centres. At the same time, we are faced with a 'stranded assets' syndrome. Even as new schools and civic centres are built in areas of population growth, whether planned or not, older facilities in established urban areas – including parts of Dublin city and its suburbs – are in danger of becoming redundant because their population is in decline. Some, indeed, have closed already. As Katherine Donnelly and John Walshe reported in April 2004, urban sprawl has already left some 26,000 second-level places vacant citywide, as well as 50,000 at primary level. One of the schools facing closure is author Roddy Doyle's alma mater, the highly regarded Greendale Community School in Kilbarrack. Cork and Limerick are facing similar problems, they reported. Dublin suburbs with ageing profiles plucked from the 2002 census include Beaumont (population down 12%), Finglas South D (17.5%), Grange C (14%), Whitehall D (15.5%) and Mounttown in Dún Laoghaire (14.2%). Even newer suburbs are beginning to see their population levels fall, largely due to the 'empty nest' syndrome as young people grow up and leave home. These include the Ludford area of Ballinteer (down 12.3%), the Rowlagh area of Clondalkin (14.2%) and the Millbrook area of Tallaght (13.4%).

In terms of gross figures, the population increases recorded by the 2002 census are more significant in Dublin's peripheral suburbs than they are in the far-flung reaches of Commuterland. The biggest single increase was in the Esker area of Lucan, where the population almost trebled in six years to reach a figure of 21,785. This is taking place in an area where development was planned, and is in line with the objective of the Strategic Planning Guidelines to consolidate the metropolitan area. What is happening in Rochfortbridge and other places outside the GDA, as well as some areas inside it, defies all planning policies. In July 2004 *Business and Finance* magazine reported that Fingal county councillors had 'signed off on proposals to rezone enough land to accommodate about 40% more than the projected 2011 population of a quarter of a million'. This will have knock-on effects on the much-vaunted National Spatial Strategy, because if more and more growth is absorbed by Dublin, the chances of other cities gathering momentum will be squandered.

These cities are sprawling unsustainably, too. A map based on the 2002 census shows great arcs of commuterland around Limerick and Galway. Yet Limerick has four railway lines running into it. In a more sensible society, its development could have been planned along these lines, stretching out towards Foynes, Nenagh, Ennis and Limerick Junction. But that would have required a commitment to higher-density living, and even today there is only a limited commuter service on the Ennis line. With six trains per day in each direction, the journey still takes 40 minutes – 10 minutes longer than travelling by car – even though there are no intermediate stations along the way. These trains are often attacked by stone-throwing youths as they pass by Moyross – a large swathe of social housing devoid of community facilities. Sprawl has also been promoted by what one observer called a 'we don't want to live in Limerick' factor, particularly among the more well-heeled. The chocolate-box village of Adare may look charmingly unspoilt, with no noticeable ribbon development along its main route, the N21, but the minor roads in every direction are littered with houses, most, no doubt, owned by commuters who drive into Limerick every day. The same is true throughout south-east Co Clare, with one-off houses spreading along minor country roads around Cratloe, Meelick and other villages. Cratloe even has its own suburban estate. There is also a clear lack of co-ordination between the mid-west's principal local authorities – Limerick City Council and the county councils of Limerick, Clare and North Tipperary. Although a common land-use and transport strategy was drafted by Buchanan & Partners in 2001, it had still not been adopted at the time of writing; Limerick County Council objected to its emphasis on reinforcing the city as the Mid-West's regional hub.

Waterford also suffers from a lack of strategic integration, as most of the land on the north bank of the River Suir is in Co Kilkenny, and moves to extend the city boundary have come to nought mainly because of intense opposition from GAA clubs. Every weekday, there is gridlock at the Ferrybank roundabout where city-bound traffic on the Clonmel and New Ross roads merges before advancing across Rice Bridge; only 8% of Waterford's commuters use public transport. Meanwhile, almost every new planning application erodes the potential for a close-knit, walkable city, and the chance to integrate the north bank into the urban area is being thrown away. Plans for a 63-acre site at Abbeylands, less than two miles north-east of the city centre, only envisage driving on or off the N25. An Taisce said this was premature, at least until the Co Kilkenny side is master-planned with a legible network of streets, but An Bord Pleanála – under orders from the Government to facilitate major housing schemes – let it through. The failure to extend our urban areas in a rational way

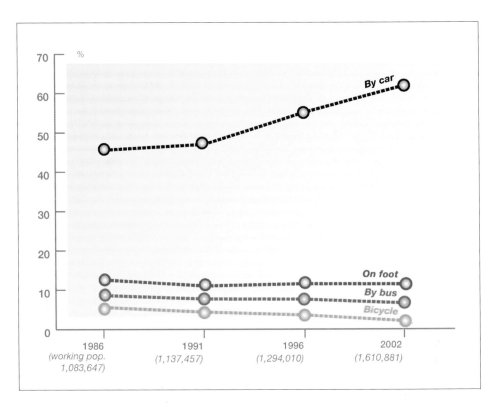

↑ *Travelling to work in Ireland, 1986-2002, and* ↓ *in the United States, 1960-2000. Commuting in Ireland seems to be following US trends.*

[*sources: Central Statistics Office, for Ireland;* National Geographic Magazine, *August 2004, for USA]*

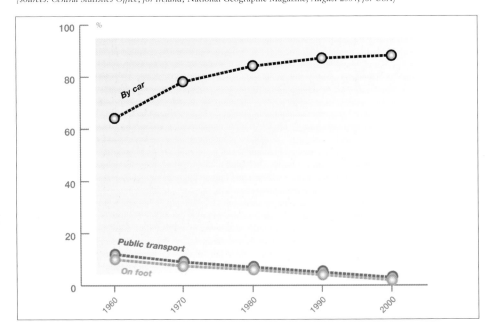

Growth Galway-style: ↑ the expansion of Terryland, with Woodies carpark in the foreground
↓ One of the roundabouts on Galway's western distributor road, fronted by some of the more
recent housing in Knocknacarra

was not the appeal board's problem. But at least it fended off the threat that Abbeylands would acquire a regional-scale shopping centre just over the 'border' in Co Kilkenny. This was seen by Waterford City Council as a 'mini-Quarryvale' in the making, something that could threaten retailing in the city centre, so it joined with Carrick-on-Suir Town Council in appealing against the proposed development. Some shape may be put on the city by the 2004 Waterford Planning, Land Use and Transportation Study (PLUTS), which proposes a new cross-city 'green route' between Waterford Institute of Technology and Belview Port – running via the quays and Rice Bridge – on which buses would have priority.

Cork prides itself as the first city in Ireland to adopt a land-use and transportation plan way back in 1979, and went on to build a major ring road, including the Jack Lynch Tunnel under the River Lee and an airport access route using the old Kinsale railway cutting. However, the LUTS plan did not deliver promised improvements in public transport, such as reopening the disused railway line to Midleton. In recent years, satellite towns in Co Cork such as Ballincollig, Ovens and Macroom have seen rapid growth, with the city and county co-ordinating planning under the umbrella of the Cork Area Strategic Plan (CASP), adopted in 2002. The plan put a strong emphasis on concentrating development along the Midleton and Macroom railway lines. After a funding famine that lasted through the 1980s and 1990s, the Government finally pledged in 2004 to invest €100 million in the Midleton line, and upgrade commuter services between Cork city and Mallow on the Dublin mainline. A public-private partnership approach is being adopted, with the county council levying developers for contributions towards the provision of new stations along the railway lines in places like Glounthane, Little Island, Carrigtwohill and Monard. Crucially, these levies will be offset by reduced contributions for roads so as not to deter investment along the rail lines. Others would go further. UCC transport specialists Dr Séamus Ó Tuama and Dr Cathal O'Connell have proposed that the Cork-Midleton line should be extended an extra half-mile into the city centre, as the original LUTS plan envisaged. CASP, too, proposes a more extensive rail network in the longer term. There are also plans for a total of 10 'green routes' – quality bus corridors with dedicated space for cyclists – and a vast park-and-ride site has opened at the Kinsale Road roundabout, offering all-day parking for €5 and a free bus into town. The initial results are impressive, with buses in the city increasing their average speed to 20kph – well ahead of cars at 8kph. These measures are designed to counteract a trend which has seen Cork end up with some of the most car-dependent dormitory towns in Ireland. Carrigaline, south of the city, topped the league in the 2002 census for the highest car-usage in the State. In 1996 some 63% of its commuters living there drove to work. By 2002 this had jumped to 74% – ahead of Dunboyne, Co Meath (70%), Tramore, Co Waterford (67%), and Naas, Co Kildare (65%).

Galway can barely contain the explosive growth it has experienced since the mid-1990s. The city is bursting at the seams, its ring road is gridlocked every day, and the Headford Road roundabout, almost as notorious as the M50's Red Cow interchange, has become known as the 'Roundabout from Hell'. As the current city plan concedes: 'We now have longer journey times to jobs and services, under-development and erosion of public transport, unequal access ... for those without a car, and unacceptable levels of congestion.' Suburban sprawl is extensive. Knocknacarra on the west side of the city has at least 12,000 residents, and this is now being matched by development in Doughiska and Oranmore to the east, as well as one-off houses stretching out in almost every direction. On the rising ground above Barna, bungalows extend in an almost unbroken ribbon along a boreen riddled by potholes with a strip of grass in the middle, and no shops or schools anywhere in the vicinity. Green Party councillor Niall Ó Brolcháin warned in August 2004 that the already-swamped village of Barna could turn into a 'mini-Torremolinos' if proposals for a new hotel, apartments and townhouses on the waterfront were approved. The new bungalows above Barna were all approved by Galway County Council, which operates a liberal regime on houses in rural areas, while slewn-out suburban estates have been tacked on to Tuam, Claregalway, Craughwell, Gort and Loughrea. Plans to develop Galway to the east along the so-called Ardaun Corridor, to house 18,000 new residents in a more sustainable way, have been stalled since the late 1990s. A new outer ring road is now proposed, extending from Oranmore to Barna, with a new bridge across the Corrib at Menlo, a picturesque, Irish-speaking village upriver of the Quincentennial Bridge. In terms of physical extent, Galway is facing the prospect that its suburbs will stretch 30 miles from Spiddal to Athenry, and northwards to Tuam. The city is becoming more and more car-dependent because of a persistent failure to invest in public transport. Though there is Government funding available for quality bus corridors in cities outside Dublin, Galway was slow to submit any plans, and the city's first bus lane – on the Dublin Road in Renmore – was only installed in 2005.

Dublin's sprawl is even more extensive, and balanced regional development will remain a hollow slogan as long as it is allowed to continue. Despite all the official guff, the Greater Dublin Area's share of the State's population has risen inexorably, from around 25% in the mid-1920s to nearly 39% today. If Dublin's tentacles reaching into outer Leinster are included, the proportion is already well over 40%. Apart from tiny Luxembourg, the only other EU member state with such a population imbalance is Greece – and it could hardly be regarded as a model of sustainable development. The SPGs that were meant to steer Dublin's development have been exposed as a paper tiger. Bringing large parcels of land together under one master plan – a common practice elsewhere in northern Europe – is hardly ever done here. Local authorities simply do not have the resources to prepare plans on a large scale – a point made repeatedly by the construction industry and planners alike. The price we are paying is a capital city sprawling out all over Leinster. The losers are you, us, and every other taxpayer who must pay for duplicating facilities. We are all living with the consequences of making it up as we go along.

–––––

3. Balanced Development

NOEL DEMPSEY DIDN'T MINCE HIS WORDS. A 1960S PLAN TO FOSTER REGIONAL BALANCE 'died a shameful death [because] local interests were put first ... by a range of people – politicians, the local media, the public – with disastrous consequences for the country as a whole and for the west and the midlands in particular. The plan was shelved because people were so parochial in their outlook that they couldn't bear what they saw as neighbouring towns benefiting at the expense of their own localities.' Dempsey, then Minister for the Environment, was speaking in September 2001 at the launch of a public consultation paper on the National Spatial Strategy, the latest effort to put some shape on how Ireland might develop in the years ahead. He chose his ground well – Charlestown, Co Mayo, birthplace of John Healy, whose crusading series of articles in the *Irish Times* in the late 1960s, 'Death of an Irish Town' (later published as a book, *No One Shouted Stop*) graphically documented the plight of the west. In 1969, as Dempsey noted, Colin Buchanan had set out to put things right by plotting a course for more balanced regional development to counter the unrestrained growth of Dublin. But Buchanan, a leading planner of the late 20th century, had his blueprint torn to shreds by parish-pump politics. Thirty years later, Dempsey saw the NSS as a chance to redress the balance, an opportunity 'too valuable to pass up'.

No one could doubt Noel Dempsey's personal commitment to the development of a coherent strategy, but he had been left high and dry more than once by pusillanimous political colleagues. And did he really need to 'reinvent the wheel' with the NSS? He could have simply put the arguments in one easy-to-digest Cabinet memorandum and presented them so cogently that his colleagues would have had no choice but to implement the plans lying around for years. Buchanan's plan proposed two 'national growth centres' – Cork and Limerick-Shannon. By 1986 the population of Cork was to have reached 250,000, while the projection for Limerick-Shannon was 175,000. These two cities were to be complemented by five regional centres (Galway,

→ *Martin Cullen's claim that life was being given to the National Spatial Strategy by the Government's decentralisation programme is belied by the mismatch between the two*

Buncrana

Gweedore

Letterkenny

DONEGAL

Donegal

LEITRIM

Sligo

SLIGO

Ballina

Carrick-on-Shannon

Monaghan

MONAGHAN

Carrickmacross

Knock Airport

Cavan

CAVAN

Dundalk

LOUTH

ROSCOMMON

Castlebar

LONGFORD

Drogheda

Claremorris

Roscommon

Longford

Navan

Tuam

WAY

Mullingar

WESTMEATH

Trim

MEATH

Clifden

Ballinasloe

Athlone

Furbo

Galway

Tullamore

Edenderry

Newbridge

Dublin

DUBLIN

Loughrea

OFFALY

Curragh

KILDARE

Birr

Portarlington

Portlaoise

Athy

WICKLOW

Ennis

LAOIS

Shannon

Roscrea

Arklow

Kilrush

Thurles

Thomastown

Carlow

CARLOW

Limerick

TIPPERARY

Kilkenny

Enniscorthy

Newcastle West

LIMERICK

Tipperary

KILKENNY

WEXFORD

Listowel

Tralee

Kanturk

New Ross

Wexford

KERRY

Mitchelstown

WATERFORD

Waterford

Killarney

Mallow

Youghal

Dungarvan

Macroom

Cork

CORK

Clonakilty

National Spatial Strategy – Gateway ■

National Spatial Strategy – Hub ■

Government Decentralisation – location ◉

3 – BALANCED DEVELOPMENT | 73

Waterford, Sligo, Dundalk and Athlone) and four growth towns (Letterkenny, Cavan, Castlebar and Tralee). Buchanan's recommendations also mirrored the conclusions on healthcare provision in the 1968 Fitzgerald Report; all but two of the locations for hospital development coincided with those recommended by Buchanan. There was also a close correlation between Buchanan and the 1965 investment strategy for third-level education that led to the development of a host of regional technical colleges, all now institutes of technology.

With projections that the State's population could be as high as five million by 2020, a 20-year vision was needed. Otherwise, we would continue to do what we have been doing for years – making it up as we go along, the very opposite of planning. The optimistic view inside the Department of the Environment in 2001 was that Irish society was now mature enough to 'buy' into it. Niall Cussen, senior planner on the NSS team, argued that people could see for themselves the consequences of laissez-faire 'planning' in the sprawl of Dublin (with all the congestion that goes with it), and the failure to develop alternative growth centres of real significance elsewhere. He pointed to the experience of Denmark, another small, but successful European country with a dominant capital city, and how the Danes sought to draw some of the heat away from Copenhagen and redistribute it to the regions.

Cussen and his colleagues had various other suggestions before them. A City of the Sacred Heart in east Mayo, 10 miles from Knock Airport, was proposed by Galway-based businessman William A Thomas. Designed by engineer John McMyler, also from Galway, this Irish version of Brazilia was to cover an area of 30 square miles, with an initial population of 100,000, rising to 250,000 within 20 years. 'Housing will be new, spatial, detached, in an infrastructured suburbia, with church-es, community centres, shops, and other recreational facilities', the promoters said. 'Wide boulevards and avenues will afford free movement of traffic and well-designed public transport and underground car-parking facilities will allow free access at all times.' In fact, it was a recipe for ultra-low-density suburban sprawl because most of the houses would be built on half-acre sites, rendering public transport unviable. Thomas, a shipping consultant, said he was confident of raising some £75 billion for the project within 12 months. 'Richard Branson has written letters of support for this proposed city. He is looking at Ireland as a potential investment location for his high-speed trains', he said in September 2000. Others claimed to be on side included Daewoo International and US multi-billionaires Bill Gates and Ross Perot. Bishop Thomas Flynn, in whose diocese the new city was to be located, said in June 2000 that he was 'very much in favour' of the plan, because he thought it would be 'a great idea if a city could be designed for modern needs, starting from scratch', instead of hav-ing to deal with the gridlock problems associated with cities that evolved from medieval times. Another backer of the scheme, Senator John Connor (FG), said Government thinking was 'still rooted in attempting to correct the totally skewed regional development pattern by pouring investment into old medieval cities like Galway, Limerick and Waterford, all of which, in their own way, were almost as bad as Dublin'. But the planners preparing the National Spatial Strategy on the attic floor of the Custom House in Dublin were not impressed. In their September 2001 consultation paper, *Indications of the Way Ahead*, they ruled out the idea of creating a new city in the west, or anywhere else, on the basis that it wasn't required.

However, without urban powerhouses, there was little chance that the west would close the prosperity gap. There was also a widespread perception that the Atlantic seaboard counties had not been getting their fair share of investment under successive national development plans, and this was to blame for the growing 'prosperity gap' with the east and what had become known as the Dublin-Belfast 'economic corridor', in particular. The Catholic bishops of Connacht were so concerned about its future that they launched their own initiative, Developing the West Together, which won widespread public and political support. A Council for the West was established, with the energetic Marian Harkin – later TD for Sligo-Leitrim and MEP for the North West – as chief executive. In response to its campaign, the Rainbow Coalition set up the Western Development Commission not long before the 1997 general election, and it was put on a statutory basis by the Fianna Fáil-PD coalition in 1999. When the National Development Plan was unveiled in November 1999, the Government stressed that redressing regional imbalance was a fundamental aim. The Taoiseach proclaimed that the NDP was for the 'whole country' – north, south, east and west. 'We are determined to end the regional imbalances that have disfigured modern Ireland', Ahern said, playing to every gallery in sight. To back this up, the per capita allocation to the Border, Midlands and Western region – the area categorised as Objective 1 for European funding – was 23% higher than the national average; of the £40.6 billion to be spent, the allocation to the BMW region was £13.8 billion.

May 2001 saw Eamon Ó Cuív, then a Minister of State, urge the Government to give greater powers and more funding to the Western Development Commission. In a major report, *The State of the West: Recent Trends and Future Prospects*, published in July 2001, the WDC found that regional disparities were continuing to grow between the west and the more developed eastern and southern regions. It was 'not primarily a question of money. It is more a question of approach and of getting promises delivered and ensuring key infrastructure is put in place sooner rather than later.' The WDC, with a remit covering the seven western counties from Donegal to Clare, emphasised the need to 'decentralise the mindset of government departments' increasingly consumed by the problems of overgrowth in the east by getting them to focus on the west. It warned that unless immediate action was taken, 'a technical and communications gap will develop that will be impossible to bridge'. Of the 13,780 new jobs announced by IDA Ireland in 2001, the Council for the West complained that less than 10% (1,246) were in the seven western counties, with half of these going to Galway city.

US multinationals based in the west often encounter serious problems. One Letterkenny-based company, which relies on high-speed phone connections, had to send their staff home after the line was damaged by a digger at Longford, 114 miles away. The fact that it was not repaired for several hours was something its bosses in the US found difficult to comprehend.

Unbalanced regional development was, in the words of the WDC's chief executive, Liam Scollan, 'as persistent as ever'. Three months after the report was published, with no sign of the Government accepting its recommendations, Scollan announced his resignation, saying it was for personal reasons. In December 2002 a review of the Commission's activities was ordered after advisers to the Minister for Finance suggested it should be abolished. Figures from the 2002 census showed that the west was not the only disadvantaged area. Dubliners were almost 17% better off compared to the State's average, but it was people in Laois rather that Leitrim who were the worst off, with only 82.4% of the average disposable income. Along with Laois, the bottom 12 comprised Offaly (82.7%), Donegal (83.7%), Mayo (84.5%), Carlow (84.7%), Kerry (84.9%), South Tipperary (84.9), Wexford (85.2%), Roscommon (85.3%), Longford (85.4%), Kilkenny (86.7%) and Leitrim (87.5%).

Back in 1972, after three years of dithering over Buchanan, Fianna Fáil ministers decided to adopt a laissez-faire approach, allowing Dublin to expand to accommodate its 'natural increase' in population, while pledging 'advance factories' all over the place. Through this cowardly decision, the Government was 'abandoning for a generation the struggle to halt the growth of Dublin', as Garret FitzGerald has put it. With a political system based on doing personal favours for individual constituents, no firm decisions could be made about how Ireland should develop. If Athlone was to be designated as a growth centre, Mullingar and Ballinasloe would be up in arms – and the same went for any other area if there was a perception of being left out. The Government actually stoked small-town rivalry. In December 1999, after Charlie McCreevy first announced that 10,000 civil servants were to be 'decentralised' from Dublin, no less than 130 areas, including some villages, became embroiled in a scramble to secure a share of the action. There was no evidence of a national vision. The very organs of the State were just cookies to be scoffed. Instead of selecting centres and explaining the choice by reference to objective criteria, the Cabinet turned what was a national challenge into a faction fight. 'Carrick-on-Suir Welcomes its Government Department', said a large sign outside the South Tipperary town in 2001. Given that ministers were already shamelessly abusing their powers to cart off State agencies to their own constituencies, there wasn't much chance the national interest would get a look-in. As Minister for Justice, John O'Donoghue had 'decentralised' the Legal Aid Board to his home town of Cahirciveen, Co Kerry, while then Minister for Defence Michael Smith moved the Civil Defence HQ from Dublin to his home town of Roscrea, Co Tipperary. Brian Cowen thought he had bagged the National Disease Surveillance Centre for Tullamore in 1999 before going from the Department of Health to Foreign Affairs; however, strong resistance from its staff led to the move being shelved some two years later. The biggest heist of that period was the relocation of the State Laboratories and Department of Agriculture laboratories from Abbotstown, Co Dublin, to Backweston Farm near Celbridge, in Charlie McCreevy's Kildare constituency. This was before the 'Bertie Bowl' project was abandoned, and the labs at Abbotstown would have been in the way. Not only would their relocation to the State-owned farm bring 400 well-paid public servants into north

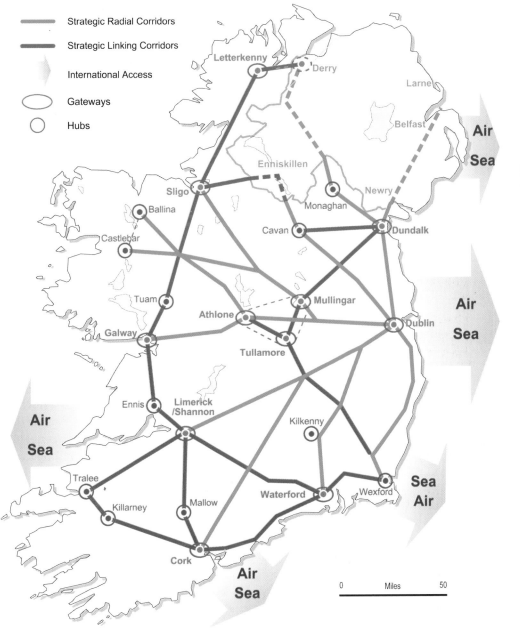

Legend:

Strategic Radial Corridors

Strategic Linking Corridors

International Access

Gateways

Hubs

↑ *The National Spatial Strategy, unveiled in November 2002, aimed to concentrate development in 9 gateways and 9 hubs. An earlier plan, with Cork's expansion as its starting point, was ignored.*

Kildare, but more than €200 million would be spent on a new laboratory complex to accommodate them, plus €50 million to fit it out.

As it was, the National Spatial Strategy was coming very late in the day, nearly half-way through the implementation period of the National Development Plan 2000-2006. It was supposed to be finalised and published early in 2002, but was put on the long finger because of the general election in May of that year, and the Nice Treaty referendum. No government would have wanted to indicate its intentions on spatial planning in such a political atmosphere, with local papers feeding on stories about 'winners' and 'losers' in the race for development. Finally published in November 2002, Bertie Ahern was able to declare, in his printed 'message from the Taoiseach', that the NSS had been 'designed to enable every place in the country to reach its potential, no matter what its size or location'. That might have been fair enough if the blueprint was clear regarding the prospective potential of urban and rural areas, but it wasn't. The NSS came so close to a 'county towns' approach that it invited attack. Not only had Dublin, Cork, Limerick-Shannon, Galway and Waterford been named as 'gateways', but also Dundalk, Sligo, Letterkenny, and a triangle carrying the abbreviation ATM – Athlone, Tullamore and Mullingar. There were also to be nine 'hubs' – Ballina, Castlebar, Tuam, Ennis, Tralee-Killarney, Mallow, Kilkenny, Wexford and Cavan-Monaghan.

The NSS pointed out that transport development formed the backbone of burgeoning links between Dublin and Belfast. While welcoming this vitality along the east coast, it noted that the Dublin-Belfast corridor tended 'to reinforce the eastwards pull of the spatial distribution of development and population of the whole island of Ireland'. The North-South dynamic needed to be sustained, but the NSS said it should be counterbalanced by developments in the south and west. 'The best prospects for establishing critical mass of the type and scale capable of competing with that of the Greater Dublin Area point to developing Cork, Galway, Limerick-Shannon and Waterford as an increasingly inter-connected and developed network of co-operating and complementary cities', according to the strategy. It referred to the way in which particular industries had formed clusters, with foreign multinationals, indigenous companies and start-ups networking around the University of Limerick. A similar phenomenon in Cork, focused on pharmachem and biopharmacy, was backed up by UCC and the city's Institute of Technology. For these two cities to share their strengths, 'greater emphasis will have to be placed on improving journey times and journey-time reliability between Cork and Limerick in terms of the roads and public transport networks', the NSS said. 'However, improving physical connections is not enough. Both areas will need to plan and act in a complementary way. Similarly, if roads and public transport connections between Waterford and Cork and between Limerick-Shannon and Galway were appropriately enhanced, the attractions of each gateway could also be seen in an increasingly shared sense.' Guided by a common vision, the aggregate population of these four cities could grow to more than a million, according to the strategy. However, no specific commitments were made to improve journey times between them. And when the Campaign for Sensible

Transport used the Freedom of Information Act in early 2003 to ask what was being done to further the intercity transport aims of the NSS, it was told: 'Your request generated no documents.'

But the central weakness of the strategy was that instead of starting with Cork, Limerick, Galway and Waterford, it designated far too many growth centres, spreading development as widely as possible, and as thinly too. As a result, the likelihood is that nowhere will develop a sufficient 'critical mass' to compete for investment with the economic engine of Dublin. It cannot credibly be maintained that any or all of the designated growth centres will be made 'similarly attractive' to Dublin, in terms of their ability to attract investment, when there are so many of them, especially with a caveat that Exchequer investment 'will need a sufficient level of economic growth to generate the required resources'. As IBEC pointed out, the fact that so many towns have been prioritised 'greatly reduces the potential' of the strategy to support ongoing economic and social development. Effectively, it would reinforce the long-established laissez-faire approach to the growth of Dublin. This was justified by its authors on the basis that Dublin had become so 'vital' to the national economy it was 'not a realistic objective' to cap its share of the State's population at 40%. The reason is simple: 'In many cases, the choice for mobile international investment would then lie between locating in the Dublin area or elsewhere in the world.' The reality is that economic opportunities outside the GDA 'would have to flourish at unprecedented levels to allow regional locations to grow faster than the GDA, make up ground and alter the scenario in which the GDA's share of the national population is likely to continue to increase', the NSS acknowledged. Indeed, all the indications are that Dublin's critical mass will continue to feed on itself and on much of the rest of Leinster. However, the Strategy would do nothing to halt the Atlanta-like sprawl of Dublin into surrounding counties and all the traffic congestion and other pressures that go with it. Atlanta itself had shown that cities can be strangled by sprawl. In the 1990s it was held up as an American model, but by the end of the decade its workers faced the longest average commuting time of any city in the US, with large corporations such as Hewlett-Packard looking elsewhere because of 'quality-of-life' concerns. But Dublin's sprawl is set to go unchecked. Based on demographic trends, the NSS projected a GDA population of 1.9 million by 2020, out of a national population of 4.4 million. But if there was stronger economic growth, it could reach 2.2 million by 2020, out of a national population of 5 million. 'If regional competitiveness is not enhanced, it is possible that up to four-fifths of future population growth could take place in the GDA, bringing its share of national population into the mid 40s. However, with the support of the NSS, this will happen at a slower rate than would otherwise be the case.'

If the Strategy was a weak-worded fudge, it was also short-lived. Twelve months later, Charlie McCreevy used his Budget statement of December 2003 to drop the decentralisation bombshell. No less than 10,300 civil and public servants, including eight entire departments, were to be relocated from Dublin to 53 centres in 25 counties. Agriculture was to go to Portlaoise; Arts, Sport and Tourism to Killarney;

Donegal:

Buncrana	120
Donegal	230
Gweedore	30

Leitrim:

Carrick-on-shannon	265

Sligo:

Sligo	100

Mayo:

Claremorris	150
Knock Airport	140

Galway:

Ballinasloe	110
Clifden	40
Furbo	10
Loughrea	50

Clare:

Kilrush	50
Shannon	400

Limerick:

Limerick	130
Newcastle West	50

Kerry:

Killarney	165
Listowel	50

Cork:

Clonakilty	150
Kanturk	100
Macroom	70
Mallow	200
Mitchelstown	200
Youghal	200

Roscommon:

Roscommon	230

To be decided:

IT Staff	835
Health Sector	500

TOTAL: 10,300

Tipperary:

Roscrea	80
Thurles	200
Tipperary	200

Waterford:

Dungarvan	300
Waterford	200

Laois:

Portarlington	110
Portlaoise	400

Kilkenny:

Kilkenny	105
Thomastown	110

Monaghan:

Carrickma-cross	8
Monaghan	2

Cavan:

Cavan	42

Louth:

Drogheda	30

Longford:

Longford	13

Meath:

Navan	10
Trim	27

Westmeath:

Athlone	14
Mullingar	30

Kildare:

Athy	25
Curragh	30
Newbridge	20

Offaly:

Birr	25
Edenderry	7
Tullamore	13

Wicklow:

Arklow	14

Carlow:

Carlow	35

Wexford:

Enniscorthy	8
New Ross	13
Wexford	32

© IRISH TIMES STU

↑ *The Government's scattergun approach to decentralisation: under the original plan, announced in the 2004 Budget, 10,300 public servants were to be dispersed to 53 locations in 25 counties.*

Communications, Marine and Natural Resources to Cavan; Community, Rural and Gaeltacht Affairs to Knock Airport; Defence to Newbridge; Education and Science to Mullingar; Environment, Heritage and Local Government to Wexford; and Social and Family Affairs to Drogheda. The scale of this dispersal was so staggering that it led Dr Ed Walsh, former president of the University of Limerick, to remark that if the Government planned to move so many departments, 'why not move all of them?' Almost 50 State agencies or companies, such as Bus Éireann, the National Roads Authority and the Land Registry, were also to be moved out of Dublin. And it was all to be done within three years. McCreevy disingenuously

↑ *Charlie McCreevy disingenuously maintained that the selected locations for decentralisation took full account of the National Spatial Strategy*

maintained that the selected locations 'take full account of the National Spatial Strategy'. But only one of the eight departments, Education and Science, was earmarked for a 'gateway' – the Mullingar point of the midlands triangle. According to McCreevy, the choice was governed not just by the NSS, but also by good road, rail or air links, the location of existing decentralised offices, and the need to create 'clusters' within each region. But transport issues had been taken into account by the NSS, and the creation of 'clusters' simply served to highlight all the driving around that would be inherent in the Minister's proposals. Mary Coughlan, then Minister for Social and Family Affairs, said the aim was to decentralise to locations where an influx of civil servants would have the greatest impact – smaller towns such as Ballina and Ballyshannon, rather than Galway where they would hardly be noticed.

It was statements like these that pointed to the clientilist nature of the project. By picking so many places it was clear that the Government was walking away from its own spatial strategy. On the opening page of the NSS, the Taoiseach pledged that the Government would 'ensure that its own policies are implemented in a manner that is consistent with the National Spatial Strategy'. In December 2003, just over a year after it was published, Martin Cullen told RTÉ: 'Now we see real life being given to it right throughout the country. It hits all of the hubs, all of the major areas that have been identified [in the NSS], the major county towns.' In fact, only a quarter of the total were being targeted for NSS gateway or hub towns. By choosing 53 centres for decentralisation, the State's largesse is spread more widely than it would have been if the Government had stuck to the 17 'gateways' and 'hubs' (excluding Dublin) identified by the NSS.

The programme had been prepared under the cloak of Budget secrecy by a tight ministerial group consisting of Bertie Ahern, Mary Harney, Charlie McCreevy

↑ *Fintan O'Toole: decentralisation programme is a classic Fianna Fáil operation*

↓ *Garret FitzGerald: decentralisation plan is a most flagrant example of the 'stroke mentality'*

and Martin Cullen. The winners would be local auctioneers, estate agents, builders, shopkeepers, publicans, car dealers, property developers and landowners with sites for sale – all of whom would gain from having a clutch of well-paid civil servants moving into an area. The only casualty would be the public interest. Fintan O'Toole saw the Government's plan as 'a classic Fianna Fáil operation, in that it appeals vaguely to a broad swathe of the population and sharply to an insider elite'. For there would be a bonanza for 'the little inner circle of property developers that has a special place in the Government's heart'. The prospect of a 'great gold rush' with massive scope for private enrichment could be detected from the first report of the Implementation Group chaired by Phil Flynn. New headquarters for eight Government departments and the Office of Public Works would be designed, built, financed and operated by private companies. O'Toole continued: 'The banks will make big profits from financing these operations. The developers will pass on these costs to the taxpayer and will receive, in return, guaranteed State tenants who can't move out for political reasons. There will of course be "an open tendering process, consistent with national and EU procurement rules", just like there was in that other great McCreevy project at Punchestown. Ask the old question *cui bono?* – who benefits? – and the whole thing starts to make sense.'

Former Taoiseach Garret Fitz-Gerald saw the decentralisation plan as 'a most flagrant example of the "stroke mentality" which afflicts so much of Irish politics and which has done such damage to our economy and society ... The blatant hypocrisy of ministers asserting that this decision has "taken into account" the National Spatial Strategy, or even claiming that it represents the implementation of that strategy, has provided further justification for the cynicism of the electorate about Irish politics.' Writing in the *Irish Times*, FitzGerald noted that the Dublin region's share of the State's population had inevitably risen further, to almost 40%, following the 'sabotaging' of Buchanan in 1972. 'We can now be certain that with this gross failure to concentrate decentralisation upon the National Spatial Strategy's chosen centres, Dublin's share of the population will continue to rise towards 45%.' As a result, the challenge of tackling the dominance of Dublin was being 'passed up' for a second time in 35 years. Though he believed there were strong grounds for relocating as much public administration as possible from Dublin, he took exception to the proposal to scatter 8 of the 15 government departments to 8 different centres, because the whole purpose of having a capital city was to facilitate interaction. 'The truth is that transfer of policy-making, involving 3,000 of the 10,300 jobs, is totally counter-productive and will be seriously damaging to the national interest. Only politicians both obsessed with political advantage and lacking in concern for the public good could have dreamt up such a hare-brained process ... Wherever they may have come from originally, most of the more senior public servants working on policy issues are now settled in Dublin with their families, often with spouses at work elsewhere in the city and with children in school or university. Few at that level are likely to be prepared to move elsewhere and if they now choose to remain in Dublin when the policy-making sections of their departments are moved elsewhere, some will leave the public service depriving it of valuable expertise. Many of the remainder who decide to remain will become supernumerary, deprived of the opportunity of useful activity.'

Another former Taoiseach, John Bruton, put it more bluntly: the Government's programme would destroy 'one of the greatest institutions of the State' – the Irish Civil Service. It would be the 'single greatest act of administrative and political vandalism' since Ireland won its independence. 'What is a capital city and why does every country have one? Capital cities exist in most democracies to make policy at national level. This is done in one place because there are inherent economies of scale in making policy in one place', he said. 'It is wrong to describe the move of 10,000 civil servants away from Dublin as decentralisation. It is recentralisation of parts of the Civil Service to a series of different places.' While it made 'excellent sense' to relocate sections involved in policy implementa-

↓ *John Bruton: the Government's decentralisation programme would destroy one of the greatest institutions of the State – the Irish Civil Service*

tion to places outside Dublin, 'the making of policy at headquarters requires constant and easy contact among decision-makers in all departments. It also requires that senior Civil Service decision-makers be easily accessible to members of the public and organisations that wish to make representations to them.' But Bruton's successor, Bertie Ahern, told the Dáil a week after the Budget announcement that 'moving a large core of departments out to regional locations is good for departments'. It would also be 'better for the staff in terms of quality of life and will make for better balanced development in the country'. With modern technology, he said, 'meetings can take place all over the world without having everyone in the one room. If those days were ever relevant, they are long out of date now. There are no difficulties with these issues.' Though not as egregiously, John Bruton had engaged in a little bit of decentralisation himself. As Taoiseach, he played a major role in securing the EU's Food and Veterinary Office for Grange, Co Meath, in the heart of his own constituency. The site is five miles outside Trim, a location that hardly lends itself to 'easy contact among decision-makers'.

The decentralisation programme was presented as a fait accompli. Senior civil servants were not involved – even secretary generals were only informed at the last minute – and, needless to say, there was no consultation with unions representing the 10,300 staff earmarked for transfer. Seán Benton, chairman of the OPW, which would be saddled with the task of implementing the programme, was first told about it at lunchtime on Budget day. Even Dublin's congestion – itself a direct result of maladministration – was used as a selling point for decentralisation. So was the prospect of cashing in on the property boom; 'bonanza' was the term McCreevy used. Martin Mansergh helpfully suggested that since some departments were to be relocated relatively close to Dublin – the OPW in Trim, Co Meath, for example – staff would be able to continue living in the capital while 'contraflow commuting' to work. He also said he knew many Fine Gael TDs and senators 'who are delighted with the localities and not shy about claiming credit for them'. But Mansergh said it was Fianna Fáil which had won a clear electoral mandate for decentralisation and it was 'the duty of civil servants to carry out the programme for government'.

Many senior civil servants were aghast at the FF-PD plan. They were well aware of the fact that some 4,500 public officials had been relocated during the 1990s. But the Government was now proposing to relocate half of all the civil servants still working in Dublin, as well as moving entire departments – something that had never been contemplated previously. Of course, 'back office' functions could easily be bundled off to other locations, but none of those in the upper echelons expected that they, too, would be dispatched. It rapidly became clear that promotion would be conditional on agreement by the appointee to relocate to wherever the relevant department was being sent; those who wished to stay in Dublin couldn't advance their careers, at least until the Government got its 10,300 heads. Despite a promise by McCreevy that the programme would be voluntary, the only element of choice was that affected staff were given an opportunity to rank locations in order of preference. But Dublin was not included among the options. This coercion mechanism was 'the

↑ *Tom Parlon was 'quick off the blocks' in putting up posters on the main Dublin to Portlaoise road in his constituency*

→ *'Parlon Delivers' posters were plastered around Laois-Offaly by its PD deputy*

↓ *Tom Parlon TD was as wise as every-body else about the decentralisation programme*

realpolitik of a decentralisation programme that is awash with double-speak and spin', wrote Arthur Beesley in the *Irish Times*. 'Despite the denials, the initiative has all the marks of a Government electioneering stunt. Remember the "Parlon country" posters?' This was a reference to the welcome extended to civil servants by Tom Parlon, Minister of State at the OPW, on billboards in his Laois-Offaly constituency put up with great alacrity on the morning after the Budget. Leaflets churned out by his supporters, headed 'Parlon Delivers!', highlighted the proposed relocation of the Department of Agriculture to Portlaoise – '400 jobs, Delivered!' – and the relocation of FÁS, the State training agency, to Birr, Co Offaly – '250 jobs, Delivered!'. But McCreevy denied that his PD junior minister had any advance knowledge of the decentralisation programme. With Parlon sitting sheepishly beside him in the Dáil chamber, the Minister for Finance said: 'As far as the process was concerned, Deputy Parlon was not involved. He was not involved in the decision-making or the preparation. He knew nothing about it and he was as wise as everybody else. He was quicker off the blocks than anybody else. That is the truth of the matter.' All he knew was that 'someone' in a hostelry near Leinster House had 'cottoned on to the fact that something might happen with decentralisation the next day'.

A week later, at the launch of the OPW's plan for a site near Heuston Station, Parlon claimed its elegant 32-storey residential tower was a foretaste of things to come in terms of the architectural quality of decentralised offices. However, it later transpired that they were likely to be procured by 'design and build' packages, under which developers call the shots. So much for the Government's 2002 commitment that architectural quality would be one of the key criteria for publicly funded projects. Meanwhile, suggestions that the Government was planning to sell landmark buildings in Dublin to raise money for the decentralisation programme were causing concern among conservationists. Buildings at risk included the Custom House, headquarters of the Department of the Environment; the Department of Defence's headquarters at Infirmary Road – another late 18th-century building designed by James Gandon; the Department of Education's headquarters in Marlborough Street, and the OPW's own offices in a terrace of Georgian buildings on the east side of St Stephen's Green. If the programme was to be self-financing, Parlon said, it would mean 'getting a plus out of our Dublin property'. Though he made it clear that the Government would not sell the Custom House, he had no reservations about flogging the OPW's offices, and even spoke of finding a commercial use for the Garda headquarters in the Phoenix Park (after staff were dispatched to Thurles, Co Tipperary). He was jubilant when a one-acre State-owned site off Baggot Street was sold for €22.5 million in February 2004, and even more delighted five months later when the mid-1960s Department of Justice building on St Stephen's Green fetched €52.3 million; the OPW had bought the building in 2000 for €36.5 million, and Parlon said the proceeds would go towards buying sites for decentralised offices. Labour's environment spokesman, Eamon Gilmore TD, accused him of behaving like the Government's 'national auctioneer'. As Arthur Beesley reported, 'there is no doubt the Government hopes to save some of its enormous rent bill for office buildings in

Dublin by moving departments away from the city.' According to the OPW's annual report for 2002, rents paid by the Government for offices in Dublin came to €98.46 million; not having to pay such a bill, it was reasoned, would free significant amounts of money to fund decentralisation. This could be illusory. In June 2004 FÁS warned that it could be left paying annual rents of over €5 million a year for empty Dublin offices after relocating to Birr, because it is locked into leases with years left to run.

There was a backlash from the Civil Service, although it took a while to manifest itself. The initial reaction of some trade unions was to give the Government's programme a guarded welcome, while warning of 'enormous' costs. The Civil and Public Service Union, which represents around 10,000 mostly lower-ranking civil servants, wondered whether staff who stayed in Dublin would have a reasonable career structure and prospects for promotion. Seán Ó Riordáin, general secretary of the Association of Higher Civil and Public Servants, representing around 12,000 higher-ranking civil servants, said 'the higher up you go, the more people are bedded down and have families and it becomes more of an issue.' The AHCPS was soon expressing its 'anger and dismay' over Tom Parlon's notorious billboards because they implied that civil servants were the property of the FF-PD Government, 'to be distributed as trophies in advance of local elections'. In a subsequent e-mail survey, the association found that 35 out of 40 principal and assistant principal officers in the Department of the Environment did not want to move to Wexford, or to any other location outside Dublin. In March 2004 a poll by the Department of Social and Family Affairs found that a majority of its staff also wanted to stay where they were rather than go to Buncrana, Carrick-on-Shannon, Drogheda or Sligo. Just over 3,000 – about two-thirds – of the department's 4,770 staff responded to the survey, many already based outside Dublin. Only 120 expressed an interest in moving to Drogheda, where its new headquarters was to be built. Significantly, the survey indicated that lower-ranking civil servants were as reluctant to move as those on higher grades; of the 2,322 clerical officers who responded, 955 said they wished to remain at their current location, while 845 did not reply.

Neither did the Government bother to listen to the concerns expressed by the Institution of Engineers of Ireland, the Royal Institute of the Architects of Ireland, the Irish Planning Institute, the Royal Town Planning Institute and the Society of Chartered Surveyors. Their joint submission said that while the decentralisation of significant numbers of operational staff was to be welcomed, 'it is essential that senior policy-making staff and Government ministers remain in close touch in the country's capital.' And although Phil Flynn's first Implementation Group report had stressed the importance of preserving 'organisational memory', it was merely talking about computer systems and 'had nothing to say about simple know-how picked up in office chit-chat', as Arthur Beesley noted. The entire programme was having a negative impact on morale. 'People are saying that we're being treated like political fodder', said one civil servant. Most worried of all were specialist staff – architects, archaeologists, engineers and other professionals – in agencies such as the Arts Council (destined for Kilkenny), Bord Iascaigh Mhara (Clonakilty), the Equality

Authority (Roscrea), the NRA (Ballinasloe), the OPW (Trim) and the Prison Service (Longford). At a public meeting in Dublin on the eve of polling day for the European and local elections in June 2004, Peter Walsh, an engineer with the NRA, said he wanted to keep his job: 'I don't want to give it away. I don't want to train anybody else to do it.' Colm Murray, a conservation architect with the National Monuments Service, said he was being expected to move with his family to Kanturk, Co Cork, where there wasn't even a crèche. The basic problem, according to Kevin Moran, an education specialist with the Prison Service, was that the Government seemed to think that all public service jobs were interchangeable when they were not. Most ludicrous of all was the case of Bus Éireann, which had been put down for a transfer of 200 staff to new headquarters in Mitchelstown, Co Cork, when less than 90 actually work at its existing head office at the former Broadstone station in Dublin. A report by Bus Éireann management noted than none of them had expressed a wish to be transferred to Mitchelstown, and warned that the whole operation would be 'extremely risky, costly, and could only be effected on a long-term basis'.

Documents obtained by the AHCPS under the Freedom of Information Act showed that at least one Cabinet minister and several high-ranking civil servants had expressed serious concerns about the decentralisation programme when it was first mooted in December 1999. In a letter to the Department of Finance in June 2000, the secretary general of the then Department of Tourism and Sport, Margaret Hayes, said the minister (Dr Jim McDaid) had considered the case for relocating the Department outside Dublin. 'However, in view of its strong policy-making content and direct supportive role for the Minister, Government and Parliament, he does not believe that the Department is suitable for decentralisation', she wrote. Tom Carroll, then secretary general of the Department of the Marine and Natural Resources, said relocation would pose major management difficulties. 'It is my considered professional judgement that any effort to relocate this Department's functions on a large scale would seriously destabilise our present organisation and capabilities which it has taken management here over ten years to bring up to its present level', he wrote. Major difficulties – the word 'major' was in bold type and underlined – had arisen in relation to the already-decentralised Marine Institute. 'These difficulties mirror/highlight in many ways what would happen if a decision was taken to relocate the whole Department of the Marine and Natural Resources and/or BIM.' As secretary general of the Department of the Environment, Jimmy Farrelly warned that there would be 'very serious detrimental consequences' if posts related to high-level policy work and specialist advice were decentralised. 'The worst scenario would be to relocate staff to an entirely new location which was not near Dublin, resulting in the disadvantages of loss of staff and increased fragmentation.' Also, locating staff away from ready access to the Oireachtas would cause such serious practical difficulties that it prompted him to ask whether consideration should be given to moving the Oireachtas itself.

In mid-January 2004 Tánaiste Mary Harney conceded that the target figure of 10,300 might be reduced if staff resistance remained strong. She was speaking after a survey in her own department (Enterprise, Trade and Employment) showed an overwhelming majority against moving to Carlow (434 out of 503 were against going there). 'If it were the case in three years' time that we hadn't hit the 10,000 civil servants we want to move, then the Government would have to reassess that target in the light of circumstances', Harney said, adding that a 'carrot approach' might be adopted to 'get over the final hurdle'. Meanwhile, her party colleague, Tom Parlon, was crowing about the strong interest expressed by some 700 property owners and developers in supplying the State with offices in 53 different locations. It only emerged in June 2004 that the Government had projected spending some €450 million on property and building work to relocate dozens of offices from Dublin – way in excess of the 'over €200 million' estimate touted previously. 'Minister Parlon is planning to splurge out taxpayers' money acquiring every available square metre of office space in the favoured areas, including his own constituency', Eamon Gilmore commented. But given the reluctance among civil servants to move, he warned of 'ending up in a situation where the OPW will have acquired spanking new office accommodation in scores of locations, with virtually nobody to work in them'. He also complained that 'despite assurances given to the contrary, the signs increasingly are that this programme will not be voluntary and the civil servants will be coerced into moving out of Dublin.' Parlon had conceded as much in an interview with RTÉ radio when he said that those who agreed to move would benefit from improved career opportunities. 'The clear implication is that those who refuse to move will suffer career-wise', Gilmore said.

Scrutiny was the last thing the Government wanted. Even the Oireachtas Joint Committee on Finance and the Public Service, whose remit covered this area, was prevented from looking into decentralisation. Fine Gael and Sinn Féin proposed that the committee should hear evidence from Phil Flynn, as well as union leaders representing public servants, management experts and Opposition deputies who had already articulated strong views on the matter. Joan Burton TD, Labour's finance spokeswoman, even suggested postponing the hearings until after the European and local elections in June 2004. But the committee's FF chairman, Seán Fleming TD, insisted that the time for debate on decentralisation was over. The whip was imposed, and the Opposition motion was defeated by eight votes to six. Fine Gael's finance spokesman, Richard Bruton TD, told the *Irish Times* it was now clear that the introduction of the measure through the Budget had been consciously designed

↓ *Richard Bruton TD: governments must not become so intoxicated with their own invincibility that they cast aside procedures built up over generations*

to bypass systems of scrutiny established to protect the public from ill-considered decisions. 'Governments have a right to make decisions, but they must not become so intoxicated with their own invincibility that they cast aside procedures built up over generations', Bruton said. 'The decentralisation agenda has never been debated in the Dáil. No Government memorandum has accompanied it. No business case has been presented for it. No risk assessment of the effect on any of the agencies has been presented. No human resource plan has been developed. No proper assessment of the financial implications has been presented. None of the selected locations has been justified against criteria for successful regionalisation. No answer has been given to those who fear a huge loss of "organisational memory". No answer has been given to those who say that the dispersal of a majority of ministries across the countryside runs counter to international best practice.' Sinn Féin's Caoimhghín Ó Caoláin TD accused the Government of 'censoring' the Oireachtas committee and running away from debate. The *Irish Times* agreed. 'The Government's refusal to allow any formal examination or impact analysis of its plans to decentralise the headquarters of eight departments and a number of State bodies reflects a mixture of arrogance, political chicanery and a determination to avoid being held to account', the paper said.

The Government had already gutted and filleted the 1997 Freedom of Information Act – precisely because it had become an effective tool in shedding light on political and administrative decision-making. The ostensible reason for changing the Act was that a clause in the original legislation would have led to the publication of some Cabinet papers that were more than five years old. The Taoiseach told the Dáil this could lead to the release of sensitive negotiating papers relating to the 1998 Belfast Agreement. But this was as fictional as his daughter Cecelia's best-selling novels, because the original Act already allowed restrictions on the release of papers dealing with security and Northern Ireland. 'Using this cover, however, the Government has taken the opportunity to run a coach-and-four through the spirit of the Act as it stands – in particular by restricting access to letters between ministers', Mark Hennessy wrote. Definitions of what constituted 'Cabinet papers' or 'Government meetings' were widened to allow a much larger range of material to be buried for ten years. In one of the most damaging changes, documents no longer need to be released where the policy process is certified as 'ongoing', which could almost apply to anything, and the right to appeal a refusal to see policy papers on these grounds was scrapped. Reports from Cabinet sub-committees and Civil Service working groups, as well as briefing material for parliamentary questions, can also be kept under wraps if departments rule they are 'for the direct support of Government deliberations'. Charlie McCreevy defended the changes, saying 'all organisations have the right to decide how to organise their business and the Government is no different.'

Presumably, this dictum could be applied to the alacrity with which pet projects were approved by ministers – most notoriously, McCreevy himself. In March 2003, following representations from a Naas GP who wanted to build a private hospital, he tabled a late amendment to the Finance Bill extending the tax reliefs available for private in-patient hospitals, covering what the GP had in mind. This spot of clientilism was worth roughly €9 million to McCreevy's constituent, and was likely to cost the Exchequer €63 million in tax foregone, assuming seven such hospitals were built, as Mark Brennock reported. But it was his committal of nearly €15 million in public money for an agricultural/equestrian event centre at Punchestown racecourse, again in his own constituency, that really raised hackles. This remarkable deal only came to light in a report by the Comptroller & Auditor General, John Purcell, published in September 2003, though it had been done three years earlier. The report queried whether the project had been 'comprehensively evaluated from a cost-benefit viewpoint prior to its approval, in particular if it met the criteria set down in the guidelines issued by the Department of Finance for the evaluation of major capital projects'. It emerged that the Department of Agriculture had approved 100% State funding in January 2000 for an event centre costing €6.8 million. However, before this approval was even notified to Punchestown, a more elaborate scheme for a €12.8 million centre was submitted, and in June 2000 it was approved by then Minister for Agriculture, Joe Walsh, and countersigned by McCreevy; they had been dealing with the promoters personally, often in the absence of officials. Much later, when the hangar-like shed was under construction, the Department kindly chipped in a further €2 million to cover the inevitable cost over-run – without at any stage securing a proper legal agreement with the promoters to protect the State's interest. The Department said it didn't need to evaluate the project because it was 'keenly aware' from farming interests, such as cattle-breeding societies, of the need for an event centre of the type proposed. It was 'a public-good development, benefits of which were long-term, reputational, and marketing through standards and presentation, and could not readily be measured in immediate and direct financial terms'. Labour Party leader Pat Rabbitte TD took a slightly different view: 'All the evidence points to a "ready-up" between the two Ministers to fast-track funding for a pet project of the Finance Minister in the heart of Mr McCreevy's own constituency.' Fine Gael leader Enda Kenny TD charged in the Dáil in November 2003 that no independent technical advice was sought on the running costs, no research was conducted on the need for it, no other potential developers were invited to express an interest, and it was never referred to the Government's legal advisers. The only positive aspect of the affair was that, in future, all departments would have to adhere to proper evaluation guidelines for funding capital projects, as recommended by the Dáil Public Accounts Committee in its highly critical report.

Punchestown was a piece of political cronyism kept under wraps for more than three years, until it was a fait accompli. With so many other ready-ups lurking within the system, there was every reason to throw a blanket over as much as possible of the Government's 'business' by filleting the Freedom of Information Act. It was the Taoiseach himself who had ordered a high-level group of civil servants to review the 1997 legislation after the FF-PD Coalition was returned to power in the May 2002 general election. Bertie Ahern felt bruised when his dream of building a national stadium and 'campus of sporting excellence' at Abbotstown, Co Dublin, was dashed by disclosures made under the Act. The eventual decision two years later to redevelop

↑ *Eithne FitzGerald, former Labour TD: restrictions on the Freedom of Information Act were a godsend for those with something to hide*

Lansdowne Road as a national stadium was 'at least an indirect result' of the Freedom of Information Act, according to the Ombudsman, Emily O'Reilly. She said it was through records accessed under the Act that the public learned of 'potential cost overruns and other problems' relating to the Sports Campus Ireland project. 'Armed with that information, the public and other interested parties could properly engage in the debate on whether the Government should press ahead with it or not. The net result is the decision that was made in January.' It is a freedom denied today.

Eithne FitzGerald, the former Labour Minister of State who shepherded the original legislation through the Oireachtas, said the restrictions imposed by Fianna Fáil and the PDs – including an up-front fee of €15 for every application – were a godsend for those with something to hide. 'Where decisions are made with the public looking metaphorically over your shoulder, there is a stronger incentive to ensure that those decisions are made in a way that can withstand public scrutiny', she wrote in March 2003. The original legislation had been introduced against the political backdrop of 'golden circle' scandals in the early 1990s involving Greencore, the Goodman group and Telecom Éireann. The proposals to water down the Act being rushed through the Oireachtas had been 'developed by insiders with the specific aim of keeping the public out'. But FitzGerald said it would be 'unfair to simply blame the Sir Humphreys, the top civil servants who reviewed the Act' as the restrictions 'go well beyond what this group recommended … All in all, these changes fly in the face of any culture of openness. The PDs doubled their seats on a promise to keep Fianna Fáil accountable. They are now colluding in a shabby attempt to make government less accountable to the public.' To reinforce her point, FitzGerald listed some of the revelations that had been made in the Act's first five years of operation. Apart from the soaring estimates for Abbotstown, they included details of politicians' expenses, the full facts on rail safety, the lucrative tax breaks created for a handful of investors in private hospitals, and the fact that only 3% of Ireland's teachers are inspected annually.

Then, in a move described by Green Party finance spokesman Dan Boyle TD as 'beyond arrogance', both Charlie McCreevy and Tom Parlon – the relevant ministers in charge – absented themselves at race week in Cheltenham while their Department's amending legislation was being rushed through the Oireachtas and simultaneously considered by the Joint Committee on Finance and the Public Service. Referring to their absence, the editor of the *Irish Daily Star*, Gerard Colleran, said he was not sure there was any point in the hearings. 'The people who decide on this matter, to curtail the flow of information to the sovereign people of this country, are not even here. The attack on freedom of information is ... going through like an express train.' McCreevy was defiant. Tracked down in Cheltenham by RTÉ, he said the Government decided to take a certain position on the matter, and in a democracy it was the elected representatives of the people who took these decisions. 'That's our Bill, that's our position, and that's democracy', he declared. Objections by the former Ombudsman and Information Commissioner, Kevin Murphy, were ignored, as were appeals by the Oireachtas Joint Committee on Finance and the Public Service. And so, in the words of Enda Kenny, ministers 'effectively applied a tourniquet to the flow of information' on how government operates. 'Freedom of information legislation is supposed to shine light into dark administrative corners; to hold politicians and public servants to account for the decisions they make, and to reassure the public that the process of government is fair and impartial', the *Irish Times* said in an editorial. But the amended Act 'is insidious in its intent and destructive in its application. It has rolled back reforms introduced by the Rainbow Government in 1997 which were designed to ensure that such economic and political scandals as were identified by the Beef Tribunal could not easily recur.'

By October 2003, while four members of the Cabinet were secretly plotting the decentralisation programme, it had become apparent how effective the tourniquet was. Figures obtained by Enda Kenny showed that the number of requests under the Act had declined significantly since the Government restricted its scope six months earlier and imposed charges that July, including €75 for internal appeals and €150 for appeals to the Ombudsman and Information Commissioner. Nearly 3,000 applications had been received between 1st January and 11th April 2003 – the date when the Freedom of Information (Amendment) Act came into force – but the number fell to 1,700 in the following three months, and to just 1,060 between July and October. As Mark Hennessy reported: 'The Department of Finance's experience since the changes were made graphically illustrates the new landscape, as it has had to respond to 85% fewer applications.' The number of requests to the Department of Agriculture had fallen by 61% since 11th April, while applications to the Department of Enterprise, Trade and Employment fell by 84%. 'The Government's policy of strangling the FoI Act has proved to be one of its few policy successes in the last 18 months', Kenny commented wryly. The Ombudsman also had something to say about it. 'If this slide continues, the implications for the FoI Act could be serious', Emily O'Reilly warned. 'In fact, I have little doubt that the scale of the charges will prove a massive disincentive to accessing what is a right – information – and, if refused, further access to an independent appeals mechanism.' The changes 'may have long-term negative effects for accountability', O'Reilly said. 'My role is to implement the legislation scrupulously and impartially. It is for others to speculate on the motivation of the Government in doing what it did.' In mid-June 2004 she reported that requests for non-personal information had declined by an average of 75%, comparing the first quarter of that year with the first quarter of 2003. Applications

↑ *Joan Burton TD: the alarming fall in the number of requests under the Freedom of Information Act is exactly what Fianna Fáil and the PDs intended*

from journalists had fallen even more sharply, by 83%, and 'still continue to decline' – a trend O'Reilly found worrying as the media were 'a key element in an open and properly functioning democracy'. She suggested that the decline in usage of the FoI Act had 'gone far beyond what the Government had intended when it decided to introduce fees'. But Joan Burton TD disagreed. As far as she was concerned, the alarming fall in the number of requests 'is exactly what Fianna Fáil and the PDs intended'.

In early June 2004, during the European and local election campaign, Tom Parlon had to concede that the Government was unlikely to complete its decentralisation programme within the three-year deadline set by Charlie McCreevy. There could be a delay of up to a year due to EU procurement rules and construction time. 'In a worst case scenario, it could be the end of 2007 before the last department moves', the former IFA president told RTÉ radio. Joan Burton said that 'people in the locations chosen for decentralisation are beginning to realise that this will never happen, certainly not on the scale and in the timeframe promised.' As if to show that it might, McCreevy joined the then Minister for Agriculture, Joe Walsh, to announce the early 'voluntary' transfer of 50 staff of the latter's department to Portlaoise; although this piece of 'good news' was delivered three weeks before polling day, both ministers brazenly denied it was a pre-election stunt.

Fianna Fáil went on to suffer its worst electoral result in 77 years. In Dublin city, the party won just 22% of the vote, a drop of 13 points, and lost half its seats. Similar percentages were recorded in other Dublin local authority areas – 21% in Fingal, 25% in Dún Laoghaire-Rathdown, and 26% in South Dublin. As Mark Brennock reported, several Fianna Fáil activists at the Dublin election count believed the party had been damaged by decentralisation. 'The anti-Dublin tone of some Ministers' utterances on the project, which was coupled with the hillbilly-style whoops of triumph from rural deputies – not least Mr Tom Parlon – over the removal of jobs from the capital grated on many city voters', he wrote. But it wasn't only in Dublin that the party's share of the vote plummeted. In Waterford, home base of Martin Cullen, who was also its director of elections, Fianna Fáil was reduced to a solitary representative on the 15-member city council. Only two FF councillors were elected to Galway and Limerick city councils. In Cork city, the party's vote sank below 30% for the first time in living memory, just about enough to take 11 seats on the 31-member city council. There was a common denominator in all four results – a public perception that the decentralisation programme had favoured smaller places instead of Cork, Limerick, Galway and Waterford, which the NSS had designated as primary growth centres. 'This Government has given the people a hundred reasons to hate us', commented Michael Mulcahy, Fianna Fáil TD for Dublin South Central. And one of those reasons was its much-criticised decentralisation programme, which the PDs had sought to pass off as 'a Fianna Fáil idea'. The Government rowed back ever so slightly after the sobering result of the elections. The Oireachtas Joint Committee on Finance and the Public Service would, after all, hold hearings on the decentralisation programme. Its determination not to do so earlier was merely a matter of timing, according to the committee's FF chairman, Seán Fleming TD. Mary Harney also did a U-turn, and now favoured examining the programme, having previously declared: 'We are not obliged to have hearings.' Tom Parlon still insisted it was going ahead, but he said his door was 'always open' for talks with staff unions and other interests.

Figures published by the *Irish Times* in July 2004 showed there was little interest among civil servants in moving, and even less among employees of State agencies. Just 2,200 Dublin-based civil servants had expressed an interest in the 6,300 posts on offer in the first round. Among employees of State agencies, the response was dismal: only 290 staff were interested in applying for some 2,200 jobs in the regions. Not a single employee of the Arts Council (targeted for Kilkenny), Bord Iascaigh Mhara (Clonakilty), the Central Fisheries Board (Carrick-on-Shannon), Combat Poverty (Monaghan), the Equality Authority (Roscrea), Fáilte Ireland (Mallow), the Higher Education Authority (Athlone), the Irish Aviation Authority (Shannon), the NRA (Ballinasloe), the National Safety Council (Loughrea), and Sustainable Energy Ireland (Dundalk) wanted to move out of Dublin. And among staff of Bord Bia and Bord Glas (both targeted for Enniscorthy), Enterprise Ireland (Shannon), FÁS (Birr) and the Ordnance Survey of Ireland (Dungarvan), just one staff member in each agency indicated that they would agree to move. Altogether, only seven employees out of the 1,900 working for 20 State agencies in Dublin were prepared to fall into line with the Government's plans. And who would do their often specialist jobs? The figures suggested that hundreds of officials would need to be retrained, at additional public expense, to fill new posts in regional locations: 'Can you imagine the chaos that that will cause?' one senior official commented to the *Irish Times*. Inducements under consideration included allowing State agency officials full rights to transfer to Government departments at their existing grade while retaining all other benefits, the aim being to generate more applications before the September 2004 deadline.

The figures showed that State bodies would suffer a 'catastrophic loss of experience' under decentralisation, according to Richard Bruton, with whole organisations being 'dismantled entirely' and reconstructed. 'You can't play God like this without proper pre-planning. The figures are a massive rejection of the Government's strategy.' Though disappointed, Charlie McCreevy characterised the preliminary results as 'a good base from which to move forward with the implementation of the decentralisation programme'. He also announced that the Government had decided on the location of five new regional offices. These included Naas, in his own constituency, which was to get 300 Health Service Executive staff, and Portlaoise, in Tom Parlon's constituency, where 125 jobs in the Department of Agriculture were to be transferred. But more cold water was poured on the overall plan. Chris Dooley reported an NRA warning of significant delays in major national road projects because none of its existing staff wanted to move to Ballinasloe. Describing the implications as 'extremely serious', the Authority told Phil Flynn's Implementation Group: 'The opinion of management is that decentralisation and the consequent potential loss of expertise will render the Authority unable to deliver on the national roads programme until such time as suitably qualified personnel, particularly in the technical area, are recruited and trained.' There would be 'corporate memory loss', the seriousness of which 'must not be underestimated'. Dooley also reported a warning by the Equality Authority that it could take years to rebuild lost capacities if its planned move to Roscrea went ahead; the loss of skilled staff and experience in case management could also expose it to the risk of court action. And the Probation and Welfare Service, earmarked for Navan, said its officers would have to travel to Dublin so regularly for court appearances and client interviews that it would still need a presence in the capital. Gamely, on foot of these reports, Dún Laoghaire-Rathdown Chamber of Commerce suggested that the Government should consider 'decentralising' a department to Dún Laoghaire. 'A large proportion of Civil Service staff currently working in Dublin city centre live in Dún Laoghaire-Rathdown. Many of these do not want to uproot their families from their community, educational facilities, etc. Why not relocate these jobs close to where these people live and also avail of the mobility provided by Luas, DART and QBCs?' asked its president, Michael Johnson.

Before the end of November 2004, the Government executed a climbdown on its decentralisation programme by announcing that only 3,500 public servants – half of them already working outside Dublin – would be relocated to 20 centres, many of them within the capital's commuter belt. Brian Cowen and Tom Parlon hung onto most of the civil servants originally earmarked for their Laois-Offaly constituency, though other ministers such as Mary Coughlan and Martin Cullen lost out. 'It is not so much a climbdown as a headlong jump', Mark Brennock wrote. 'There will not ... be a "big bang" implementation of the decentralisation programme ... There will not be a small bang. Indeed, it is arguable whether there will be a bang to be heard at all.' According to Richard Bruton, the Government's plan was 'in tatters' less than a year after it was announced with such fanfare. 'This decentralisation programme has set back the cause of genuine regional development. Staff have been used as political pawns, no preparation was done before the stunt was announced [and] the cost in financial and administrative efficiency terms has been ignored.' Indeed, Phil Flynn's Implementation Group conceded that even the more limited dispersal plan would not be 'self-financing', as Charlie McCreevy had maintained, and it could take 20 years to break even. (Flynn, a former vice-president of Sinn Féin, resigned as chairman of the Implementation Group in February 2005 following reports that he was under investigation by the Criminal Assets Bureau, though he strongly denied any involvement in 'laundering' money stolen by the IRA. Six months later, he was charged with possession of a 'pen gun' that fires mini-tear gas canisters.)

Where did all of this leave the National Spatial Strategy? In the bin, or so it seemed. Immediately after that supposedly over-arching framework was published in November 2002, Martin Cullen instructed the nine regional authorities to draw up planning guidelines to give effect to it. But with such a terrible headline set by the Government itself, why should any regional authority pay attention even to the broad thrust of the NSS, never mind the letter of it? It was clearly a flexible policy that could be bent on a whim. Cullen tried to insist that they would be reined in. 'I won't hesitate to act if what is a reasonable, fair overall strategy for the country is to be ignored, because I'd be failing, the Government would be failing and, worst of all, we'd be failing the people themselves', the Minister told the *Irish Times* in May 2003. But the only time he used his power to intervene under the 2000 Planning Act was to direct Dún Laoghaire-Rathdown County Council to zone more land for residential development after it adopted a county plan which its manager, Derek Brady, regarded as deficient on housing provision.

After the Government turned its back on the NSS, the regional authorities pretty well drove a coach-and-four through it. The Midlands Regional Planning Guidelines, for example, departed from the exclusive designation of Athlone-Tullamore-Mullingar, saying their development as a triangular 'gateway', as envisaged by the NSS, could only be done at the expense of other towns in the region. It would 'cut against the grain' of development trends in the midlands and, by failing to build on the strengths and potential of Portlaoise and Longford, 'hinder the achievement of critical mass ... and balanced regional development'. The scenario favoured by the midlands plan was to drive forward implementation of the three-town gateway 'in conjunction with the development of Portlaoise and Longford as principal towns' – officially described as a 'polycentric five-town model'. This was based on replicating the success of a similar planning strategy in Denmark, where eight small and medium-sized towns came together to form the 'Triangle Region' with the aim of securing a larger slice of economic development. The combined population of Denmark's Triangle is exactly the same as the midlands, at 225,000. The big difference is that the midlands has a very weak urban structure, and none of its five main towns has a population greater than 20,000. At the end of March 2004 Laois County Council made its bid for a share of the action by launching plans to turn Portlaoise into a main hub for warehousing and distribution. County manager Martin Riordan described the Portlaoise Interchange initiative, centred on a 250-acre transport and logistics centre near the M7 and the Dublin-Limerick railway line, as 'the first step in ensuring sustained economic growth for Co Laois'.

This initiative could hardly disguise the fact that Laois's growth is largely driven by its relative proximity to the capital. Dr Edward Walsh, founder and former president of the University of Limerick, realised that the midlands was being drawn into Dublin's orbit, and put forward an alternative. In June 2003, referring to satellite images showing Ireland at night, he observed: 'There is no doubt where Dublin is

↑ *Cork City Council commissioned Catalan architect Beth Gali to revamp St Patrick's Street and Grand Parade. With its new lighting and paving, it is now a pedestrian-friendly environment.*

located: a large pool of light extends far west towards the midlands.' The outer limits of Cork, Limerick and Galway, he noticed, were surprisingly close, 'triggering the thought that if these three cities were encouraged to merge in a creative and collaborative way the resultant conurbation – let's call it the Atlantic Technopolis – could be a vibrant counterpole to Dublin'. The quality of life in the capital had deteriorated, and bold initiative could have political rewards, both in Dublin and the regions, he argued. The cities in the west and south 'could offer a most attractive alternative to Dublin that would attract the mobile research talent and knowledge-driven enterprise so vital to Ireland's future'. Identifying transport and communications as crucial, Walsh said a motorway from Cork to Limerick and Galway would serve as its backbone, while upgrading the railway line from Cork to Limerick and reinstating it to Galway would be a bonus. Road and rail links to a Euroferry port in Waterford would give direct continental access, taking some of the pressure off Dublin.

However, instead of pursuing such a 'win-win' strategy, Walsh said there was 'serious reason to fear that a "lose-lose" strategy was now emerging. On one hand, the National Spatial Strategy will not generate the desired major counterpole to Dublin, while on the other, the Government decentralisation programme threatens to fragment the national policy team that can take much credit for shaping Ireland's

↑ *A computer perspective of the new Cork School of Music, which is going to cost a lot more under a public-private partnership*
↓ *New apartments on Pope's Quay, Cork: a good example of urban regeneration*

↑ *Dr Edward Walsh, former president of the University of Limerick: any prospect of rational regional planning had been undermined by the 'hurriedly prepared' decentralisation programme*

remarkable economic success story.' Relocating the Oireachtas and 15 government departments to a new western counterpole was unrealistic, but 'it would make admirable sense to concentrate on devolving functions to new regional administrations while focusing effort on the Cork, Limerick, Galway corridor as the most likely means of creating a viable counterpole to Dublin.' Walsh said any prospect of rational regional planning had been undermined by the 'hurriedly prepared' decentralisation programme, in what he saw as a pre-election gimmick similar to the abolition of domestic rates in 1977. And he warned that the current plan could 'seriously endanger the future effectiveness of central government and Ireland's well-being'. Walsh's view, put forward in a speech to Limerick Chamber of Commerce in December 2003, should have carried some weight as he was chairman of the Irish Council for Science, Technology and Innovation, which advises the Government. But nobody was listening, at least not in the corridors of power.

Spurious arguments were advanced to defend the decentralisation programme. Martin Mansergh cited the European Union as an entity that 'functions partly on the basis of summoning delegates from widely dispersed locations to regular meetings'. But this overlooked the fact that all 25 delegations to an EU summit typically fly from airports serving cities of one million or more. The same can't be said of an official in the Department of the Marine after it is relocated to Cavan. To make a fisheries meeting in Brussels, he or she would face six or eight hours of additional travelling on a round trip. Mansergh went on to state that 'most countries avoid concentrating power and higher level services in one place', but gave no examples to flesh this out. Perhaps the FF senator would have been on firmer ground if he had pointed to countries where the seat of government differs from the nation's largest city – Australia (Canberra rather than Sydney), the Netherlands (The Hague / Amsterdam), Switzerland (Bern / Zurich), South Africa (Pretoria / Johannesburg). There's a similar situation in the US with the location of many state capitals: California is governed from Sacramento, and New York's legislature is based in Albany, and so on. But had he taken these on board, Mansergh would have confirmed the case made by Ed Walsh – relocation should occur not a splintered basis but with a unified move. Instead, he contended that Walsh 'always had a liking for the soapbox', again without offering any support for the statement. In fact, Walsh had been spelling out workable policies for the growth of regional cities at low-key events (such as UL graduation ceremonies) since the mid-1990s. It was only after the Government declined to accept good advice that Walsh turned to higher-profile venues.

The change of venue didn't make any difference: Cork, Limerick, Galway and Waterford were left to fend for themselves. Cork took on the mantle of European Capital of Culture for 2005, brimming with a new air of confidence that saw it twin-ning with Shanghai – a city more than 90 times larger. Following an international design competition in 1999, the city council commissioned Catalan architect Beth Gali to revamp St Patrick's Street and Grand Parade, and was confident of receiving Exchequer funding for the project, then estimated to cost €9 million. But three years passed without any word; a massive overrun (to €25 million) on the refurbishment of Cork's great neo-classical courthouse was believed to be behind the delay. Eventually, the Department of the Environment relented, agreeing to provide 50% of €13 mil-lion in funding for the first phase to enable the part-realisation of Gali's vision, which city manager Joe Gavin said would reflect the city's 'pride and spirit'. Astonishingly, Cork was overlooked by the Government's decentralisation programme. Instead of recognising it as a real asset by relocating 920 public servants to the city, they were to be dispersed throughout the county to Clonakilty, Kanturk, Macroom, Mallow, Mitchelstown and Youghal. Cork was to get a new School of Music as the centrepiece of its European starring role, but two years of 'foot-dragging' by the Government meant this deadline was missed. Construction work on a new building designed by architects Murray Ó Laoire was to have started in March 2002, but the Department of Finance became alarmed about the likely cost of this public-private partnership (PPP) project and how it would affect the Government's balance sheet.

The Cork School of Music was one of five pilot PPPs for new schools pro-moted by Micheál Martin in 1999 when he was Minister for Education. Four of those projects were secondary schools, all of which are now completed. The new school in Cork, a third-level facility, was billed as 'the jewel in the crown' of the PPP pro-gramme, under which the capital cost of new buildings is funded by a private-sector partner in return for an annual fee from the State over a number of years. Jarvis Ireland Ltd, a subsidiary of Jarvis UK, which has experience of similar PPP arrange-ments in Britain, was chosen as the partner. Under the proposed PPP, it would build the school at a cost of €60 million – much more than originally thought – and also assume responsibility for operating and maintaining the building for 25 years. In return, the State would pay Jarvis €8.2 million a year, which put the total cost to the Exchequer at more than €200 million (over the duration of the PPP). It was not until March 2004, with the local elections just ten weeks away, that approval for the proj-ect on these terms was finally announced by the then Minister for Education, Noel Dempsey, and his Cork-based Cabinet colleague, Micheál Martin. By then, however, Jarvis had run into financial difficulties, and in December 2004 sold its contract to Hochtief, a German construction company, which hoped to start work on the school in early 2005. Until it is built, the 3,500 students and 100 staff will have to operate from 16 buildings throughout the city, as they have been since early 2001.

The biggest challenge in Cork is redeveloping its docklands, where there is at

↑ *Steamboat Quay and the Clarion Hotel in Limerick, symbols of how the city has been turned around to face the River Shannon*

→ *The new Riverpoint office tower in Limerick, designed by BKD Architects. At 58.9 metres, it is currently the third tallest building in the State.*

least 300 acres of land available, stretching out for two kilometres on both sides of the River Lee. Just as Rome wasn't built in a day, the 25-year plan envisages some 6,000 new homes and six million square feet of commercial space, including offices and retailing, as well as leisure facilities. It has been kick-started by belated plans to redevelop the 17-acre site at Horgan's Quay, owned by CIÉ, with Manor Park Homes in the driving seat.

Limerick has improved enormously since the late 1980s when Jim Barrett, as city architect, set the goal of turning it around to face the Shannon. Since then, numerous civic, commercial and residential projects have sprung up along the city's quays. Nearly €1 billion has been invested in hotels, restaurants, shops and apartments, stretching from Arthur's Quay to Steamboat Quay, where the iconic 17-storey Clarion Hotel is located. King's Island, which had already seen substantial rejuvenation throughout the 1990s, is targeted for further development as a tourism, commercial and cultural centre, with an investment of up to €50 million by the public and private sectors. Limerick plans to turn itself into a 'great European riverside city for this millennium', in the words of one of its most successful sons, Pat Cox, former

president of the European Parliament. He was speaking at the launch in April 2003 of the Riverside City project, which will provide a framework for a range of developments along the waterfront, including the redundant docklands area. The project is a partnership involving Shannon Development, local authorities, the Shannon Foynes Port Company, the University of Limerick and Waterways Ireland. Limerick's docklands, an important component of the Riverside City project, is seen as offering huge opportunities. The aim is to turn this area into a hub of industry and commerce, balanced by a strong residential element. Other projects envisaged by the plan include an arts and performance centre, a 'tourism campus', and the restoration of the Park Canal to link the medieval city with the University of Limerick, which is expanding to the north bank of the Shannon, in Co Clare. That's what Limerick City Council would like to do, too. The city development plan, adopted in November 2004, seeks to absorb 11,590 acres of Co Limerick and 3,890 acres of Co Clare, arguing that the 'partitioning' of the city from its immediate environs is 'inimical to the ... well-being' of Limerick and its strategic role as the urban hub of the Mid-West Region. But Limerick faces a difficult financial future. In June 2005 an arbitrator ruled that the city council had wrongly fired a contractor from its main drainage scheme. The €50 million compensation bill is equivalent to nearly 80% of the council's annual budget, and one of the beneficiaries is set to be Paddy Whelan, the Clare-based quarry owner. Unless this massive bill is shouldered by the Government – just like the cost overruns on Luas, Cork's courthouse, and other major projects – the fear locally is that major retail stores will flee the city to avoid the imposition of crippling commercial rates.

In Galway, a bitter row erupted over plans to revamp Eyre Square after they were approved by An Bord Pleanála in November 2002. Most people were not aware that the landscaping would mean removing many of its trees, some of which were planted by former mayors and visiting politicians, including John F Kennedy. The appeals board specified that 11 of the square's 100 trees be retained or transplanted close to their present positions, and that the disembodied Browne doorway – originally from the family mansion in Abbeygate Street – be relocated within the square. Since the project was initiated in 1999 by the then city manager Joe Gavin (who later moved to Cork), it was clear that most of the trees were to be replaced by new trees in a European-style redesign by Dublin-based landscape architects Mitchell & Associates. The Galway Environmental Alliance held a series of protests, including a 24-hour 'vigil' to save the trees. In a GEA-organised 'referendum' on the issue in June 2003, almost all of the 2,329 people who took part – a Soviet-style 98% – agreed 'that the Eyre Square enhancement scheme be amended to incorporate the existing trees'. Few would dispute the verdict of Derrick Hambleton, chairman of the Galway branch of An Taisce, that the square should have been 'redesigned around the trees, rather than the other way round'. The cost of the project also escalated, from €3.2 million in 1999 to €10 million by February 2005. Worse was to come. In June 2005 Cork-based contractors Samuel Kingston Construction walked off the job and threatened to sue the city council, claiming that 'extraneous difficulties' had not been kept within 'tolerable limits'. For Hambleton, the débacle over Eyre Square under-lined the need for Galway to have a City Architect with enough authority to 'bring some order to the planning process'.

Waterford has been working hard to capture development opportunities on the strength of a more positive perception – aided by the arrival of the Tall Ships race in July 2005. Red Square, renamed John Roberts Square in honour of the city's eminent 18th-century architect, was beautifully re-laid in limestone and granite as part of an extensive pedestrianisation programme. So, too, was Barrowstrand Street, outside one of the cathedrals designed by Roberts. A municipal marina was also provided at Merchants Quay, and a maritime Millennium Plaza on Clyde Wharf, near Reginald's Tower. But the most ambitious project involves regenerating the redundant docks area on the north bank of the Suir, directly opposite Waterford's mile-long south quay. Nearly 17 acres of land, owned by the Harbour Commissioners and IAWS, and currently occupied by wharves, lifting cranes, storage sheds and silos, was targeted for development to provide a mix of apartments, offices, light industrial units, a hotel, and even a 'landmark venue building'. A conceptual plan drawn up by the Office of Public Works, while Martin Cullen was Minister of State in 1999, envisaged that the north quays would also include a docking station for cruise liners – and Cullen suggested at the time that this fantastical €100 million project might even attract some public funding. His close associate, Monica Leech, got her first public contract as PR consultant to promote it, receiving nearly €20,000 in fees and expens-es. In October 2002, after he had been promoted to the Cabinet, Cullen announced that London-based architects IDOM UK had won a major international competition to provide a 'development vision' for the area. However, no commitment was given that their 'vision' would ever be realised, even though the cost of holding the compe-tition was put at €1 million. The port company raised well over €1 million per acre for the site, which had become surplus to requirements following the transfer of com-mercial shipping downriver to the deep-water port at Belview. But 18 months later, Waterford Port's chairman, Ben Gavin, said the development was being held up by the 'wholly unreasonable' stance taken by Iarnród Éireann on a proposed access route over its sidings. A spokesman for the rail company said it fully supported the regen-eration plan, but had concerns about safety. But at least Martin Cullen was able to arrange that, even though Wexford got his Department's headquarters under the decentralisation programme, 200 of its staff were scheduled to move to Waterford.

In May 2003 it was revealed that Cullen raked in close to €35,000 over the pre-vious year in political donations – higher than any other TD – prompting the Green Party leader, Trevor Sargent TD, to describe him as 'the most corporately sponsored politician in this country'. Among his donors were several prominent builders, including Noel Frisby, who made a €2.4 million settlement with the Revenue Commissioners in 2001, claiming that a tax scheme 'came adrift'. Cullen received almost twice as much as the second-highest beneficiary of political donations in 2002, his Fianna Fáil colleague Eoin Ryan TD (now MEP), and nearly three times more than Bertie Ahern who declared €13,000 for that election year. By mid-August

↑ *A photomontage of the European-style revamping of Galway's Eyre Square by Dublin-based landscape architects Mitchell & Associates*
↓ *Aerial view of Waterford, with the docks site in the foreground*

↑ *Dusk at Christmas on John Roberts Square in Waterford, the centrepiece of the city's extensive pedestrian zone*
↓ *Millennium Plaza on Clyde Wharf, near Reginald's Tower, in Waterford*

↑ *Architects IDOM UK's competition-winning project for Waterford North Quays*

2003, Cullen was talking about the 'need' to drop the cap on corporate donations. 'I'm not convinced of the value of limits', he told Alison O'Connor. 'We need to start with a blank sheet of paper and simplify the way in which things are done, so that we have a fair and open system that is easily understandable and we don't get caught up in discussions on the end of a pin head.'

He also continued to show extraordinary generosity to Monica Leech, who had fund-raised for him in Waterford. After he became Minister for the Environment in June 2002, Leech was engaged on a part-time basis at €1,000 per day. Six months later, she was adjudged to beat Carr Communications and awarded a longer-term contract. Leech got the job, even though her fees were higher than Carr's. By the end of 2004, when the story broke, Leech had been paid €310,000 by the Department of the Environment. Her role, apparently, was to advise on selling the National Spatial Strategy and the Race Against Waste campaign – even though two other experienced PR companies, Drury Communications and Mary Murphy Associates respectively, were already handling these areas. It also emerged that she had accompanied Cullen on numerous foreign trips to such destinations as Johannesburg, Kiev, New York, Paris, Singapore, Stockholm, The Hague, and the 'paradise resort' of Langkawi on the Andaman coast of Malaysia. But Cullen's bacon was saved in February 2005 when the Standards in Public Office Commission decided there was 'not a prima facie case which would have warranted an investigation within the terms of the legislation' – a reference to the 1995 Ethics in Public Office Act. An earlier report by Dermot Quigley, former chairman of the Revenue Commissioners, found that Cullen had merely left himself open to 'a perception of impropriety' over the Leech contracts. 'In any country, however, the Minister would have been long gone out of office because of his record of incompetence', the Labour Party commented. Cullen, who had squandered €52 million on electronic voting, seemed oblivious to irony in June 2005 when he lashed out at objectors for 'robbing money out of the taxpayers of the country' by holding up major infrastructure projects in the courts.

Meanwhile, the State's nine regional authorities – none of which has any authority – submitted their planning guidelines to the Department of the Environment by the end of April 2004. One of the key issues was to ensure at least some measure of compliance with the NSS, for the guidance of local authorities in preparing their own development plans. Asked what would happen if they all ended up as toothless as the Greater Dublin Area SPGs and growth continued haphazardly, Martin Cullen said: 'Well, what happens then is that we would have a disaster, and that's what I don't want.' Yet just over 12 months after publishing the NSS – and pledging that it would form the basis of public policy – the Government itself had effectively disowned the spatial strategy with its scatter-gun approach to decentralisation, which was also ham-fisted.

In its latest report, published in July 2005, the Implementation Group conceded that new jobs would have to be found for 6,000 public servants in Dublin when the decentralisation programme is complete because the number applying for transfers was so low. The Group – now headed by Finbarr Flood, former chairman of the Labour Court – blamed lack of progress in talks between management and unions on an elusive deal that would allow Civil Service staff to transfer freely to State agencies, and vice versa. But even by the end of 2004, it was clear that 29 of the original 53 destinations had been 'relegated to "long-finger" status', as Richard Bruton said, while over 60% of the jobs in the first phase would be relocating to towns in the Dublin commuter belt. As Michael Bannon, former professor of planning at UCD, told Urban Institute Ireland in June 2004: 'If the current Irish relocation proposals survive beyond next week and if they are to be implemented without a radical rethink, then the major impact will be further expansion of the Greater Dublin Area. In themselves, the Government's proposals are ill-considered. They will damage the coherence and efficiency of the public service. They fly in the face of the National Spatial Strategy, and they are likely to sound the death knell for regional policy in Ireland. This reckless dispersal of government work is a follow-on from years of scattering industrial plants in every town and village, with the disastrous consequences we have today. Would an Irish government go to a corporation such as Intel and propose that it should break up its Leixlip campus in favour of 30, 40 or 50 dispersed locations? Not only does this adventure give us all a bad name, but it represents a tragic lost opportunity to do the right thing, to do it with wisdom and to do it well.'

—

4. Rural Housing

IN AUGUST 2001 A FORMER PRESIDENT OF THE IRISH PLANNING INSTITUTE PROPOSED THAT the Government should establish a special commission to investigate the scale of Ireland's rural housing phenomenon, which he believed was 'spiralling out of control'. Writing in the institute's journal, *Pleanáil*, Fergal MacCabe said such a commission would need to set out clearly 'the nature and scale of the situation, analyse why it is happening, the probable consequences and the possible solutions'. In an article entitled 'How We Wrecked Rural Ireland', MacCabe wrote: 'Go up any rural road and you will find nests of bungalows all over the place. It is now out of hand and many planning authorities ... have thrown in the towel.' Donegal and Kerry were 'beyond redemption', while Kildare was 'heading that way'. Some counties, such as Westmeath, had 'tried to hold back the tide', while An Bord Pleanála 'generally rejects any unjustified rural housing that comes to it on appeal'. At local level, numerous county councillors 'regard it as their aggressive duty to see that as many one-off houses as possible are provided in the countryside, regardless of any longer-term consequences'. In his home county of Offaly, MacCabe noted that the once-unspoiled 13-mile route from Tullamore to Croghan Hill was now lined with 'uniformly awful' bungalows, while the sites in between them were 'festooned with notices' seeking permission to build more. The few farmhouses he remembered were now abandoned and decayed, and, ironically, the only part of the whole route where no housing had occurred was where you might expect it – in the little village of Kilclonfert with its church and school. Although nearly every county development plan had 'pious policies' restricting rural housing to farmers' children or others with locational needs in rural areas, MacCabe said it was 'as plain as a pikestaff that the amount of rural housing built bears no relationship to that policy'. What was happening, he suggested, was that 'applicants must tell lies and planning authorities must turn a blind eye. Everybody knows that the permission granted to the local will be sold on to a non-

→ *A new dormer bungalow stands even more starkly than its neighbour against the relatively wild landscape of Connemara*

local, and nobody objects because they might want to do it themselves next week.'

MacCabe felt compelled to speak out after the revelation, in April 2001, that 36% of new homes consisted of one-off houses in the countryside. And since output at the time was running at 50,000 annually, this meant that 18,000 new homes were being built in the countryside – equivalent in straightforward numerical terms to *six times* the annual output of one-offs in the whole of Britain. Finian Matthews, principal officer in the Department of the Environment's planning division, explained that the estimate was based on data from ESB connections. And the 18,000 figure for 2000 came on top of 10,000 one-offs built in 1997, 11,000 in 1998, and 14,000 in 1999. A planning paper published by the Department in August 2001, in the context of preparing the National Spatial Strategy, noted that the number of planning applications for rural housing went up between 20% and 70% in the period 1997-99, depending on the county. It also conceded that virtually all of Ireland's small villages were suffering significant population decline as the countryside around them became suburbanised, a trend it described as 'worrying'. Based on official estimates, the housing built in rural areas during 2000 alone consumed 2,700 hectares (6,480 acres) of agricultural land and resulted in the loss of an estimated 540km (337 miles) of natural hedgerows to create new site boundaries. It also added 18,000 septic tanks to the national total, estimated at 400,000. This raised fears for the protection of groundwater sources, especially in more vulnerable areas where development pressures tend to be stronger. 'This issue is one of the more pressing ones relating to dispersed rural settlement, particularly as it affects one of the basic requirements of life – the availability of clean water', the Department's paper said.

↓ *Finian Matthews, principal officer at the Department of the Environment, explained that the full extent of one-off housing in rural areas was revealed by ESB connections*

The paper found urban-generated rural housing 'generally unsustainable' because of the energy it consumes, the traffic it generates, and the pressure it puts on water supplies. That's why it said there 'must be a presumption against' urban-generated housing in rural areas for a variety of reasons, including 'the need to preserve outstanding landscapes'. Unless housing in rural areas was associated with the needs of rural communities, then 'the energy needs and landscape, transportation and environmental impacts of dispersed settlement patterns render these contrary to the principles of sustainable development'. The Government's Sustainable Development Strategy, formulated in

1997, also flagged the negative impact on the fabric of towns and villages of unlimited development in the countryside – and this point was taken up by the Department's paper, which warned that small villages were being turned into 'doughnuts'. Figures showed that the 448 villages with less than 1,000 in population had fewer residents because new housing development has been lost to the surrounding countryside.

As the authors noted, rural housing is predominantly car-dependent, with consequential increases in greenhouse gas emissions, as well as generating more pressure on rural roads and more demand for parking in towns. Its transport impact was, therefore, 'a significant and long-term issue'. They saw the debate about urban-generated housing in the countryside as a 'battlefield of hearts and minds' between the interests of individuals, on the one hand, and sustainable development principles, on the other. Controls borrowed from Britain had been resisted by the 'indigenous enthusiasm for a laissez-faire approach to rural housing'. They identified the fact that farmers can sell sites for 'many multiples' of their agricultural value as one of the main driving forces. 'The desirability of a rural site has increased its value to a point where there is now a very real incentive to abuse the planning system by persuading a planning authority to grant permission on the basis, say, of local need and then to sell [the site]', according to the paper. 'Occupancy conditions offer little resistance to this.' In general, the Department's paper said, the contentiousness of rural housing as an issue for local authorities 'has been leading to a situation where development plan policies are increasingly being framed in a loose manner' in order to accommodate the pressures for building in the countryside. Almost half of all county development plans had no specific policies requiring any controls on the occupancy or use of new housing in rural areas, while only a third had any particular requirements giving guidelines on the siting and design of houses. Its authors also queried whether the Government's 1999 White Paper on Rural Development, which espouses the objective of maintaining a dispersed population in the countryside, can be reconciled with the overriding requirement to achieve sustainable development. But the trend which the planners found so worrying in 2001 intensified over the following years, with the proportion of one-offs rising from 36% of housing output nationally in 2000 to 43% in 2003, when a record 68,819 new homes were built. The proportion of one-offs is higher in some counties than others, accounting for 65% of all housing in Mayo, 68% in Wexford, and some 70% in Galway. On average, 85% of all planning applications for one-off houses are granted, and only a tiny minority – less than 1% – are appealed by An Taisce. The coast road between Galway and Carraroe is a classic example of the spread of suburbia. Up to a few years ago, you could turn off the main road from Casla and see a bit of the Connemara landscape, with its blanket bog and mountain backdrop. Now the road to Screebe is dotted with suburban-style houses, including one 'magisterially overlooking a lake as if it was a feature in its own back garden', as one local critic complained in September 2003. 'After Screebe, we have more undistinguished bungalows ... Then just before the holiday village at Glynsk, note the clutter of houses, all suburban in style, that have been allowed on the seaward side of the road – a ghastly sight.'

However, despite all the evidence of an indulgent planning regime, the impression was put about that there was some sort of 'ban' on building one-off houses in the countryside. This was largely based on a relatively small number of 'hard cases' where farmers' sons or daughters had been refused permission to build on their land, often due to reasons of visual amenity, water quality or road safety. Some were very high-profile, such as the case of a young couple in Co Kerry, who had been refused planning permission for a two-storey house on a scenic site near Kenmare, but went ahead and built it anyway on foot of a Section 140 motion requiring the county manager to approve the plan. The only problem was that An Taisce successfully appealed this decision to An Bord Pleanála, leaving Kerry County Council with the unpleasant task of serving the couple with an order requiring the demolition of their completed home as an 'unauthorised development'. It was finally demolished in March 2004, after a three-year legal wrangle that went all the way to the Supreme Court. In the meantime, they got planning permission to build a single-storey house on the same site.

What many councillors found so galling was An Taisce's strikingly high success rate on appeals, and, even worse, the fact that this was based on declared public policy. In nearly every case, An Bord Pleanála upheld appeals where issues of road safety and public health were the main grounds. It even turned down initial plans by the President, Mary McAleese, for a two-storey lakeside home near Carrick-on-Shannon in 2001 on the grounds that it would be 'prejudicial to public health' as well as 'visually obtrusive'. (The McAleeses later got permission for a more sensitive single-storey house, designed by Arthur Gibney, a former president of the RIAI.) An Taisce also zeroed in on plans by Niall Callan, Secretary General of the Department of the Environment, for a holiday home on Sherkin Island, off the Co Cork coast. In

↑ *A 1987 aerial photograph of the sprawl of one-off houses outside Carraroe, in Connemara*
↙ *One becomes four: a row of 'one-offs' in north Co Galway*

June 2003 An Bord Pleanála upheld an appeal against Cork County Council's decision to grant permission, saying the county plan strongly discouraged new houses in scenic coastal areas. Callan made it clear that he would not be contesting the board's decision in the High Court. 'They have a job to do, and that's what the system is there for', he said. Others, however, were not so understanding. Every time a planning refusal came through, incensed applicants would complain to local councillors about An Taisce's intervention costing them the 'right to build' on their own land. In Mayo, even though it had appealed relatively few one-off cases, the trust found itself excoriated at a county council meeting in February 2002, when the members voted unanimously for a motion calling on the Minister to 'de-list' it as a prescribed body under the Planning Act. 'Oliver Cromwell is remembered for saying "To hell or to Connacht", but what An Taisce is now saying is "To hell out of Connacht". It's outrageous', fumed Johnny Mee, a Labour councillor. According to Cllr Al McDonnell (FF), also an estate agent in Castlebar, 'they want to see empty, barren hillsides with no lights after 5pm. They will oppose vehemently the construction of one simple hamlet in the countryside.' When it was put to him that An Taisce had appealed against only one house in Co Mayo in the previous five years, he said it was the 'mentality it represents' that he was criticising and its 'growing influence' on planning

↑ *The holiday home near Rooskey, Co Roscommon, built for Minister for Justice Michael McDowell and his wife, Prof Niamh Brennan. They successfully challenged the county council's refusal to extend its planning permission.*

↓ *President Mary McAleese and her husband Martin's first application for a one-off house in Co Roscommon was judged to be visually obtrusive and prejudicial to public health*

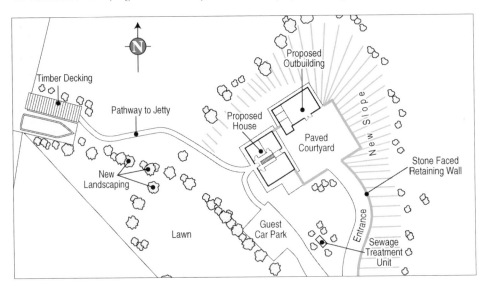

decisions generally. When permission was refused to a local man for a new house on Ely Bay on the Erris peninsula because it was in an area of high scenic amenity (a candidate Special Area of Conservation) and also had a Blue Flag beach, Cllr Frankie Leneghan (FF) said: 'It's time we took the blue flags and tossed them into the sea. If the flags come at the expense of local people living in local areas, then they're not worth it.'

At a protest meeting in Foxford in March 2002, councillors made it clear that they also wanted Vincent Roche, chief executive of the North Western Fisheries Board, 'reined in' because of its success with planning appeals. The track record of the fisheries board was the reason. In 1999 it took seven appeals and won them all. The following year, 11 of its 14 appeals were upheld. In 2001 it won 14 out of 15. At the Foxford meeting, Beverley Cooper Flynn TD (FF) said it was 'wrong to have so much power invested in one man', adding that he should be 'more under the control of his board members'. One of her associates, Cllr Jimmy Maloney (FF), who described himself as an 'outspoken' member of the fisheries board, agreed wholeheartedly. Roche was uncontrite. 'Nobody at that meeting seemed to ask the fundamental question about why these permissions are being turned down. It's to do with water quality and public health', he said. 'Angling tourism is virtually finished because trout stocks have been virtually wiped out in Lough Cullin and are down to about a third of what they were in Lough Conn. And though our concern is fish stocks, many group water schemes are contaminated, so there's a public health issue involved, too.' Char had survived in Lough Conn for 10,000 years, but stocks were 'wiped out' during the 1990s by pollution from agriculture, town sewage and septic tanks. For whatever reason, the number of planning appeals made by the fisheries board fell from 15 in 2001 to nine in 2002 (of these, five were upheld and four withdrawn), and three in 2003 (of which one was upheld and tw0 declared invalid). Stephen Neylon, fisheries environmental officer with the board, pointed out that some appeals were withdrawn when an upgrade of Castlebar's severely overloaded sewage treatment plant was brought forward. As for the overall fall in the number of appeals taken, he said this reflected a substantial increase in the number of applications being refused by Mayo County Council's planners on water pollution grounds.

In the meantime, Mayo councillors

↓ *Beverley Cooper Flynn was critical of the North Western Regional Fisheries Board's defence of water quality*

↑ *Glenveagh National Park, Co Donegal: its very existence as a protected landscape seems to have led to the declaration of an 'open season' for one-off houses in the rest of the county*

removed most of the remaining restrictions on housing in the countryside, including landscape controls, before adopting a new county development plan in November 2003. They also ditched design guidelines prepared by Paul Keogh Architects on the basis that they were too restrictive. Asked to explain why they had done this, one councillor said: 'We have to give the people what they want.' The *Western People* commented: 'Sadly, our politicians of all hues have said very little about the notion of good planning, about all the different ingredients that should be involved in proper planning or, indeed, about the need to satisfy the common good.' Anna O'Malley Dunlop, a leading member of An Taisce in Mayo, accused the councillors of disregarding 'the well-informed and painstaking work of their own technical staff who have had the humiliating experience of preparing a sound County Development Plan in accordance with best planning practices ... only to see deleted all those elements in the plan which would render it workable'. They had abandoned their duty to the wider public interest by 'yielding shamelessly to the pressure of a noisy body of landowners, auctioneers and developers'. And she called on those who had 'spoken up for a balanced view of the future development of this beautiful and fragile part of God's earth to declare themselves now and let us know if there is any hope that democracy exists in Mayo'. None did.

↑ *Under bare Ben Bulben's head: a dormer bungalow near Rosses Point, Co Sligo*
↑ *A large house trading as a B&B on the N4 near Kinnegad, Co Westmeath*
↑ *Just one of the many new houses built in recent years in scenic locations on the Fanad peninsula in Co Donegal*

In Donegal, the very existence of Glenveagh National Park as a protected landscape seems to have led to an 'open season' in the rest of the county. Bloody Foreland, in the Rosses, has 'the worst continuous coastal strip development in the country', according to Ian Lumley, An Taisce's heritage officer. 'Strings and strings' of houses had also spread over the landscape in places like Creeslough, Falcarragh, Fanad and Portnablagh. Letterkenny, the county's largest town, has become something of an octopus, with tentacles spreading out all over the landscape, while the town itself has only one or two coherent streets. Donegal councillors traded in Section 4 (now Section 140) motions – the device used by local politicians to secure permission for developments which would otherwise be refused on planning grounds. And though the planning regulations now require that these motions must have the support of three-quarters of all elected members, there is still not much problem in putting them through – especially when they win the undying gratitude of the beneficiaries. But Donegal's planners also can be quite indulgent. Jim Harley, the county council's senior planner, saw nothing wrong with plans to build 38 two-storey houses on the seaward side of the coast road between Moville and Greencastle – something that would have gone ahead but for an appeal by the local environmental group. In January 2004 An Bord Pleanála said the proposed development 'would interfere with the character of this scenic coastal landscape and detract from views of Lough Foyle'. And because the five-acre site was outside Moville's town boundary, with undeveloped land in between, it would also 'prejudice the orderly planned development and consolidation of the town'. Moreover, Moville has no sewage treatment and there is a shortage of water in the area.

Wexford County Council also liberalised its policy on housing in the countryside in its August 2003 development plan. Members of the council voted through a series of amendments to make it much easier for applicants – including people working in Dublin – to get planning permission for rural one-off houses. The amendments, tabled by the council's Fianna Fáil group, included the omission of any 'local needs' requirement for new housing. 'It's going to be a free-for-all', said Cllr Anna Fenlon (FG). 'The prices of sites are going to go sky-high and who is going to benefit? The landowners and the IRDA' – a reference to the Irish Rural Dwellers Association, which lobbied for the changes. According to Wexford County Council, the amended plan 'will facilitate the provision of single rural houses and cluster development in rural areas'. It would also allow development closer to road frontages and permit the sharing of

↓ Ian Lumley of An Taisce: 'It's all to do with landowners being able to sell sites'

septic tanks. A provision sterilising sensitive areas was removed, and the amended plan also provided for a review of all scenic routes where development is currently restricted. Declan MacPartlin, the IRDA's Co Wexford chairman, said he was very pleased that the county council had adopted its proposals on residency, sightlines, road frontage and 'the right to build' – changes he described as 'most encouraging for the democratic process'. But Adrian Doyle, the council's director of services, said some of the amendments 'completely contradict' planning advice and were also contrary to Government guidelines on sustainable development, as well as the National Spatial Strategy. 'It's all to do with landowners being able to sell sites', said Ian Lumley. The *Wexford Echo* agreed. In an opinion piece headed 'Can't eat scenery? Well you sure can't eat bungalows!', the paper said the people of Killarney had been 'eating pretty well off it now for 200 years'. Commenting on the proliferation of housing in rural Wexford, it said: 'Unless the farming community is particularly fecund, not all of the one-off houses are being built by farmers' sons and daughters ... In Wexford, the relevant figures are: 70,000 people live in the rural electoral divisions, of whom a mere 5,000 are farmers.' The pattern of development also posed an important question: 'What happens in 20 years time when most of these stand-alone houses are occupied by elderly people, living alone and afraid, without the comfort of neighbours and miles from medical services, shops and other supports?'

Intimidation also crept in. According to An Taisce, people in rural areas who raised their heads above the parapet were being intimidated by landowners, developers and their agents, including county councillors. A German couple with an organic farm in Dowra, Co Leitrim, went to the High Court in mid-2002 claiming that they were being terrorised by gangs of local men after they objected to new housing in the area. Their barrister told the court how gangs had 'ploughed' their land using 4x4 jeeps, driving over plants, ramming feed troughs and scattering sheep in their path. The couple had also been photographed and videotaped day and night. In other areas, according to Breda Keena of An Taisce, even the children of objectors have been bullied at school by the children of those who stand to gain, while their parents are subjected to 'malicious whispering campaigns'. These efforts 'are always led by people with a vested interest – farmers selling sites, local councillors who also act as auctioneers or publicans and local builders who offer sports halls and the like in return for a community's support'. In Co Mayo, one woman feared losing her job. After lodging an objection against a proposed two-storey house in the countryside, she was contacted by her employer and told that the applicant had threatened to boycott his business if she didn't withdraw it. Tony Lowes, founder of Friends of the Irish Environment, received threatening phone calls when FIE appealed against a 60ft mast beside Myross graveyard, a listed archaeological site on a 'magical' hillside above Leap, Co Cork. One man left a message on his answering machine saying, 'if you don't withdraw the appeal, I'll bust your fucking head in.' Some days later, a spent bullet was posted to Lowes' house with a note saying 'from Leap, Co Cork'. Shortly afterwards, Dr Sara Dillon, another founder-member of FIE, who had also received threatening phone calls, wrote to An Bord Pleanála withdrawing its appeal because it was 'no longer safe or wise to continue'. In Co Wicklow, one couple who objected to a proposed development had gunshots fired over their house and torches shone through the windows at night. Later, they were menacingly asked if they had protection. In Vicarstown, Co Laois, another objector was told that her house would be burnt. In other counties, according to An Taisce, people who merely look up planning files are asked who they are, only to have their names passed on to applicants or their agents. 'Then they get a call from their local councillor querying why they're doing this.'

Planners were also feeling the heat. When An Bord Pleanála advertised six planning inspectors' posts in May 2002, there were more than 70 applications – most of them from planners in rural local authorities who wanted out. In one western seaboard county, several councillors were offering a 'complete service' to people planning to build in the countryside – from the design of individual houses to tabling a Section 140 motion to secure planning permission. Some councillors in Louth and Galway hired their own planning consultants to prepare alternative plans, and then, in the case of Dunleer, brazenly participated in voting them through. 'Councillors in Kilkenny, Leitrim and Roscommon have taken an active part in having planning control and amenity provisions dumped in the review process [of county plans] to make it easier for applicants to secure permission for one-off houses in rural areas.' What these councillors were arguing for, in effect, was to have no planning at all, as Ian Lumley saw it. 'They are seeking to replace a weak planning system with a completely laissez-faire approach so that anyone can build whatever they like wherever they like.' This is what had came across from the spate of rural development and 'planning action' meetings which, he said, were 'orchestrated by landowners with an axe to grind or by councillors who are more than happy to act as their planning agents'.

What Lumley found most disheartening was the stance of the two main farming organisations, the IFA and ICMSA. 'Instead of being concerned about the loss of farmland to ribbon development and contamination by septic tanks, they are craven in their attitude to short-term vested interests.' Pat O'Rourke, president of the ICMSA, summed up their view: 'As far as we are concerned, if a farmer gets full planning permission for a house on his farm and then sells the site, he's entitled to do that.' (The IFA's only qualification is that anyone building in the countryside must accept the rural way of life.) But this is hardly surprising when those who own land in rural areas could collectively be making as much as €810 million a year from the sale of sites for housing – an estimate based on 18,000 sites at an average price of €45,000 per site. With such staggering sums at stake, rational dialogue between rural planning action groups and those seeking to protect fragile or sensitive landscapes became impossible. *The Jaundiced Eye* column, hosted on www.castlebar.ie, took the *Connacht Telegraph* to task over the issue. The local paper had given Fianna Fáil TD John Carty free rein. In welcoming the Taoiseach's commitment that the Government intended to relax the planning regime, Carty had said that the failure by young people to get planning permission on family farms was now one of the biggest issues in Mayo. 'And lots more of the same disingenuous rubbish in the press statement pub-

↑ *Site for sale in Co Donegal, with a panoramic view over Lough Swilly and 'full planning permission' for development*

lished without comment by the *Connacht Telegraph*', said to the always acerbic columnist. 'Why can't we just say what we mean: "We farmers need this fine cash crop of building sites" and be done with it? The nice myth that all one-off houses are built by the sons of farmers is a load of cow manure – and indeed it smells just like the kind that regularly wafts across into the kitchens of these one-off houses ... Just look at the "Sites for Sale" signs littered all along any road in the country. Check the names of those erecting them. How many belong to that other vested-interest species of TD and County Councillor – the auctioneer or "developer"? If all these houses are built for just the immediate offspring of farmers, how come there are "for sale" signs all over the place? Do they have so many children that they have to auction the sites off to their children? Do we really have that many farmers with children that want or need to build a house on their farm? You gotta be kiddin' us!' As Brendan O'Mahony, Connacht IFA president, told a public meeting in Leitrim in November 2002, 'selling a site can be the means of getting a farmer out of a corner or putting a son or daughter through college.'

For home-buyers, too, the economics are attractive. Even allowing for the cost of a site, a young couple could provide themselves with a new home for less than the average price of nearly €320,000 in Dublin. As Labour's environment spokesman

↑ *Minister for Community, Rural and Gaeltacht Affairs, Eamon Ó Cuiv: farmers have become 'used to selling sites' for houses in the countryside*

↓ *Eamon Gilmore TD: a young couple working in Dublin would have to earn over €100,000 a year between them to be able to raise a mortgage on an average house*

Eamon Gilmore pointed out in June 2004, a young couple working in the capital would have to earn over €100,000 a year between them to raise a mortgage on an average house, never mind one costing €400,000 or €500,000. 'For many, the only way to get on the property ladder is to build the first rung themselves', wrote Laura Slattery in the *Irish Times*. 'Some choose to hire the services of a timber frame company who will supply stock housing plans that can be purchased online, and an engineer who will check that the plans comply with local building regulations.' Many others pick their design from pattern books such as *Bungalow Bliss*, by Jack Fitzsimons. Very few hire architects, mainly because their fee could amount to 10-15% of the cost of a project. Slattery quoted the example of a four-bedroom bungalow planned for a site with sea views, south of Midleton, Co Cork. The site cost them €100,000; the estimate for building the house came to €150,000; a local development levy could add another €8,000 to the bill; and there was a further €5,000-€10,000 for self-build insurance. The total cost worked out at under €270,000, but the 2,500 square foot bungalow would be worth between €350,000 and €400,000. No wonder financial institutions will advance up to 80% of the price of a site with full planning permission. 'If the borrower already owns the site, lenders will fund 100% of the build cost as long as the overall loan-to-value ratio is less than 90%', according to Sarah Wellband, of REA mortgage brokers. 'Given that the end value of the house is normally well in excess of the combined site price plus build costs, most lenders are happy to advance top-ups if the costs over-run.'

→ *The* ABS Book of House Plans, *one of the early competitors to Jack Fitzsimons'* Bungalow Bliss

The one-off housing lobby had a voice at the Cabinet table through Eamon Ó Cuiv, who articulated a homespun philosophy about populating rural areas. Ó Cuiv, as Minister for Community, Rural and Gaeltacht Affairs, said his 'vision of rural Ireland is a populated countryside', following the Celtic pattern of dispersed settlement; this was better than 'forcing people' into cities, towns and villages. He also predicted in August 2002 that the long-awaited National Spatial Strategy would contain 'a clear statement that rural people with connections in the countryside will be allowed to build their own houses there'. Ó Cuiv's line on rural housing was criticised by An Taisce, which called for his resignation in March 2002 for espousing 'voodoo planning' theories that were at odds with public policy. It said Ó Cuiv 'represents the interests of a vociferous vested minority who hope to farm sites as once they farmed agriculture. There is no academic, professional or empirical justification for his opinions ... In these circumstances, he should put up or shut up.' When questioned on the issue in May 2002, Ó Cuiv no longer grappled with the substance of the argument. Instead, he noted that farmers had become 'used to selling sites' – though he was careful to distance himself from the vast sums of money at stake. 'I'm about settlement patterns, not about handing bucks out to people', he told a special meeting of Kerry County Council.

Planning in Kerry was already way out of control. The N22 between Killarney and Farranfore will have to be replaced by a new road, at a 2003 estimate of €90 million, because so many houses have been built along the original route – largely on foot of Section 4 (now Section 140) motions tabled by councillors. By permitting these houses, the councillors ignored a long-standing rule that ribbon development should not be permitted on national primary or secondary routes, to allow for future upgrading. Engineers said widening the existing N22 would directly impact on 140 properties and require 17 houses to be demolished, while the cost of land acquisition would come to €6 million. Also, the number of established entrances and exits is too high. Along the 15km stretch between Farranfore and Killarney, 15% of all accidents occurred at private entrances, all of which would have to be maintained as part of any realignment of the existing roadway. A study for the National Roads Authority noted: 'Development is particularly dense on the section of road between Lawlors Cross and Killarney. On this 5.5km section of roadway, there are approximately 110 residential/commercial accesses, representing 20 accesses per kilometre or one access every 50m', and the potential for accidents would increase with rising traffic volumes. No wonder the N22 case prompted the NRA to tell local authorities they should insist on a road safety audit in all planning applications for new houses fronting onto national primary and secondary routes.

Kerry councillors had already been warned, in a legal opinion by Dermot Flanagan SC, that they could be personally liable if they failed to 'act judiciously' in dealing with developments which threaten public health or safety. But this grave warning had no impact in reducing the abuse of Section 140. In March 2004 the council had 27 such motions on its agenda – all directing the county manager to grant per-

↓ *Jackie Healy-Rae TD, with his two sons Danny and Michael*

↑ *The Meadowlands housing estate, 10km from Killarney, consists of very large and obviously very expensive detached two-storey houses in their own enclave*

mission for one-off houses, most of which merited refusal for sound planning reasons. It was three months before the local elections, and the councillors were clearly trying to out-do each other ingratiating themselves with their constituents. In south Kerry, Section 140s had become ammunition in an ongoing political struggle between Fianna Fáil and the Healy-Rae dynasty. Fine Gael councillors were also active. And the council's planners were so severely stretched producing reports on each case, with no measurable effects, that some of them left in despair. At the March 2004 meeting, no less than 21 of the motions were adopted by the required majority of three-quarters of the council's membership, and the other six were adjourned. Cllr PJ Donovan (FG) moved a motion to grant permission for a house on an elevated site above the Ring of Kerry, near Cahirciveen. A planning report noted that the site was part of a small farm owned by the applicant's father, where 15 houses had already been permitted since 1997 and a further 13 refused; he had 'kept the best site for his son', the council was told. A month earlier, councillors granted outline permission for a scheme of three houses with septic tanks on a boggy site at Gneeveguilla, Killarney, despite being advised that percolation tests had failed and the development would be 'prejudicial to public health'. An Taisce and anyone else who objected were just standing in the way of Kerry people's 'God-given right to build on their own land', according to Cllr Michael Healy-Rae (Ind).

The Kerry landscape is being inundated with housing – including suburban estates remote from any village or town – and this has little to do with providing new homes for the sons and daughters of farmers. Septic tanks are contributing to the pollution of Lough Leane, Killarney's principal lake, which frequently suffers from an algal bloom in summertime. Housing has been built right up to the boundary of the National Park, particularly on the Muckross road. This has eliminated any buffer zone, and means the park can never qualify for designation as a World Heritage Site. One-off houses are scattered all over the high ground in Fossa, 5km from Killarney, some on the brows of hills, and most of them orientated to avail of views towards the Magillicuddy Reeks and Gap of Dunloe. Around Faha, off the main road from Killarney to Dingle, one-off housing is being intensified by building clusters of sub-urban-style homes. One estate called Meadowlands, 10km from Killarney, consists of very large and very expensive detached two-storey houses in their own enclave, behind a low stone wall. Not far away, near Laharn Cross, five identical bungalows have been laid out around a keyhole driveway, with footpaths on each side, but not a shop, school, community centre or other social facility in sight. In Flintfield, built by Cronin Developments, each house has its own driveway off a private estate road. All along the road from Firies to Killarney there is a real sense that an entire rural area is being colonised by suburban housing that should have been built on the immediate outskirts of Killarney. And since there are no shops to serve any of it, cars are essential for getting around. Cllr Danny Healy-Rae (Ind), a vocal supporter of one-off housing in the countryside, said the 'exorbitant cost' of land on the edge of Killarney was driving people further out. Ian Lumley, who visited the Faha area in late 2003, was taken aback by what he saw there. 'I'm not easily shocked because I'm used to seeing bad planning all over Ireland, but the pattern of development in this area is totally new in its sheer shocking impact. We've now moved from one-off houses to one-off housing estates', he said. 'Killarney has long been recognised for the scenic beauty of its landscape, but if this sort of development continues it may become notorious as a planning fiasco.' Lumley was being polite. Because most of the new houses are serviced by septic tanks rather than town sewerage, groundwater is at risk. Firies, where the population has exploded in recent years, has a primitive sewage treatment plant which is overloaded and cleaned out by a tractor once a week. 'You wouldn't see it in Morocco', one of the new residents said.

Martin Cullen did nothing to halt the abuse of Section 140 in Kerry. In fact, he heaped fuel on the fire by further liberalising the planning regime for one-off housing in March 2004. And he was so anxious to get the ball rolling that planning authorities were instructed to implement the so-called Sustainable Rural Housing Guidelines even while they were still in draft form. 'The policy move and directional change is clear', Cullen said. 'These new guidelines now being issued are based on a presumption that people who have roots in or links to rural areas, and are part of and contribute to the rural community, will get planning permission for houses.' This would apply even in rural areas where there is already strong pressure for urban-generated housing, subject to 'the normal requirements of good planning' such as road safety and proper treatment of sewage. 'New houses in rural areas should, of course, be located and designed to integrate well with their physical surroundings and be generally compatible with the conservation of sensitive areas such as natural habitats.' But Cullen made it clear that the statutory designation of Special Areas of Conservation, Special Protection Areas and Natural Heritage Areas 'is not intended to operate as an inflexible constraint on housing development'. In addition, 'anyone wishing to build a house in rural areas suffering persistent and substantial population decline will be accommodated, subject to good planning practice in siting and design' – even if they have no roots in the area. The Minister denied that the new policy would 'open the floodgates by abandoning any sense of a planned approach to rural housing'. It was 'not a panacea to concrete over Ireland', and people would not be allowed to 'build on top of mountains'. Given that groundwater in Ireland is identified in the guidelines as a 'key asset', he said he was 'considering' whether any additional measures were required to ensure that septic tanks and other sewage treatment systems were monitored and maintained. Cullen said the new regime was intended to ensure a 'vibrant future for all rural areas', and he called on all planning authorities to review their development plans so that they would be consistent with the Government's new policy on rural housing. 'Significant population decline in rural areas should trigger the need for ... policies aimed at encouraging housing development at appropriate identified locations in parallel with promoting development and economic activity in smaller villages and towns.'

The guidelines say past experience has shown that planning policies need to make a distinction between 'urban-generated' and 'rural-generated' housing, particularly when close to cities and towns, in order to avoid ribbon or haphazard development. But in considering those with rural-generated housing needs, planning authorities 'should avoid being so prescriptive as to end up with a very rigid development control system'. Those who are intrinsically part of the rural community include 'farmers, their sons and daughters, and/or any persons taking over the ownership and running of farms, as well as people who have lived most of their lives in rural areas'. Others would qualify if they worked full-time or part-time in rural areas – and reference is made to those engaged in forestry, inland waterway or marine-related occupations, as well as teachers in rural schools. Ultimately, however, it would be up to local authorities to define eligibility. In rural areas under strong pressure for urban-generated housing, the guidelines say it would be reasonable for planning authorities to impose conditions specifying that a new house must be occupied by the applicant, rather than sold on to others. Though the document admits that there are no figures available on the extent of holiday home

↓ *Bertie Ahern at the FF parliamentary party meeting in Sligo in September 2003. According to him, rural housing was the biggest issue around Ireland.*

development in the countryside, it suggests that this is growing and that it should be clustered in appropriate locations to avoid damage to sensitive scenic areas. According to the Minister, the guidelines were an attempt to 'introduce some balance into what has been a very polarised debate'.

One-off housing had become a hot political issue, not because rural landscapes were being despoiled by the suburbanisation of the countryside, but because of a myth that it was extremely difficult to get planning permission for houses in the countryside. The myth made all the difference. In September 2003 the Taoiseach told astonished journalists that it was 'the biggest issue around Ireland at the moment'. Bertie Ahern was in Sligo for a Fianna Fáil parliamentary party meeting in advance of the new Dáil session, and felt he had found something useful for FF councillors to latch onto eight months from the June 2004 local elections. The previous year, a similar parliamentary party meeting in the wake of the 2002 general election was seething with discontent over TDs and senators taking brickbats from the public due to the Government's string of broken promises. Now, amid complaints that there was no money to spend and fears that the party would lose seats in the local elections, they were being told that the demand for rural housing would be satisfied. Ahern made it clear that he strongly supports people who want to build one-off housing on their family farms, saying there was 'no justification' for preventing them from doing so. 'I can understand all the arguments about aesthetics and about natural beauty and environmental issues, [but] there is a case for people who have land ... people in the

↓ *Claims that it is difficult to get planning permission for houses in rural areas are belied by this map of Co Limerick showing the locations where one-off houses were approved in 2000-03*

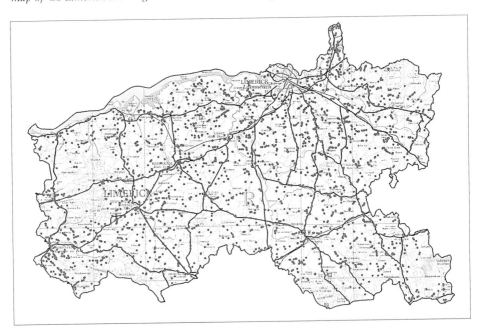

heart of rural Ireland where their family thankfully don't now have to emigrate, yet when they marry they are forced to move into towns and move away from areas because they can't get planning for ordinary houses.' This did not make sense in the context of the National Spatial Strategy, which he perversely interpreted as an effort to get people to move out of cities. As far as the Taoiseach was concerned, Eamon Ó Cuiv – in pitting himself against environmentalists and planners alike – 'represents the Fianna Fáil view'.

Six years earlier, just before the 1997 general election, the Rainbow Coalition government published a strategy to achieve sustainable development in Ireland, which included a presumption against urban-generated housing in rural areas. This strategy was never explicitly disowned by Fianna Fáil and the Progressive Democrats, though they began chipping away at it with Ó Cuiv's 1999 White Paper on Rural Development, which said planning policy 'should, as far as possible, facilitate people willing to settle in rural areas, especially those wishing to remain in their own areas of origin'. But such development would have to be 'sensitive to the conservation of the rural environment, including preservation of natural beauty spots and natural habitats'. The National Spatial Strategy also recognised the 'long tradition of people living in rural areas', while drawing a distinction between housing that catered for those who were 'an intrinsic part of the rural community' and housing in rural locations sought by people living and working in urban areas, including holiday homes. 'Smaller towns and villages have a key role in catering for these types of housing demand in a sustainable manner', it said, adding that development plans 'must include measures to improve the attractiveness of towns and villages' as residential locations. 'The long-term answer to strengthening structurally weak areas requires the strengthening of the structure of villages and towns in these areas.' Thus, it was by no means clear from the NSS that the Government was going to declare an open season for housing in the countryside.

And that's what Martin Cullen did when he launched the disingenuously titled Sustainable Rural Housing Guidelines. The day the guidelines were published, 4th March 2004, was a day that would live in infamy, according to Kevin Myers. Writing in his 'Irishman's Diary' slot in the *Irish Times*, he described it as 'the day the death sentence was pronounced upon the green fields of Ireland'; short-termism was 'the axe glistening in the executioner's shed'. Qualifications in the guidelines about having 'roots in' or 'links to' rural areas were 'barn doors swinging open wide to allow just about anyone to build a house where they like'. Myers pulled his readers up, saying there was no natural right for anyone to live in the area where they were raised. 'There never has been, and it is fantasy to insist that there should be such a right today. No one maintains that, because you were raised in Killiney, the State should therefore enact whatever provisions are necessary for you to set up home there. Why should the countryside be any different?' What we were witnessing, said Myers, was 'the creation of an environmental and visual catastrophe ... With rural suburbanisation, our water-tables will in time be underground e-coli paradises, our country lanes speedways for parents getting their children to school before rushing to work. Houses and ESB cables everywhere, our scenery despoiled, and bungalow blitz back with a vengeance. Hallelujah!'

Shane Coleman of the *Sunday Tribune* agreed. The new rural housing guidelines were 'a shameful example of a political party shirking the responsibilities of office and pandering to populism', he wrote. 'Despite all his waffle about creating a more "balanced approach", Cullen has given carte blanche to one-off housing and the suburbanisation of the countryside.' Fintan O'Toole was even more scathing: 'The backing track that accompanies politics these days is a soft scratching noise. It is the sound of boxes being ticked as the Government works its way through a list of populist measures designed to buttress its sagging support. One-off houses in rural Ireland and the designation of An Taisce as the Spawn of Satan – tick. Playing the race card – tick. Pulling back from the Hanly Report by pretending that every local hospital is going to get everything – tick. Finding a new form of local patronage through a massive decentralisation programme – tick. All of these boxes contain woeful consequences in the medium term, but who cares so long as they tickle the fancy of key constituencies over the next three years?'

One of those constituencies was the Irish Rural Dwellers Association, which had been campaigning hard for a more liberal planning regime to cater for the 'right to build', irrespective of its impact on the landscape. If tourists were after the unspoiled scenery portrayed for years by Bord Fáilte, they should 'go to places like Scotland', according to Jim Connolly, the IRDA's spokesman. He made this comment to the *Irish Letter*, an Irish-American publication, in March 2004. An article titled 'Goodbye to the Countryside?' noted that Americans who visit Ireland these days 'come back singing a slightly different tune. The people, the pubs, the humour are as great as ever. But there's less talk about the scenic beauty, and more about the scatter-shot home-building that's rapidly eating up the landscape. In real estate terms, a kind of "perfect storm" is going on in Ireland that combines sudden wealth with a decline in farming, weak zoning laws and a popular architectural style that looks wildly out of place. It's threatening to turn west Ireland, in particular, into one of Europe's less attractive suburbs', with the economic boom fuelling 'a land-grab as intense – if not quite as large – as America's housing boom after World War II'. Describing Connolly as 'the best-known voice against tighter zoning laws', the article said he 'stands hard by the cultural argument' that the traditional Irish townland for thousands of years was 'a scattered community, although its people are tightly knit'. As for any negative impact the proliferation of one-off houses might have on tourism – now Ireland's second largest industry, employing 150,000 people – 'Connolly says, simply, "if people want to see the green fields, they should go to places like Scotland".' Asked by the *Irish Times* if this was his view, he said it was an 'off-the-cuff remark' in the context of what he described as the 'desertification' of the Scottish highlands as a result of these areas being 'denuded of people' by clearances and, more recently, large corporations. 'Tourism disappears where there's no people.' But a survey of 515 overseas and domestic tourists published by the Kerry Fine Gael frontbencher, Jimmy Deenihan, in November 2003 ranked environment/scenery among Ireland's greatest strengths as a tourism destination, and registered complaints about 'ugly holiday homes along the coast'. Another survey carried out as part of the South East River Valleys project found that two-thirds of overseas tourists were attracted by Ireland's natural environment, with 'beautiful landscape and scenery' cited as the top reason for coming here.

The vision of a countryside 'bright with cosy homesteads', in Eamon de Valera's old phrase, has long had a resonance in Ireland. Eamon Ó Cuiv is not only Dev's grandson, but his spiritual successor too, at least in terms of rural housing. Ó Cuiv's views on the issue were informed by Séamus Caulfield, former professor of archaeology at University College Dublin. Caulfield had spent years uncovering the prehistoric Céide Fields, near Ballycastle, Co Mayo, which bills itself as 'the most extensive Stone Age site in the world'. Covering an area of 24 square miles, its stone field boundaries show evidence of a dispersed pattern of settlement in Ireland 5,000 years ago. Taking his inspiration from prehistory, Caulfield argued that the dispersed village, known as *baile fearann*, was 'a characteristically Irish phenomenon', four times older than the *sráidbhaile* (street village). His passionately held view, expressed at numerous conferences, seminars and public meetings, was that Ireland should maintain at least one-third of its population in rural areas. After all, hadn't the countryside sustained many more people before the Great Famine? But Caulfield's thesis overlooks the fact that until the arrival of the railways in the mid-19th century, most people in rural Ireland rarely travelled outside their own parishes. Even as late as the 1960s there were elder-

↑ *Fianna Fáil Senator Martin Mansergh: what people want is more important than what experts think*

↓ *Jim Connolly, of the Irish Rural Dwellers Association: people will not be told where they can or cannot live*

ly people living in the west of Ireland who had never visited Dublin. Modern travel has changed all of that. For most people, whether in urban or rural areas, a trip to the cinema, take-away, dry cleaners, video shop or sports centre is a regular occurrence. There is simply no parallel with pre-Famine Ireland. Yet Senator Martin Mansergh argued precisely that point in his *Irish Times* column: 'Some 160 years ago, this island had a population of 8.2 million, most of whom lived in the countryside along now sparsely inhabited peninsulas that once teemed with life and in once congested districts now depopulated. Where once people lived, they apparently may live no more ... Luckily, we live in a democracy. Whether it is trains or one-off rural houses, what people want, rather than all the time what different experts determine is good for them, still counts for something.'

Mansergh had become a fellow traveller of Jim Connolly, who had pioneered the idea of providing homes in rural areas for people living in Dublin and other urban centres as founder and chairman of Rural Resettlement Ireland Ltd. Based in Kilbaha, near Loop Head, Co Clare, RRI has resettled more than 500 urban families in rural areas since 1990. In May 2002 Connolly set up the IRDA to campaign for 'the survival of a populated countryside', picketing Clare County Council's offices in Ennis in protest against a proposed ban on 'outsiders' building houses in certain parts of the county. 'The frustration I am feeling over this is driving me out onto the streets for the first time in my life at the age of 65', he told Gordon Deegan. 'RRI is trying to operate a Government-backed programme specifically aimed at bringing families into depopulated areas, but we are being prevented from doing so by this crazy planning policy [which is] anathema to the Irish psyche and the Irish way of life.' A 'locals only' rule would bestow 'special privileges on local people by virtue of where they were born', and this would make nonsense of the planners' own official line – 'the proper planning and development of an area'. He also asked how a 'locals-only' rule could be justified in a multi-cultural society protected by anti-discrimination legislation. Complaining in October 2002 about a similar move by Wicklow County Council, Connolly said: 'People will not be told where they can or cannot live.' In February 2003 he accused Clare County Council of 'attempting to criminalise' farmers and other landowners for selling on newly built houses in rural areas. The council's director of services, Ger Dollard, said prosecutions under the Planning Act had been taken after it emerged that houses approved on the basis of strict occupancy conditions were being offered for sale on the open market. Connolly insisted that it was 'a legitimate form of income for farmers to sell off sites and houses in order to remain on the land' – even in areas of high scenic amenity. He told a forum organised by the Wicklow Uplands Council in Glendalough in September 2003 that the IRDA was considering a constitutional challenge to the right of local authorities to designate areas of outstanding natural beauty, claiming that they had become an obstacle to building houses in the countryside. Connolly also complained that planners in Ireland were operating on the basis of 'imported ideas'. Their third-level courses were 'accredited by the Royal Town Planning Institute in London', which had set up a committee to look into 'our planning laws', though he neglected to mention the fact that everyone on the committee was an Irish planner and that almost every professional planner here is a member of the home-grown Irish Planning Institute. The IRDA's line on planners' qualifications was parroted by Jim Higgins (FG) during his successful run for the European Parliament in June 2004: 'It means that planners are forced to adapt UK-orientated policies … alien strategies … to the Irish situation. The end result is that the fabric of rural Ireland is being eroded and the culture and history of a predominantly rural society is being ignored. We need to take radical steps now to overturn the current system before rural Ireland is completely extinguished.' As for his own initiative in setting up the IRDA, Jim Connolly said: 'I had to persuade no one to become involved. There is nothing new in rural communities uniting, we did it through the Land League. It is a battle for survival, it is as stark as that.'

The IRDA later expanded its philosophy in a publication, *Positive Planning for Rural Houses*, which characterises building houses in the countryside as a 'basic human rights issue'. It claims that 'a whole raft of rules, regulations, environmental groups, journalists, planning authorities, officials, the National Spatial Strategy, regional, county and local area development plans' are 'conspiring to thwart people's rights and choices'. The imposition of restrictions by such 'elitist establishment groups who believe that they alone carry the torch of superior wisdom from generation to generation' on people's 'right to build' could no longer be tolerated in a modern democratic society. 'In the present situation, the constitutional right of the ordinary citizen to build a home, to sell a site or otherwise develop their property is completely outmatched by the weight and strength of those authorities who are determined to control and restrict that right.' There were 'many cases now of people leaving Ireland because they cannot get permission to build'. The IRDA, according to a foreword by Jim Connolly, is opposed to people 'being herded like animals into towns and villages' – a policy he describes as 'enforced … urbanisation and villigisation' (sic) – by a bureaucratic planning regime in which 'large numbers of professional planners are non-nationals who have no knowledge or understanding of Irish culture and history'. As for the theory that towns needed a critical mass in population terms

Facility	Minimum population
Shop	150
Primary school	700
Post Office	1,500
Library	2,000
Doctor	2,000
Dentist	3,000
Secondary school	4,000

→ *Critical mass: the number of people needed to sustain key services*

[source: An Foras Forbartha, 1976]

to support the provision of a wide range of public services, this was 'so nebulous as to be meaningless', according to the authors. But six pages on, they have this to say: 'Rural community life, like urban life, requires essential services. Schools, shops, post offices, doctors, gardaí, transport, professional and many other services need sufficient people in order to keep going.' The publication is rich in imagery. Nearly all the pictures hint at the ever-greater demands we can put on space, and the capacity large sites have to accommodate these demands. One set of pictures is accompanied by large font text: 'The typical modern family with children will own a car or two, a buggy or pram, lots of clothes, children's and adults' bikes, a child's swing, large toys, a dog and cat, often a garage full of equipment and possessions associated with leisure activities or hobbies, a clothes line, perhaps a caravan, the list can go on and on.' Another picture shows a boy peddling a go-cart attached to a trailer. His friend is sitting on the trailer making it next to impossible to peddle the go-cart. The two lads are having a laugh. The picture brings home two points. First, how pathetic Ireland has been in providing for shared public space, and how a determined effort by individuals, or a group of individuals, to carve out large private spaces can scarcely answer this failing.

However, each member of the IRDA appears to have a different vision of when and where housing should or shouldn't be allowed. According to Joe McDonnell, 'there is no need to allow building at every site and crossroads in the countryside, many areas should be left untouched. Also sound planning practices should not be abandoned, e.g. skylines should not be broken, buildings kept off main roads and other well established rules.' This formula would still leave 'a lot of space out there to accommodate peoples' desires', he writes. Caulfield sees different constraints: 'In places like Mayo where dispersed villages are separated by miles of unoccupied land where there is no record of habitation in recent times, these areas should be preserved free of housing', he suggests. But how recent is recent? The IRDA's proposed amendments to Martin Cullen's guidelines recommended 'rural populations to match 19th-century patterns'.

But other organisations also had contradictory positions. The IRDA drew attention to an apparent gulf between the official stance of the Royal Institute of the Architects of Ireland in advocating that towns and villages should be reinforced, and its involvement in the publication *Build Your Own House and Home*, which is aimed at those wishing to build in rural areas. 'Ireland's finest one-off houses from €150,000', the cover proclaims. 'Escape to the country. Many urbanites harbour dreams of a retreat to the quiet life of the country, and more and more are making that dream come true' – in an architect-designed home, of course. Yet, in November 2003, an RIAI delegation told the Oireachtas Joint Committee on the Environment that the sprawl of 'unsustainable scattered peripheral housing' would weaken the life of urban centres as well as putting public services under strain. 'The only problem the IRDA have with the RIAI – and it is an extremely serious problem – is the way in which they openly use their professional weight at conferences and at the Oireachtas Joint Committee to criticise and condemn ordinary people wishing to build in the country while they themselves shamelessly tout for similar business among the wealthy', Jim Connolly wrote in a circular letter to TDs, senators and councillors. In fact, only 10% to 12% of one-off houses are designed by qualified architects. Subsequently, the two sides met for what turned out to be useful round-table discussions on the whole issue, and found a surprising measure of agreement – at least on the need for more clarity in how the planning laws are applied. But it seems unlikely that the IRDA would reach a similar accommodation with An Taisce, which has taken a hammering for its restrictive policy on housing in the countryside. 'To confine planning permissions for rural houses to those with a connection to the land/agriculture is the most philosophically barren, culturally impoverished, anti-rural community, racist and basically unconstitutional policy that has been attempted in Ireland', was Connolly's take on it. One of the contributors to the book, TC Lynch of the IRDA's Kerry branch, even uses An Taisce's name in quotation marks.

An Taisce was strongly challenged over its claim, in November 2002, that landowners were engaged in 'massive fraud' to get planning permission for houses in the countryside. In many cases, Ian Lumley told a conference in Dublin, applications were being made on behalf of sons or daughters and then the sites sold as soon as permission was granted. This practice was facilitating the spread of holiday homes in the west, while in the counties around Dublin, sites were being snapped up by commuters. An IFA spokesman insisted there was no evidence for Lumley's claim and accused him of polarising the debate with anti-farmer rhetoric. Eamon Ó Cuiv also lashed out. Maintaining that the vast majority of applications were bona fide, he said An Taisce was more interested in 'invective and insult' than genuine debate and research. But the chairman of An Bord Pleanála, John O'Connor, said it would not be unusual for its inspectors dealing with planning appeals on one-offs to find 'for sale' signs on the sites, even in cases where occupancy conditions were being imposed. 'Some applications were even being made on behalf of children who turned out to be as young as six', he said. According to the Irish Planning Institute, there was also 'no doubt that applicants who are well-connected politically or skilled in the art of lobbying have a much better chance of success in applying for a one-off house than applicants without these connections or skills.' Councillors lobbying on behalf of their constituents were causing public frustration, anger and confusion over an already contentious issue, though it conceded that some of this frustration arose from 'a high degree of inconsistency in the application of planning policies throughout the country and even in specific local areas'. But the IPI insisted that there was no 'ban' on one-off housing in rural areas. 'On the contrary, there is a largely laissez-faire approach, the evidence of which can be all too clearly seen throughout rural areas of Ireland', it said.

Iain Douglas, the institute's president, said Cullen's rural housing guidelines were 'an attempt to dismantle the planning system so carefully built up over the past number of years'. The basic problem was that they 'set out to override the interests of the common good and the principles of sustainable development where these conflict with the desire of individuals to build housing where they wish'. There was 'no empirical evidence' to justify a policy change, as the Department of the Environment's own figures showed that 85% of applications for single rural houses were granted. Douglas said the Department should look at rural housing in the wider context – including the impact of up to 250,000 new one-off houses in the next 20 years. But how could it have done that when the planning agenda was being driven by short-termism – 'the complete antithesis of what planning should be about'? As for the abuse of Section 140, Douglas said it 'would lead one to question whether those elected members have any cognisance of planning for the common good rather than simply vote-catching at the expense of the environment'. The lack of overall vision in planning, he continued, 'is well exemplified by the ongoing investment in rural towns and villages of water and sewerage infrastructure, which is subsequently negated by the free-for-all for housing in the countryside'.

Among planners, Martin Cullen had become known as 'the Minister for No Environment'. Just as he had declined to meet the IPI while the rural housing guidelines were being framed (though he met the IRDA twice), Cullen spurned an invitation to address its annual conference in April 2004. He sent along one of his junior ministers, Noel Ahern, who made a ludicrous attempt to portray the guidelines as good news for planners. Ahern, an elder brother of the Taoiseach, had to sit through Iain Douglas's opening speech, with its use of such bald terms as 'gerrymandering' and 'railroading' to characterise the Government's approach to decentralisation and rural housing. By the time Douglas had finished, 'Noel Ahern looked as if he had swallowed a lemon', one of those attending acidly observed. 'All we can do is hope that it's more optical than real', one senior planner said of the guidelines. 'Morale is low, there's no doubt about that', another planner said. 'It's as bad as it was in the mid-1970s when Jimmy Tully was in the Custom House signing planning permissions for bungalows all over Meath. But just as Tully's name lives on, so will Cullen's.' Another planner said the rural housing guidelines 'play to the worst element of clientelist politics' because they were 'all about fixing up individuals' with planning permissions.

A long-practising planner said she had spent her professional life 'preaching the principles of good planning practice', and one of their central tenets was that a permission attached to the land, rather than the individual landowner. 'That's now being turned around, so we're into a free-for-all where planners will come under emotional blackmail to consider the "needs" of individual applicants for houses in rural areas. Urban kids haven't a hope of getting the same treatment. If all the children of the nation are to be cherished equally, as the 1916 Proclamation says, surely they have an equal right to live near their parents in the areas where they grew up, if they choose to do so. But they can't because of high house prices.' Just because someone had land 'shouldn't make them more privileged', she said, referring to the Taoiseach's view that people with roots in rural Ireland had a right to build houses in their own areas. 'Why doesn't he apply that to Drumcondra?' she asked. The regime introduced by Cullen would 'turn the system on its head', according to another planner. 'Instead of looking at what a community needs to be vibrant and sustainable, we're meant to look at what individuals want.' Planning had suffered more than merely a lack of support from politicians in recent years, another said. 'What's happening before our very eyes is that Martin Cullen is actively dismantling Ireland's planning and environmental infrastructure.' Apart from the rural housing guidelines, 'he's broken up Dúchas, he wants to strip An Taisce of its prescribed status, and it's all being done in the interests of short-term electoral gain and the rights of property owners over the common good.' Another planner commented: 'Noel Dempsey must be tearing his hair out as he watches his successor dismantle the policies and sys-

↑ *Jimmy Tully suppressed a critical 1976 study of one-off housing*

tems he put in place to advance the cause of planning and sustainable development. It's very sad really.'

Attempts to curb one-off housing in the countryside go back a long way – to a 1976 study, *Urban Generated Housing in Rural Areas* by An Foras Forbartha (AFF), the National Institute for Physical Planning and Construction Research. Because its findings would have been politically unpalatable, the report was suppressed; 'Confidential: Not For Publication' was bold-stamped on the few copies that did leak out. At the time, Jimmy Tully was Minister for Local Government. In the period before An Bord Pleanála was established in 1977, Tully became notorious for abusing his appellate jurisdiction to grant planning permission for one-off houses – particularly in Meath, his own constituency – which had been refused on sound planning grounds. AFF's 1976 study compared the relative costs of servicing close-knit communities with dispersed one-off housing, and queried 'the extent to which the public costs involved are borne by the community at large, thus providing a form of hidden subsidy to the individual ex-urban generated dweller'. This sort of stuff was not something Tully wanted to hear. Ten study areas were selected – three for their scenic beauty and seven because they were under pressure from a nearby urban centre. The first three were the coastal road between Moville and Greencastle on the Inishowen peninsula in Co Donegal; the scenic route from Bantry to Glengariff in west Cork; and the Milltown road near Newbridge, Co Kildare. The seven other areas examined in detail were Cratloe, north of Limerick; the Barna-Spiddal road, west of Galway; the Strandhill road, west of Sligo; the Dublin road near Blessington, Co Wicklow; Beech Road, west of Arklow; Bennetsbridge, Co Kilkenny; and an area along the Waterford road, east of Clonmel. The survey was piloted in Mornington, about 6km (4 miles) from Drogheda, Co Louth, where it found that 64% of all one-off housing had been built after 1964 – the year Ireland's first comprehensive Planning Act came into force. Only 5% were farmhouses.

The report contained more than cost data. It sought to paint 'a picture of the ex-urban generated dweller, his socio-economic status, lifestyle'. And it aimed to analyse 'the social forces which determine why people decide to live in a rural area'. A total of 255 people were interviewed in the 10 areas: 96% of respondents were married, most of them parents of young children; the vast majority – 71% – originally came from a city, town or village; 63% of husbands worked in the nearest town or city. Of the women who worked, 69% did so in the nearest town or city. Two pages into the body of the report, the authors concluded: 'Much of the urban-generated housing in rural areas is not simply satisfying local need but involves housing for people with no connections with the rural area who are working in the urban centre.' As well as recording the reasons for moving, the survey sought to relate these reasons to peoples' backgrounds. Unlike a traditional poll where people are given a slate of options and asked to rank them, An Foras Forbartha allowed the reasons to flow from the survey. The answers were assembled into categories afterwards. The two top reasons given were 'privacy' (21%) and 'to get away from the built-up environment' (19%), with scenic beauty ranking third (16.5%). 'People originally from the inner city and suburbs put most emphasis on privacy and getting away from the built-up environment, while those originally from rural areas put most emphasis on scenic beauty.' Other reasons were minor by comparison: convenience to work (12.6%); originally from the rural area (12.3%); lack of sites in the urban area (6.5%); only house available (5.5%); individuality (5%); convenience to recreation (1.5%). Some 79% alluded to the disadvantages of rural living. These related mainly to the lack of social and recreational opportunities and/or the expense or inconvenience of getting to and from these activities. However, if moving again, 80% of respondents said they would go to a similar type of area. Just 12% would move to an urban area, 6% would move to a more rural area, while 2% would settle in a village. Interestingly, 65% of respondents stated that they would not like to have more people moving into the area they now lived in. This sentence is succeeded by the observation: 'It will be seen, however, that the very nature of this type of development is that more neighbours will continue to come into the area.'

Examining the relative costs, An Foras Forbartha looked first at the postal service. In 1976 Ireland had one post office for every 1,300 people. This compared favourably with Britain, where there was one post office per 2,300, or France, with one for every 2,900 people. The report recommended a catchment area of 1,500 people for post offices. It found that postal deliveries to widely dispersed houses were 3.5 times more expensive than to houses in an urban area. More than 25 years later, Dr Diarmuid Ó Gráda, an independent planning consultant, found rural mail delivery to be four times more expensive. No wonder An Post, faced with massive losses year after year, sought to introduce a roadside delivery system to rural areas, and issued a tender for the supply of 500,000 theft-proof letter boxes in January 2003. As Jamie Smyth reported, the plan was An Post's response to a paper by the Commission for Communications Regulation (ComReg), which suggested that it should develop strategies to deal with the proliferation of one-off housing. But even though this would produce savings of €20 million a year, it was widely seen as 'another blow to rural Ireland' in many of the 1,000-plus submissions to ComReg's chair, Etain Doyle. In May 2003 she said An Post would be breaking the law if it went ahead with the provision of roadside letter boxes without first obtaining the consent of rural customers. The company responded saying this made a rise in the price of stamps inevitable.

In its 1976 study, An Foras Forbartha found that 93% of respondents drove to work in the areas it surveyed, compared to 26% in a town of 10,000 or more, the latter figure taken from the 1971 census. More than half of all children (51%) in one-off housing were taken to school by car, compared to 9% in urban areas. One quarter of children from one-off houses walked to school; in urban areas, the figure was 89%. Some 24% were taken by bus in the areas surveyed, 12 times the urban figure. 'The significance of the school bus service is clearly evident', the authors said. A draft of the report dated August 1975 said: 'The fact that the present financial outlay on the provision of school buses is costing as much as the schools capital programme emphasises the potential of the situation.' This sentence was dropped from the final report of June 1976. Updating this data, Ó Gráda was informed by the Department of Education that 96% of pupils using State-funded school buses are outside Dublin city and county. The budget for the service was €111 million in 2004. Each school day, 140,000 pupils are carried at State expense, of whom 9,000 have special needs.

The cost of domestic waste collection largely depends on the number of bins emptied into a refuse truck per minute. An Foras Forbartha drew on work done by Kildare's local authorities showing that five bins could be collected per minute in an urban area compared to 1.4 bins per minute in a rural area. In the Kildare study, there was one bin every three metres in urban areas, with a bin every 93 metres in rural districts. Drawing on this data, An Foras Forbartha contrasted houses with 5-metre and 58-metre frontages, and found rural bin collection to be 2.5 times more expensive. The further apart people live, the higher the cost of bin collection.

With telephone lines, distance does not dictate cost to the same extent, but each new house must be connected in turn. And when a one-off house is being wired up to the network, is it not known how many more houses might be built in the area. 'It is impossible to provide the entire system at one time because of the lack of knowledge of what is going to happen in the future. While spare capacity is always allowed for in any scheme, this might never be used up in a rural area.' But if spare capacity is not provided and additional development does take place, the study noted that the cost of 'adding on' is considerable. To install two cables at different times, each serving 15 houses, was found to be 50% more expensive than connecting 30 houses at once. Comparing 5-metre house frontages with dispersed development (58-metre frontages), the capital cost of telephone provision was five times lower in an urban area.

For electricity, as with telephone connection, it is not so much the diffuse nature of development that gives rise to high cost, it's the unpredictability. As the AFF study said: 'While it can be seen that the costs are greater for scattered development than concentrated development, the cost of sporadic scattered development is even greater. This involves the impossibility of locating the high tension lines strategically ... duplicating lines through doubling back, replacing transformers, changing the type of cables, relocating poles and changing cross-arms on poles. The cost increases involve both material and labour and consequently [our] figures should be regarded as minimal'. Again, comparing house-frontages of 5 and 58 metres, the capital costs serving the dispersed housing with electricity was 2.4 times higher.

Ó Gráda's paper explored the same topic. He found the capital cost of electricity connection in an urban area was subsidised to the tune of €390. However, the subsidy for rural connection was more than double this at €865. In 2003 the ESB levied an annual standing charge of €61 in rural areas and €38 in urban areas. But have the higher costs of meter-reading been factored in? Ó Gráda noted that urban meter-reading mainly entails short door-to-door walks. Rural areas involve much more time driving around. In 2003 meter readers were paid 41 cent for each urban home and 96 cent for rural visits. Taking meter-reading alone, rural costs are 134% higher, but the annual charge is only 60% more. The higher costs incurred in serving one-off housing because of storm damage – mostly falling trees – must also be factored in, Ó Gráda said. As for public lighting and footpaths, An Foras Forbartha's study found that only 22% of the areas it surveyed in 1975 had public lighting, and almost double that number (42%) were actively seeking it. Power cables are usually routed underground in an urban area and this reduces the cost of erecting lamp standards, as well as minimising visual obtrusiveness. In rural areas, on the other hand, the power has to be taken from an overhead line and then from pole to pole. Based on 5 and 58 metre frontages, capital costs in the rural area would be 12 times the urban area. Day-to-day running costs would be 10 times higher. Footpaths in the study area were rare (8%) but widely sought (57%). For one-off housing, the capital cost would be 12.5 times that of urban homes.

The AFF study did not examine the septic tank issue in great detail. It looked at what it would cost to link a rural area to a sewerage scheme and calculated it to be five times the cost of urban housing. A greater possibility of complications also arose. 'In providing a public scheme, the costs depend on, *inter alia*, length and size of pipes, pumping and excavation required, number of manholes, type of soil and topography. While these vary with individual sites, the cost per house clearly increases as density declines, because of the increased length of pipe and number of manholes per house, and the increased possibility of topographical and soil difficulties.' Examining the issue in 2004, Diarmuid Ó Gráda noted that Ireland has the highest level of microbial groundwater pollution in the EU, for which he believed farming and domestic sewage were equally to blame. What figures are available indicate that 250 million litres of effluent is discharged by homes with septic tanks each day, according to Ó Gráda. This is based on the national estimate of 400,000 septic tanks. But how many of these work properly? Ó Gráda pointed to a 2002 study by engineers at Trinity College Dublin showing 95% of septic tanks are located in areas with insufficient natural percolation. A total of 74 tanks were tested, all randomly chosen. 'If

95% of Leinster sites are in need of intervention, what can be expected from poorer conditions west of the Shannon?' he asked. Should more advanced small-scale treatment systems be mandated to replace the dysfunctional 95%? With help from the companies involved, Ó Gráda reviewed the operation of four of the most up-to-date proprietary sewage treatment units for one-off housing. The companies provide a one-year warranty. After that expires, it is up the homeowners themselves whether they sign a service agreement with the company to maintain the system. Annual maintenance agreements are offered by all four companies, but the take-up rate at the end of the warranty period is low, ranging from 20% to 40%. Worse still, for the two most prominent companies, figures show that the number of customers signing a second or subsequent maintenance agreement is below 5%. One of the companies expressed great concern about the situation; its system is often specified for marginal sites. Where there is no professional maintenance, the first sign of trouble tends to be overflowing sewage, Ó Gráda said. This led him to recommend that all septic tanks should be tested once every two years. In terms of potential harm to others, he argued that there is 'an analogy between septic tank testing and the National Car Test'. (Presumably, under this proposed system, inspectors engaged to examine septic tanks would also be empowered to issue a maintenance notice and levy fines in the case of default.) But 'Official Ireland has walked away from the problem', according to Ó Gráda. One county council actually took the time to assess sewage treatment in two areas. In one village, half of the systems were discharging directly into a watercourse. In the other area, 27 systems were surveyed (among them two pubs, a grocery store and a butcher's shop) and three-quarters were found to be discharging directly into a local stream.

The 1976 Foras Forbartha study also focused on the safety implications of locating entrances sporadically onto roadways; it found one-off housing was much more hazardous, but did not put a cost on it. Ó Gráda drew attention to the €2 billion allocated to non-national roads since 2000, and particularly to the €500 million allocated in January 2004. Of this, only 12% is going on urban roads. If just half the rural spend is linked to new one-off houses, this would put the cost per house at €8,500. Not surprisingly, he also highlighted the case of the N22, which is going to have to be replaced by a new road costing €90 million because of the proliferation of one-off houses between Killarney and Farranfore. Perhaps it is too blunt to say each new householder along the road has cost the State almost €500,000. Blame must surely fall with councillors who, against all advice, pushed through Section 4 or Section 140 motions for one one-off house after another, and the National Roads Authority, which failed to discharge its duty to maintain a 'safe and efficient network of national roads' by appealing against any of these decisions (at least until March 2004 when it was shamed into doing so by An Taisce). Ó Gráda's research also found that young couples buying new houses in the Dublin area are paying an extra €30,000 towards the provision of social and affordable housing, while those building homes in rural areas contribute nothing. He attributed a third of the price differential between new houses in Dublin (average €300,000) and new houses in counties outside the GDA (average €210,000) to the burden of financing housing under Part V of the 2000 Planning Act. And it was in the GDA that 96% of the 'social and affordable' housing under Part V was being built.

Dealing with the consequences for farming of suburbanising the countryside, An Foras Forbartha drew on a study of the Slough/Hillingdon area in England where rubbish dumping and damage to fencing were identified as serious problems for agriculture. It wasn't so much a question of monetary loss. 'Trespass-damage disrupts farming more by virtue of its interference with day-to-day management than by the extent of financial loss.' And 'inflated land prices, caused either by planning permission having been granted for the development of the land or by "hope value" for future development, tend to hamper the purchase of land by bona fide farmers.' An Foras Forbartha said the impact in Ireland had never been quantified, 'but experience suggests that the Minister [a reference to Jimmy Tully] has on occasion upheld planning applications for residential development in what might be termed traditional agricultural areas, in spite of evidence presented by agricultural economists and others.' According to the AFF study, it was apparent that 'inflated prices often cause farmers to sell sites simply for the quick financial return without sufficient thought being given to the long-term implications.' Since 1997 Irish agricultural land values have overtaken Denmark and Germany, and risen significantly ahead of Scotland and Wales. A Canadian solution, referred to in the AFF study, was to limit new rural house-building to those working full-time in the countryside, farm family members working the land on a full or part-time basis, and landholders who retire or sell their land with the intention of remaining in the countryside. The AFF study ended by quoting from a 1975 planning guidance circular issued by the UK Department of the Environment: 'The fact that a single house on a particular site would not be very noticeable is not by itself a good argument for permission. It could be repeated too often. If people were free to build houses wherever they wished in rural areas, they would soon be dotted all over the countryside and strung out along the roads. The face of the countryside as we know it today would be lost, and the cost of extending water, drainage and other services over long distances would be immense.'

An Foras Forbartha got no thanks for its advice in 1976. Ray Burke, Minister for the Environment in 1981, sought to move the institute to Cork. There it was to become the anchor tenant in an office development planned by Robin Power, dentist-turned-property tycoon. AFF staff simply refused to go, and that was that. However, when Fianna Fáil returned to government in 1987, its savage cuts in public expenditure included the abolition of An Foras Forbartha, even though it had been established with assistance from the United Nations in 1964. According to Senator Martin Mansergh, it would 'probably never have been abolished if its staff had agreed to move to Cork'. Pressed by hard times, the State ditched its best researchers in the planning arena. Research by the private sector is invaluable, a point Tánaiste Mary Harney has been keen to stress. But for the public sector, research became something of an optional extra, and policy drifted further and further away from any evidence that might be adduced to support it.

When a delegation from An Taisce appeared before the Oireachtas Joint Committee on Agriculture in September 2003 to discuss the issue of one-off housing, the organisation was likened to the 'British landlords' who evicted their tenants in Famine times. Johnny Brady (FF, Meath), the committee's chairman, ruled out an attempt by one of the authors of this book (James Nix) to draw on the AFF report on the basis that it had 'no bearing' on the issue. Neil Blaney (Ind FF, Donegal North East) characterised the research as 'rubbish' and said An Taisce had become a 'dictatorship'. It was 'disgraceful' the way it was 'undermining rural people's lives and their rights' to build houses on their own land. Senator Peter Callanan (FF) said it was 'irrelevant' for An Taisce to quote examples of planning in Britain, Canada, the US and the Netherlands. Referring to Britain, he said: 'We fought to break that link. We have our own culture here, thank God.' Ollie Wilkinson TD (FF, Waterford) said: 'It is ironic that in Famine days, hundreds of Irish people lost their lives through eviction, hunger and bad treatment. Yet now, in modern Ireland, we have this faceless body of serial objectors. This is a shocking state of affairs.' Denying that An Taisce was a 'faceless body', its president, Frank Corcoran, said all of its appeals to An Bord Pleanála were lodged by named officers of the trust. It was also suggested to the committee that there was an urgent need to establish how much housing in rural areas was actually 'urban-generated'. If that could be done, it might then be possible to reach a consensus on how to cater for genuine rural housing needs. No committee member acknowledged that one-off houses now account for nearly two out of every five new homes, apart from the Green Party's Ciarán Cuffe TD. This wasn't acknowledged either in the preparation of the Sustainable Rural Housing Guidelines. Fianna Fáil milked the issue of rural housing for what it was worth, and Fine Gael hadn't the gumption to do anything other than join in.

In other European countries, the concept of 'rural development' would be all about strengthening villages and towns, not filling the countryside with houses. German and Swiss local authorities purchase land in and around villages, service it and then sell it on to people who want to build there. This would also be more in line with the 'proper planning and sustainable development' criterion laid down by the 2000 Planning Act. That's why An Bord Pleanála upheld An Taisce's appeals in 90% of all one-off housing cases – usually because of the risk of groundwater contamination from septic tanks, the creation of traffic hazards, or simply visual obtrusiveness. As a pattern of development, it is inherently unsustainable. Narrow country roads colonised by housing are remote from public services, such as shops and schools, and dangerous – because of the absence of footpaths and lighting – for walking with a baby-buggy. The inevitable increase in traffic on rural roads was one of the reasons cited by Michael Smith for An Taisce's opposition to dispersed housing in the countryside. Writing in the *Irish Times*, Smith, An Taisce's chairman from 1999 to 2003, referred to US literature which suggests that every extra 10 minutes spent commuting carries with it a 10% reduction in social interaction. The knock-on effect was less time spent with children and friends. One-off housing was also 'beginning to undermine our tourist industry' as well as creating a 'demographic time bomb',

Smith wrote. 'As people grow old, and sometimes too infirm to use cars, it is crucial that they should not be far from local services.' The alternative he suggested was to provide incentives to encourage development in villages.

What annoyed those championing more one-off housing was the fact that An Taisce's spectacular success with appeals to An Bord Pleanála was based on declared public policy. The policy would just have to be changed, and that's what Martin Cullen did – to make it more difficult for the appeals board to say no. Even the statutory designation of nature protection areas under EU legislation will 'not necessarily represent an obstacle to rural housing'. And though he insisted that the new guidelines had been in gestation for some time, it was obvious that they were published to coincide with the Fianna Fáil ardfheis, where Cullen got a rousing reception. On the eve of its opening, the Taoiseach repeated the canard that it was difficult to get planning permission for housing in rural Ireland. 'As we all know, it is extremely difficult to get planning. I adhere strictly to the proper planning laws, but when you have a situation where you have three-quarters of the applications where the planning authorities are giving permission being rejected by An Bord Pleanála, that's unreasonable for people living in rural communities.' What Bertie Ahern said was pure fiction, as An Taisce pointed out. The true figures are that 85% of all applications for one-off houses are granted by local authorities. A tiny minority of these are appealed, and the 75% success-rate figure refers only to that minority. Although the appeals board was set up as an independent body, Cullen publicly stated that he wanted to see its 'overturn rate' drop from 75% to 10%. He also pretended that there was some sort of crisis. 'We want to end the tears, and we have all seen this, of people from families who have lived on farms for hundreds of years and who are being told that they cannot build', he told a cheering ardfheis. 'Everybody that wants to live, work in rural Ireland should be able to do so. We will continue to deliver for the people of this country without fear or favour, and we won't be dominated by any exclusive group.'

Cullen claimed that the new guidelines would help to achieve the National Spatial Strategy's 'balanced regional development' goal. But this is nonsense too, because it stands to reason that every urban-generated house built in a rural area means one less home built in an urban area. So why, then, is planning policy so skewed? Building up villages would mean that only a few landowners benefit from a rise in speculative land values. Allowing unrestricted development everywhere means that everyone in the countryside would be able to cash in. In some places, notably west Cork, where planners have managed simultaneously to restrain the bungalow blitz and build up towns like Clonakilty and Skibbereen as vibrant urban centres, Cullen's guidelines threaten to unravel this achievement by introducing a free-for-all. Yet the National Spatial Strategy seeks to accommodate housing need within existing settlements: 'Unmanaged, the projected growth in housing demand could lead to more urban sprawl and miss the opportunity to develop Ireland's urban structure', it said. There were some who maintained that the Minister had not gone far enough. Two Fianna Fáil councillors in Clare complained that the guidelines were too prescriptive in laying down that future development with direct access to national roads should not be permitted outside the 30mph speed-limit zones of towns and villages, and that regional roads should also have their routes safeguarded. Another unwelcome restriction was a seven-year occupancy clause, intended to discourage the short-term sale of sites.

Nobody would argue with the right of farmers to provide sites for sons and daughters taking over the family farm, but as the *Irish Times* said in an editorial, 'most of what is built, including increasingly ostentatious mansions, has nothing to do with meeting genuine rural housing needs. Neither have the holiday homes dotted all over counties Donegal, Galway and Kerry, to name but three. But the new guidelines mean that *anybody* would be eligible to seek permission to build a house in rural areas suffering population decline purely because they wished to do so ... At a time when agriculture is in decline and farmers are getting less for their produce in real terms than they were 10 years ago, it is hardly surprising that they would be tempted to sell half-acre sites for one-off houses. Under the Fischler reforms of the EU Common Agricultural Policy, many farmers will be compensated for managing the landscape. It would be a tragedy if that landscape – the main asset of our tourism industry – were to become even more disfigured than it already is by a reckless relaxation of the planning code.' Only a fair system to finance good management of the landscape will allow proper planning to take root and gain respect.

Those opposed to one-off housing tend to focus on the economic implications and the long-term burden on the Exchequer. But what about the impact of sustained site sales on Irish agriculture? – still the third largest unsegregated employment category in GNP terms, behind pharmaceuticals and computers respectively. The sale of sites for housing is sometimes presented as having benign effects on farming. In reality, nothing could be further from the truth. The transfer of agricultural land on the premise that virtually everywhere has 'development potential' is a recipe for the frustration and stagnation of Irish farming. Between 1997 and 2002 the price of Irish agricultural land rose by 142%, even though farm incomes have fallen in real terms. The Celtic Tiger saw huge leaps in the years of greatest economic growth (25% in 1999 alone), with the increases tapering off to 14% during 2000, and 9% in 2001. While farm incomes dropped 8.5% in 2002, the price of agricultural land rose by roughly the same amount. Dr Nicholas Bielenberg, president of the Irish Landholders' Association, was not alone in pointing to 'non-agricultural forces' boosting its value. Indeed, there is some evidence that the price of agricultural land in Ireland is tracking the housing market rather than the value of agri-produce. There is also no doubt that many farmers are offering land for sale with an eye to its development potential. A random selection of advertisements in mid-2002 included 'extensive road frontage' and/or easy access to national primary routes among their selling points. Some were even more explicit. In Ballycumber, Co Offaly, 32 acres of land in one division located just outside the 30-mile speed-limit zone was said to have 'building potential', while seven acres near Clooneyquinn, Co Roscommon, on the main Elphin-Tulsk road, had 'good site potential'. Yet good road frontages and/or access to national primary routes are not relevant to farming. Dairies send milk transporters to collect produce from suppliers. Tillage crops are delivered once or twice a year. In livestock farming, the long-distance transport of animals takes place infrequently. Weighed against soil quality or field attributes, proximity to a national road is a minuscule factor. Road frontage is even less relevant to agri-business. But because non-agricultural selling points have been allowed to feed into land values, young farmers find themselves bidding against those willing to pay a premium, or 'hope value', to secure the land for development. And such hope value is directly attributable to Ireland's pliable planning regime.

This underlines the point that only a stable agricultural sector can prevent the countryside filling up with houses. According to the ICMSA, a farmer producing 44,000 gallons of milk in 2001 could earn €25,000, but the same output in 2005 only brought in an income of €13,500. Over the same period, by contrast, the average industrial wage increased from €27,000 to €32,000. Agriculture in general, and dairy farming in particular, is in the throes of a relentless price-cost squeeze. Not only are farmers getting lower prices for their produce, but they are also paying higher costs right across the board, with animal feed up by 7%, fertiliser by almost 20%, energy by 33%, and veterinary fees by more than 40%. Compliance with the EU Nitrates Directive is set to push up costs still further. Ireland had sought a derogation to allow 250kg of nitrogen per hectare – considerably higher than the EU standard of 170kg. This bid was completely unrealistic, as Denis Brosnan, ex-Kerry Group chief executive, made clear to Agriculture Minister Mary Coughlan and Environment Minister Dick Roche in late 2004. Brosnan recommended a lower derogation target of 230kg – the level achieved by Denmark. Ignoring Brosnan's advice with a misguided initial submission, the Government lost all credibility and left itself with neither the time nor the room to negotiate anything other than the standard 170kg per hectare. Allied to the price squeeze is the erosion by inflation of what's known as the Single Farm Payment, the main outcome of the Fischler reforms. Designed to replace produce subsidies, it will give farmers a 'rolled-up' annual sum from 2005 onwards. But the payment is not index-linked and its value is likely to diminish in real terms over time – perhaps by as much as 25% by 2010. To redress this and discourage farmers from selling sites, there is a strong case for Ireland to make Landscape Protection Payments, tightly focused to ensure that only those who confine building development to the footprint of existing farmsteads would be eligible.

The Irish tax code also operates to encourage one-off housing in the countryside. Under Section 598 of the 1997 Taxes Consolidation Act, as amended, a farmer aged 55 or more can dispose of all or part of his or her farm, up to a value of €426,250 without incurring any liability for capital gains tax. The section is unfocused, and even applies to rezoned land which will be lost to farming forever. Its continued existence in this form negates a plethora of policy pledges to release agricultural land to young farmers. Even more bizarre is Section 603A of the 1997 Taxes Consolidation Act (as amended by Section 93 of the 2001 Finance Act), which exempts a parent from capital gains tax where s/he transfers a site to a child which is valued at not more that €254,000. But if both parents do it simultaneously, the child may be able to receive €508,000 worth of property without his/her parents incurring capital gains tax. Section 603A is problematic in other respects. 'Site' is not defined, so there is no ground area restriction to limit how much land may be transferred. Given the tax-efficiency of section 603A, parents may increase the amount of land transferred until they reach the €508,000 ceiling. In this way, Section 603A allows sons and daughters to sell on further sites (albeit incurring capital gains tax in the normal way) and proliferate one-off housing on a scale that its drafters could not have anticipated. Usually tax legislation has a principled focus. But this provision seems based on the view that just because someone happens to own land they should be able to transfer some or all of that property to their children free from tax. This is hardly a sound basis for granting tax relief. The continued existence of the provision sug-

↑ *David McWilliams: will we have anything left to sell in the countryside?*

gests that, in spite of all the policy pledges, the State has yet to find an inter-departmental understanding of sustainability.

'Farming in Ireland is jeopardised by the high cost of land – a cost buoyed by the fateful failure to distinguish agricultural and development land', broadcaster and columnist David McWilliams wrote in the *Sunday Business Post*. 'Global forces are at work too, scale economies from south American pampas to eastern European steppes. These threats will grow. And as they do so does the case to pay farmers as custodians of the countryside.' He framed it in terms of finding a balance between 'soft' and 'hard' economic power. The former is 'not captured by the hard and increasingly inappropriate language of mainstream economics, [and] will be crucial to Ireland's well-being in the future', McWilliams said. 'Across the Tuscan landscape, no one-off houses scar the hilltops and valleys. Small towns ban cars from their narrow streets and the architectural heritage is safeguarded like a vulnerable child. Even the local farmers are in on the act; replicating perfect pastoral scenes for the benefit of visitors. In return, tourists plough millions of euro back into Tuscany each day. They spread the word every week.' And by unashamedly positioning itself at the upper end of the tourist game, Tuscany had ensured that it would keep its medieval private banks in business for years yet. If Tuscany excelled at soft economic power,

↑ *Andrew Lloyd Webber: Ireland's landscape is marred by some of the most 'hideous and inappropriate housing anywhere in the world'*

Ireland had a lot to learn: 'Following the decision in favour of one-off housing, what is the likelihood that rural Ireland will again offer uninterrupted views?' he asked. 'When a combination of Polish and Argentinian farmers finally buries Irish farming, will we have anything left to sell in the countryside? We will have a once wild landscape blighted by ugly houses. This is an example of short-term expedient politics literally bulldozing soft economic prestige that could stand to us for decades and centuries.'

Composer Andrew Lloyd Webber, who owns the 12th-century Kiltinan Castle in Co Tipperary, told the *Irish Independent* that Ireland's landscape was already marred by some of the most 'hideous and inappropriate housing anywhere in the world', and he was 'gobsmacked' that planning regulations were being changed to allow thousands more to be built. Lloyd Webber, whose credits include *Cats* and *Phantom of the Opera*, said he realised that there were few things more infuriating than 'some outsider pontificating about the affairs of another country. But I plead a huge affection for Ireland and it grieves me to see such a special landscape besmirched by houses that have absolutely no sympathy for local vernacular architecture whatsoever.' He suggested a scheme of grants to encourage designs that respected local traditions 'if there really is a need for new housing on the scale suggested'. Stephen Rhys-Thomas, planning officer of the Heritage Council, warned that the countryside 'could come to resemble a dispersed suburb from which people travel by car to work, shops and schools, with worsening congestion at peak time, even on rural lanes', which already carried so much traffic that it was 'no longer safe to walk to school or to the local shops'. But according to *Irish Times* columnist John Waters, the whole debate about rural housing had been 'conducted on the basis of metropolitanism, prejudice, spurious aesthetics, snobbery, dinner party politics and a fundamental lack of perspective on what life is about'. Concerns about car-reliance and groundwater were 'red herrings', and revealed the 'essentially elitist' nature of complaints about one-off housing.

Waters must think that the EPA was spinning a yarn when it said in a 2002 report: 'Inappropriate single house dwellings in the rural countryside result in greater car-usage, increased energy needs and greater use of … septic tanks which have the potential to pollute groundwater.' And though Martin Cullen acknowledged the septic tank issue, he did not pledge to do anything about it; he was merely 'considering' whether any further measures were required to protect groundwater supplies. When Marian Harkin, the Independent TD for Sligo who won a seat in the European

Parliament in June 2004, suggested that homeowners in rural Ireland should get grants to maintain their septic tanks, there was no official response. Friends of the Irish Environment pointed out that a county-by-county groundwater protection survey had been suspended with 11 counties still to be examined because of a 'chronic lack of resources' at the Geological Survey of Ireland. The Government just wasn't willing to hire more people.

In April 2005, when Dick Roche published the Sustainable Rural Housing Guidelines in its final form, he said it was 'critical' that local authorities identify areas of groundwater pollution risk in their development plans. Just as disingenuously as his predecessor, Roche denied that the guidelines would open the floodgates for suburbanising the countryside or contravene the principles of sustainable development, even though they clearly do. 'Planning for the provision of rural housing must recognise the strong and continuing tradition of people living in rural areas and should promote andsupport vibrant rural communities', he said. Though the broad thrust of Martin Cullen's draft guidelines remained, some additional qualifying categories were introduced, such as returned emigrants seeking to build houses in their home area and people with health problems who might need more fresh air; apparently there was a 'hard case' like that in the Minister's Wicklow constituency. The final version also included some new and relatively unspecific text on the need to promote affordable housing in smaller towns and villages, though how this can be squared with the main purpose of the guidelines – to promote housing in their hinterland – is a conundrum.

The only hope planners had was that the European Commission would intervene, at least to enforce protection of habitat and wildlife areas that are meant to be protected under EU legislation, because they too are up for grabs. Yet the Taoiseach himself held out the prospect that civil servants decentralising from Dublin would be able to afford 'mansions' in rural areas after selling their homes in the capital at inflated prices. If this is the Government's vision of 'planning' in rural Ireland, we will end up with a land where towns never end and countryside never begins.

———

5. Heritage

IT WAS DEEPLY IRONIC THAT THE FUTURE OF IRELAND'S HERITAGE SHOULD TURN ON THE fate of an English Pale fortress at Carrickmines – or, rather, the remains of its outer enclosure. Built by the Anglo-Norman Walshes in the 13th century, Carrickmines Castle was crucial in protecting Dublin against marauding raids by the O'Byrnes and O'Tooles of Wicklow. After the Walshes changed sides to lead a revolt by south Dublin against the Crown in the Great Rebellion of 1641, the castle was sacked by an English force led by Sir Simon Harcourt, who perished in the assault. Though later levelled and replaced by a manor house, its approximate location was known. There was 'ample evidence already published to suggest that caution be exercised' before an alignment was chosen for the South Eastern Motorway, as Tim O'Brien wrote. This evidence included a 1983 Foras Forbartha report by archaeologist Paddy Healy which Dún Laoghaire-Rathdown County Council and the National Roads Authority later insisted had been 'taken into account and adhered to' in designing the final phase of the M50. The council's project engineer, John McDaid, told the *Irish Times*: 'There was always going to be an interchange at Carrickmines, although it would not have been planned in detail on the early Dublin County Council maps.' The Foras Forbartha report had been commissioned for a plan to realign Ballyogan Road, 'a completely different kind of animal', he said, adding that route selection for the South Eastern Motorway had regard to significant archaeological remains in Laughanstown. The fact that the route bisected land owned by Jackson Way Properties – a mysterious shelf company under investigation by the Planning Tribunal – was 'a separate conspiracy theory', according to McDaid.

An extensive excavation involving 100 archaeologists, some from as far away as Australia and New Zealand, failed to find physical remains of the castle itself. What it did unearth were large sections of the outer enclosure, parts of a fosse (walled ditch), the remains of workshops, houses, kilns and wells, as well as 20,000

→ *Ireland's heritage – interior of Muckross Abbey, Killarney, as depicted in 1823 by George Petrie*
[illustration from George Petrie – The Rediscovery of Ireland's Past *by Peter Murray (Gandon Editions, 2004)*]

↑ *Dr Mark Clinton, director of the excavation at Carrickmines Castle: the site would have been bulldozed 'within 48 hours of me leaving' if it wasn't for an occupation by conservationists.*
↓ *Some of the 'Carrickminders' who tried to protect the archaeological remains*

pieces of medieval pottery, coins, textiles, musket rounds, cannon balls, and even some human skeletons. Though only the rubble granite foundations of its enclosure remained, Dr Mark Clinton, who headed the dig, could still point to where a drawbridge was located during more troubled times. If these remains lay on a greenfield site unaffected by motorway plans, he had no doubt they would be preserved as a national monument. The two-year archaeological excavation, carried out by consultants Valerie J Keeley Ltd, was certainly expensive, but a drop in the ocean compared to the mind-boggling over-run on the project as a whole. The dig, when it came to an end in November 2003, had cost €6.5 million – some €5.8 million more than anticipated. Total spending on the South Eastern Motorway, excluding archaeology, ran to €589 million – nearly *four times* what the NRA had budgeted for in 1999. The increased archaeological cost accounted for 1.3% of the total overspend – information that only came to light in June 2004 with the publication of a report by the Comptroller & Auditor General. The real reason why it cost so much was attributable to the huge expense of acquiring land at the height of the property boom.

Admittedly, the dig itself would have ended in late 2002 but for an occupation of the site by a group of conservationists, the 'Carrickminders', some of whom were also involved in legal battles to re-route the road. 'If they hadn't intervened, the site would have been bulldozed in August 2002 within 48 hours of me leaving', Mark Clinton told Paul Cullen of the *Irish Times*. 'That's what went wrong for them. I'm a soldier of the old school, and I stood my ground.' As the dig continued, he came under strong pressure to wrap things up. 'Do you not feel guilty? How many dialysis machines could you buy with the money being spent?' he was asked. The real blame lay with those who refused to countenance a realignment of the Carrickmines interchange, he replied. 'At an early stage, they should have said: "We're in trouble, this is a huge site. Move the road now." But that didn't happen.' He also insisted that there was sufficient information available, including a 1998 geophysical survey, to show that the site was 'colossal' and should have been given a wide berth by the motorway. 'I'm not an obsessive who's bitter about Carrickmines ... what I do see is our heritage being whammied across the board. Perhaps it's time for the country to redefine itself in an honest way and to end the hypocrisy. You learn all this stuff about history and culture at school, and then we go and sacrifice it for a poxy third-rate motorway.'

A draft European Commission report on the Carrickmines case, leaked to the media in December 2003, was highly critical of the way the site was handled. It described the environmental impact assessment as 'flawed', with significant shortcomings on 'some points of vital importance'. Prepared on foot of a formal complaint by Prionsias De Rossa, Labour MEP for Dublin, it also queried why no compromise solution was found after the extent of the archaeological remains became apparent. Among the report's more damning findings was that Dúchas, the State heritage service, 'was more concerned about the road construction programme' than it was about archaeology. 'The important question is why the new large roundabout on the castle site became (for engineers) such an immovable component' of the motorway plan, especially as another interchange further south at Laughanstown had been redesigned to suit a property developer. Noting that Carrickmines had become 'the cause célèbre of Irish archaeology', the report speculated on how this could have happened 'in a country with a mature archaeological profession, a Government and roads authority fully aware of the needs of archaeology and committed to proper treatment of sites'. The Department of the Environment defended its handling of the case, claiming that the draft report contained 'serious mistakes, and deals with issues outside the scope of the assignment', but no substantiation was offered for these assertions.

The Carrickminders first sought a High Court injunction after it emerged that plans to partially destroy the site had not been sanctioned by the Minister for the Environment. This action was taken when the protesters were anticipating an 'imminent push' into the archaeological site once excavations had finished, following a five-month time extension. Indeed, Dún Laoghaire-Rathdown County Council's embattled director of transport, Eamon O'Hare, announced that the next stage would involve removing part of the fosse from the line of the motorway for conservation elsewhere on site. The creation of a 'heritage park' at Carrickmines was a response to public pressure, and only conceded by the Minister for Transport in September 2002. In January 2003 up to 30 protesters blocked archaeologists from removing parts of the fosse, and the county council responded by seeking a trespass order against Gordon Lucas, Vincent Salafia and other protesters on the basis that this impasse was costing between €50,000 and €100,000 a week in claims for compensation by the contractors, Ascon.

Negotiations to reach a compromise between the council and the protesters continued until early 2003. The Friends of Carrickmines Castle group submitted a plan designed to allow the motorway to go ahead while preserving most of the site. It would have involved raising the roadway 1-1.5 metres and dropping plans for a feeder road and roundabout to service lands owned by Jackson Way Properties. Dr Pat Wallace, director of the National Museum and veteran of the Wood Quay dig, said such a compromise 'should be possible'. Though Carrickmines Castle 'may not be Wood Quay, it is a site of national importance and should therefore be fully recorded'. Preserving the stone enclosure, rather than relocating part of it, would also have been in line with Dúchas guidelines for protecting archaeological heritage; these refer to maintaining in situ 'masonry structures of particular archaeological or historical interest'. In the case of Carrickmines Castle, the NRA's senior archaeologist, Daire O'Rourke, said it would be sufficient merely to record the site as fully as possible. She later said it was only because of the road that there had been an archaeological excavation at all. 'No road, no excavation. No excavation, no knowledge of the extent of the castle. This is the dilemma.' But the roads authority came in for serious criticism from Dr Eamon Kelly, keeper of antiquities at the National Museum. In October 2002 he publicly accused it of attempting to 'exclude the museum from the information loop' on motorway projects, saying this 'amounted to an attempt to limit the museum's ability to perform its statutory role, which we cannot accept'. A code of practice on archaeology, published by the NRA and Dúchas in July 2000, specified that ancient sites lying in the path of new roads should be 'archaeologically resolved', at least by record, before being tarred over. The National Museum pressed urgently for more detailed guidelines for archaeologists and others working on road projects. Dr Kelly said the NRA raised objections to the museum's proposed role 'at extremely short notice' – presumably because of its independence. But compared to Dún Laoghaire-Rathdown County Council, the NRA was more open to change, according to Carrickminders spokesman Ruadhan MacEoin, youngest son of veteran conservationist Uinseann MacEoin. This was rejected by Michael Egan, the NRA's head of corporate affairs, saying the Authority stood 'four-square' behind the council.

After Dr Kelly visited the site, he said the licence issued by Dúchas was invalid because the National Museum had not been formally consulted, as required by law. Kelly's view was highlighted by Ciarán Cuffe, Green Party TD for Dún Laoghaire-Rathdown, and the issue found its way to the courts. In late February 2003, the Supreme Court held that Section 14 of the 1930 National Monuments Act required Dún Laoghaire-Rathdown County Council to get the consent in writing of the Minister for the Environment to remove the medieval fosse. In the wake of this ruling, the problem facing the council was that a 1994 amendment to the original legislation said consent could only be granted if it was in the interests of archaeology – a change intended by the then Minister for Arts, Culture and the Gaeltacht, Labour's Michael D Higgins, to avoid a repetition of the Wood Quay débacle. (Previously, mere expediency, like building a road, could be cited as a justification for interfering with a national monument.) The Supreme Court ruling was hailed by Prof Terry Barry of Trinity College, who specialises in medieval castles, as 'a great day for Irish archaeology'.

However, in April 2003, Dún Laoghaire-Rathdown County Council duly applied to Martin Cullen for his consent to allow it to resume work on the Carrickmines interchange – a request granted on 3rd July 2003. The council subsequently applied to the High Court to overturn the previous order preventing it from demolishing or removing archeological remains at Carrickmines Castle. When work resumed in mid-December 2003, the Carrickminders threatened to seek a new judicial review on the basis that the Minister had no right to permit its destruction because he was supposed to be the State's archaeological guardian. They also claimed that the motorway interchange was some 50% larger than that approved in October 1998 by Cullen's predecessor, Noel Dempsey, and required a new planning application. But An Bord Pleanála had ruled in March 2003 that the county council need not prepare a revised environmental impact statement for these modifications because they would not 'significantly alter' the road scheme as approved. 'People have had their day in the sun', said the council's Eamon O'Hare. 'They used the legal channels to make their opposition known, and that's good. We have responded in the same way and now hope that will be the end of it.' The continuing delays were having 'a serious impact on the Irish Exchequer, the taxpayer, and on all the people who are trying to do business and who need the motorway completed'. O'Hare claimed he was speaking for 'the silent majority trapped in their housing estates' by traffic congestion. 'Life in this area can't go on as it is at the moment. How can people invest in this region with the traffic chaos as it is? It's time to put the rest of the motorway jig-saw in place.' His view was enthusiastically endorsed by Olivia Mitchell, Fine Gael TD for Dublin South. She said people in the area could no longer be 'expected to tolerate the current appalling traffic congestion while a small group, with no personal financial exposure, seek every legal effort and other means to frustrate efforts to solve the traffic problems'.

But on 29th January 2004, after considering the conservation aspects of the case, the High Court quashed Cullen's consent for partial destruction of the Carrickmines site. The Minister knew then that the only answer was to move the legal goalposts. On 15th June 2004, the day before the Bloomsday centenary, he published a Bill to amend the National Monuments Act, saying it aimed to 'protect heritage, deliver infrastructure and safeguard the taxpayer'. Effectively, the legislation gives the Minister the power to decide what level of protection a national monument needs, if any. If a monument is discovered during the construction of a road, the Minister is empowered to give directions concerning its preservation, restoration, excavation, recording or demolition. And he can consider any factors 'to the extent that they appear to the Minister to be relevant in exercising discretion' about whether to 'demolish or remove wholly or in part or to disfigure, deface, alter, or in any manner injure or interfere with' a monument. As Vincent Salafia pointed out, the new Act 'gives the Minister unlimited discretion, reduces the number of parties involved in deciding the fate of a monument, and removes the requirement that a ministerial demolition order be placed before the Oireachtas for 21 sitting days. These amendments eviscerate the core democratic checks and balances put in place by the 1994 Act.' Friends of the Irish Environment feared that enacting legislation to deal with one case would undermine heritage protection as a whole, quite apart from being 'a recipe for future court battles'. Frank Callanan SC, who represented the Carrickminders in the Supreme Court, found it 'reprehensible if not indeed sinister'. According to him, the amendments would allow the Minister to 'piggyback a licence to destroy other national monuments on the back of completion of the motorway at Carrickmines'. Mark Clinton, now speaking for An Taisce's National Monuments and Antiquities Committee, pointed to the absence of consultation. 'If Minister Cullen's intervention is ultimately going to destroy the heritage of the nation, surely he should encourage a proper debate so that the public can decide whether they want to maintain our heritage or destroy it?' By granting himself the power to decide on the necessity and level of preservation, as well as the power to bulldoze, Clinton said the Minister had made the archaeological community 'dependent on what side of the bed he gets out of in the morning'. Dr Seán Duffy, head of medieval archaeology at TCD, said this would 'push the clock back to the period before the National Monuments Act' of 1930. Dr David Edwards of UCC's history department said the legislation came from 'the ideological mindset which views heritage as a problem'.

Even before the Bill was published, conservationists had 'zero trust' in Martin Cullen, as Clinton put it. After all, he had abolished Dúchas a year earlier and subsumed its functions into his department – probably to underscore its lack of independence. Responsibility for heritage policy and Dúchas had been transferred to the Department of the Environment when the Taoiseach allocated ministerial posts in June 2002. At the time, Bertie Ahern told the Dáil there would be a review of the heritage area to determine the final distribution of functions, but nobody foresaw the dismemberment of Dúchas. Just three months earlier, Síle de Valera published the Government's National Heritage Plan, under which the Heritage Service was to be given 'a more coherent and integrated structure' – the exact opposite of what actually happened under Cullen. DeValera's plan referred to the 'unprecedented rise in the demands placed on Dúchas' by the pace of development. The 'need to support the work of Dúchas through the provision of new structures and a greater level of resources has been recognised for some time'; the aim of the plan was 'to provide a more efficient, integrated and regionalised service'. Many people might also have been misled by the Government's pledge to place heritage protection 'at the heart of public life' and to recognise that 'each form of heritage is unique and is of value in its own right'. But there were too many complaints from the development lobby that Dúchas was 'getting in the way', so the Government got rid of it. Cullen said the decision to 'reorganise and re-resource and re-manage Dúchas' was taken by the Taoiseach himself. 'What we wanted to do was get a structure that would give us the best outcomes, and that's what's now happened', he told RTÉ radio.

Cullen sought to dispel the fears among conservationists about this change in policy by saying that 'in carrying out my functions I will continue to be advised by my Department's professional archaeologists'. However, as the *Irish Times* reported in January 2004, he rejected recommendations to appeal a third of the planning cases he was urged to take to An Bord Pleanála. According to documentation obtained by the paper under the Freedom of Information Act, Cullen allowed his Department's heritage division (formerly Dúchas) to proceed with appeals in 19 of the 28 cases which crossed his desk between June 2002 and November 2003. These represented a tiny fraction of planning applications referred by local authorities to the heritage division over the same period. Previously, when Dúchas was part of the Department of Arts and Heritage, planning appeals were typically handled without reference to its Minister, Síle de Valera. But Cullen decided to involve himself personally. In November 2002 alone, he vetoed four of the five recommended appeals. In the previous five months, he had consented to all 12. There was also a marked decline in the number of cases where the heritage division recommended an appeal – from 18 in the period of June to December 2002, to just 10 for the whole of 2003 – and a corresponding increase in the number rejected. When it came to Jim Mansfield's controversial convention centre at the Citywest Hotel complex, the heritage division recommended that all ground works should be monitored by a qualified archaeologist. Yet when South Dublin County Council omitted this requirement in its decision to approve the scheme, there wasn't a peep from the Department. Professional heritage officers such as archaeologists and architects wondered what was the point of preparing reports on threatened national monuments or historic buildings when they would get such a frosty, even hostile, reception in the Minister's office. As for the supposedly independent Heritage Council, which used to lodge a few planning appeals of its own, it took 'a policy decision to be polite', in the words of one insider, after seeing Dúchas bite the dust; Mary Moylan, assistant secretary in charge of the Department of the Environment's planning division, sat on the council as a ministerial representative. The Heritage Council certainly proved to be very accommodating when it came to selecting a location for the National Biological Records Centre – the Waterford Institute of Technology, in Cullen's own constituency. One of its members, Desmond Crofton, resigned over the 'indecent haste' with which this decision was made. No one else did.

So why did Cullen become so proactive on the heritage front? Interviewed on RTÉ radio, the Minister himself said it was when he realised that 'a lot of objections' were being made in his name by the heritage division of his Department that he decided to get involved. 'It would be totally remiss of me not to understand why I'm involved in this process.' But Ciarán Cuffe TD said there was 'a conflict of interest between the Minister's role in safeguarding heritage and promoting development', and Cullen should not be 'acting as judge, jury and executioner' on heritage issues. Bernard Allen TD, Fine Gael's environment spokesman, wanted the Oireachtas Joint Committee on the Environment to examine all relevant papers relating to the planning cases on which heritage officials recommended appeals to An Bord Pleanála. Cullen's 'more hands-on approach and his political involvement in the planning process should be carefully monitored', he said.

The most alarming case on which Martin Cullen ordered no further action to be taken involved plans for a four-storey hotel directly opposite Trim Castle. Ireland's largest and most important medieval fortification, and a monument of international significance, the castle provided one of the main backdrops for Mel Gibson's film *Braveheart*. Heritage officials, still trading as Dúchas, wrote to Trim Town Council expressing serious concern about the 'adverse and unacceptable' impact on the castle's setting if the proposed 58-bedroom hotel was built just 17 metres (56 feet) across the road. 'The scale and bulk of the design is, in our opinion, inappropriate in this highly sensitive location', they said. Even with revisions, which included 'pulling back' the top floor, the scheme was still seen as unacceptable. They expressed particular concern about a corner element, four storeys tall, which would be higher than the medieval curtain wall of the castle and considerably higher than a protected terrace of estate cottages on Castle Street. An appeal to An Bord Pleanála was recommended, but none issued. Cullen's spokesman denied that the heritage division had been 'nobbled' in the exercise of its functions. 'On the contentious issue of the size and scale of the hotel, the Minister asked that it be scaled back and this was done to our satisfaction.' The spokesman also said the 1.3-acre site, formerly known as the Nun's Garden, was in a designated urban renewal area and that the town council had agreed to sell it to David O'Brien Development Ltd after a competitive tender. That was not the full story. At the council's request, Dublin architects Hassett Ducatez had prepared an urban plan for the area, showing how sympathetic, small-scale development might be accommodated, but this was ignored when the tenders were being assessed for the town council by a panel that included Jimmy Farrelly, former secretary general of the Department of the Environment. Two proposals were submitted, one for a hotel and the other for a civic theatre and small hostel. Not only did the hotel win out, but its promoters were informed almost immediately that their tender for €868,000 had been successful. This effectively precluded the elected members of the council from having their say on the disposal of public property – something they were entitled to do under local government law. The hotel is located in an Architectural Conservation Area in Trim's development plan, and its construction will impinge on a supposedly protected view. But Aidan Collins, the town council planner who recommended permission, said in his report that the principle of building a hotel on the commercially zoned site was quite acceptable, and the revised design submitted by Trim-based planning consultants Christopher Flynn & Associates was one of 'high quality'. When it was put to Flynn by one of the authors that the Tower of London is protected by an old but still operative rule that no new building may be erected within a longbow shot of its ramparts, he said: 'Why are you quoting an English example? We're not ruled by Elizabeth Windsor here.'

A third-party appeal was made, but An Bord Pleanála never got the opportunity to hear it. The appeal was lodged by Dermot Kelly, a native of Trim who studied its medieval heritage for a master's degree at UCD. He was supported by Cllr Philip Cantwell, an independent member of Trim Town Council, who described the hotel scheme as 'absolutely horrendous', and Prof Anngret Simms of UCD, who has mapped medieval towns for the Royal Irish Academy. But neither Cantwell nor Simms managed to have their objections registered in time by the town council, so only Kelly – who had objected within the prescribed five-week period – could pursue an appeal. However, Kelly worked as a senior planning inspector with An Bord Pleanála. Christopher Flynn & Associates pointed this out to the appeals board and expressed their client's 'utmost concern relating to the potential conflicts which may arise in the assessment and determination of the appeal'. Following a meeting with the appeal board's chairman, John O'Connor, Kelly withdrew his appeal. With no valid appeal before An Bord Pleanála, the hotel scheme went ahead on foot of Trim Town Council's grant of permission in September 2003. Cllr Cantwell told the *Irish Times* he was 'absolutely gutted' to discover that the appeal had been withdrawn. 'This was the only hope that many people, not just myself, would have of redressing this development.' Branded by a fellow councillor, Vincent McHugh (FF), as 'Mr No' when he threatened to seek a judicial review, Cantwell insisted that he had every right to appeal so that the issues would be properly ventilated. Europa Nostra, which awarded a cultural heritage prize for the €4 million restoration of Trim Castle in 2002, agreed that the hotel would have an adverse impact on what it described as 'the most significant Anglo-Norman castle in the Republic of Ireland'. In a letter endorsing An Taisce's submission on the failed appeal, it said the EU directive on environmental impact assessment had been violated because the views of Dúchas had not been taken into account by Trim Town Council. But neither this nor any of the other issues

↑→ *Trim Castle, Ireland's most important medieval fortification, will soon find itself looking at a four-storey hotel after Martin Cullen declined to intervene to stop the controversial development*

involved were scrutinised because the appeal collapsed and the judicial review route was never pursued.

The inconsistency of Martin Cullen's approach to conservation was illustrated by the case of Clondalkin's 9th-century round tower, also a national monument. In June 2004 some 1,200 people attended a rally to save its setting after a developer lodged plans for an apartment block, bar, restaurant and heritage centre on an adjoining half-acre site. 'The tower is acknowledged as one of the oldest and best preserved in the country. They are going to be excavating within 12 metres of it', Bernardine Ní Giolla Phádraig, chairwoman of Rally Round the Tower, told Olivia Kelly of the *Irish Times*. Even though the developer, Rory Burgess, had been given to understand that a commercial scheme would be permitted on the site, South Dublin councillors from all parties decided to cut the ground from under him by removing a specific objective to develop the lands around the tower from the county plan. They also called for immediate negotiations on a possible land swap with the developer. The arguments used by the Department of the Environment's heritage division in objecting to the proposal for Clondalkin were curiously similar to those employed in the case of Trim. A letter to the council said the proposed development could have 'a seriously damaging impact' on the character and setting of the round tower. But then,

↑ *While a billboard advertises 'The Heritage' housing scheme, bathers are banned from swimming due to sewage pollution* ↓

it was easy for Cullen to row in behind the campaign to save this ancient landmark; the local political establishment, under pressure from the public, wanted to see it saved too. In Trim, it was the other way around, or, at best, Cllr Cantwell represented the minority view.

The clash between conservation and development was also evident in Ardmore, Co Waterford, Cullen's own constituency. For 800 years, this historic seaside resort was dominated by its slender 12th-century round tower, a powerful symbol – alongside the ruins of a cathedral – that this picturesque place briefly had its own bishop. It was reputedly the first Christian community in Ireland, as local people proudly maintain. Even before the arrival of St Patrick, Christianity had been established in Ardmore by St Declan in 416. Though St Declan's Well still attracts hundreds of pilgrims every year, Mammon rules in Ardmore now, as symbolised by the new housing estate built on the brow of the hill above the round tower, dominating everything in sight. On the western approach from Youghal, the scheme conspicuously intrudes on a centuries-old view of the round tower, yet this insensitive development was approved by Waterford County Council and by An Bord Pleanála. A billboard marketed these 'luxury four-bedroom detached houses ... in a wonderful location', without a hint of irony, as 'The Heritage'. The 24 'exclusive homes' built in 2002 constituted merely the first tranche of many more that would march across the hill to join a burgundy-coloured trophy house built by one of the developers, Tom Collier, right above the cliff path to capture views over the bay. 'Barbarism' is how Fergal Keane, the award-winning

BBC journalist who has a holiday home in Ardmore, characterises what's happening there today. It seemed to show that there was nothing sacred in Ireland anymore. Ardmore still has no sewage treatment plant (though one is promised). Down by the beach, a sign over a culverted stream warns the public not to paddle anywhere near it. The reason is that it becomes polluted by sewage effluent whenever a rudimentary pump fails. Ardmore lost its Blue Flag in 1998 and has not regained it since.

The profoundly negative turn of heritage policy under Martin Cullen, and the increasingly frequent battles being fought to protect sensitive sites from insensitive development prompted academics to enter the fray. Academy for Heritage, which involves Dr Roy Foster, Carroll Professor of Irish History at Oxford University, pledged to counter what he called the 'profit-driven approach to planning', saying historians, archaeologists and other academics needed to protect 'what is left of our historical environ-

↑ *Dr Roy Foster: a concerted effort is needed to protect what is left of our heritage*

ment'. Dr David Edwards of UCC said the Academy aimed to 'speak up for heritage' by getting involved in the planning arena. In April 2004 Foster told the *Irish Times* the moment was ripe for such intervention, not only because of the number of threatened sites, but also because of 'clear evidence from the tribunals and elsewhere how corrupt and careless the entire area of planning has been in the past'. Academy for Heritage would draw attention to 'outrages' such as the hotel plan for Trim Castle, 'and make An Bord Pleanála look very carefully at decisions that have been made by local authorities'. Layers of historical wealth once protected by Ireland's poverty were now, ironically, being destroyed by prosperity, Foster said.

The Waterford-born Oxford don first got involved in the struggle to save Ireland's heritage in 2001 when the settings of two historic buildings intimately associated with WB Yeats came under threat. He joined an international group of Yeats scholars to oppose plans to build a bungalow some 70 metres from Thoor Ballylee in south Co Galway where the poet had once lived and worked. Other objectors included Ireland West Tourism, the Galway branch of An Taisce, and the Irish Georgian Society. According to the IGS, the proposed development would 'diminish every aspect' of the 16th-century tower-house – a national monument and protected structure under the county plan. But Noel Treacy, then Minister of State and TD for

↑ *The elegant round tower in Ardmore, Co Waterford*
↓ *The round tower in Ardmore, with new suburban-style houses built on the ridge above it –*
approved by Waterford County Council and by An Bord Pleanála

↑ *At Muckinish, on the road to Ballyvaughan, Co Clare, a mini-estate of townhouse-style holiday homes nudges the ruin of a medieval castle*

Galway East, lobbied for the applicant, a local farmer, and secured a letter from Dúchas stating that it had 'no archaeological objection' to the development. Treacy urged the county council's planners to give 'immediate and urgent priority attention' to the application with a view to it being 'granted at the earliest date possible'; he also asked for prior notice of the decision, Lorna Siggins reported. The council decided to grant permission but this was appealed to An Bord Pleanála by Linda O'Connell Satchwell, a California-based Yeats scholar, who said the poet's best work, *The Tower*, had been written there, and that Yeats himself had declared Thoor Ballylee to be the symbol of his life and work. Foster, author of an acclaimed biography of Yeats, told an oral hearing in February 2003 that the construction of 'a glaring new house on an elevated site less than 100 metres away would be an appalling intrusion into a landscape'. He noted that the proposed Gort bypass was already threatening to ruin nearby Coole Park, while a battle was being fought in Dublin to save the poet's last residence, Riversdale, an 18th-century farmhouse off Ballyboden Road, from 'demolition and redevelopment'. An Bord Pleanála allowed the Thoor Ballylee appeal, agreeing with senior planning inspector Dermot Kelly that the proposed bungalow would 'seriously detract from the literary interest, character, heritage value and setting' of the tower.

↑ *A baby protests against the demolition of Riversdale House, final home of WB Yeats*

There was less joy for Riversdale. The house and its three acres of grounds were acquired in 1999 by developers Roy Begley and Gerard Clarke for £1.53 million (€1.95 million). Their original application sought to demolish the period house and build 28 apartments in its place. After protests by An Taisce and a group of academics and writers, including Foster, this plan was turned down because the house was a protected structure. But in mid-2003, permission was granted for the conversion of Riversdale House into offices, as well as the construction of three substantial detached houses, three mews houses and car parking in the grounds, and the demolition of derelict outbuildings. It had been Yeats's home from 1932 until his death in 1939. In the second volume of his biography, *The Arch Poet*, Foster described Riversdale as 'picturesque, but without pretension'. As Rosita Boland wrote in the *Irish Times*, the poet's lemon yellow study 'opened out onto what was then 13 acres of grounds: rose gardens, orchards of apples and cherries, a croquet lawn, bowling green, tennis court and conservatory. The family kept hens. They installed a phone. Michael Yeats went to school in nearby St Columba's. It was, quite simply, their home.' In a piece entitled 'No homes to go to', Boland contrasted the treatment of Riversdale with the way writers' homes are 'preserved, open to the public, and taken seriously as cultural landmarks' across Europe. Examples include the house in Paris where Victor Hugo lived for 26 years, or Dostoyevsky's last apartment in St Petersburg, which is filled with memorabilia relating to his life. Roy Foster said Riversdale would have made an excellent Yeats museum, or perhaps a residence for visiting writers. The fact that it was being turned into offices, and the grounds developed for housing was 'very symbolic as an example of profit being valued above cultural identity'.

Tourism-related 'heritage projects' have been among the worst offenders, with Powerscourt in Co Wicklow being a notable casualty. Eagle Gate, its main entrance near Enniskerry, has been irreparably scarred by an estate of pretentious 'luxury' houses, built on land hived off by the Slazengers – ostensibly, to raise funds for the restoration of the original house, gutted by fire in 1974. But instead of being faithfully restored, the building was simply re-roofed, complete with green PVC domes, and turned into a shopping mall, while a crude mock-Palladian golf club was plonked in its grounds. 'The ignorance of conservation is rife nearly everywhere you go', James Howley, a Dublin-based architect who has written dozens of reports for the Heritage Council, complained in August 2002. 'Churches and other historic buildings are being destroyed left, right and centre. It's really shocking.'

Even in designated 'heritage towns' such as Tyrrellspass, Co Westmeath, just one of the houses on the picturesque village green still has its original windows. In Kilkenny, developers have bulldozed remnants of medieval walls to make way for infill schemes; one of the casualties here was a view of the Black Abbey framed by the last surviving city gate, now lost forever. In Granard, Co Longford, the new enamel street signs carry Pat the Baker logos; as the town's largest employer, the company sponsored them all as a job lot. The Burren in Co Clare has been littered for years by large billboards advertising the otherwise unobtrusive Ailwee Caves visitor centre, including one right in front

↑ *Street signs in Granard were sponsored by Pat the Baker, the town's largest employer*

of Leamaneh Castle. At Muckinish, on the road to Ballyvaughan, there's the extraordinary sight of a mini-estate of townhouse-style holiday homes cheek-by-jowl with an earlier medieval castle. At the other end of Co Clare, Killaloe is overlooked by serried ranks of new houses rising up above its sister village of Ballina, on the Co Tipperary side of the Shannon. Outside Westport, Co Mayo, suburban housing estates are creeping out towards the foothills of Croagh Patrick, while in nearby Murrisk four houses have been built right on the edge of the strand. In the picturesque village of Inistioge, south of Kilkenny, a favourite for holiday homes, local people set up a watchdog group to prevent it becoming 'a weekenders' paradise and a weekday ghost village'. In Youghal, a previously uninterrupted view of the Blackwater estuary from the Cork road has been obscured by a long block of tax-shelter apartments, five storeys high. And in Connemara, Leo Hallissey could point in 1997 to the Errislannan peninsula, south of Clifden, where some 39 of the 44 houses were second homes. One German owner of a holiday home overlooking Derryinver Bay, near Renvyle, reacted to two burglaries by securing it with roller shutters, which are pulled down over the windows and doors while he is away. How long before these devices become commonplace?

But holiday home developers haven't always got their way, not least because of

↑ *Suburban housing outside Westport, Co Mayo, stark against the backdrop of Croagh Patrick*
↓ *Ailbe McDonnell, a resident of Killaloe, Co Clare, with the serried ranks of new houses
marching up behind him in Ballina, on the Co Tipperary side of the Shannon*

↑ *Four new houses at Murrisk Strand, near Westport, Co Mayo. In 2001 both An Taisce and Coastwatch warned that a 'tidal wave' of development was sweeping Ireland's coastal areas.*
↓ *In Youghal, a view of the Blackwater estuary has been obscured by these tax-shelter apartments*

↑ *Neil Jordan successfully appealed twice against a holiday home scheme on the Beara Peninsula, saying it would militate against the area's rural environment*

the sceptical view taken by An Bord Pleanála. It has refused permission for several schemes, including a major development at Ventry Strand, on the Dingle Peninsula, citing 'the cultural heritage of this Gaeltacht area'. So when film-maker Neil Jordan objected to a proposed holiday village near his own retreat outside Castletownbere, the appeals board twice overturned it, most recently in June 2004. An Bord Pleanála said the proposed 41 holiday homes, clubhouse, swimming pool and leisure centre 'would militate against the existing rural environment and the proper development of nearby towns and villages'. The local community desperately wanted the swimming pool and had rowed in behind the developer, John Burke. 'We have people who come down here a few times a year trying to dictate what Beara should or should not have, and that's not acceptable. In Dublin, where they live, they have all the facilities within a five-minute walk', said a dismayed Denis Regan, chairman of the Beara Action Group. But Jordan maintained there was no guarantee that the pool would ever be built. Following the board's earlier refusal of a somewhat larger scheme in May 2003, An Taisce called for 'effective planning policies to protect the remaining unspoilt areas of Cork's coastline, while at the same time sustaining local housing and development needs, including tourism development'.

As for historic buildings, 'the overwhelming trend is the destruction of real heritage and its replacement with mock heritage', according to Ian Lumley, An Taisce's heritage officer. 'Old buildings are losing original features such as slate roofs and timber sash windows to mock-Georgian plastic, even in designated heritage towns like Kinsale, with new buildings designed in the same bastardised style.' The 'massive scale of loss and abandonment' was illustrated by An Taisce's *Buildings At Risk* register at the height of the Celtic Tiger boom. 'Thatched houses and mill buildings are having a terrible time. Even State-owned schools and Garda stations have been hideously altered in breach of the Department of the Environment's guidelines.' In the wake of a victory in July 2004 when An Bord Pleanála refused Hanlon's pub on Dublin's North Circular Road permission to retain 14 mock-woodgrain PVC windows, Lumley told the *Sunday Tribune* that An Taisce would be pursuing public bodies which had carried out similar 'improvements' to listed buildings. These included courthouses in Carrick-on-Suir, Dungarvan, and the towns of Tipperary and Wicklow, as well as a number of Garda stations where PVC windows had been installed. 'Carrick-on-Suir has one of the few surviving RIC barracks in the country, because most were burned down', Lumley said. Other public buildings being target-

↑ Old buildings are losing
original features such as
slate roofs and timber sash
windows, even in designated
heritage towns like Kinsale

→ A German holiday-home
owner near Renvyle reacted
to two burglaries by securing
his house with roller shutters

↑ *Durrow Abbey, near Tullamore, Co Offaly, was purchased by the State in December 2003 for €3.17 million*

ed by An Taisce for reinstatement of their timber sash windows include town halls in Cobh, Enniscorthy and Trim, as well as the Castleknock gate lodge in Dublin's Phoenix Park. It is also opposing plans by Kells Town Council to demolish 18th-century outbuildings to make way for an extension of its town hall, originally built by the National Bank in 1852.

The State's purchase of Durrow Abbey in Co Offaly in December 2003 was obviously designed to suggest that the Government had some commitment to preserving Ireland's heritage. Three years earlier, An Taisce and the Heritage Council had successfully appealed against plans by Radleigh Developments Ltd, run by a Roscrea-born developer, John Maher, for a 105-bedroom hotel, 475 houses or apartments, an 18-hole golf course and Champneys-style leisure centre on the 300-acre estate, some six miles from Tullamore. Describing Durrow Abbey as having 'major international significance', the council said the scale and character of the €170 million scheme would 'overwhelm' such visible monuments as the abbey's 9th-century high cross. Yet Offaly County Council had unanimously approved the plan, which also had the support of Fianna Fáil heavyweight Brian Cowen. The local PD deputy, Tom Parlon, was in charge of the Office of Public Works, which bought Durrow Abbey and some 73 acres of land around it for €3.17 million. But whatever the

↑ *Constance Cassidy and Edward Walsh with their children in Lissadell House, Co Sligo, which they purchased for a reported €3.75 million in September 2003*

motive, it was no more than a gesture in the context of continuing losses right across the board. From Tara to Trim Castle, from Carrickmines to Clondalkin, major elements of Ireland's heritage were threatened with destruction or, at least, of having their context seriously compromised. And there was no State agency with the required level of independence to do anything about it. Dúchas was never capable of acting on its own, though it had a freer hand under the more benign regime run by Síle de Valera. Now absorbed into a restyled Department of the Environment, Heritage and Local Government, it has much less freedom of action – certainly nothing to compare with the clout of English Heritage or Bâtiments de France.

While it did purchase Durrow Abbey, the Government baulked at acquiring Lissadell in Co Sligo, despite its provenance as the childhood home of Constance Markievicz and its close association with WB Yeats. In this case, the OPW advised Martin Cullen that the cost of renovating the early 19th-century stately home could be as high as €25 million – a guestimate coloured by the lavish sums spent on Farmleigh House, beside the Phoenix Park. In September 2003 Lissadell was sold by Sir Josslyn Gore-Booth for a reported €3.75 million to Edward Walsh SC, and his wife, Constance Cassidy SC. But when the vendor rejected their offer of €750,000 for the contents of the house, they appealed to the State for support. In this case, Cullen was advised by Joe McGowan, chairman of the Constance Markievicz Millennium Committee, that all of the items of historical significance relating to the Rebel Countess had already been sold and there was nothing left in the house but 'the trappings of decadent wealth from a vulgar and oppressive past'. The new owners were in regular contact, with ministers Cullen and McCreevy, but both declined to intervene. A Christies auction for the contents raised more than €2 million, and that excluded the purchase by Walsh and Cassidy of Lissadell's famous gasoliers (gas-fired chandeliers) for an undisclosed sum. They shelled out €800,000 to buy as many of the other 628 lots as possible, including furniture made for Lissadell by Dublin cabinet-makers Williams & Gibton. The new owners also pledged to keep it open to the public, and said they would invest €5 million in restoring the house to its original condition by 2010 – a fifth of the OPW's overblown estimate.

Sligo councillors played a prominent role in the campaign to save Lissadell, but would they have done the same if commercial interests were at stake? Although the Minister for the Environment has the power under Section 53 of the Planning Act to request that threatened buildings are given protected status, this can be thwarted by local councils. The first such request (in March 2000) to save the mid-19th-century Harper Campbell warehouse complex in Sligo was rejected by the town's borough council, one of whose members described the warehouse as 'a relic of slavery'. Council officials wanted to get rid of it anyway because it stood in the way of Sligo's Inner Relief Road. The 2000 Planning Act made the designation of historic buildings as protected structures a 'reserved function' – i.e. a power exercised by councillors rather than officials.

Often, clientilist politics get in the way, even in a town as important in heritage terms as Kinsale, where councillors bowed to vested interests in 2004 by agreeing to list only 24 of more than 200 historic buildings recommended for inclusion in its Record of Protected Structures. Back in September 2000, a headline in the *Mayo News* proclaimed: 'Commercialism rules the day as Ballina UDC "delists" heritage buildings'. James Laffey reported that councillors had unanimously decided to withdraw legal protection from one of the oldest buildings in the town because its owner, Eddie Melville, wanted to get rid of it. 'If we list this building, we will imprison this man', said Cllr Johnny O'Malley (FF). 'We cannot marry what he wants for the building and what Dúchas wants. There is a need for business in this town and we cannot stifle development', he declared. A very impressive Victorian bank premises, which Dúchas recommended should become a protected structure, was also delisted on the basis that it had been converted into a private house and listing it would be 'an invasion of privacy'. According to Cllr O'Malley, owners of old buildings feared that they would not be able to 'cut the grass' if their properties were registered as protected structures. Galway witnessed a similar example of clientilism, with one councillor managing to have 100 buildings removed from the city's draft list in response to representations from constituents. There is, of course, an element of 'playing to the gallery' in all of this; what ultimately happened in Ballina was that most of the buildings recommended by Dúchas were listed as protected structures.

Under the architectural heritage provisions of the 2000 Act, local authorities are obliged to protect buildings of artistic, architectural or historical interest, and to identify them in a Record of Protected Structures. Where owners fail to maintain protected buildings, councils can direct that necessary conservation works be carried out and use their compulsory purchase powers to intervene in extreme cases of neglect. Only one local authority, Dublin City Council, has availed of these powers. It concluded that the landlord, Marie Underwood, was neglecting two 18th-century town palaces in Henrietta Street, and issued a CPO. Under the Act, lanning permission must be obtained for any renovation work, unless it is deemed to be exempt. High-profile property owners who objected to the new regime included the flamboyant former *Riverdance* star Michael Flatley and billionaire financier Dermot Desmond. In 1999 Flatley bought Castle Hyde near Fermoy, Co Cork, the ancestral home of Ireland's first president, for a reported £3 million (€3.8 million). Two years later, he announced his retirement and embarked on a major renovation of the early 19th-century stately home. Immediately he ran into trouble. In September 2002 An Bord Pleanála upheld an appeal by An Taisce and refused Flatley planning permission to install a sweeping flight of steps with an elaborate balustrade at the main entrance to his mansion, saying the scheme would involve 'the removal and replacement of a significant architectural element' of the building, which dates from 1801 and is a protected structure under the 2000 Planning Act. The new steps would 'materially and adversely affect the character' of the neo-classical house, and 'would, therefore, be contrary to the proper planning and development of the area, including protection of its architectural heritage'. Welcoming the decision, An Taisce's then planning officer, John O'Sullivan, said the case was 'symptomatic of problems we're having throughout the country because relatively well-off people are buying historic buildings with the notion that they can add vast extensions and completely modernise them'. Although the trust welcomed the fact that people were purchasing period houses, 'what we're saying is that they must respect the character of the house and adapt themselves to the property rather than the other way around'. Unusually, Castle Hyde is the subject of a Section 38 covenant under the 1963 Planning Act between its former owners and Cork County Council under which they agreed to conserve the house and what is left of its once extensive estate.

Things went better for Dermot Desmond, but his alterations were less radical than Flatley's. So he was understandably livid in 2003 when both Dublin City Council and An Bord Pleanála refused permission to retain elements of a lavish refurbishment of couturière Sybil Connolly's house, No. 71 Merrion Square. His Gibraltar-registered company, Illium Properties Ltd, bought the 1791 house in July 2000 and had invested €6 million in it, by Desmond's own estimate. But a bitter row erupted over Illium's five planning applications and what could or couldn't be done to the fabric of the house – including the interiors, all of which are protected. 'We practically had to get down on bended knees to get the planners, who are supposedly interested in historical buildings, to visit the site', Desmond complained to the city manager, John Fitzgerald, in August 2001. If this was happening generally, there was 'a real danger

↑ *Former* Riverdance *star Michael Flatley was refused planning permission to install a sweeping flight of steps at the entrance to Douglas Hyde's ancestral home in Co Cork*

that potential investors are going to run a mile from listed properties'. The planners took exception to the installation of an electrically operated dumb-waiter and matching service duct on either side of the chimney breast in the main rooms to the rear. Refusing permission, they said retaining these alterations would 'cause unacceptable damage to the original fabric of a protected structure of national architectural heritage importance', and set an undesirable precedent that could undermine the character of Dublin's Georgian houses. An Bord Pleanála agreed, upholding the council's decision in March 2003. Illium took the council to the High Court, challenging its right to seek further information on elements of the renovation scheme. In an affidavit, the financier spoke of his life-long fascination with Georgian architecture and how No. 71 Merrion Square was 'truly unique'. During a three-day hearing in July 2004, Judge Seán O'Leary was told that what began as a project of great promise for Desmond had turned sour as a result of the council's handling of the matter, resulting in considerable difficulties, frustration and 'huge unnecessary costs'. But, as Mary Carolan reported, John Rogers SC, representing the council, said Illium was seeking to have it both ways in this 'extreme case'. Ultimately, Desmond won the action.

Under the 2000 Planning Act, the curtilage of a protected structure is also covered by its listing, though this is not always a guarantee that it will actually be pro-

↑ *Dermot Desmond, pictured in his Merrion Square house, warned that potential investors are going to run a mile from listed properties due to strict planning regulations*

tected. In the case of the Casino in Malahide – a very rare example of the early 19th-century cottage orné style, best exemplified by the Swiss Cottage outside Cahir, Co Tipperary – both Dúchas and the Heritage Council took back-seat roles when the land surrounding it came up for development. The site, on the tree-lined approach to Malahide, had been acquired by Gannon Homes Ltd, which drew up plans to build 140 apartments in five blocks. Fingal County Council granted permission subject to a reduction to 115 units. The thatched cottage itself was to be surrounded by a new stone boundary wall within an area equivalent to about half of its acreage. While An Taisce, the Malahide Community Forum and others appealed to An Bord Pleanála in 2002, Dúchas and the Heritage Council merely made 'observations'. Dúchas said the significance and appreciation of this well-maintained thatched house was 'largely dependant on the pastoral nature of its setting' and it was 'not acceptable to separate off the protected structure and its immediate surroundings from its original site'. Michael Dillon, the planning inspector who dealt with the appeal, agreed with Dúchas and recommended that Fingal's decision should be overturned. But An Bord Pleanála decided to grant permission subject to 22 conditions, saying the proposed development as amended 'would not adversely affect the character or setting of the adjacent protected structure'.

A National Inventory of Architectural Heritage was established by statute to identify heritage buildings in a systematic way, with a view to having them designated as protected structures. It started out compiling an inventory of towns with every single building listed – something that would have taken years to finish – but the effort is now concentrated on more broad-brush county surveys. Ten have been completed since 2002 – Carlow, Fingal, Kerry, Kildare, Laois, Leitrim, Meath, Roscommon, South Dublin and Waterford – with some 10,000 historic buildings recommended for protection. Even though some of these buildings are under imminent threat, councils have been slow to amend their development plans so that they can be included in the Record of Protected Structures. Incredibly, there is no procedure to follow up whether all or any of the recommendations made have actually been adopted. 'With the notable exception of Dublin City Council, few local authorities have adequate Records of Protected Structures. Almost all have been deficient in scheduling architectural conservation areas or using the positive provisions of the Act to curtail dereliction', An Taisce told the Oireachtas Joint Committee on the Environment in November 2003. The trust argued that giving councillors the power to alter or delete entries in the lists of buildings is contrary to the Council of Europe's 1985 Convention for the Protection of Architectural Heritage, known as the Granada Convention. 'In certain towns, the web of property, family, financial and client relationships between individual councillors and properties in their area would require almost all members of the council to absent themselves in voting on a Record of Protected Structures', An Taisce suggested.

For decades, listed buildings had virtually no protection. But now, the owners of protected structures are under a legal obligation to prevent them falling into decay. Ostensibly, there are grants covering up to 50% of the cost of approved works. But the annual amount allocated for this scheme was slashed from an initial £3.9 million (€5m) in 2000 to just €2.9m in 2004 – mere pittances compared to the scale of need. 'The purchase of Farmleigh and subsequent lavish spending on its refurbishment cannot atone for the Government's miserly approach to funding in this area – especially as ministers barely bat an eyelid when confronted by massive cost over-runs, running into tens of millions of euro, on major infrastructural projects', the *Irish Times* commented. Barrister Brendan Kilty didn't get a cent in official assistance towards the restoration of No. 15 Usher's Island, the 'dark gaunt house' from 1775 that provided such a memorable setting for James Joyce's most famous short story, *The Dead*. As Shane O'Toole wrote in the *Sunday Times*, its fanlight, fireplaces and doors had all disappeared by mid-2000. 'The place was a wreck. The top floor of the house had been removed during the 1970s. The back wall was falling out, its foundations probably undermined by one of the rivers and millstreams that defined Usher's Island until the 17th century. The interior had been ransacked and vandalised by squatters. Fires were lit. The once-fashionable address was reduced to a den for prostitutes and junkies.' Kilty had established his credentials by salvaging the bricks of Joyce's down-at-heel home in Millbourne Avenue, Drumcondra, after it was illegally demolished in 1998, and used the bricks as 'calling cards' to raise funds for his restoration project;

one of them was presented to Bertie Ahern, who said it should be incorporated into a seat in a local park. But it was down to pot luck that No. 15 was restored. John Heagney, later to become Deputy City Architect, had been scouting around for an old building to survey for his MA in conservation at UCD – 'something that was in danger of disappearing forever'. With the aid of his drawings, Kilty's architects, Murray Ó Laoire, were able to reproduce much of what had been lost.

Unfortunately, while the Taoiseach has championed individual projects – the restoration of the Victorian glasshouses in the National Botanic Gardens being the most notable example – the overall disposition of his government leaves so much in peril. No one was hired to cover for Dublin City Council's conservation officer when she took a sabbatical in 2003; planners had nobody to advise on applications affecting any of the city's 9,000-plus protected structures for a period of six months. Limerick City Council lost its conservation officer in 2003, while vacant posts in counties Limerick and Leitrim were not re-advertised. According to Peter Cox, of the Irish branch of ICOMOS, the International Council for Monuments and Sites, these glaring gaps showed that the Government has 'no commitment to the protection of our heritage'. It didn't seem to matter that the Taoiseach had promised legislation in September 2003 to establish a National Trust to secure the future of at least 50 great Irish houses, with tax breaks for business interests investing in them. Ahern was speaking to the *Irish Times* after the publication of *A Future for Irish Historic Houses?* by Dr Terence Dooley, a report jointly sponsored by the Irish Georgian Society and the Department of the Environment, which recommended that a trust should be set up. The move is long overdue, especially as Ireland is one of only four countries in Europe that does not fund such an institution to look after significant elements of its architectural heritage. However, An Taisce hotly disputed Dooley's contention that, as currently constituted, it was 'not feasible for it to become a major property-owning trust on the scale of the National Trust in Britain'. Within three weeks, Martin Cullen announced that consultants were being appointed to examine the most appropriate 'trust-type organisation' to acquire and manage heritage properties in the State. The project had the backing of one-time Tory Party treasurer Sir David Davies, proud owner of Viscount de Vesci's former seat, Abbeyleix House in Co Laois. Saving big houses would be a start, but won't change the overall picture.

The Heritage Council, set up in 1995 to advise the Government, warned four years later that Ireland's archaeological heritage 'is now more under threat than at any time in history'; a third of recorded sites were already destroyed and the rate of destruction had increased to an unprecedented 10% per decade. Prof Barry Raftery of the department of archaeology in UCD complained that prosecutions were rare, even though the scale of destruction was 'horrific'. Although the motivation was different, he said the principle was the same as the Taliban's destruction of Buddhist monuments in Afghanistan. In May 2001, for example, a pair of adjoining forts near Templemore, Co Tipperary, were destroyed. One was a ring fort and the other a raised square fort, but more importantly it was the traditional site of the Synod of Rathbreasil, held in 1111, where Ireland was divided into its present-day dioceses.

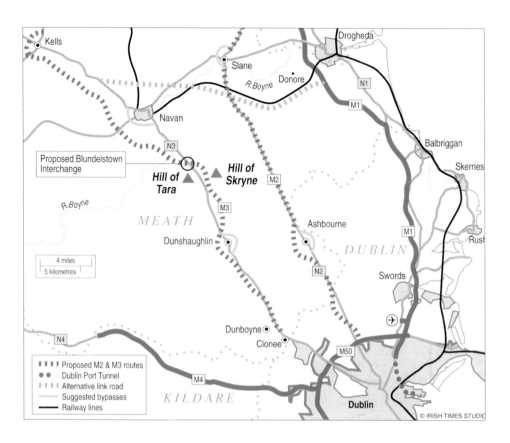

Kells

Slane
R.Boyne
Donore
Drogheda
N1
M1

Navan

N3
Proposed Blundelstown
Interchange
Hill of
Tara
Hill of
Skryne
M2
Balbriggan
Skerries

M3
Ashbourne
M1
Rush

R.Boyne
MEATH
Dunshaughlin
DUBLIN

4 miles
5 kilometres
N2
Swords

Dunboyne
Clonee
M50

N4

M4
Dublin
KILDARE

Proposed M2 & M3 routes
Dublin Port Tunnel
Alternative link road
Suggested bypasses
Railway lines

© IRISH TIMES STUDIO

↑ *Map showing the M1
and proposed M2 and M3
motorways, as well as an
alternative link road
between Navan and
Drogheda and earlier plans
to bypass Ashbourne and
Dunshaughlin*

→ *The ancient earthworks
on the Hill of Tara in
Co Meath, looking south*

← *The Hill of Tara could
end up facing 'a huge 34-acre
floodlit intersection' if the
M3 motorway is forged
through the landscape just
a kilometre away*

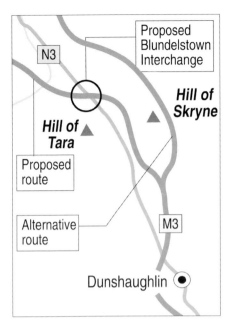

↑ *A possible alternative route for the M3 motorway, running east of the Hill of Skryne*

↓ *The Hill of Tara is graphically represented in the logos of Artists for Tara, and – ironies of ironies – the State-funded Discovery Programme for archaeological research*

[Artists for Tara who donated work in aid of the campaign against the route of the M3 include Robert Ballagh, Liam Belton, Melanie le Brocquy, Cliodhna Cussen, Anna Duncan, Jim Fitzpatrick, Trevor Geoghegan, John Jobson, Brian Maguire, Tom Matthews and Imogen Stuart.]

According to archaeologist Donal O'Regan, about 12 ring forts in the area have been lost since the 1960s. A pilot survey of south Meath, published by Riocht na Midhe in 2004, showed that a third of monuments were destroyed over a 25-year period, mainly due to pressures from farming. In June 2004 Martin Cullen made a preservation order under the National Monuments Act to protect a prehistoric promontory fort at Dún Mór, on the Dingle Peninsula. Archaeologists confirmed that a double earthen bank had been levelled over a distance of 82 metres and that a standing stone had been removed. The damage was discovered when a local tour guide, Con Moriarty, arrived with a group of American visitors to show them the fort, which looks out towards the Blasket Islands. It was 'an act of cultural sabotage', according to archaeologist Michael Gibbons, who blamed 'aggressive farming activity', in the form of land reclamation for the destruction of such important sites. The owner of the land, Denis Dowd, would not comment to the media, but one member of his family insisted that no damage had been done to the main part of the fort. The chances of a successful prosecution are significantly reduced if the landowner has not been notified of the presence of an archaeological site on his or her holding. Some 140,000 archaeological sites have been identified. Is it really too great a task to send 140,000 letters by registered post?

Whatever about Cullen's willingness to act in the Dún Mór case, conservationists feared that the powers given under the 2004 National Monuments (Amendment) Act were intended to be used to 'railroad' major road projects such as the proposed M3, irrespective of the archaeological impact. The green light for this controversial tolled motorway through the Tara-Skryne valley was given by An Bord Pleanála in August 2003 despite the fact that its corridor was known to contain no less than 141 archaeological sites. It is so sensitive, indeed, that an archaeological report for the NRA said it was 'not possible to suggest a preferred route' between Dunshaughlin and Navan if the motorway was to run within 1km of Tara. Yet the archaeological survey in the environmental impact statement only highlighted 27 sites, of which five were recommended for investigation, four to be surveyed, and 11 to be the subject of watching briefs. Dúchas had also criticised the EIS. In submissions to An Bord Pleanála before the oral hearing on the motorway plan in August 2002, it said that 'all those parts of the EIS dealing with architectural heritage need to be reviewed'. Dúchas also requested a new assessment of archaeological features and sought to be involved in 'a meeting between the NRA and the project archaeologist prior to any assessment being made'. Even Brian Duffy, who later became the Minister's chief archaeological adviser, conceded that environmental impact statements for road schemes 'could be improved'. Despite all of this, the appeals board failed to lay down a single archaeological condition in its approval of the €680 million scheme; it simply rubber-stamped what was proposed by Meath County Council and the NRA. Yet just over six months later, in March 2004, An Bord Pleanála refused permission for a golf course in the Tara-Skryne Valley mainly because it would be 'visually intrusive in this sensitive landscape … and would detract from the character, appearance and interpretative experience of the region'. Its ruling also noted that one of the objectives of the Meath county plan is to protect the hills of Tara and Skryne from 'visually damaging development or proposals that would cumulatively erode landscape quality'. The fact that a four-lane motorway snaking through the same valley was not considered 'visually intrusive' graphically illustrates the board's craven approach to the Government's road-building programme.

Archaeologists and conservationists were outraged when the appeals board failed to stop the project, likening it to 'putting a motorway through the pyramids', though, in fairness, it should be noted that many of those most prominent in the campaign to save Tara did not make their case at An Bord Pleanála's oral hearing. Vincent Salafia, bloodied but unbowed from the battle for Carrickmines, set up the Save the Tara-Skryne Valley campaign and persuaded numerous academics, many from overseas, to come on board. Salafia is a determined campaigner and has a tendency to do his own thing. He had fallen out with Ruadhan MacEoin and other Carrickminders, who issued a

↓ *Vincent Salafia: the 2004 National Monuments (Amendment) Act 'gives the Minister unlimited discretion'*

← *Aerial view looking south across the earthworks on the Hill of Tara, with St Patrick's Church of Ireland church in its tree-filled enclosure to the left*

→ *The route of the M3 motorway showing its relationship to archaeological sites in the area, with the largest clusters around Tara (to the left) and Skryne (to the right)*

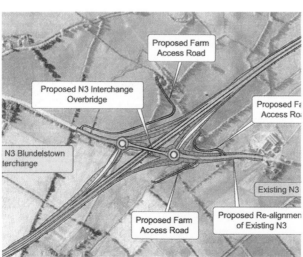

Proposed Farm Access Road

Proposed N3 Interchange Overbridge

Proposed Fa Access Ro

N3 Blundelstown terchange

Existing N3

Proposed Farm Access Road

Proposed Re-alignmen of Existing N3

← *The proposed M3/N3 interchange superimposed on the landscape just north of Tara*

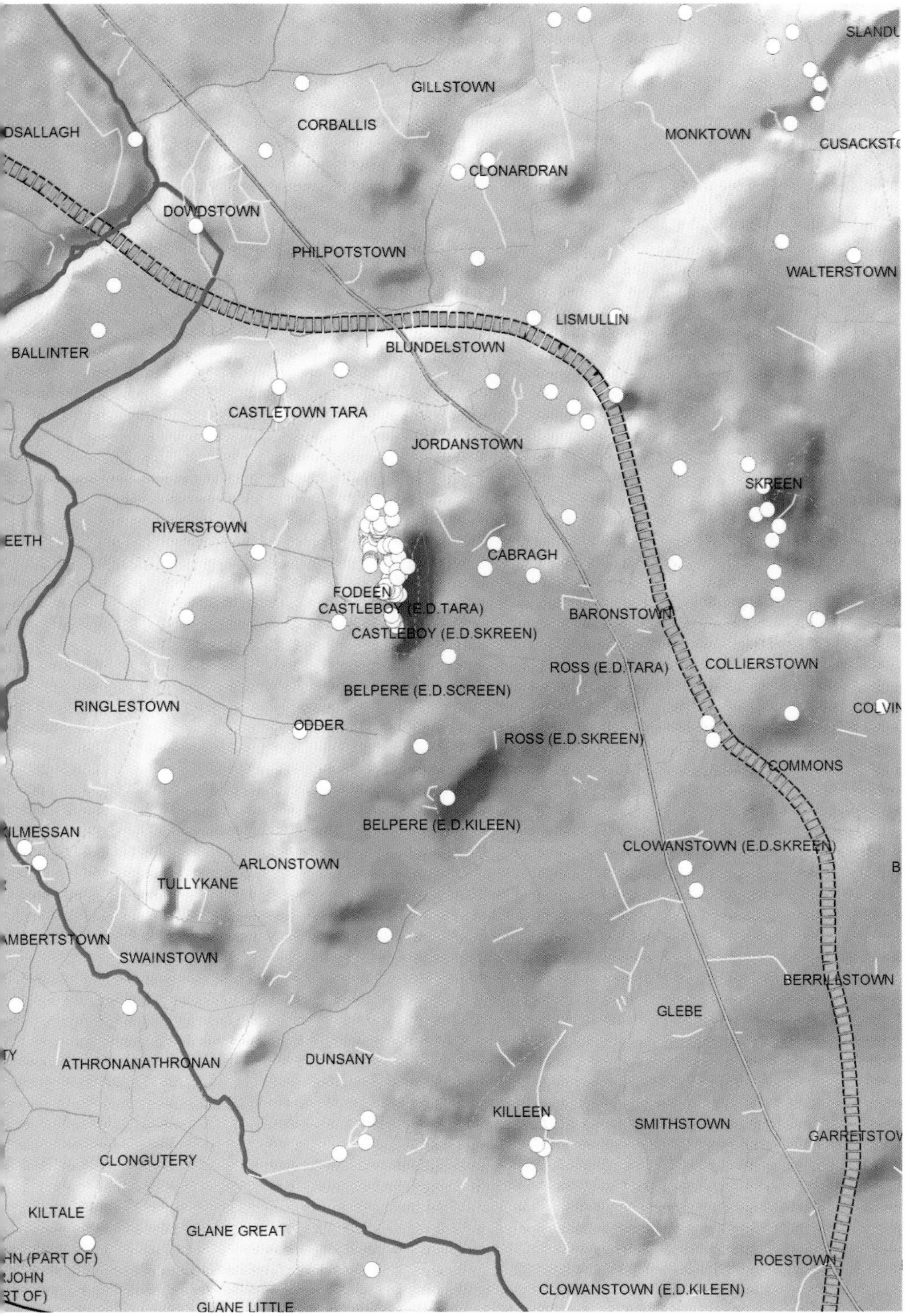

GILLSTOWN

CORBALLIS

SLANDU

MONKTOWN

CUSACKST

DSALLAGH

CLONARDRAN

DOWDSTOWN

WALTERSTOWN

PHILPOTSTOWN

LISMULLIN

BALLINTER

BLUNDELSTOWN

CASTLETOWN TARA

JORDANSTOWN

SKREEN

RIVERSTOWN

EETH

CABRAGH

FODEEN
CASTLEBOY (E.D.TARA)

BARONSTOWN

CASTLEBOY (E.D.SKREEN)

ROSS (E.D.TARA)

COLLIERSTOWN

BELPERE (E.D.SCREEN)

COLVIN

RINGLESTOWN

ODDER

ROSS (E.D.SKREEN)

COMMONS

BELPERE (E.D.KILEEN)

KILMESSAN

CLOWANSTOWN (E.D.SKREEN)

ARLONSTOWN

B

TULLYKANE

BERRILLSTOWN

AMBERTSTOWN

GLEBE

SWAINSTOWN

ATHRONANATHRONAN

DUNSANY

KILLEEN

SMITHSTOWN

GARRETSTO

CLONGUTERY

KILTALE

GLANE GREAT

HN (PART OF)
JOHN
RT OF)

ROESTOWN

CLOWANSTOWN (E.D.KILEEN)

GLANE LITTLE

press advisory saying he had 'no consent to either act on our behalf or imply any approval to do the same'. There was a similar contretemps in the Tara-Skryne Valley campaign, and for the same reason – Salafia had been making 'solo runs' to the media, so he was dismissed as spokesman, according to a statement issued on behalf of the committee. But not for long. He retaliated by serving a solicitor's letter on its members, with the result that he was instantly reinstated. He later sought a nomination to run against President Mary McAleese, convening in Buswell's Hotel to seek support from TDs and Senators; none was forthcoming. 'Using our experience at Carrickmines', Salafia said in October 2003, 'we hope to facilitate and refocus the efforts of the many diverse groups and individuals who are concerned with the situation at Tara, such as the hundreds who made submissions as part of the EIS for the motorway.' Hallowe'en 2003 saw a gathering at Tara to heighten awareness of 'the archaeological and cultural damage the proposed M3 motorway will do to the area surrounding our most famous public monument'. This came just three months after it was announced that the Heritage Service and Meath County Council had hired consultants to draw up a management plan for Tara, once the seat of the high kings of Ireland. But the area was confined to the State-owned 100-acre plot on the hill, whereas campaigners argued that it should cover the wider archaeological landscape. Dáithí Ó hÓgáin, author of *The Sacred Isle: Belief and Religion in Pre-Christian Ireland*, noted that Tara had been 'a sacred centre from time immemorial' – a point reiterated in a letter to the *Irish Times* by 21 academics describing it as 'one of the most culturally and archaeologically significant places in the world ... it holds a special key to understanding the continuous progression of European civilisation.' According to Fintan O'Toole, 'the plans to drive a big motorway through this sacred landscape are the epitome of the crass, vulgar values that now hold sway here' – not least because the route would include 'a huge 34-acre floodlit intersection a kilometre from the Hill of Tara'. In his *Irish Times* column, O'Toole wrote: 'A few decades ago, there was a living memory in County Meath of things that stretched all the way to prehistoric times. Now, memory itself – the sense that there are layers of meaning both literally and metaphorically beneath our feet – is a bloody nuisance. There is money to be made and the prospect of cutting a few minutes off a journey. Anything else is an irrelevance. People, history, cultures, landscapes, the delicate web of connections that binds us to one another and to the earth, are so much debris to be bulldozed aside.'

Former Taoiseach John Bruton urged the NRA in March 2004 to examine whether it was prudent to route the M3 through the Tara-Skryne Valley. 'Recent archaeological studies suggest that Tara – which is globally unique – is not just the monuments on the hill itself, but is the centre of a sacred space of interlinked monuments stretching over a comparatively large area', he said. 'Short of the motorway actually going over the Hill of Tara itself, it is difficult to conceive of a route more likely to run into delays generated by archaeological excavations than this one.' In a letter to the roads authority, Bruton pointed out that the route had been 'identified from the very outset as the least desirable from the archaeological point of view'. And though it had been approved, this did not mean it was the right decision. Picking an alternative route was 'not an easy thing to contemplate, but in the long run it could prove to be a much less expensive option' for a road project which he still believed was needed. Six weeks later, archaeologists found an early prehistoric cemetery on the route. Discovered at Ardsallagh, just north of the River Boyne, this ring-ditch site yielded pottery, cremation pits, and evidence of traditional burial practices. Mary Deevy, the archaeologist in charge of test-trenching for Meath County Council and the NRA, said it was probably the remains of a burial mound. The Tara-Skryne Valley campaign wasn't surprised, as the area around Tara had been Ireland's 'national graveyard' for centuries.

Leading experts on Tara, such as Joe Fenwick and Conor Newman of the department of archaeology at NUI Galway, underlined its importance to the Oireachtas Joint Committee on the Environment in April 2004, and called for work on the M3, including test-trenching, to cease immediately. Fenwick and Newman also disputed the NRA's estimate that it would cost €20 million to have the route archaeologically resolved, saying this was likely to be 'the tip of the iceberg' because it was running through one of the richest valleys in the world. The Authority's chairman, Peter Malone, responded by insisting – quite erroneously – that the new motorway would be 'twice the distance from the Hill of Tara as the current N3'. He also criticised the media for listening to 'those who make noise, but not those who operate quietly'. Bertie Ahern was equally blind. In November 2004 he dismissed claims that the motorway would destroy a mystical landscape; he had stood on its route and couldn't even see the hill from there. Ahern seized on the fact that the M3 won't actually run *through* the ancient seat of Ireland's kings as sufficient to permit the NRA to proceed with its controversial plan. Similarly, Cllr Tommy Reilly, Fianna Fáil chairman of Meath County Council, illustrated his ignorance of what was at stake – Tara's landscape – when he sneered that archaeologists hadn't even found any 'pots and pans' along its 61km route. But the Taoiseach's belief that there was no better option than running the motorway through the Tara-Skryne Valley was flatly contradicted by the NRA's own route selection report, as the *Irish Times* reported in December 2004. This report, compiled by consultants Halcrow Barry in 2000, examined a range of alternatives, and showed that a route to the east of Skryne would have 'the least impact' archaeologically. Such an alignment would also be 'the least visually intrusive in terms of the Hill of Tara ... The route does not come particularly close to, or cross through, any of the archaeological features in the area.' By contrast, it said routing the motorway through the Tara-Skryne Valley would have a 'profound' effect on the Hill of Tara and on its outlying monuments, and would have 'severe implications from an archaeological perspective'. Brendan Magee, of the Meath Roads Action Group, which has been monitoring the M3 since its inception, said he was 'astonished' to discover that the route eventually chosen was not recommended, on *any* of the environmental criteria against which it was assessed – not just the archaeological ones.

It also emerged that plans to extend the archaeological protection zone around

↑↓ *Support for the M3: posters put up by Kells Chamber of Commerce on the N3, asking commuters to back the chosen route*

the Hill of Tara were abandoned after it became clear that the M3 would run through the expanded zone. As revealed by the *Irish Times*, an archaeological report by Dr Annaba Kilfeather of Margaret Gowen & Co, compiled in August 2000, explicitly referred to a proposed expansion of the zone of archaeological protection around Tara. Largely as a result of the research carried out under the State-funded Discovery programme, 'the extent and number of the archaeological monuments in this region has been greatly expanded', the report said. 'This in turn has led to an expansion of the zone of archaeological protection afforded to Tara, which now encompasses not only the hill itself, but also includes an area approximately six kilometres in diameter.' Kilfeather's report was compiled as part of a route-selection study by Halcrow Barry for the Dunshaughlin-Navan section of the M3, commissioned by the NRA and Meath County Council. It stressed that the monuments around Tara 'cannot be viewed in isolation, or as individual sites, but must be seen in the context of an intact archaeological landscape, which should not under any circumstances be disturbed'. For these reasons, 'the only unreservedly recommended route' would run east of Skryne because 'it avoids the area of highest archaeological potential ... and has the inestimable advantage of being largely invisible from the Hill of Tara'. However, this advice 'fell on deaf ears', said Conor Newman, who carried out the research for Discovery with his colleague, Joe Fenwick, and UCD-based historian Dr Edel Bhreathnach. The NRA, in its defence of the M3, said the chosen route 'sought to avoid the important core zone around

Tara' by running east of the N3 – something Newman likened to 'a doctor telling you that you're wife is dead but the bus swerved to miss her'. All of this clearly rattled the NRA, not least a statement by Seán Haughey TD, newly elected chairman of the Oireachtas Joint Committee on the Environment, that the route chosen for the M3 was 'bordering on vandalism'. The Authority took out full-page advertisements in national newspapers to respond to the 'misinformation' allegedly put forward by opponents of the scheme. It claimed that running the M3 east of the Hill of Skryne would place 'dozens of homes' within 25 metres of the centre line of the motorway, and also insisted that archaeological advice had been heeded in choosing the preferred alignment. But when members of the Oireachtas Committee visited Tara in December 2004, they were limited to meeting representatives of the NRA and Prof George Eogan, the distinguished archaeologist who had spent much of his life excavating the Neolithic passage tombs in Brú na mBóinne. He also made it clear to the TDs and senators that Tara was not just a hilltop, but an entire area that should be left untouched by road-building. 'To put something as intrusive as a roadway is very, very strange – I'd even go as far as to say a very odd decision.'

Inevitably, the M3 became a hot issue in the Meath by-election to fill the Dáil seat left vacant after John Bruton was appointed EU ambassador in Washington. The chambers of commerce in Navan, Kells and Trim banded together to back the route chosen by the NRA, arguing that any change would lead to further delays and leave Meath's commuters snarled in endless traffic jams on their way to and from Dublin. 'Fed up sitting in your car?' roadside posters asked passing motorists on the heavily congested N3. 'Support the M3', said follow-up posters, which also gave a number for text messages (at 60c per message). There was no number to text in support of alternatives – such as a rail link to Navan or a new road linking the N3 to the M1, for example. The results of an 'opinion poll' commissioned by the chambers of commerce showed that 8 out of 10 people in Meath backed the existing route, including many who were under the impression that it ran right over the Hill of Tara. The

↓ *Martyn Turner's 'take' on the M3 and Tara*

Taoiseach rowed in with a trite comment about not wanting to upset Tara's kings. 'If I had known they were there, I would have gone around them', he said. Fianna Fáil's by-election candidate, Shane Cassels, accused 'serial whingers' of holding up construction of the motorway, and said that 'people moving camp from Carrickmines ... will not stand in the way of progress'. Despite his fulsome support for the M3, he went down to defeat. Julitta Clancy of the Meath Archaeological Society, one of the most outspoken critics of the motorway route, conceded that traffic congestion on the county's roads was appalling, but said: 'We have not the right to destroy one of the richest and most important archaeological landscapes in Europe to achieve the long-overdue relief.' A more fundamental point was made by the leaders of 12 Irish clubs and associations in England, France, Germany, Switzerland, Belgium and the Netherlands in a letter to national newspapers on 15th March 2005. 'Perhaps what is unclear in the detail of the debate in Ireland has greater clarity when viewed from abroad: a four-lane motorway through the Tara landscape will destroy the integrity and beauty of a priceless cultural treasure ... not just of importance to Ireland but to the whole world.' Noting that WB Yeats had described the hill as 'probably the most consecrated spot in Ireland', the letter continued: 'Both of the Irish national symbols, the harp and the shamrock, originated at Tara.' These had become 'readily recognisable motifs for Ireland and for what it is most prized internationally – its culture, rich history and beautiful landscape.' For Tara was 'the place where St Patrick first used the symbol of the three-leafed shamrock in his teachings to signify the Divine Trinity. To put a motorway through the grounds of royal Tara is to deface a national icon, akin to removing a leaf from the emblem of the shamrock. The landscape of Tara is indivisible and must remain entirely intact and undisturbed.'

Rumours abounded about land deals along the route of the M3, particularly around the proposed Blundelstown interchange. In February 2005 the *Sunday Business Post* revealed that more than 200 acres of land adjoining the interchange had been acquired by Cathal McCarthy, joint developer of the main shopping centre in Navan. 'In the mid-1990s', Ciarán Buckley reported, 'McCarthy and property developer Eamonn Duignan bought a property in Navan with Fianna Fáil fund-raiser Des Richardson and Frank Dunlop, the former government press secretary. Duignan, Richardson and Dunlop have no involvement in the land transfers near the interchange at Blundelstown.' Two weeks later, *Ireland on Sunday* fleshed out the story by revealing that McCarthy and Duignan had contributed £30,500 to Fianna Fáil in 1999 by attending party fund-raising functions. Others with land along the route include 'a company controlled by multi-millionaire builder Joseph Murphy Jr, whose main business, JMSE, was exposed as corrupt by the Flood Tribunal', according to John Lee, the paper's political correspondent, who gathered this information from the Land Registry. 'Tara Tycoons', the report was headed; 'Political cronies poised to make fortunes as controversial motorway runs close to ancient site and right through their land'. Lee said Murphy 'stands to make even more substantial profits from the hundreds of acres of land which he owns within a few miles of the motorway route which may well be opened up for development once construction is completed'.

Newland Properties Ltd, owned by Murphy and former JMSE managing director Frank Reynolds, had bought up more than 130 acres of land in Ratoath, Dunshaughlin, Dunboyne, and other parts of south Meath that would be served by the M3. This includes 26 acres near Roestown, Ratoath, of which just over five acres are subject to compulsory purchase by Meath County Council for construction of the motorway; this is expected to net the company about €5 million. According to the report, JMSE 'has made huge financial contributions to Fianna Fáil and the Progressive Democrats'.

There is, of course, no suggestion that Environment Minister Dick Roche would be influenced by such considerations. However, he was statutorily obliged to consider the views of Dr Pat Wallace, director of the National Museum. Wallace's 18-page report, delivered to the Minister in mid-March 2005, dealt in detail with the archaeological sites along the route, but also made it clear that the setting of Tara would be 'demeaned' by the M3 and the visual impact of the Blundelstown interchange, in particular. 'Tara is a unique cultural landscape which has a significance for our national heritage that extends beyond the sum of its individual components ... It is one of a small number of monumental complexes that are of more than usual cultural importance from the standpoint not only of archaeology, but also of history, mythology, folklore, language, placenames study, and, in the case of Tara, even of national identity.' He challenged the conclusion reached by former Cork county engineer Brendan Devlin, the Bord Pleanála planning inspector who dealt with the case, that the route as proposed 'would not have a significant impact on the archaeological landscape associated with the Hill of Tara' – a view repeatedly cited by the NRA and Meath County Council in defending the M3. 'I fail to see how the inspector could be so certain about the lack of impact on the archaeological landscape ... given that the archaeology of the area ... still remains to be fully defined.' Wallace suggested that an attempt had been made to 'downplay the importance' of archaeological sites along the route – a claim described as 'disingenuous' by Brian Duffy, the Department of the Environment's chief archaeologist – and he also took exception to the use of 22-tonne mechanical excavators in stripping topsoil to expose archaeological features, saying 'the chances of retrieving archaeological objects in the face of heavy machinery of this sort are ... very limited indeed'. But his primary concern was that the planning process was too narrowly focused 'because it chose to confine its deliberation on Tara on the basis of the requirements of individual sites, and ignored the importance of the place as a complex'. Duffy took a different view: 'It could be argued that the M3 will be a monument of major significance in the future and be seen as a continuation of the pattern of route development through the valley.'

Long before this unusual argument was publicly revealed, Roche had signalled his intentions to the *Irish Times*, saying there was 'no way' he was going to re-visit An Bord Pleanála's decision: 'I am where I am ... This has gone through the planning process.' He conceded that a decision by him not to issue licences would leave the NRA and Meath County Council with no option but to find an alternative route for the motorway, but claimed that it would be 'a very serious misuse of ministerial power [to] attempt to stymie a properly approved project'. He was anxious to portray himself as a man with a 'limited' role and less room for manoeuvre than he actually had. Yet even the 1994 National Monuments Act explicitly states that it is 'at the discretion of the Minister' whether he issues his consent. The possibility of changing the route of an 'approved road development' is also provided for under Section 14 of the Act, which lays down that any such alteration must be referred to An Bord Pleanála to determine if it is 'material'. And 'as a consequence of the directions of the Minister', the board may require the submission of a revised environmental impact statement 'for the purposes of permitting any changes to the route or design of the approved road development,' according to the Act. The fact was that Pat Wallace had shown up serious deficiencies in the planning process, something that would have left a conscientious minister with cause to exercise his discretion. Had Roche chosen not to grant licences for the archaeological excacvations, he would have spared a mystical landscape and forced the NRA to come up with an alternative. He didn't.

An so, on 11th May 2005, Roche announced his approval for the excavation of 38 archaeological sites along a 15.5km stretch between Dunshaughlin and Navan. At his news conference in the Government Press Centre, he said the excavations would be 'onerous', taking at least two years to complete at a cost of up to €40 million. Steps would be taken to reduce the visual impact of Blundelstown interchange by omitting its tall lamp standards from the final design of the scheme, and he was delighted to announce that this had been agreed with the NRA. There would be 'extensive landscaping', including the use of embankments, to minimise its impact still further. The Minister said he would also 'consider' using his power under the 2000 Planning Act to direct Meath County Council to curb commercial developments gathering around the interchange. In other words, all he was prepared to consider was damage-limitation – even after reading the entire file, including Pat Wallace's letter, and meeting some of the objectors in private, in one case accompanied by the Taoiseach himself. Roche refused to be drawn on when the motorway was likely to open to traffic; the best guess was 2010 at the earliest – and that made no allowance for the possibility that a High Court judicial review of his order would be successful. The three leading scholars on Tara – Edel Bhreathnach, Conor Newman and Joe Fenwick – said Roche's decision to allow the M3 to go ahead would be recorded and remembered as 'not only a dark day for Tara, but a dark day for Irish culture. Ireland's premier landscape, an icon of our nationhood, is about to suffer an act of vandalism that will see a four-lane motorway, a large intersection and undoubted secondary developments obliterate its landscape.' And all in the name of 'progress'. It was 'a shameful decision that will have repercussions far and wide ... Let there be no doubt that this event will receive the attention of future historians and that the judgment of history will be harsh.' More than 300 academics and scholars from Ireland and abroad had also appealed for a 'mature approach' to balancing transport needs and heritage protection. 'If the motorway is constructed as currently planned, what does that say to the world about the cultural sensitivity of the Government?' they asked. 'How can it be justified in what is now one of the richest countries in Europe that such a sensitive landscape is destroyed rather than subjected to proper landscape management ... as has been done with the comparable landscape of the Boyne Valley?'

During an earlier UNESCO fact-finding visit to the Boyne Valley in February 2004, which mainly focused on the controversial Indaver incinerator planned for a site near Duleek, the Tara-Skryne group pressed for the entire valley to be designated as a World Heritage Site and placed on the 100-most-endangered-sites list. At present, the Boyne Valley protected area is confined to Brú na mBóinne, incorporating Newgrange, Knowth and Dowth. A report by the UNESCO mission in July 2004 concluded that the incinerator 'will not have a major effect on the outstanding universal value and the visual integrity of the archaeological ensemble', nor would its construction 'preclude any interpretation' of the Battle of the Boyne. It had nothing to say about the impact of the M3. Yet the Tara complex is as large, and arguably as significant, as Brú na mBóinne, which is one of only three designated World Heritage Sites in Ireland. The others are Skellig Michael in Co Kerry, and the Giant's Causeway in Co Antrim. Skellig is relatively well-protected, but plans to intensify tourism-related development have given rise to controversy in north Antrim.

In Co Clare, there has been a similar brouhaha over plans by Clare County Council to build a new visitor centre at the Cliffs of Moher. This €25 million project by a debt-ridden local authority, had been strongly opposed on environmental grounds by Shannon Development. It was also used as an excuse for expensive trips to Portugal and Australia. The councillors' junket to Portugal was of no help, as Gordon Deegan reported in December 2003, because the Sagres cliffs were not very tall by comparison – 200ft as against 700ft – 'and the only visitor facility available to inspect was a small, modern building housing a café and shop inside a fort originally built in the 15th century.' The official report on the trip said the Portuguese site 'was a good example of what one should *not* do rather than what one should do'. Nothing of note came from the trip to Australia either. With Clare's debts mounting, the 'dream scheme' for the Cliffs of Moher looked dead and buried, and was only rescued in mid-2004 by the Minister for Arts, Sport and Tourism, John O'Donoghue, with a €10.5 million grant to the council in advance of the European and local elec-

↓ *Aerial view of the Cliffs of Moher with existing visitors' centre and car park*

tions. He said the development would deliver a 'world-class visitor experience' at the cliffs, which currently attract some 600,000 visitors a year. Martin Cullen had earlier breached a national cap on local authority borrowing by giving the county council approval to raise a loan for the remaining €15 million. When it was first mooted in the early 1990s, the estimated cost was less than €4 million. Ironically, the visitor centre is to be managed by Shannon Development, which had appealed against it to An Bord Pleanála on the grounds that it would have a negative impact on the environmentally sensitive landscape of the cliffs. The semi-State company also pointed out that it was best management practice internationally to locate tourist facilities away from environmentally sensitive areas – a point made repeatedly by the Burren Action Group in its long and ultimately successful campaign against the controversial visitor centre planned for Mullaghmore, in the heart of the Burren National Park. But An Bord Pleanála ruled that the Cliffs of Moher visitor centre was in line with a sustainable tourism strategy for Co Clare and would not seriously injure the visual or natural amenities of the area. Donough O'Riordan, of Cork-based Reddy O'Riordan Staehli Architects, who designed the 3,000m² (32,290 sq ft) facility, said the fact that it would be built into the hill on the site was 'a fantastic solution to the challenges posed by the location'. Nuala O'Faoláin was dubious. 'Go up to the visitors and ask them whether they feel the need for an audio-visual theatre. Guess what: they don't', she wrote in February 2002.

← *Ask visitors to the Cliffs of Moher if they want a visitor centre and 'Guess what: they don't', Nuala O'Faoláin wrote*

↓ *A computer-generated view of the proposed visitor centre at the Cliffs of Moher*

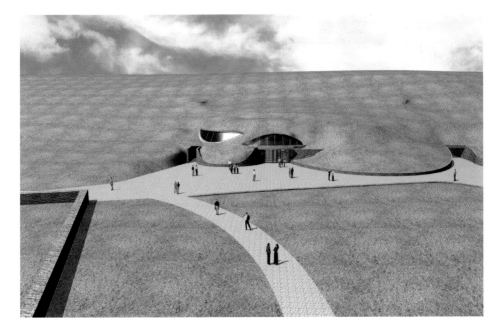

SO WHAT IS 'HERITAGE'? ACCORDING TO A COMPREHENSIVE DEFINITION IN THE 1995 Heritage Act, it includes monuments, architecture, archaeological and other heritage objects. Flora, fauna, wildlife habitats, geology, inland waterways, heritage gardens and parks, landscapes, seascapes and even shipwrecks are also covered. Passage tombs, ruined abbeys, medieval castles, stately homes, imposing neo-classical public buildings and the streetscapes of planned towns are no longer contaminated by alien associations with invaders, landlords or 'belted earls'; they have all been embraced as part of what we are. But we still have our blind spots. Developers were allowed by Kildare County Council and An Bord Pleanála to turn Carton Demesne, the most intact 18th-century landscape in Ireland, into an upmarket golf resort, with dozens of 'villas' dotted through the trees planted by Lady Emily FitzGerald, 1st Duchess of Leinster, in the 1790s. An Taisce maintains that transformation into luxury golf resorts may not be the right recipe for heritage properties such as Carton, but has had little success in persuading An Bord Pleanála of this view, as shown by the board's string of permissions for such developments at Powerscourt (Co Wicklow), Killeen Castle (Co Meath), Luttrellstown (Co Dublin), Lough Rynn (Co Leitrim) and, of course, Carton. The challenge with estates such as these is to find a way to make them self-financing so that they can be kept intact. The trouble is that golf appears to be the only option to bring in the revenues needed for their survival.

The case of Lough Rynn, ancestral home of the earls of Leitrim, is worth look-ing at in some detail. An Taisce's heritage officer, Ian Lumley, described the surviving 105-acre estate near Mohill as 'one of the most important, romantic, picturesque landscapes from the 19th century in Ireland'. The house and gardens had been opened to the public by its Irish-American owner, Michael Flaherty, with the aid of a €94,000 grant from the International Fund for Ireland, though Lough Rynn never did draw crowds like Strokestown Park in Co Roscommon. In 1999 he sold out to Capsivale Ltd, a consortium headed by the Hanley quarrying group based near Elphin, Co Roscommon, and the company put forward plans to develop an 18-hole golf course, a conference and leisure centre, and 168 houses and apartments on the estate. Lumley said the proposed development was 'fundamentally incompatible with the natural heritage, historical and landscape quality of the site', given that Lough Rynn House is a listed building and the site includes part of two Natural Heritage Areas. In particular, the Nick Faldo-designed golf course, with the first fairway locat-ed between the house and the lake, was 'as intrusive as you could get'. But Capsivale, which also stood to benefit from the tax incentives available under the Upper Shannon Rural Renewal Scheme, had powerful local support. Enda Stenson, an inde-pendent county councillor, told the *Irish Times* in March 2001: 'Mohill has been a dead, sleepy town where nothing ever happened. There is only one small factory here. People see the estate as the only thing we have to bring people in.' John Tiernan, then county manager, said Leitrim needed the development to 'boost its tourism product' and to provide a venue 'where people and local businesses, both indigenous and for-eign-owned, can entertain and show the best side of the county'. After the county council's decision to approve the scheme was upheld by An Bord Pleanála in October

2002, An Taisce was roundly condemned by local politicians for threatening to take legal action in the High Court, which it didn't, and to pursue a formal complaint in Brussels about the handling of the case, which it did. John Ellis TD (FF) accused the trust of 'trying to stop Mohill from developing'. However, Ian Lumley defended An Taisce's stance, saying the development proposed for Lough Rynn 'brings to a head the environmental concerns raised by us and others' when the 'ill-advised' Rural Renewal Tax Incentive Scheme was introduced in 1999. Subsequently, after work on the site got under way in September 2003, including earthworks, vegetation removal and drainage of lake areas, An Taisce claimed much of it was being carried out in defiance of conditions attached to the planning permission. The trust also said that its complaints to Leitrim County Council and the Department of the Environment in relation to these alleged breaches of the Planning Act had been ignored.

When the Upper Shannon Rural Renewal Scheme was introduced in 1999, the Heritage Council warned that it 'could harm the national heritage' in Leitrim and Longford, as well as west Cavan, south Sligo and north Roscommon – the areas covered by it. Expressing 'serious concern' that no Government department or agency would oversee the scheme, the council said there was 'a clear need for a cohesive strategic plan for the development of the designated area as a whole'. Seven months earlier, in June 1998, Charlie McCreevy rejected a proposal from Noel Dempsey that the scheme should be administered by the Department of the Environment, saying it was 'a pilot scheme and I would like to oversee it myself so as to ascertain how it is progressing'. One wonders how much attention McCreevy paid to the way it panned out. As well as dismissing the serious reservations expressed by the Heritage Council, he spurned advice from his own officials that the scheme would prove 'very costly'. Michael Tutty, then deputy secretary general at Finance, told McCreevy that its introduction would 'inevitably increase the pressure' to extend this pilot scheme throughout the State; indeed, the department had been 'inundated with representations' to designate other areas, including north Mayo, south Galway, north Sligo, south Roscommon and even north Cork. And though similar reliefs were available under the Urban Renewal Scheme, Tutty noted that they were aimed at 'limited rundown areas', whereas the Rural Renewal Scheme applied to 'two entire counties, half of another county, and significant portions of two further counties'. But McCreevy's mandarins were simply wasting their time writing reports for him; the Minister knew what was best.

He also ignored the dreadful precedent of an earlier pilot scheme for 14 seaside resorts, in operation since 1995. Under this scheme, tax incentives applied to a wide range of development, including hotels, guesthouses, hostels, B&Bs, self-catering accommodation and all-weather facilities in Bundoran, Enniscrone, Achill, Westport, Salthill, Lahinch, Kilkee, Ballybunion, Clonakilty, Youghal, Tramore, Courtown, Arklow, Bettystown, and Clogherhead. According to Enda Kenny, who introduced it as Minister for Tourism, the scheme would 'contribute significantly' to the regeneration of these resorts, enabling them to 'play their part' in meeting Government targets for tourism. But the then Minister for Finance, Rúairí Quinn, a

↑ *Entire estates of tax-designated holiday homes sprung up in places like Courtown, Co Wexford*
↓ *A roadside cluster of billboards advertising new holiday homes plonked in fields around*
Bettystown, Co Meath

↑ *Dooagh, Achill Island, now with more than its fair share of tax-designated holiday homes*
↓ *A large billboard advertising a scheme of 15 holiday cottages on the slopes of Slievemore,*
Achill Island, in 1997

↑ *Fine Gael leader Enda Kenny claimed the Seaside Resorts Scheme would 'contribute significantly' to their regeneration. An interdepartmental group found otherwise.*

qualified architect and town planner, should have known better; if holiday homes were covered – and they were – the likely result was that they would account for the bulk of new development. And so it turned out. Even by mid-1997, entire estates of holiday homes were being shovelled into places like Courtown, which didn't even have a sewage treatment plant at the time. People in Kilkee felt they were being overwhelmed by 'tourist houses'; there was a tower crane in Lahinch for the first time in its history, and new housing was popping up in fields around Bettystown and Enniscrone, or marching across rising ground on Achill Island. In the case of Courtown, 890 self-catering units were built in an area which had a population of just 364 in 1996. And though there was a review of the scheme in 1997, two years after it was introduced, the report was never published (it pre-dated the Freedom of Information Act), and the evident damage it was doing was let fester until the end of 1999.

If the seaside resort tax incentives had generated new hotels, hostels, B&B accommodation and much-needed indoor leisure facilities, its effects would have been beneficial. Instead, as Friends of the Irish Environment said in June 1999, it had served only as 'a tax avoidance vehicle for rich non-residents' of the areas, and pushed property prices beyond the reach of local people. 'It is scandalous that the public should be subsidising such a scheme, which violates every principle of sustainable tourism.' An expert inter-departmental group subsequently concluded that the effects of the scheme were probably contrary to national tourism policy, because they detracted from the unspoilt beauty of the designated areas. It had also failed to achieve a key tourism objective to attract more overseas tourists. Holiday homes – a total of 5,295 of them – accounted for four-fifths of the estimated total investment of €800 million levered by the scheme, mainly involving top-rate taxpayers from outside the 14 localities. An investigation by the Revenue found that it was also being milked by 'partnerships' claiming double-rent allowances against the income of their members. There was also evidence that many of the new self-catering units were not genuinely on the rental market, as required by the scheme. Private holiday homes for Irish people accounted for most of the houses and apartments built in the resorts, Colm Keena reported. Altogether, it was estimated that the scheme had cost the Exchequer a whopping €315 million – much more, proportionately, than the Urban Renewal Scheme which levered a total investment of nearly €3 billion in its first 10 years (1986-96), for a ballpark bill of €525 million in tax foregone. It cost the Exchequer just 17 cent in lost revenue for every euro invested, compared to 44 cent for every euro sunk into the seaside resorts. Courtown turned out to be the most costly location, with development there resulting in €52 million in tax revenue foregone – or the equivalent of €140,000 for each of its permanent residents in 1996.

But the enormous amount of tax forgone wasn't really the worst aspect of the Seaside Resorts Scheme. Anyone can make a mistake once. The fact is that McCreevy decided to repeat it. He junked advice from his own officials to push yet another poorly anchored scheme, this time designating whole counties. Yet there was every reason why the Upper Shannon Rural Renewal Scheme should have been cast differently. A 1996 review of the Urban Renewal Scheme recommended that future tax incentives should be linked to area-based plans encompassing community development, employment, urban design and conservation. The Department of the Environment took this advice, and integrated area plans were required for later urban renewal schemes, to avoid repeating such disasters as befell Athlone and Portlaoise, where the tax-designation of greenfield sites for shopping centres undermined their main streets. But this was all ignored when it came to the Upper Shannon. Instead, the approach was laissez-faire and 'clearly not in line with the principles of sustainable development', as Paddy Matthews, then planning officer of the Heritage Council, said in letters to McCreevy and Dempsey in July 1999. Using blunt language that would be inconceivable for the since-cowed council, he said the Department of Finance was 'solely concerned with the enhancement of economic growth' and had 'failed to grasp the essential characteristics of good planning'. In the light of what happened with the Seaside Resorts Scheme, and given that the Upper Shannon region was 'particularly susceptible' to damage by inappropriate development, Matthews concluded: 'We can no longer afford to embark upon a scheme which offers lucrative financial incentives for property developers without first putting a strategic plan in place.' The Department of the Environment agreed with the 'broad thrust' of the Heritage Council's criticisms, but nothing was done. A memo in January 2000 by Finian Matthews, principal officer in the Department's planning division, noted that the Rural Renewal Scheme was 'now well up and running [and] it is too late at this stage to put many of these suggestions in place'. A round-table meeting sought by the Heritage Council was finally held at the end of April 2000 and attended by the departments of Finance and Environment and the five local authorities. Dom Hegarty, the senior architectural adviser who chaired the meeting, expressed concern about sporadic construction: 'Buildings are not like plants; they can't be shifted around when they're built. Local communities are going to have to live with any mistakes for a long time.' The five county managers from Leitrim, Longford, Roscommon, Sligo and Cavan all insisted they could cope and that they were conscious of the need to avoid a repeat of 'the problems that may have arisen' with the Seaside Resorts Scheme. As things turned out, their confidence was misplaced.

Leitrim bore the brunt of criticism from conservationists over what was unfolding on the landscape. Desperate to secure its share of development, the county council had already rolled out the red carpet for Masonite's huge fibreboard fac-

↑ *A fly-fisherman in front of a new housing estate at Tullaghan on part of Co Leitrim's short coastal strip, which was becoming saturated with development according to Ian Lumley*

tory on the east bank of the Shannon, near Drumsna. Some 280 jobs were created, but there were also complaints from farmers and other residents in the vicinity about noise, odours and excessive discharges of formaldehyde, with the US-owned company prosecuted on at least one occasion. Now, fuelled by Upper Shannon tax incentives, development had arrived along Leitrim's short coastline. In and around Tullaghan was becoming 'saturated' with one-off houses, as An Taisce's Ian Lumley said in October 2001. 'What's happening ... is tax-subsidised coastal development at its worst.' By then, up to 100 houses had already been built and more were being planned, many as holiday homes. 'The housing developments at Tullaghan now run into the already sprawling outskirts of Bundoran, with the result that it is now impossible to distinguish the town boundary as more and more countryside disappears', Theresa Judge reported. Bundoran had acquired some 470 new holiday homes as a result of its designation under the Seaside Resorts Scheme – and most of these were occupied for relatively short periods of the year. Now this phenomenon was spilling over into Leitrim. 'This is completely at variance with the ideals of the Rural Renewal Scheme which was designed to bring people back to live and work in an area', said a spokesman for local residents. 'At least the seaside resorts can be served by upgraded sewerage, but in Tullaghan it's all individual houses with septic tanks',

Lumley said. 'This must surely be creating a water pollution time-bomb, with implications for groundwater supplies and, ultimately, bathing water quality' – a charge rejected by the county manager, John Tiernan. Even in cases where Leitrim's planners recommended a refusal, they were under instructions to supply a list of conditions that might be attached to a decision to grant permission, should the manager exercise his power to overturn their recommendation. Tiernan often did. Referring to a scheme where houses were being built just yards from the sea, he maintained that this constituted good development because they were replacing an unsightly caravan park. Asked by Theresa Judge whether tighter planning controls might be useful, he said: 'I wouldn't like the train to leave the station while we are scratching our heads.' As far as he was concerned, the Upper Shannon Rural Renewal Scheme was 'the most positive intervention in Co Leitrim in modern times'.

In June 2003 An Taisce issued a statement deploring Leitrim County Council's decision to dump its heritage officer when a three-year pilot programme funded by the Heritage Council came to an end. This was a 'retrograde step' because of the major challenges Leitrim faced in regulating such developments as rural housing, coniferous forestry, wind farms and tourism projects, all of which needed to be 'reconciled with strategic heritage protection', according to An Taisce. However, the trust claimed some credit for the role it had played in saving the relatively unspoiled shoreline of Lough Allen from 'scatter-gun' holiday homes. 'We took the view that schemes outside service centres were unsustainable and An Bord Pleanála mostly agreed with us.' The response of Leitrim County Council was to downgrade areas of outstanding natural beauty or high visual amenity, even as Ireland was signing the draft European Landscape Convention in March 2002. An Taisce also pointed to the 'exceptionally poor quality' of the design and siting of new houses in Co Leitrim, and said the management of the Shannon as a natural and amenity resource 'needs an active co-ordinated role with other counties and agencies, where the role of the local authority heritage officers was intended to be crucial'. In August 2000 the trust called for amenity designation for the entire Shannon catchment to curtail the spread of insensitive development. It told the Oireachtas Committee on the Shannon that decades-old attempts to drain the river to provide flood-free farmland have been 'wholly destructive' of wildlife habitats in the callows. And with the River Shannon classified as the sixth most polluted in the country, restoration of its water quality must be 'a national environmental priority'. An Taisce identified excessive use of phosphate and nitrate fertilisers and poorly controlled intensive farming as the main culprits, and called for an end to 'environmentally destructive agricultural methods' by switching subsidies to more sustainable farming practices. The 'irrevocable' destruction of landscapes in Kerry, Donegal and Galway had not yet been visited on the Shannon catchment, but a major initiative was needed to avoid repeating these mistakes. In August 2004 Lough Derg was closed to bathing for the fourth consecutive year due to persistent toxic algal blooms. Complaining about this threat to human and animal health, An Taisce said it was clear that the Shannon was being 'treated as an open sewer' by farmers spreading slurry and too much fertiliser on their

↑ *A slurry tanker using a standard 'splash-plate' attachment, and using the alternative 'trailing shoe' system*

land, silting caused by industrialised turf-cutting, and towns discharging raw sewage into the waterway. And it called yet again on the Government, the Mid-West Regional Authority, the EPA and local authorities to enforce the law on water quality in line with EU directives. There are measures that can be taken to curb the run-off of slurry, such as 'trailing shoe' application. This method deposits the slurry in little ravines in the soil rather than splashing it out all over the place. In vulnerable counties like Cavan, it would reduce run-off as well as cutting ammonia emissions by 60%, and make the usually obnoxious odour imperceptible. While costly, the amount of money would be small in the context of the benefits involved.

Ireland's natural heritage is under relentless development pressure. No landscape outside the handful of national parks seems to be safe, not even Special Areas of Conservation designated under the EU Habitats Directive and Natura 2000 programme. Priority Irish habitats include raised bogs, upland blanket bogs, native woodlands, heaths, machair, sand dunes, lakes, turloughs, rivers, estuaries and sea inlets. Far from seeking to protect such areas, the Government dragged its feet for so long that the European Commission had to take legal action in a bid to ensure compliance. Only the least contentious of the SACs were approved initially, often involving State-owned land or sites where there were no development pressures; strong opposition from landowners frustrated progress elsewhere. The designation of Natural Heritage Areas, not quite as rigorous as SACs, has also been painfully slow for the same reason. As part of the Natura 2000 programme, Ireland proposed designating 364 SACs under the Habitats Directive, and 109 sites as Special Protection Areas under the Birds Directive, from March 2003. The total land area covered amounted to 9,953 square kilometres for SACs and 2,236 square kilometres for SPAs, or 14.3% and 3.2% of the national territory respectively. But the information and mapping was incomplete, with 'significant gaps' particularly in relation to SPAs. In January 2004 the Commission decided to refer Ireland to the European Court of

Justice for failing to designate a sufficient number of SPAs and for failing to adequately protect sites that have or should have SPA status. Several threatened and vulnerable bird species, such as corncrakes, choughs and hen harriers, were poorly covered by site protection measures. In particular, the Commission claimed that Ireland failed to cut back on overgrazing by sheep in the Owenduff-Nephin Beg upland blanket bog complex in Co Mayo – the State's largest protection zone for birds – two years after being ordered to do so by the European Court. Upland blanket bog in the west of Ireland was once purple with heather, but now it's dull brown as a result of massive overgrazing. Red grouse numbers have dwindled to such an extent that this protected species is fighting for its survival. And not just because of overgrazing: serious problems are also being caused by a new breed of joyriders on quad-bikes. The Commission also zeroed in on the 'wide exemptions for damage and disturbance caused by farming and other activities' in the laws we enact purporting to transpose EU environmental legislation. In fact, the way Ireland brought in these laws inhibited the protection of a number of species, including the lesser horseshoe bat and the natterjack toad.

Ireland has made more progress on SAC designations. Since 1997, with the aid of EU funding, the National Parks and Wildlife Service has been preparing draft management plans for the various sites; about 250 had been prepared by mid-2004. But environmental NGOs (non-governmental organisations) regard the published plans as weak and the process of consultation inadequate. The NGOs were also less than impressed by the National Biodiversity Plan, published in April 2002 to fulfil the requirements of a UN Convention. 'It was released invisibly by Síle de Valera at the height of the general election campaign', Michael Viney observed. He contrasted this with Northern Ireland's Biodiversity Strategy, launched 'at a big green gathering' with a pledge by the then Environment Minister, Dermot Nesbitt, to reverse decades of biodiversity decline. Viney also found that the North's strategy 'responds with enthusiasm to an open, consultative process', whereas the Republic's plan 'crept to completion with plenty of NGO recrimination'. Though it was supposed to be an 'action plan', bureaucratic foot-dragging bedevilled the setting up of a 'stakeholders' forum' involving NGOs such as An Taisce, Birdwatch Ireland and the Irish Peatland Conservation Council. This forum was to have a role in overseeing implementation of the 2002 plan, but the Department of the Environment simply wants it to consist of the biodiversity working group of Comhar – a very low-profile advisory council on sustainable development, chaired by RTÉ's John Bowman.

The NGOs were also kept in the dark during negotiations between the Department and the main farming organisations – IFA, ICMSA and Macra na Feirme – over implementing the EU Habitats Directive. 'We tried to find out what was going on by using the Freedom of Information Act, but didn't get anything', according to Shirley Clerkin, environmental consultant and An Taisce's natural environment officer. The deal, announced in July 2004 after 12 months of haggling, was widely seen as a sell-out to the farming lobby. Even while the talks were under way, farmers dramatised their opposition to habitat designations by denying wildlife rangers

↑ *Greg Norman walks towards a helicopter about to land at the controversial golf links he designed in Doonbeg, Co Clare*

access to their land. Now they had an agreement that the process of designating sites for nature conservation would be completed as speedily as possible, 'having full regard to the need for consultation with landowners and users'. Procedures for notifying landowners of designation proposals were to be improved and a code of practice developed covering contacts between them and conservation staff. Neither was designation to become 'an inflexible constraint on development'. Mimicking the so-called Sustainable Rural Housing Guidelines, local authorities were told by Martin Cullen to 'allow sustainable rural development while maintaining designated areas at a favourable conservation status' – whatever that means. The extent of protection for SAC rivers was also limited to 2.5 metres from their banks 'except where special features are present'. Most importantly, the deal pledged that 'fair and proper levels of compensation will be paid for any costs, income losses or capital losses which result directly from restrictions on farming or other existing activities'.

The loss of habitats went on. In July 2004 the European Commission issued a formal notice to Ireland after a complaint was lodged by Friends of the Irish Environment about the unauthorised filling of a proposed wetlands SAC at Oranmore, Co Galway. In its letter, the Commission pointed to the 'apparent lack of enforcement action with regard to unlawful infilling of wetlands', and went on to say that FIE's complaint 'appears to reflect wider legislative and administrative weaknesses in relation to the safeguarding of proposed Irish Natura 2000 sites'. As an FIE spokesman noted, the construction of the Oranmore bypass resulted in the partial infilling of Moneymore Fen with construction waste, despite its SAC designation. This opened the way for explosive development, with hundreds of new houses built on the seaward side, many on reclaimed fen. Infilling began at the neighbouring Carrowmore marsh – also designated – in May 1999 and continued until May 2003, with mounds of excavated material spread over pristine wetland. Correspondence obtained by FIE showed that the National Parks and Wildlife Service had repeatedly written to Galway County Council about this illegal activity. The council did not resolve the problem.

The Irish authorities must now convince Brussels that measures are being taken to ensure that Ireland's wetlands receive effective protection, or face the prospect of huge daily fines as they lose cases before the European Court. But even if the fens at Oranmore and other SAC or SPA sites were protected, Shirley Clerkin regards the idea of creating 'little islands of wildlife' with no buffer zones around them as piecemeal and tokenistic – especially if development is let rip immediately outside their boundaries. And these boundaries are not necessarily fixed in stone; environmentalists claim that they have been 'changed all over the country'. Take the case of a proposed SAC at Doonbeg, Co Clare, where a major golf-based leisure scheme could only proceed if the boundaries were redrawn by Dúchas. Another State agency, Shannon Development, was promoting the plan by Landmark National, a US company with an Irish subsidiary chaired by Senator George Mitchell, a key player in the Good Friday Agreement. According to planning consultant Bernard McHugh, who represented Landmark National at the Bord Pleanála oral hearing in 1999, plans for the Greg Norman-designed golf course on the rare dune system of White Strand were amended to meet the 'exacting requirements' of Dúchas. But FIE, which joined An Taisce in appealing against the £12.5 million scheme, pointed out that Dúchas – then answerable to Síle de Valera as Minister for Arts and Heritage (and also a Fianna Fáil TD for Clare) – had chopped off more than three-quarters of the White Strand SAC, reducing it from 638 acres (266 hectares) to 125 acres (52 hectares). FIE claimed that the change, made in February 1998, was done at the behest of Landmark National. Dúchas rejected the allegation, saying it would not permit the adjustment of any site boundaries other than for scientific reasons. Because of the informal nature of the appeals process, it's just the word of Dúchas against FIE; the reasons for reducing the size of an SAC don't have to be documented. Pointing to a Dúchas report, An Taisce and FIE maintained that the proposed development at Doonbeg, which included a 51-bedroom hotel, conference centre and 80 holiday homes, would 'destroy the ecology of a priority conservation area ... of considerable scientific interest'. As it turned out, Landmark National did discover a rare snail, *Vertigo angustior* – one of three land snails protected by the EU Habitats Directive. But Dúchas asserted that the snail was 'not threatened by the development', and An Bord Pleanála granted permission subject to measures being taken to protect the 2mm creature. The appeals board also reduced the number of holiday homes to 46, and required Landmark National to submit a management plan to protect the entire SAC. Doug Barton, chief executive of the company's subsidiary, Irish National Golf Club Ltd, pledged that it would act as 'good managers of the SAC' and good neighbours to the people of the area. The project had strong support from the local community development association, which said the objections were 'tantamount to telling the young people of Doonbeg that they are not entitled to a job and a future in their own community'. However, FIE's Tony Lowes maintained that spin-offs for local people were likely to be few and far between, as most golf tourists were 'car-based visitors who just drive into the area, play a game and then leave again; any jobs created as a result of these developments tend to be low-skilled and low-paid.' Nature, rather than the Habitats Directive, seems set to have the final say at Doonbeg. In December 2003 the golf club lodged plans for coastal protection works to counteract anticipated erosion caused by climate change – a gradual retreat of the dunes in the face of rising sea levels. 'Soft' dune stabilisation works had already been washed away in a storm in 2001. As Gordon Deegan reported, the club sought to place a barrier containing over 80,000 tonnes of rock at three strategic locations along the beach to protect the €150 million golf links. After running into strong opposition from An Taisce, local people and surfers, it scaled down its plans. In any event, Landmark National seems locked into an eternal battle with global warming.

The most bitter struggle on the golf front was fought over the Old Head of Kinsale in Co Cork. For years, there had been informal public access to this headland, off which the *Lusitania* was sunk. However, its acquisition in 1989 by brothers John and Patrick O'Connor ultimately led to the Old Head being sealed off to everyone other than those who stump up €300 for a round of golf, or €50,000 (2003-04 prices) for membership of what has become one of the most exclusive clubs in the world. In 1996, while the greens and fairways were being laid out, Kevin Myers wrote a lament in his 'Irishman's Diary'. 'How was it possible that the Old Head of Kinsale could be ravaged? Why did the OPW not do anything to preserve this most wonderful headland in Ireland so that others might enjoy it for generations to come as generations in the past have been able to enjoy it? ... The substance of what made the Old Head magical, what lifted the soul on mad, storm-tossed days, were the 240 acres of tussock grass, bogland and heather, which nourished a huge wildlife – choughs in wheeling numbers, calling through the gales at one another; puffins and kestrels, gannets and fulmars, wheatears and whinchats and stonechats and nameless armies of darting small birds that rewarded long waits with binoculars and a bird book ... Builders have come with a heavy hand and bridged and ruled and ruined the land – ruined it not just for this golf-playing generation, but for all time. What has been done to the Old Head of Kinsale is the eradication of thousands of years of ecological history ... And all needless, needless. If the OPW had been half as vigorous in defence of the existing natural parkland as it was in getting involved in the silly, footling heritage interpretative industry, the Old Head would now be safe in public hands. The State, too busy with its damned fool enterprises elsewhere, did not act, and a private developer bought the Head over. He did not need planning permission to build a golf course in those days, and he proceeded to ravage the soil and the sub-soil, moving tens of thousands of tons of soil to restructure the surface, to provide a false local environment for close cropped greens, to plough fairways through the wide acres and to gouge out bunkers to ensnare fat, frustrated visitors. No doubt golfers like links golf; but there is no reason on earth why they should be given a monopoly over one of the most priceless parts of our coastline. Merely because a small group of powerful people want something desirable should not mean they get it.'

But the O'Connor brothers, through Ashbourne Holdings Ltd, had one thing on their side that overwhelmed all others – the right to run a golf course on private property. They threatened to close it down if the courts upheld a condition laid down by Cork County Council (and endorsed by An Bord Pleanála) requiring public access to be maintained. According to the O'Connors, if people were roaming the land, they were doing so illegally, and the campaign being waged against their golf course was led by 'cranks and headbangers' with a political agenda. 'We are serious about closing the course, because quite simply you cannot have people rambling around a golf course', John O'Connor told the *Irish Times*. 'We tried in the early days to accommodate public access. We charged a nominal fee, but it just didn't work, and our insurers warned that they wouldn't underwrite us if the public was allowed on the land.' The High Court agreed with them. In March 2001 Mr Justice Kearns said such a condition would effectively allow the public to wander over the playing area, and was so 'manifestly unreasonable' as to render the use of the Old Head as a golf

↓ *Protesters climb a fence at the exclusive golf links on the Old Head of Kinsale, Co Cork. The Supreme Court ended public access to the scenic headland in March 2003.*

↑ *Aerial view of the Old Head of Kinsale, when it was open to the public to enjoy what Kevin Myers described as the 'most wonderful headland in Ireland'*

course 'potentially inoperable'; walkers and golfers were 'inimical to each other'. An Bord Pleanála thought the issue was so important that it appealed to the Supreme Court, but to no avail. Delivering its judgment in March 2003, Mr Justice Adrian Hardiman struck down the condition requiring public access saying it had nothing to do with the development of the clubhouse, road and equipment shed, for which permission or retention had been sought. It was an outright victory for the O'Connors, whose €20 million in developing the Old Head was already paying off handsomely. They were also planning to invest a further €20 million in the development of a five-star hotel in the heart of Kinsale to cater for the burgeoning luxury golf market. But An Bord Pleanála twice rejected their proposals, ruling in June 2004 that the scale, bulk, massing, design and footprint of the scheme, as well as its relationship to the harbour, would make it 'visually intrusive, out of character with the pattern of development in the area, and incompatible with the urban grain of the town centre'. An Taisce said the revised plans had merely reduced the number of bedrooms by doubling them into suites, and 'failed to address the original grounds for refusal – the sheer scale of the project on what was the site of an old fish market'. But the O'Connors were shocked, and considered putting the property up for sale.

Golf developers didn't always get their way either. In November 2003 FIE

↑ *Aerial view of the Old Head of Kinsale, after it was developed as an exclusive golf links with no free access to the headland by members of the public*

hailed a decision by An Bord Pleanála to refuse permission for an 18-hole golf course on Inchydoney Island, in west Cork, on the grounds that it would have 'significant negative impacts' on nature conservation in an area of 'high ecological value' as a habitat for wild birds. The site, at Clogheen Strand Intake, also adjoined Clonakilty Bay SAC, and the appeals board was concerned that the main feeding area for black tailed godwits would be lost if the development went ahead. FIE said the ruling, which overturned a grant by Cork County Council, was a 'landmark decision for nature conservation' and contained a 'clear message' for the controversial golf links planned for Bartragh Island, in Killala Bay, on the north Mayo coast. Nick Faldo was a member of the consortium that acquired the 357-acre island in 1997. The champion golfer had earlier been rebuffed in a bid to lease Ballyliffin Golf Club in Co Donegal for 33 years. His proposal was overwhelmingly rejected by its members on the basis that the twin 36-hole links course was 'part of their heritage and not for sale'. On hearing of Faldo's plans for Bartragh, business interests in Ballina expressed huge enthusiasm, with the chamber of commerce predicting that the island would become 'a mecca for golfers'. But Michelle Mulherin, a Fine Gael member of Ballina Urban Council, feared that 'people might just drop in and out in their helicopters and not frequent the mainland at all'. An Taisce said Ireland was already well-served by golf links and there was 'a serious question whether any development is appropriate' on Bartragh, given the island's ecological significance as a special protected area – especially if it involved a range of ancillary facilities, including a clubhouse, golf chalets and the like. A bridge might also be needed, as the dune-laden island is accessible only by boat or on foot at low tide. Faldo pledged in November 2003 that the proposed golf course would be 'hand-crafted ... and extremely sensitive to the environment'.

In late 2001, An Taisce and Coastwatch warned that a 'tidal wave' of development was sweeping Ireland's coastline. Whole stretches had already been so blighted by unrestrained development, particularly housing, that An Taisce regarded them as 'irredeemable'; indeed, it effectively wrote off large parts of counties Donegal and Galway. The worst areas are the Gaeltachtaí, where rural housing for local people has been subsidised for decades. Much of the more recent development in these areas consists of holiday homes – and there is no evidence of additional Irish speakers. Lumley paralleled the consumption of landscape by housing with the way the Gaeltacht was being diluted by English-speaking weekenders. Here and elsewhere, 'entire areas of the coast are being turned into Beamer colonies for the Dublin 4 set', he said. Prime examples were Schull, Co Cork; Ballinskelligs, Co Kerry, and the areas around Clifden, Roundstone and Renvyle in Connemara. The Wicklow coastline between Brittas Bay and Arklow was 'filling up quite a bit' with one-off houses and this phenomenon had also become 'quite conspicuous' around Clew Bay, in Co Mayo, particularly on the way to Louisburgh. Karin Dubsky, co-ordinator of Coastwatch, contrasted Ireland with Denmark, where nobody is allowed to build within one kilometre of the coastline. Every Irish coastal county, on the other hand, provided numerous examples of houses being built too close to the shore – in turn, leading to demands for coastal protection measures. A lot of erosion control is done on a freelance basis without any consideration of its impact. In Co Wicklow, she complained, the European Club golf course 'poured cement all over part of the shore where tern and plover used to nest. Now it looks like a concrete slipway.' Illegal access points are also widespread, as holiday home-owners make their own paths to the sea instead of using established, more circuitous routes. Many caravan sites in coastal areas are also illegal, and Dubsky noticed an increasing trend where individual caravans 'metamorphose, lose their wheels and sprout decks, effectively becoming permanent dwellings'. At Blackwater Head, in north Wexford, the operation of mechanised sand quarries threatens the dune system. In Mullaghmore, Co Sligo, local people were in tears over what happened to their dunes, Dubsky said. An area of over 100 acres with a carpet of scented orchids had been 'wrecked by slurry spreading'. In Cahirciveen, Co Kerry, rock for a marina breakwater was excavated from the headland without a licence, even though the county council and local Leader group were partners in the €3.5 million project. In August 2004 environmental scientist Richard Nairn drew attention to widespread damage inflicted on the Portnoo sand dunes in Co Donegal by extending the golf links without either planning permission or an environmental impact assessment. Photographs showed a digger levelling the dunes in an area subject to an EU-funded project by Donegal County Council and the University of Ulster. The project team erected a sign on the beach describing the dunes as internationally important for wildlife, but under threat from intensive recreation and other inappropriate uses. After inspecting the site, Nairn said the work should be stopped immediately and planning permission sought. 'If this was taking place on the Bull Island in Dublin Bay, there would be a public outcry', he said. 'Sand dunes are a priority habitat for protection under the EU Habitats Directive ... Beach-dune systems are very fragile and easily damaged by heavy machinery. Once permanently under a golf course they are lost forever to the natural environment.'

The penalties for destroying protected habitats are risible, and the number of prosecutions small. In June 2004, for example, CW Shipping Ltd, a subsidiary of the Whelan Limestone quarrying group, was fined €1,900 in Ennis District Court for infilling a saltmarsh SAC at Cahercon on the Shannon Estuary, with Judge Timothy Lucey describing the maximum penalty as 'paltry'. He ordered the company to pay costs of €2,750 and to restore the site under the supervision of the National Parks and Wildlife Service. The use of the Cahercon site allowed the Whelan group to secure a €2 million contract to supply 140,000 tonnes of rock to stabilise a natural gas pipeline under the Shannon estuary, Gordon Deegan reported. Paddy Whelan, the group's chief executive, said he had 'used that site at Cahercon for a long time, and just because it is made an SAC shouldn't stop me using it'. He confirmed that he was appealing the SAC designation, and said all of his companies had a very good environmental record. At the time, Clare County Council was carrying out separate investigations into alleged breaches by Whelan Limestone Quarries. Its flagship quarrying operation at Fountain Cross, near Ennis, featured in an RTÉ *Prime Time* special, broadcast in April 2004. Though the quarry pre-dated the 1963 Planning Act, it underwent huge expansion to become one of the biggest suppliers of road construction material in the west of Ireland. Local residents complained that various extensions to the quarry had no planning permission, but it took the county council seven months to issue a warning notice and to follow this up with an enforcement notice in January 2003. Reporter Mike Milotte established that extensive blasting had continued for five days after the enforcement notice was served – under the licence and supervision of the Gardaí. Millions of euro worth of limestone was excavated from the site during this five-day period. If local people felt 'fobbed off' by officialdom, one of their own TDs, Tony Killeen (FF), had the explanation: 'There are fears that road projects under the National Development Plan would be seriously disrupted.' As Milotte commented: 'It's official then. The NDP needs illegal quarries.' Again, no effective action was taken against the operators of an unauthorised quarry in Ballynahallia, near Moycullen, Co Galway. A karst limestone protected habitat known locally as 'the Little Burren' was turned from a rough grazing area for feral goats into an illegal five-acre quarry. It became the subject of an investigation by the European Commission, after an official complaint by FIE. Local residents who objected to it were told that the crushed stone being taken out was needed to provide fill for an EU-funded realignment of the N59 between Moycullen and Clifden.

↑ *A truck pulls out of the illegal quarry in Athleague, Co Roscommon. Bertie Ahern urged the county council to go easy on the quarry owners.*

This was the backdrop for an extraordinary intervention by the Taoiseach in another case involving an illegal quarry, this one near Athleague, Co Roscommon. There was nothing new about clientilist politicians intervening in the planning process by making 'representations' on behalf of their constituents. Though in operation for many years, local residents – many living in new houses built nearby – were complaining about blasting and about lorry-loads of excavated material leaving the site every day. They also claimed that the county council itself had purchased gravel from the quarry for work to improve the Roscommon stretch of the N4. But then, as Friends of the Irish Environment pointed out, Section 261 of the 2000 Planning Act requiring the registration of all quarries has still not been implemented. What prompted the Taoiseach's interest was that one of the Murray brothers, owners of the Athleague quarry, is secretary of a local Fianna Fáil cumann. Another is a resident of Ahern's Dublin Central constituency, and after Roscommon County Council issued an enforcement notice under the 2000 Planning Act, he dropped in to Bertie's 'clinic' in Drumcondra. Within a month, a planning enforcement officer on the council's staff received a letter signed by the Taoiseach requesting that any further action be deferred. According to Senator Cyprian Brady, who runs Ahern's constituency office, it was a 'humanitarian gesture' because Brian Murray was undergoing treatment for

↑ *T&J Standish Sawmills, right beside Leap Castle, Co Offaly, has been operating for several years with no planning permission*

cancer. There was 'no question of interfering in the planning process', and Senator Terry Leyden (FF) had also made 'representations'.

Yet it was the FF-PD Coalition that piloted a consolidated Planning Act through the Oireachtas – legislation that ostensibly ushered in a tougher line on law enforcement. Fines for unauthorised development were increased to £10 million for convictions on indictment, and from £1,000 to £1,500 for summary convictions in the District Court. The Act also attempted to remedy what was seen as a serious deficiency in the planning system by obliging local authorities to follow up complaints from the public about breaches of development control within a given time-frame. Previously, councils were not required by statute to take any action on unauthorised developments. As with so many other things in Ireland, a blind eye was turned – even towards flagrant breaches of the planning laws, particularly by quarry owners. In the case of Athleague, the new Roscommon county manager, John Tiernan, said there was no question but that the Murrays' operation was illegal; a small quarry had been intensified in its use and this required planning permission. Tiernan also confirmed that quarrying at the site continued a month after the enforcement notice was served.

What's the point of having planning laws unless there is a commitment to enforce them, especially at the highest levels of government? Otherwise, we might just as well say 'you can build whatever you like, wherever you like, and there'll be no one stopping you'. Illegal development is rife, as *Prime Time* established, because of the extraordinary reluctance of local authorities to enforce the law. 'Around the country, non-enforcement is commonplace, as illegal developers know well', Mike Milotte reported. 'While local authorities have their eye off the ball, those who play dirty just keep going, as the scoresheet shows. In 2002, the most recent year scanned, over 1,800 illegal developers were served with notices under the 2000 Act ordering them to cease. Over 1,300 failed to comply, but only 46 were convicted. In some counties, the compliance rate actually hit zero. In 2002 five councils – Dún Laoghaire-Rathdown, Mayo, Waterford City, Westmeath and Wicklow – between them issued 350 enforcement notices. None [of them] was complied with that year. A further six councils – Galway City, Kilkenny, Leitrim, Limerick, Monaghan and Roscommon – together issued 400 notices and just 25 were obeyed.'

Right beside Leap Castle in Co Offaly's Aghancon Valley, as *Prime Time* showed, T&J Standish Sawmills had been operating for several years without planning permission. The owners maintained that they were operating a long-established business and didn't need permission. But they let it slip to the *Farmers' Journal* that they had 'diversified into sawmilling during the 1990s, having previously been involved in tillage and beef farming'. Timber fencing is their main product now. When local residents complained, Offaly County Council first tried to insist that it wasn't a factory at all. 'What do you want us to do about that? It's a business', one official said in February 2003, adding that it was 'not the council's intention to commence enforcement proceedings at this time'. By contrast, its website says: 'We act decisively to halt and rectify unauthorised development.' Just days before taking office as Minister of State in charge of the Office of Public Works in June 2002, newly elected TD Tom Parlon posed for a photograph with Tom Standish, one of the company's directors, at its new staking plant – constructed, incidentally, without any notification to the Environmental Protection Agency. Parlon told Tim O'Brien of the *Irish Times* that the Standish family were 'very significant employers', having 'invested heavily in their enterprise over the past few years', and now ran a '24-hour, seven-day-a-week operation'. As far as he was concerned, they were 'a very good company' and he was not worried about his own farm, which is nearby, being polluted by the sawmill. At the end of February 2004 T&J Standish had accumulated profits of €720,000, with the two directors paying themselves €169, 000.

The EPA had just discovered that chromium VI, a carcinogenic used as a wood preservative, was polluting the Fuarawn river and a number of wells in the area, and attributed this potentially lethal contamination to T&J Standish. Five weeks later, the agency advised local residents to stop using water from 12 private wells; those affected by the EPA advice included Tom Parlon's mother. His response was to issue a statement describing the test results as 'a matter of serious concern'. In February 2003 tests carried out by the company's own consultants recorded the presence in local wells of polyaromatic hydrocarbons (PaHs) – 'carcinogenic and genotoxics of the kind which are monitored and regulated in urban air, vehicle and industrial emissions', as Tim O'Brien reported. In October 2000, the EPA secured a District Court conviction against the company, which was also successfully prosecuted the following year for polluting local ground and surface water. A further notice of non-compliance was served in January 2002 after the agency found 'treated product was still dripping treatment liquor when removed to stockpiles'. And when Tom Standish was convicted of damaging Leap Castle's outer defensive wall, he said the £100 fine represented a victory over 'those who wanted thousands'. He blamed a 'vendetta' by local people for the close interest the EPA was taking in his company, and also for the fact that it had to make a planning application to retain the sawmills; in his view, getting permission would be a simple formality. But Offaly County Council's decision to grant was appealed by the Aghancon Concerned Residents' Association and Friends of the Irish Environment. Some of those involved got Mass cards in the post containing handwritten messages, in block capitals, saying 'You will be fixed begrudger'. The company issued a statement denying it used 'subversive tactics to get our way'. When the objectors arrived for a Bord Pleanála oral hearing in Tullamore in May 2003, they had to run the gauntlet of a picket mounted by 50 sawmills workers; FIE's Peter Sweetman said he was 'spat at and jostled'. Whatever about the success of the business, the objectors' planning consultant Stephen Dowds told the hearing, it was being operated in 'complete flagrant disregard of the planning laws' at considerable nuisance to local people. The appeals board agreed, and in July 2003 overturned the council's decision, noting that 'no part of the existing development on the application site is authorised by way of planning permission'. The noise and general disturbance caused by the plant, particularly at night, would 'seriously injure the amenities of property in the vicinity' and 'seriously detract' from the setting of Leap Castle, a protected structure.

Following this adverse ruling, the company thumbed its nose at An Bord Pleanála by placing advertisements in local newspapers reassuring its staff and customers that it would remain in operation. And, indeed, four months later, the county council had still not taken enforcement action or even visited the site, as the *Irish Times* reported. The council's director of services, Jack Keyes, said the legal proceedings were 'complex', and officials weren't going to 'tie ourselves down' on when they would be served. He also acknowledged that they had held a number of pre-planning meetings with T&J Standish over the previous few months regarding a new application for retention of the sawmills. Then, just before Christmas 2003, the company again applied for permission to retain the facility, this time including a new low-level timber storage area and an extension to the sawmill itself. Before the county council had made a decision on the application, the EPA warned that the whole operation was in breach of its IPC licence – contrary to Standish's claim that it was in line with the agency's requirements. 'What do you have to do to win?' a spokesman for the local residents association commented to the *Irish Times*. 'This business failed in its application for retention, it has been successfully prosecuted by the EPA, and now we must face a planning battle all over again while the business continues.' Despairing of the county council taking effective action, local residents took their

↑ *Jim Mansfield, proprietor of Citywest Hotel and Leisure complex in Saggart, Co Dublin, and Weston Aerodrome*

own proceedings to force the illegal sawmills to close. But even though the Countess of Rosse was among the plaintiffs and their case seemed clear-cut, Judge Henry Abbott merely adjourned it in July 2004 while T&J Standish made another planning application to retain the unauthorised development. True to form, Offaly County Council again decided to grant permission, and the Aghancon Concerned Residents – with the support of historian Roy Foster – appealed for a second time to An Bord Pleanála. In October 2005 the board shocked everyone involved in the appeal by legitimising the entire operation – essentially on pragmatic grounds – in a decision that sent out the wrong message to those who flout the planning laws.

A lot of developers find the planning laws frustrating, but few flout them quite so flagrantly as Jim Mansfield, proprietor of the Citywest Hotel complex in Saggart, Co Dublin; much of it was built first and got planning permission later. Mansfield takes risks – it's what he does for a living. He made his first fortune by buying British war material from the Falklands and selling it on at a huge profit. He went on to develop the Clondalkin Mills shopping centre, and then built up his Citywest complex from nothing, turning it into the biggest money-spinning conference, leisure and golf resort in Dublin. When Fianna Fáil and Fine Gael book Citywest for ardfheiseanna, it doesn't seem to matter that much of it was built illegally. South Dublin County Council effectively turned a blind eye to unauthorised development by failing to take enforcement proceedings while the complex was under construction during the mid-1990s. Mansfield later retained the county manager, Frank Kavanagh, as his planning consultant within days of the Wexford-born official's retirement in January 2002. 'I never knew him when he was in the council, but when he retired I thought if I could get a hold of this fellow he'd know all the rules', said the man branded by one councillor as a 'rogue developer'. Mansfield is usually in a hurry to get things done. Whole bedroom blocks at Citywest were the subject of retention applications. 'There was a lot happening at the time', he told the *Irish Times* in November 2002. 'I would love to be able to put in for planning, but it could be a year before you get it.'

By the time Mansfield lodged plans for a new convention centre at Citywest in June 2003, the complex already included a sprawling hotel with more than 1,000 bedrooms, a leisure centre, two 18-hole golf courses and conference facilities with seating for 4,000. To this, he was proposing to add an enormous portal-frame building with capacity for almost 6,000 people – more than enough to accommodate the ardfheiseanna of the main political parties. HSS Ltd, Mansfield's company, actually started site development work in September 2003, two months before the county council issued its decision to grant permission. When the council became aware of this, it served an enforcement notice requiring the work to stop. But as soon as the planning decision was issued, Mansfield felt entitled to go ahead with building work because – as he explained to the *Irish Times* – even the council was 'reasonably happy that there couldn't be an appeal'. However, it is illegal to begin work until a period for appeals to An Bord Pleanála expires. Mansfield's bravado was based on the assumption that none of the statutory bodies which had made observations on the application – the National Roads Authority, the Dublin Transportation Office or the Heritage Service – would appeal. And when none of them did, he thought he was home and dry. What he didn't anticipate was that An Taisce would be able to lodge an appeal by invoking Article 28 of the Planning Regulations. As a prescribed body, the trust is entitled to receive copies of planning applications affecting amenities or historic buildings – in this case, an archaeological zone associated with the historic village of Saggart. The application by HSS was not referred to An Taisce by the county council, even though it clearly was referred to the Heritage Service and the NRA for their observations. The first An Taisce knew of the plan was through a report in the *Sunday Business Post*, in which Mansfield declared his intention to proceed on foot of the council's decision to grant permission. Abe Jacobs, the senior planning official who dealt with it, saw the same report and made contact with HSS the next

↓ The unauthorised portal frame structure of Mansfield's proposed convention centre at Citywest. He claimed: 'I would love to be able to put in for planning, but it could be a year before you get it.'

day, warning that it would begin work at its peril. The council followed this up by initiating legal action in the District Court for non-compliance with its enforcement notice. A High Court injunction could have been sought to stop the work in its tracks, but the council did not choose that route as it had just approved the scheme. After it became clear that An Taisce had appealed – and, moreover, that its appeal was accepted by An Bord Pleanála – the council got an undertaking from HSS that construction work would cease, pending the board's final determination.

Mansfield had already had his wings clipped by An Bord Pleanála. In December 2003 the board ruled out plans for a major expansion of Weston Aerodrome, which would have turned it into an 'executive airport' for business travellers. Now his gamble to steal a march on other prospective developers of the long-delayed National Conference Centre was at serious risk. If the appeals board ruled against his plans, he would face the grim prospect of having to demolish the partly built shed-like structure at Citywest. The bad news came in April 2004, when the board overturned South Dublin's decision and its own planning inspector's recommendation by a majority of seven to one. It did so on the basis that a convention centre of national or international importance should be located in Dublin city centre or other major town centre, rather than in an area remote from public transport and other complementary facilities. The second reason given by the board was that the proposed convention centre would contravene the open space and recreational amenity zoning of the site, and would, therefore, be contrary to proper planning and sustainable development. So what was the county council's response? Though Abe Jacobs conceded that the structure on the site was now an unauthorised development and said the council hoped it would be removed 'by agreement', it subsequently gave Mansfield an undertaking not to take any action pending the outcome of a High Court judicial review of its planning status, in proceedings taken by HSS. Furthermore, as Liam Reid reported in August 2004, the council's management proposed rezoning the site to facilitate completion of the unauthorised convention centre as 'a valuable addition to the tourist infrastructure of the county'. A spokesman denied that this amounted to 'back door' planning.

In the meantime, Mansfield had suffered another setback when An Bord Pleanála overturned his plans for a 290-bedroom hotel, 1,200-seat conference centre, 65 tourist apartments and a substantial business park at Palmerstown Demesne, in Co Kildare. Former estate of the earls of Mayo, its listed neo-classical mansion and 700 acres of land had been acquired by the developer in 1999 for £10 million (€12.7 million) with the intention of replicating the success of Citywest. But all the appeals board was prepared to permit was an 18-hole golf course, which had already been laid out, and a clubhouse. Mansfield's plans for Weston Aerodrome were also thwarted. After a protracted action in the High Court by South Dublin County Council, the developments his companies had carried out there after purchasing the property in 2002 for almost €13 million were deemed to be unauthorised. Local councillor Derek Keating (Ind) described Judge William McKechnie's July 2005 decision as a 'significant victory' for the community, which would send a 'clear message' to all developers. The court subsequently ordered that the unauthorised works – including hangars and an extended car park – must be removed, and gave the offending companies three months to get rid of them.

There was also the curious case of Marie and Joe Donnelly. The former chair of the Irish Museum of Modern Art and her wealthy bookmaker husband, a noted collector of contemporary art, got planning permission in 1994 to build an 'art gallery' within the grounds of Mount Eagle Lodge, on Vico Road, a site with panoramic views over Killiney Bay. At the time, it would have been nearly impossible to get permission for a house because of the restrictive zoning then being applied by Dún Laoghaire-Rathdown County Council to protect the scenic amenity of the coastal strip. U2's The Edge, for example, was refused permission for a substantial two-storey extension to his house on Vico Road because it would be visible from the sea. What the Donnellys got approval for was an art gallery and caretaker's flat in single-storey terrace form, 'having regard to the nature of the proposed development' and the 'significant tree cover on the site'. One of the planning conditions, which was confirmed by An Bord Pleanála after a third-party appeal, was that 'the gallery shall be open for viewing by appointment on at least 60 days per year'. Another condition specified that 'the residential use of the caretaker's apartment shall be solely ancillary to the use of the building as an art gallery' – even though, as was clear from the drawings, this 'apartment' is substantially larger than the 'gallery' itself.

The striking modern building by Claudio Silvestrin, a renowned Italian-born minimalist architect based in London, is simply described on his website as 'House D: Dublin'. The total floor area is given as 1,000m² (10,764 sq ft), roughly eight times the size of an average suburban house. But the breathtaking scale of the building, with 'expansive clear glass along the full front', stretching nearly 90 metres (297 feet), is partially concealed by the rich vegetation on the site. As for public access to the Donnelly 'gallery', Aidan Devon, of Glenageary, who has been pressing to have the planning conditions enforced, told the *Irish Times* in October 2003 that it was 'an absolute joke' because of the arbitrary restrictions being imposed. Responding to his complaint, a spokesman for the council said it had requested evidence on the issue of public access, but 'so far we haven't got the evidence required'. After a lot of to-ing and fro-ing, Devon managed to get in. He described the 'exhibition' as very limited. 'There are just four oil paintings, two drawings, a bronze sculpture and some "art" furniture in the "gallery" space – minimalist indeed.' He condemned the county council for its failure to enforce the planning conditions. 'This is a huge building that was cleared for planning specifically on the basis that it be an art gallery, not a private mansion', Devon said. Since it was completed in 2000, the council failed to inspect and confirm its proper use. 'They have thus allowed developers of substantial wealth and influence to abuse the planning laws', he declared. When contacted by the *Irish Times*, Ms Donnelly said: 'I have no comment to make.' Then she hung up. The county council's handling of the case was being investigated by the Ombudsman, Emily O'Reilly, at the time of writing. Meanwhile, anyone wishing to visit the exclusive 'gallery' should telephone the administrator, Penny Grey, at 01-6768200.

↑ *The Claudio Silvestrin-designed 'art gallery' built by Marie and Joe Donnelly in Killiney, Co Dublin, as seen from the sea*

More grievous, because it involved State authorities, was what happened at Shannon Airport. In March 2004 Ennis District Court heard that Aer Rianta was pumping untreated sewage into the Shannon estuary, a candidate SAC. The airport authority had simply ignored a planning condition requiring the installation of sewage treatment facilities in Clare County Council's 1998 permission for a new terminal. A report by the EPA in January 2003 found that the airport was pumping more than 100,000 cubic metres of raw sewage, much of it from visiting planes, into the estuary every year. Billy Leen, an independent Kerry county councillor, sought a High Court order to stop the discharges, but Aer Rianta claimed that his real agenda was to prevent US troops landing at Shannon on their way to Iraq. Although Clare County Council had served a warning notice ordering the company to comply with the planning conditions, the District Court case was actually taken by the Shannon Regional Fisheries Board. Judge Gerard Haughton regarded it as a very serious matter, but did not impose the maximum fine after being told that Aer Rianta had approached the council with a solution to the sewage problem six years earlier, only to be advised to await the local authority's own plans for an upgraded sewerage system. There was more: while a new planning application for a €2.25 million sewage treatment plant was under consideration in October 2003, Gordon Deegan reported that an unpublished Aer Rianta report from 1995 showed the company operating an illegal dump on Dernish Island, near the airport. It continued to dump waste – some of it hazardous – at the site for a further three years until the EPA told it to stop. An analysis showed 'unacceptably high' levels of arsenic, aluminium, iron and zinc; hazardous waste, including fluorescent tubes, paint and primer cans, was visible. There was also evidence that biological waste from aircraft had been doused in diesel oil and burned at the site. 'It is obvious that Aer Rianta was operating a private unlicensed dump at Shannon Airport for years and had a fly-by-night attitude towards waste disposal', Ian Lumley commented. But when the council decided to approve the new sewage plant, An Taisce lodged an appeal on the basis that it did not provide full biological, or tertiary, treatment. Asked by *Prime Time* to account for Clare County Council's failure to enforce the planning laws, its director of services, Ger Dollard, sought to minimise the problem by characterising the discharges as 'domestic' rather than 'industrial'. In fairness, Clare's planning enforcement record is not the worst. In 2003 the council issued 179 enforcement notices under Section 154 of the 2000 Planning Act, the fourth highest number in the State. Of these, 38 were complied with during the period, 19 prosecutions were initiated, and 13 convictions secured in the District Court. Many other councils were much more willing to turn a blind eye to breaches of the planning laws.

This was all of a piece with a conclusion reached in 2001 by the then Ombudsman Kevin Murphy that there was a 'marked reluctance' among local authorities to take action against errant developers. 'This increases public cynicism and the tendency to give credence to unfounded allegations of corruption and conflicts of interest on the part of public officials', he said. (Murphy's comments predated the findings of the Flood/Mahon tribunal showing some of these allegations to be true.) While the Ombudsman recognised that the planning departments of many councils are understaffed, he also cited a deeper reason – that the 'thrust of economic and political pressure is towards the completion of developments in as short a time-frame as possible'. In his final report as Ombudsman in April 2003, he again drew attention to the failure of local authorities to respond adequately to valid public complaints about abuses of the planning laws – although he attributed this to a lack of knowledge and resources, rather than indifference, official arrogance or bias in favour of developers. But the *Irish Times* said in an editorial that a 'pro-development mindset' among county and city managers must also be a factor. 'Builders and developers are frequently well-connected, powerful individuals within local communities, and there is little political or official appetite to hold them to account for their actions or omissions. The balance between a need for commercial development and compliance with planning regulations has been badly struck'. Even worse, as Murphy himself said two years earlier, 'the overall impression is one of a system which is in a state of collapse.'

onjectural extent of D-shaped town area

Waterford City

Area of current test excavation

↑ *Bird's-eye view of Woodstown, the internationally important Viking site near Waterford city, showing area of current test excavation and conjectural extent of D-shaped town area*

Sometime in 2003, Martin Cullen was told something that would put a great strain on the system – that a major Viking site had been discovered upriver of his home city of Waterford. He knew that *something* had been found at Woodstown, a beautiful, bucolic site on the southern bank of the River Suir. The problem lay in its location on the route of the N25 Waterford city bypass, for which the estimated cost almost doubled from €179 million to €300 million within four years. At first, the authorities thought they would get away with a minimalist approach to Woodstown, but this hope turned out to be misplaced as archaeologists came to realise that this was the site of a Viking *longphort* (ship fortress) established in the 9th century. 'We have always known about Viking activity in this area, and a site fitting this description on the banks of the Suir is well documented', Dr Mark Clinton told the *Irish Times* in May 2004, when the discovery at Woodstown was finally revealed. 'How, then, they decided to build the road right through the area is amazing.' He claimed that Martin Cullen had known about Woodstown for 10 months 'before news was leaked out by good people saying "do you know what we've got here?".' Yet this is the minister who is now saying give all the power for conservation to me.' Incredibly, the NRA denied any knowledge of the site before May 2004. Its head of corporate affairs, Michael Egan, said the Authority had fully complied with official guidelines

→ *Martin Cullen steering a bulldozer, with Alderman Tom Cunningham, Mayor of Waterford, after the Minister turned the sod for the city's bypass*

→ *Map showing the Waterford bypass and outer ring road, with the Woodstown Viking site at left*

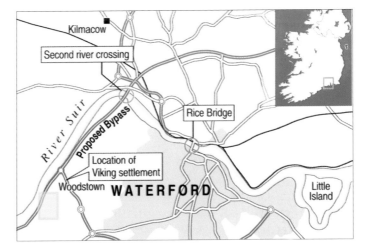

→ *Some of the finds from an exploratory archaeological excavation at Woodstown*

on archaeological protection in this case. At the time, a spokesman for Cullen said he was 'aware of the broad outline of the situation'.

Predating the foundation of Waterford, Woodstown was hailed by archaeologists as one of the most significant Viking sites to be discovered in Europe. It was the base from which raiding parties would have travelled up the Suir, Barrow and Nore – the dreaded 'Waterford fleet' referred to in annals of the time. Even work carried out under an exploratory licence recovered some 2,500 items, including Viking spears, swords, gaming pieces, weights and ships' nails. Numerous locks and keys were also found, suggesting to Dr Donnchadh Ó Corráin, professor of archaeology at UCC, that large numbers of slaves were kept there. Dr Pat Wallace, director of the National Museum, also made it clear that Woodstown would have to be fully excavated because it was 'a site of exceptional international importance'. But the museum had been consulted very late in the day, and it was not until May 2004 that Dr Wallace actually met senior heritage officials at the Department of the Environment. Martin Cullen visited the site for the first time in the run-up to a meeting of the EU Council of Environment Ministers in Waterford later that month, and was briefed on its significance by archaeologists. The Minister might have proudly shown Woodstown to his EU colleagues, especially those from Scandinavia. But there was 'not enough time' in their packed programme, which included a visit to the Waterford Glass factory and a leisurely lunch in sun-drenched Dunmore East. However, Cullen acknowledged that the site was of 'enormous importance internationally', and had already yielded some 'quite extraordinary' finds.

The key issue was whether there would be an extensive archaeological excavation – not one limited to the 'road take' alone. After Cullen indicated that an excavation of some kind would take place, An Taisce stressed that it 'must be carried out in a scientific manner, to the highest European standards'. Donnchadh Ó Corráin, who became prominent in the campaign to protect Woodstown, proposed that the National Museum should undertake the dig because it was 'the only truly independent institution of the State that is above reproach'. But everyone involved expressed disappointment that 'nine months of precious planning time have been frittered away', as An Taisce said, claiming that the NRA first became aware of the nature of the site in August 2003. Dr David Edwards, of Academy for Heritage, said it would be 'a much better use of public funds' to re-route the bypass than hold the project up for two or three years to allow for a proper excavation. 'Most of us own cars and drive, and we all want better roads. But we also want better planning. If we put our heads together there is no reason why we can't have both.' The NRA, however, was 'moving ahead with the tender process', its spokesman, Michael Egan, told the *Irish Times* in May 2004. 'I won't say we have crossed the Rubicon but we are in the final building stages.' And while the possibility of realigning the bypass was not ruled out, he said it would be 'difficult to come up with a viable alternative'.

The advice given to the NRA by its own archaeologists and engineering consultants was that the site could somehow be 'preserved' while it was covered over by the road, leaving it for future generations to explore in, say, a few hundred years time.

The risk with such a cover-up is that the archaeological layers would be compacted by pounding from decades of heavy traffic. Yet this 'solution' was backed by the Department of the Environment's chief archaeologist, Brian Duffy, on the basis that it would be the 'most cost-effective' option. Documents obtained by the *Irish Times* under the Freedom of Information Act show that Duffy continued to advocate this 'preservation in situ' approach, rather than a full-scale excavation, even after Woodstown was recognised as being of international importance. He cited engineering advice from consultants Mott McDonald, indicating that 'a design solution can be developed with archaeologists which can disperse loads so that the impact on the site [of building the road over it] is less than an individual standing in a field.'

Earlier, in September 2003, he had dismissed the view that Woodstown was a Viking *longphort* as a 'speculative notion of the site's nature, with absolutely no archaeological evidence to support it'. In this, Duffy was wrong. The discovery of the previously unknown site in March 2003 was kept under wraps for 13 months, and its significance was also downplayed in internal reports, which referred to it as 'Hiberno-Norse / Early Medieval'. But the archaeologists who were working on the site had no doubt that they had stumbled on something of enormous significance – a 'pre-urban' Viking site from the raiding period. As far as the National Museum was concerned, there was no question of covering it over. 'To "preserve" it in a potentially damaging way seems to fly in the face of science, archaeology and knowledge, not to mention being negative publicity for the Minister for the Environment in his own front yard when there is an opportunity to capitalise upon it both in scientific and PR terms', Dr Wallace told the Department of Arts, Sport and Tourism in April 2004. 'Only full-scale open excavation can reveal to us the true nature of the activities carried out on this site.' To him, Woodstown was so important that he was 'prepared to argue the case for the total and rapid excavation of this site in public or in private with the other State archaeologists, who for some inexplicable reason, seem to think it would be better covered over.' He warned that 'nobody can afford another Carrickmines situation, and in international terms this is a far more important site ...

↑ *Dr Pat Wallace, Director of the National Museum of Ireland. He said of Woodstown that only a full-scale archaeological excavation could reveal the true nature of the site.*

The so-called "preservation" route is entirely wrong in this instance. I have, anyway, a sincere doubt about the policy of "preserving" the site under the weight of thousands of tons of hardcore, gravel and other treatments', which even the consultant engineers had conceded would reduce its 'culture layer' by 35cm. What really mattered to Dr Wallace was the extent of the excavation – whether it should be confined to the 'road take', a strip of land some 40 metres wide, or be extended laterally in each direction.

Attention was initally focused on an area of marsh beside the Suir, on the lower part of the site. If Viking ship timbers were discovered there, it would add greatly to the sum of archaeological knowledge about what a *longphort* was really like. In the summer of 2004, this area was being explored through test-trenching, boreholes and a geophysical survey. Given that the only other Viking *longphort* sites discovered so far have all been in Russia, Woodstown is of European significance because it 'must have a great deal to tell the Scandinavians themselves about the nature of transplanting urban and other settlement forms, building types, craft pursuits and other occupations in their 9th-century westward expansion', according to Dr Wallace. One of the interesting conundrums to be explored is why Woodstown didn't become Waterford. 'Excavation rather than "preservation" of the site will throw light on the probable different nature of the two settlements ... and on why this settlement at Woodstown was established in the first place', Dr Wallace wrote. There would be real economic benefits, too. 'Full excavation would also allow the development of a major cultural attraction in Waterford which would place it firmly on the map in terms of Viking and Early Medieval archaeology.' The National Museum's director was holding out the prospect of giving Waterford a visitor draw that would put it firmly on the European map.

After the initial media reports in May 2004, the NRA warned that 'any departure from the approved strategy to preserve the Woodstown site in situ [would have] implications for the delivery of the Waterford city bypass.' In a letter to the National Monuments section of the Department of the Environment, Michael Egan said the 'apparent absence of consensus' on how to deal with it raised 'significant risks', especially as the bypass was a public-private partnership (PPP) project. The statutory Heritage Council, in its submission to the Department, argued against rolling over the site, saying there were 'compelling reasons' for a full archaeological excavation to examine the role of the Vikings in urbanising Ireland. But the Department was still committed to 'preservation in situ'. Officials were told by Dave Fadden, then principal officer in the National Monuments Section, to 'trawl through the library to see if [they] can find anything' from abroad to support this approach. Even after the discovery of a Viking warrior grave with a battleaxe, sword and shield boss, Brian Duffy continued to advocate rolling over the site. His stance caused consternation at a meeting of the Heritage Council in early June 2004, so much so that the Department's observer, Liam O'Connell, was 'taken by surprise by the ferocity of the reaction'. But he saw this as 'a good thing' because it 'accelerated openness on a simmering major controversy whose time to be outed had well and truly arrived'.

↑ *Environmentalist David Cabot at Pollardstown Fen. The Government was berated by Europe for approving the Kildare bypass without studying the environmental impact on the fen.*

A determined campaign by the Save Viking Waterford Action Group helped to turn the tide, and eventually the NRA relented. The Authority calculated that 'looping' the proposed bypass around the highly sensitive site would be both cheaper and faster; one of the main factors was that the cost of an archaeological excavation had been put at €10 million. In January 2005 the NRA decided to re-route the road, clearing the way for environment minister Dick Roche to exercise his discretion under the 2004 National Monuments (Amendment) Act to make a preservation order, which he finally did on 11th May 2005. This followed a revised recommendation by Brian Duffy that the Minister should issue 'directions' under the Act to 'secure the site and ensure its preservation pending the formulation of a long-term strategy for the National Monument' at Woodstown by an expert group. Apart from the overwhelming evidence of its importance, the only factor cited by the chief archaeologist for his change of tune was that the NRA had identified an alternative route for the bypass and indicated that this was now the Authority's 'preferred option'.

As for Carrickmines Castle, the fate of its unearthed outer defences had been sealed in August 2004 when Martin Cullen – using the same powers under the National Monuments (Amendment) Act – signed an order clearing the way for work to resume on this section of the M50/South Eastern Motorway. Commenting on

Cullen's decision, Kealin Ireland, a Green Party councillor in Dún Laoghaire-Rathdown, said the Minister 'should have identified many years ago the existence of this important archaeological site and moved the route of the motorway. Instead, he delayed making this fundamental decision, and the public and our heritage have suffered unnecessarily.' After work resumed on the site, Ciarán Cuffe TD was appalled to witness heavy earth-moving equipment being used to remove sections of the medieval fosse. Hundreds of years of history were being 'wiped away with every scoop of the JCB bucket', something he characterised as 'barbaric'.

So how did Cullen's action, and the entire handling of the Carrickmines saga, square with the overriding objective of the National Heritage Plan 'to protect and promote appreciation of the built and natural heritage and to promote their enjoyment by all'? Like so many of his other actions as Minister, it just made the fine words in the heritage section of his own Department's website ring hollow. 'Ireland is endowed with a rich heritage. That heritage is inextricably linked with our sense of identity, and affirms our historic, cultural and natural inheritance. For present and future generations, that inheritance has the ability to enhance and enrich the context of everyday existence. Heritage in all its manifestations is one of our key assets and is, therefore, deserving of the highest levels of protection and management thus securing its future for coming generations.' These statements exist only in cyberspace. Inevitably, there was a last-minute court challenge to forestall the bulldozers at Carrickmines. Dominic Dunne, plaintiff in the earlier proceedings, claimed that Section 8 of the 2004 National Monuments (Amendment) Act was unconstitutional. When the case came before the High Court in August 2004, Rory O'Sullivan, project engineer for the South Eastern Motorway, claimed that further delays would cost €350,000 per week. The action failed and work resumed on the road on the morning after the judgment was delivered by Ms Justice Laffoy. But Vincent Salafia took some comfort from her finding that there was a 'constitutional imperative' to safeguard national assets, including 'monuments of cultural and historical significance', and he believed this opened the door to a full constitutional challenge to the 2004 legislation. Unusually for a losing plaintiff, Dunne was awarded costs; the judge said the issues he had raised were 'truly of general public importance'.

It wasn't as if the Government didn't know about the dangers of proceeding with major road schemes without first taking their impact into account. Back in February 2001, the European Commission officially berated the Irish authorities for approving the Kildare bypass without studying its effect on nearby Pollardstown Fen, a protected habitat, and the regionally important Curragh aquifer, one of the largest groundwater sources in Ireland. Its natural springs feed the summit of the Grand Canal at Lowtown, as well as providing pure water for Guinness at its St James's Gate Brewery in Dublin. The minister responsible for this 1996 blunder was Labour's Brendan Howlin. Even Dúchas recommended that the bypass should not go ahead as planned. An assessment by the Office of Public Works concluded that the EIS was 'unreliable' in its predictions about the impact on Pollardstown Fen, and recommended that plans be put on hold pending more detailed groundwater, geotechnical and ecological investigations. In April 1999 the Taoiseach himself simplistically suggested that the project had been held up for years by a snail. There was a snail involved alright, *Vertigo angustior*, but the real issue revolved around the danger of draining the Curragh aquifer, something that would cause a drop in water levels in Pollardstown Fen. For a distance of 3km, the Kildare bypass runs in a cutting through the aquifer up to six metres deep – a measure taken to reduce its impact on the National Stud. It was estimated that five million gallons of water would have to be pumped out each day to keep this cutting dry – many times the threshold at which an EIS would be required for a public water supply. A hydrological scheme on this scale had never been attempted in Ireland, and the OPW warned that experience elsewhere suggested it would be expensive and fraught with technical difficulties. At the public inquiry into the bypass scheme in 1993, Kildare County Council's then senior planner, Philip Jones, also expressed concern that the cutting could 'seriously affect' Pollardstown Fen. If the only reason for it was to protect the amenities of the National Stud, it was his view that this should be weighed against the need to protect the aquifer and fen. 'In this regard, it can be stated that the Curragh and the Fen – both of which are unique and cannot be replicated – must be regarded as of much greater importance than the stud, which is man-made and could be relocated', Jones said. But that would have required a radical redesign, something his road engineering colleagues would not contemplate. Nonetheless, the Department of the Environment inspectors conducting the inquiry recommended that the county council should 'immediately design and implement' a groundwater monitoring programme, with 'particular attention being paid to Pollardstown Fen'. However, when An Taisce made a complaint to Brussels in 1998 over Ireland's failure to implement the Habitats Directive, it was accused of holding up a vital piece of infrastructure. The European Commission got involved because the fen was designated as an SAC under the Habitats Directive, and the Commission was also aware that there wasn't another fen in Ireland of comparable importance. Ultimately, it accepted An Taisce's view that precious resources had been placed in peril, and the result, as Judith Crosbie reported, was yet another public reprimand for Ireland. There was also a cost overrun of €20 million due to the half-baked approach to hydrology.

Less than 18 months after the bypass opened in late 2003, the critics were proved right and the engineers wrong. The construction of the road in a cutting had resulted in a partial draining of the aquifer, causing 'serious ecological risk to critical fen habitats', according to Terrascope environmental consultants, as Michael Viney noted in his *Irish Times* column. In the long term it would have been much cheaper to re-route the bypass further south, something all those championing the flawed plan were not prepared to consider. And all the Taoiseach could do was to trivialise the issue.

———

6. Kyoto and Waste

HAILSTONES THE SIZE OF GRAPEFRUITS KILL PEOPLE ON THE STREETS OF TOKYO, TORNAdos rip through Los Angeles, and New York city is engulfed by a massive tidal wave. These are among the cataclysmic events dramatised by *The Day After Tomorrow*, Hollywood's take on global warming. If climate change is going to mean more 'extreme weather events', it couldn't get more extreme than this. A background news broadcast reports that Europe is blanketed by 15ft of snow and Dublin is among the cities being evacuated. The film's scenario – that climate change could happen in weeks rather than decades – is so wildly improbable that it may be dismissed as just another disaster movie. It is based on the notion that warm ocean currents – including the Gulf Stream, which gives us our temperate climate – will be diverted south by melting polar ice-caps, plunging the Northern Hemisphere into a new Ice Age 'just like that'. Go outside and you freeze to death – instantly. By telescoping the timescale, the 2004 film pretends that climate change will happen in weeks. In reality, it will occur over decades.

Environmentalists seized on *The Day After Tomorrow* to drive home the message they've been spelling out for years – that action must be taken. 'The film is fiction, but climate change is real and humans are causing it', said Will St Leger, spokesman for the Stop Esso campaign in Ireland. The amount of ignorance about global warming is startling. An opinion poll commissioned by the London-based Carbon Trust, which works to cut carbon dioxide (CO_2) emissions, found that nearly a third of adults in Britain wrongly believe climate change is reversible. Another third see its threat as minor or non-existent, while a fifth are so confused that they blame plants for causing it. Missions to space, second-hand tobacco smoke, meteors and genetically modified organisms were also wrongly thought to cause climate change. And of the three in 10 who believe that global warming can be reversed, many were just hoping that 'Mother Nature will somehow sort herself out'.

Among experts there is little certainty about the pace and scale of change. 'It

→ *Energy from fresh air: new wind turbines on the Arklow Banks, off the coast of Co Wicklow*

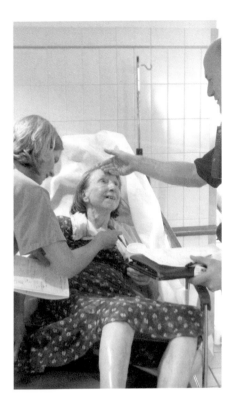

↑ *An elderly woman is treated in hospital in Paris during the August 2003 heatwave when 10,000 people died in France*

is likely that some aspects and impacts ... will be totally unanticipated as complex systems respond to ongoing climate change in unforeseeable ways', according to a comprehensive assessment in 2000 by the US Global Change Research Programme. Another report commissioned by the US Department of Defence – intended to be secret but leaked to *Fortune* magazine – suggested that imminent catastrophic climate change is 'plausible and would challenge United States national security in ways that should be considered immediately'. Average temperatures in Europe and North America would fall, creating a 'Siberian' climate for all of us, while some major cities would be submerged by rising sea levels, the Pentagon was told. As early as 2005, the report warned, widespread flooding caused by a rise in sea levels would create major upheaval for millions. By 2020, 'catastrophic' shortages of water and energy supplies will become increasingly difficult to overcome, leading to the outbreak of 'resource wars' on an already over-populated planet. 'Disruption and conflict will be endemic features ... Warfare may again come to define human life.' As the report gloomily put it: 'History shows that whenever humans have faced a choice between starving or raiding, they raid. So we must assume that, after the great climate change, an ancient pattern re-emerges: the eruption of desperate, all-out wars over food, water and energy supplies.' One of the authors, Doug Randall, called climate change a unique national security threat 'because there is no enemy to point your guns at'. Prof Bob Watson, chief scientist for the World Bank and former chairman of the UN Intergovernmental Panel on Climate Change, said the report could not be ignored by a US president who had made national security his single highest priority. And, as Watson told the *Observer*, the Pentagon 'is no wacko liberal group'.

The US is the biggest emitter of greenhouse gases, accounting for 24% of the global total – six times more than its share of the world's population. But in 2001 the Bush administration pulled out of the Kyoto Protocol on Climate Change, insisting that cuts would damage the US economy. This position has been strongly criticised by, among many others, Sir David King, chief scientific adviser to the British government. Writing in the journal *Science*, he said President Bush was wrong to discount the reality of climate change, which he believed was 'more serious even than the threat of terrorism'. Enumerating the evidence, Sir David noted that the 1990s was the hottest decade on record: ice-caps are melting, sea levels rising and flooding has become more frequent. In the 1980s, the Thames barrier was used once a year to protect London, but the early years of this decade have seen it used more than six times a year. During the summer of 2003, an estimated 20,000 Europeans died in a suffocating heatwave – 10,000 in France alone. 'As a consequence of continued warming', the British scientist said, 'millions more people around the world may in future be exposed to the risk of hunger, drought, flooding and debilitating diseases'. A major study commissioned by the UN Environment Programme warned in January 2004 that more than a million species will become extinct over the next 50 years due to dramatic changes in their habitats as a result of global warming – unless we begin reducing our greenhouse gas emissions, particularly carbon dioxide.

There has been close to a 40% increase in the concentration of CO_2 in the atmosphere over the last 200 years, mainly due to burning fossil fuels. The trouble with CO_2 is that it accumulates; no feasible way has been found to let it escape or render it harmless. In the 1990s, the level of CO_2 in the atmosphere had reached 360 parts per million (ppm). By 2004 it stood at 379ppm, and current trends see it increasing at the rate of three ppm a year, as Paul Brown reported in July 2004. The result is an ever-warmer planet and more unpredictable weather generally. Global average temperatures are now rising faster than at any time since the end of the last Ice Age, 10,000 years ago. In mid-latitude areas such as Europe and the US, a rise of one degree Celsius is equivalent to relocating 500km further south. One of the great imponderables is the speed at which the giant glaciers of Greenland and the Antarctic will break up as temperatures rise. With most of the world's fresh water trapped in these glaciers, their disintegration would add significantly to sea levels. Elsewhere, the effects of global warming are already being felt. Some Alpine resorts are wary of investing in a new set of ski-lifts because the glaciers on which they depend are visibly receding year by year. And the retreat of these glaciers sends more water into Europe's rivers and, ultimately, the oceans.

Sir David King has no doubt that climate change is 'the biggest problem civilisation has had to face in 5,000 years ... We are moving from a warm period into the first hot period that man has ever experienced since he walked on the planet ... Delaying action for decades, or even just years, is not a serious option. I am firmly convinced that if we do not begin now, more substantial, more disruptive and more expensive change will be needed later on.' A rise in sea levels of just 50cm would inundate low-lying coastal areas in Bangladesh, Egypt and the coral reef islands of the Pacific, such as Fiji. Other idyllic holiday islands in the Indian Ocean, notably the Maldives, could be wiped off the map. In Egypt, a one-metre rise in sea levels would result in the loss of at least 10% of its productive land, with up to 10 million people losing their homes. Even as it is, some 40 million people in the world are flooded every year as a result of storms – a figure set to treble over the next century, according to insurance industry projections.

↑ *A queue forms for food after serious flooding in Bangladesh. Egypt and the coral reef islands of the Pacific, such as Fiji, are also threatened by rising sea levels as a result of climate change.*
↓ *Hollywood film,* The Day After Tomorrow, *features a tidal wave engulfing New York city*

↑ *An Taoiseach, Bertie Ahern, standing up to his coat tails in water after floods hit Drumcondra in November 2002*
↓ *A collapsed road in Kilgarvan, Co Kerry, following flash floods in July 2004*

Although Sir David was upbraided by Downing Street for being so candid about the Bush administration's refusal to face up to the facts, Tony Blair himself has described climate change as 'the single most important long-term issue that we face as a global community', and pledged to cut Britain's greenhouse gas emissions by 60% before 2050. He also planned to put climate change at the heart of his 2005 chairmanship of the G8. As early as 1996, John Gummer, Environment Secretary in John Major's Conservative government, declared that action needed to be taken now 'not tomorrow, but now'. Within the lifetime of today's children 'the climate will change to a degree which will utterly alter the basis of their lives', he said. The world's leading insurance companies have been calling on governments to cut greenhouse gas emissions since 1995. In November 2000 the industry's leading expert on global warming said the bill for property damage caused by storms, floods and other natural disasters was rising exponentially by 10% per annum. Andrew Dlugolecki, Scottish-born director of CGNU, one of the world's six largest insurance groups, warned that if this rate of increase was sustained, it could bankrupt the world economy by 2065. The UN Environment Programmes's Finance Initiatives group reported in October 2002 that losses occasioned by natural disasters were doubling every decade. The group, which includes 295 banks, insurance and investment companies, found that such losses amounted to €1,000 billion in the previous 15 years, and forecast that the economic cost would reach €150 billion a year by 2012 if current trends continued. While most of these losses would not be insured, the industry would incur annual claims of €30 to €40 billion – equivalent to one World Trade Centre attack every year. As Dick Ahlstrom noted, the massive economic losses stemming from flooding in central Europe in summer 2002 were typical of the events predicted by climate change modelling, as was the near-total failure of the Indian monsoon season in the same year. March 2004 saw the world's second largest reinsurer warn that the cost of weather-related natural disasters could spiral out of control, plunging the human race into a catastrophe of its own making. 'There is a danger that human intervention will accelerate and intensify natural climate changes to such a point that it will become impossible to adapt our socio-economic systems in time', according to Swiss Re. Because when climate change really begins to kick in, 'it will happen at a frightening pace', Andrew Dlugolecki told the *Irish Times*. Asked whether the industry would continue insuring property in high-risk areas, he said that it would, once other measures were taken, such as improving flood defences. But even where additional measures were taken, there would be changes in cover and higher premiums.

No more than any other nation, Ireland cannot escape some of the unpleasant consequences of climate change. There has already been some very freakish weather. In June 2004, for example, just 3.3 millimetres of rain fell in the Kilkenny area, 30 times less than the 101 millimetres recorded for the same month a year earlier. After one huge downpour in August 2004, a flash flood caused a landslide that engulfed a mile-long section of the road between Bantry, Co Cork, and Kilgarvan, Co Kerry. Around the same time, Ireland's cereal farmers were told by tillage experts to 'smash and grab' what they could as soon as possible, otherwise they risked losing the best grain harvest on record to bad weather, Seán MacConnell reported. And who can forget that photograph of a forlorn Bertie Ahern, standing up to his coat tails in water after the Tolka burst its banks in November 2002? Mark Twain once observed: 'Everybody talks about the weather, but nobody does anything about it.' Not everyone is just talking, however. Dr John Sweeney, lecturer in geography at NUI Maynooth, is co-author of two seminal studies for the Environmental Protection Agency on what might be in store. His second report, *Climate Change: Indicators for Ireland*, published in November 2002, fell prey to media sensationalism. The likelihood of increased flooding in parts of Dublin, Cork and Clonmel was highlighted, with speculation on what this would mean for the property values of these areas. Reactions from residents became the big story, with little attention on what needs to be done. As well as the threat of more flooding, climate change brings a greater risk of water shortages due to reduced rainfall during the summer. A water crisis in Dublin is not far off; indeed, the City Council started a preliminary feasibility study in 2004 on piping water from the Shannon to Dublin. Sweeney queried the sheer cost of building facilities to pump and store water, pointing to the enormous expense of operating and maintaining water supply lines in more arid places like California and Spain. With water availability set to be stretched throughout Leinster, he believes that developing Ireland's other cities would 'make a lot more sense'. If population growth in the east continues unchecked, the demand for water in the capital will be 'unable to be met in the medium term'. Also, work that local authorities should be undertaking is not being done because of complacency. For example, some sea defences built to protect our cities in the 1800s haven't even been assessed in 60 or 70 years, never mind strengthened. Judgment calls need to be made: coastal golf courses aren't worth protecting, cities are. According to Sweeney, we need to 'start thinking about the precautionary heights necessary for floor levels' in new buildings – designing basements and ground floors mindful that they may become flooded once every 20 or 30 years. Depending on the pace of climate change, what is now a one-in-200-year 'extreme weather event' may occur once every 35 years, or even less. A lot hinges on variables such as the resilience of polar ice caps in a warmer climate, and the extent of global action taken to arrest global warming. Sweeney advises against reclaiming more land from the sea, putting new buildings within 50 metres of a coast subject to erosion, and extracting sand from estuaries or the seabed. These may seem like simple precautionary measures, but they are so often ignored. The EPA's director-general, Dr Mary Kelly, put it starkly: 'Decisions about what crops to grow, what landscapes to protect, where to build transport corridors in coastal zones, and, perhaps most importantly of all, where to build new residential areas urgently require to be "climate change-proofed".' According to her, Ireland was 'facing the most severe test yet of its resolve to deal with environmental issues'. Even Martin Cullen described the EPA's assessment of the risks posed by climate change as 'credible and worrying'. And he went on to make what is surely the central point in dealing with the problem – that our emissions of greenhouse gases are 'simply unsustainable'.

Viewed in overall terms, Ireland's cities are not anywhere near as vulnerable as major population centres such as London. Even apart from rising sea levels, the British capital is subsiding, and, according to Sweeney, has undertaken some ill-advised development east of the city along the Thames. The storm surge faced by London also comes from the North Sea, which is much more potent than what Dublin has to contend with from the Irish Sea. Cork and Limerick are also located some distance from Atlantic swells, while Galway and Sligo are sheltered from its full force. But with rising sea levels, how wise is it to develop in coastal cities in the first place – be they on the east coast or the west? Sweeney points out that in recent years all of Ireland's cities have developed to varying extents towards the sea. But he doesn't view building in remote or upland areas as an alternative because of the issues this would pose in terms of sustainable development. Cities are easier to serve with every-day facilities – drinking water being a prime example – so provided the precautions are observed, we should continue to develop them. With vital resources at stake, trade-offs are inevitable. Across the south and east of Ireland, competition for water will become acute, while lack of rainfall will retard grass growth. As a result, the pro-file of crops grown in these areas is set to change, with Sweeney predicting that farm-ers will turn to maize and sweetcorn – crops that require less rain during the summer months. At the same time, winters will be wetter, particularly in the west, where more rainfall is projected over the coming years, again with significant consequences for agriculture. Low-lying land will be waterlogged for longer in winter but will then dry out more in summer. Throughout the countryside, fields and hedgerows will take on a different complexion as our flora and fauna changes. Farmers may be unable to put cattle out as early as they now do, something that will pose challenges for farm man-agement. Towns prone to flooding, such as Clonmel and Kilkenny, have been carry-ing out flood relief schemes. The Kilkenny scheme has turned part of the River Nore into a stone-faced concrete channel at a staggering cost of €48 million. This was nearly four times the original estimate in 1998, and even at that, a 'design error' by the Office of Public Works and its engineering consultants led to the wrong type of fish-pass being installed to allow salmon to swim upriver. According to one well-placed source, no more than 30 houses are set to be 'saved' by these works – over €1 million per house. With calls for more and more flood defences, the Kilkenny project is an early example of appalling cost-benefit analysis.

Climate change is much more complex than any other environmental problem we have faced. It cannot be solved by a simple technical fix, like banning fluorocar-bons in an effort to save the ozone layer. The industrialised world, particularly the US, is addicted to oil and other fossil fuels. Cutting energy consumption – and the green-house gases it generates – is not something most countries are prepared to do, because it means making sacrifices. But under an EU burden-sharing agreement struck in Luxembourg in June 1998 to implement the Kyoto Protocol, Ireland is required to limit its increase of greenhouse gas emissions to 13% on top of their 1990 levels in the period 2008-12. Six months before this ambitious target was agreed by Noel Dempsey, then Minister for the Environment, the ESRI warned that emissions would be 28% higher because of strong economic growth. Without changes in government policy, it forecast that CO_2 emissions from traffic would rise by 115% on 1990 levels to 10.5 million tonnes in 2010, while emissions from electricity generating stations would increase by 74% to 18.5 million tonnes. According to the ESRI report, *The Cost to Ireland of Greenhouse Gas Abatement*, cutting back on emissions without slowing down economic growth would involve spreading the burden over all sectors of the economy. It also proposed levying a 'greenhouse gas tax' on all polluters, preferably on an EU-wide basis. The report recommended a 5% across-the-board increase in energy prices, including electricity charges, to meet EU targets for curtailing emissions. Authors John FitzGerald and Sue Scott estimated that new carbon taxes would cost the average Irish household €247 a year and raise more than €860 million in revenue. But in this and later reports, the ESRI emphasised that the new levy would be matched by reductions in income tax, with exemptions for the less well off. Dealing with traffic, now the fastest-growing sector, the institute advocated 'greatly increased' investment in public transport, especially in urban areas. But it said this would need to be matched by some form of road pricing.

The Government's National Climate Change Strategy, published in October 2000, set out what Noel Dempsey called 'a radical blueprint for decoupling economic growth from the growth in greenhouse gas emissions'. Under the programme, carbon taxes designed to achieve emission reductions were to be phased in, and environmentally perverse subsidies such as cheaper electricity for large industrial users were to go. The strategy noted that Ireland needs to achieve a reduction of 13 million tonnes in CO_2 emissions to meet its Kyoto target, and recognised that the burden of achieving this, and the much more ambitious targets likely to be set for the years after 2012, must be borne equitably across all sectors. It also included a commitment to promote sustainable development and maximise economic efficiency, with a preference for the use of 'no regret' and least-cost measures. Apart from the introduction of 'appropriate tax measures' aimed at curbing CO_2 emissions, it said Ireland would also participate in the pilot EU trading scheme beginning in January 2005. In the industrial, commercial and services sectors, the emphasis was to be on market instruments, such as emissions-trading, targeted taxation and 'negotiated agreements'. Firms that agreed to reduce their emissions were to get tax benefits.

To reduce emissions from agriculture, which accounted for 35% of Ireland's output of greenhouse gases in 1990 – much higher than the European average – the strategy called for a cut in methane emissions from the national cattle herd 'equivalent to a reduction in livestock numbers by 10% below 2010 projected levels'. The use of fertilisers was also to be reduced by 10% below expected 2010 levels, and best practice guidelines were to be developed to change farming practices. The strategy also called for a stronger relationship between agriculture and forestry policy under the Rural Environmental Protection Scheme, known as REPS. Given the value of trees as CO_2 'sinks', a more intensive afforestation programme was envisaged to maximise their carbon sequestration potential. In the late 1990s, Irish forests were expanding so fast that they would 'prove to be one of the key ways to lock up more carbon dioxide and so help Ireland meet its targets for controlling greenhouse gases', according to

Kevin O'Sullivan, of the *Irish Times*. Writing in June 2000, he quoted Dr Eugene Hendrick of Coford, the national council for forestry research, as saying that a tree could absorb more than 9kg of CO_2, 'equal to that produced by a car travelling non-stop for 18,300km'. According to Prof Jack Gardiner of UCD, Irish forests have the potential to consume 30% of our surplus greenhouse gas emissions. The Rainbow Government realised the value of trees, and in its 1996 *Strategic Plan for the Development of the Forestry Sector in Ireland: Growing for the Future* it pledged to plant 25,000 hectares of new forests every year for the first five years, and 20,000 a year thereafter to 2035. But in 2003, an industry-funded report by Peter Bacon & Associates found that planting in the period 1996-2002 had fallen short of the targets by 34%, and calculated that there would be a shortfall of 300,000 hectares over the period of the strategic plan, based on current planting rates. Estimates in 2000 showed 9% of the country covered in forest, some 60% of it owned and managed by Coillte Teoranta, the State forestry company. But despite some increase in the planting of traditional broadleaves, fast-growing conifers such as Sitka spruce remained the principal type of tree being planted, accounting for just under 85% of new planting in the period 1997-2002.

The strategy also set out definite measures for other sectors of the economy. In transport, where emissions were expected to rise by 180% in the 2000-10 period largely due to dramatic increases in car numbers, the climate change strategy proposed 'rebalancing' Vehicle Registration Tax to favour more fuel-efficient vehicles. Other proposals included fuel economy labelling for all new cars, the purchase of less polluting vehicles for public transport, and the possibility of raising fuel taxes to cut consumption. (It had nothing to say about the fact that flying is the most detrimental form of travel in terms of aggravating global warming. It emits 'almost seven times more carbon dioxide per person than taking a train, and some three times more than driving', wrote Iva Pocock in the *Irish Times*. Yet aviation fuel everywhere remains untaxed.) In the construction sector, the Building Regulations were also to be amended to reduce energy use in new housing by up to 40%, while an energy rating system was to be introduced for pre-existing homes. Measures in the waste management sector were to include a requirement that all waste generators – including households – would have to pay the full cost of waste collection, treatment and disposal, though the strategy was suitably vague about incineration. In the energy sector, it called for a switch to 'less carbon intensive fuels' for power generation and throughout industry. This would involve the use of more CHP (combined heat and power) plants, where energy efficiency of up to 80% can be achieved, as well as an expansion in the use of renewable sources such as wind. The options of closing down the ESB's coal-burning power station at Moneypoint on the Shannon Estuary or converting it to run on natural gas were also mooted. An Taisce had described the 900-megawatt station, which supplies around 20% of the State's electricity, as 'the single most problematic greenhouse gas and acid-rain-producing stack in Ireland'. As the largest individual contributor to Ireland's greenhouse gas emissions, accounting for more than five million tonnes a year, Moneypoint was also identified as the biggest 'single hit' in reducing emissions. 'Replacing it with a combined cycle gas-fired plant would yield the largest emission reduction and potentially could be achieved at a negative cost, i.e. it would be a profitable investment at current fuel prices', a report commissioned by the Department of the Environment and the Department of Enterprise and Employment found in May 1998. Compiled by Oxford-based consultants Environmental Resources Management, in association with Byrne Ó Cléirigh and the ESRI, it also identified phasing out the use of peat for power generation as a 'no cost' option. However, this didn't prevent An Bord Pleanála granting permission in December 1998 for what amounts to the biggest CO_2 factory yet built in the midlands. The 120-megawatt Europeat-1 plant near Edenderry, Co Offaly, had been held up for a number of years because the European Commission was concerned about its environmental implications – particularly the fact that it would emit 634,000 tonnes of CO_2 a year. The Commission eventually agreed it could go ahead after reaching an understanding with the Irish authorities that older, less efficient peat-fired power stations such as Portarlington and Ferbane would be closed down. Not that the ESB's new 'state-of-the-art' peat plants are much better. Compared to a new gas-fired power station, electricity is 27% more expensive to generate at Lanesboro, Co Longford, and 50% dearer at Shannonbridge, Co Offaly, according to business analyst Charlie Weston. Writing in the *Irish Independent* in August 2005, he calculated that each job in the new peat plants is subsidised to the tune of €500,000 a year. If regional employment was the key issue, as he observed, then the scale of this subsidy 'would go a long way to creating sustainable and environmentally friendly jobs in the Midlands'. Weston also noted that the peat station at Edenderry – run by British energy company Powergen – doesn't get a subsidy, and, in contrast to the ESB plants, it was licensed to burn bonemeal and woodchippings, something that would cut CO_2 emissions.

At Moneypoint, the issue of fuel security raised its head. If the station was converted to run on natural gas, 80% of the State's generating capacity would then be gas-fuelled and 'we could be held to ransom over gas supplies', as Dempsey said at the time. (Europe's natural gas now comes mainly from Russia and Algeria.) In the end, the fuel security argument won out. And so, the ESB's €250 million upgrade of Moneypoint is limited to reducing sulphur dioxide emissions by 80% and nitrous oxide emissions by 50% in 2008, as required by the terms of its licence from the Environmental Protection Agency. The station's then manager, Paul Mulvaney, told the *Irish Times* that fuel security and diversity of supply were critical factors. 'We're already heavily reliant on natural gas, so it makes sense to keep Moneypoint because we can store a million tonnes of coal on-site, which is a six-month supply.' The ESB had also made 'an economic decision', as there was 'no known commercially viable technology to reduce CO_2 emissions' from coal-fired power stations. In any case, Moneypoint is designed to burn coal, and it 'does that efficiently', Mulvaney said. The fact that it emits five million tonnes of CO_2 was 'a global issue, not a local issue' which needed to be looked at in the context of flexibility in complying with the Kyoto Protocol. So too was the fact that the clean-up technology being installed would actu-

↑ *Moneypoint, on the Shannon Estuary, where the ESB's huge coal-fired power station is allowed to belch out five million tonnes of carbon dioxide every year for the next twenty years*

ally add a further 126,000 tonnes to its CO_2 emissions. Prof John FitzGerald of the ESRI agreed it was 'probably sensible' to keep burning coal at Moneypoint if the price of CO_2 was fixed at €20 per tonne under the EU carbon trading regime – though this would change if it rose to €40. He argued that shutting down peat-fired power plants, which emit more CO_2 per tonne of fuel burned, should have a higher priority, as well as expanding wind power and building more gas-fired plants to back it up when the wind is low. Moneypoint is also worth €10 million a year to Clare County Council, or 42% of its total revenue from commercial rates. In August 2004, having secured Government approval, the ESB awarded the €250 million 'clean-up' contract to a German company, thereby ensuring the station's future until 2025. It also decided to proceed with a nine-turbine wind farm on the site. But this is small potatoes in the context of two more decades of prodigious CO_2 emissions from Moneypoint.

An official review of Ireland's environmental performance, published in the run-up to the 2002 UN World Summit on Sustainable Development, sought to suggest that many of the measures proposed in the climate change strategy were already being implemented. But the EPA reported that our emissions were already 24% above 1990 levels by 2000 and could increase to 37% by 2012 under a 'business-as-usual'

↑ *The new peat-fired power station outside Edenderry, Co Offaly, was held up for a number of years by the European Commission because it will emit over 600,000 tonnes of CO_2 a year*

scenario. Prof Frank Convery warned in August 2001 that Ireland was at risk of becoming 'the dirty man of Europe', and could face 'punitive financial sanctions' if it overshot its Kyoto target by a factor of three. Eighteen months later, with no sign of any move to introduce carbon taxes, Martin Cullen told his Cabinet colleagues in an *aide memoire* that failure to comply with Kyoto could cost Ireland €260 million a year over the 2008-12 period. 'There is no "get out of jail" card on this one', Cullen told the *Irish Times*. 'But we have a window of opportunity between now and 2008 to get our house in order and we're just going to have to do that.' He stressed the importance of introducing a carbon energy tax regime, saying it 'can no longer be avoided'. Without the political will to take such steps, he warned that Ireland would have its emissions rights reduced by an amount equivalent to its overshoot of the Kyoto target, plus a further penalty of 30%. But the Minister had an imperfect understanding of what was driving climate change. Cullen seemed to be under the impression that it all had something to do with the ozone layer. Asked on *Morning Ireland* if the severe storms and flooding of late 2002 could be symptoms of climate change, Cullen replied: 'All of the experts are saying all of this is the greenhouse gases having an effect on the ozone layer and it's causing major changes in weather.' Fintan O'Toole corrected him, pointing out that the hole in the ozone layer is caused by chlorofluorocarbons found in aerosols, air-conditioning units, fridges and plastic foam, while greenhouse gases result mainly from using fossil fuels. 'We expect children as young as 12 to know all of this. It is on the school curriculum presumably because we think it is the kind of thing that a functioning citizen needs to know. For any national politician not to know the difference between the ozone layer and the greenhouse effect would therefore be pretty alarming. For the Minister for the Environment, it's ludicrous. That a man like this doesn't have a clue about an issue that has been in the news for 20 years now gives us an insight into the world of the professional politician. It suggests a complete absence of curiosity about the world.' O'Toole asked if it mattered that the Minister's sense of these issues was as hazy as the gases in the air, and as empty as the hole in the ozone layer? 'Yes it does. For one thing, this compete lack of curiosity is almost certainly one of the reasons why the Government is only now waking up to the commitments it made in Kyoto. For another, it is impossible to ask the public to take the pain of paying environmental taxes when the man who is proposing them has only the vaguest notion of what they're for. Major changes in attitude don't come about without passionate leadership. How could anyone attach any credibility to a politician who hasn't bothered to acquire even a basic grasp of his subject?'

Cullen found himself being ribbed at European Environment Council meetings over Ireland's profligacy. The EU had signed up to reduce its greenhouse gas emissions by 8% on the baseline year of 1990 over the period 2008-12. The burden of meeting this undertaking was shared out among member states, based on their capacity and relative level of development. Germany, committed to reducing its own emissions by 21%, took a hard line on feckless countries. It noted that Ireland's per capita emissions of 18 tonnes per annum were way above the EU average of 11 tonnes, making it the world's fifth-largest emitter of carbon dioxide and other greenhouse gases, on a league table headed sequentially by Australia, the US, Canada and New Zealand. By 2001 the Germans had already succeeded in reducing their emissions by 18%, largely by shutting down highly polluting factories in what used to be East Germany; the last 3% is proving more difficult to attain. Britain, France, Luxembourg and Sweden are all on course to meet their targets. There is no magic formula; each of them is fulfilling its obligations in different ways. Britain has turned in a reasonably solid performance across all sectors – to give two examples, green energy has been pushed, and rail use is up, spectacularly so in the case of freight. France did not have to reduce emissions at all, largely due to its heavy reliance on nuclear power. Sweden was allowed to produce 4% more greenhouse gases, but is on target to cut emissions by 3%. Luxembourg is the European champion in terms of combating climate change. The tiny country agreed to reduce emissions by 28%, but is set to achieve close to a 45% drop. All other EU member states are off-course at least to some extent, but Spain and Ireland stand out. Both countries are equally bad in terms of exceeding their Kyoto targets, but Ireland's per capita CO_2 emissions are double those of Spain.

Given that we were clearly at the back of the class, Cullen not only had the

ESRI's support for a move to carbon taxes, but also that of the Organisation for Economic Co-operation and Development. In its first-ever review of Ireland's environmental performance, published in November 2000, the OECD, which represents the world's 29 richest countries (a group that includes Ireland), recommended that more use should be made of 'eco-taxation'. Six months earlier, Noel Dempsey gave a strong signal that energy taxes were on the way. 'We have to modify people's behaviour. We have seen from litter and various other things that appealing to their sense of care for the environment, or anything like that, is just not sufficient. You have, in a sense, to hit them where it hurts and that's in their pockets.' He noted there were also moves at EU level towards energy taxation. Ireland had been one of two countries in Europe which objected to the concept but 'we have removed our block and are prepared to consider it'. However, there was no joy from Charlie McCreevy or Mary Harney. While McCreevy accepted that carbon taxes would have to be introduced sooner or later, he was putting off the day. As Liam Reid reported in July 2003, McCreevy had been warned by industry and by his own officials that proposals put forward by the Department of the Environment could damage Ireland's competitiveness. Cullen's officials had proposed a minimum carbon tax of €7.50 per tonne of CO_2 across the board on all fossil fuels, rising to €20 per tonne over a four-year period. But though the Tax Strategy Group endorsed this regime in 2002, McCreevy stalled on introducing it because of concerns about the effect on the economy. And Harney, despite her creditable record as Minister of State for Environmental Protection from 1989 to 1992, vehemently opposed her old Department's proposals and insisted that carbon taxes be brought in at a lower rate, with an advance notice of two years before they were introduced.

A lot of faith is being put in emissions-trading, whereby Irish industrial enterprises can purchase CO_2 credits to offset their own emissions. IBEC constantly emphasised that major industry in Ireland is among the most modern and energy-efficient in Europe; that explained why, although industrial production rose a remarkable 225% in 10 years, energy consumption rose a mere 32%. IBEC sees emissions-trading as a 'least-cost method' to achieve the Kyoto target, although Donal Buckley, head of its environment unit, thought the system would put EU companies 'at a considerable competitive disadvantage'. Writing in the *Irish Times*, he said Irish companies could either reduce emissions by lowering production or improving efficiencies, buying allowances from other EU sites if available, or paying the pilot phase penalty of €40 per tonne, rising to €100 per tonne thereafter. But lobbying by IBEC's heavy-hitters led the Government to long-finger carbon taxes. As a result, McCreevy did not make any commitment on the issue until his 2003 Budget, when he said plans would be advanced for a carbon energy tax with a view to introducing it from the end of 2004. The EPA, in its 2002 review, had said fiscal measures, both incentives and disincentives, would become 'increasingly important tools' in sustainable development policy, and pointed to the enormous success of the 15 cent plastic-bag tax. However, 'key sustainability issues' were raised by Ireland's increasing consumption of energy, its high dependence on imported fossil fuels, the use of these fuels for electricity gen-

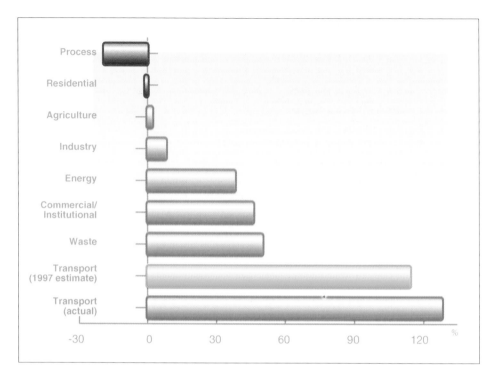

↑ *Kyoto emissions: percentage change by sector in Ireland, 1990-2003*

[sources: Environmental Protection Agency, 2004; Economic and Social Research Institute, 1997]
Note: The 1997 projection by the ESRI relates to 1990-2010; the EPA figures show what has actually happened in 1990-2003.

eration and the carbon dioxide emissions they generate. 'It has always been recognised that, with no action, Ireland would rapidly and substantially exceed its [Kyoto] Protocol target', the review said, adding that 'significant action' was now required over this decade to limit the rise in emissions to 13%.

A 2004 report by the European Environment Agency was more emphatic: Ireland was among the EU countries 'heading towards missing their burden-sharing targets with domestic policies and measures'. For energy supply, Ireland was bottom of the EU table. In terms of using renewable energy, Ireland was fifth from the bottom. For taking measures to capture heat generated by power plants, Ireland came second from the bottom. When it came to action to reduce emissions from agriculture, Ireland was bottom of the table – the only member state not expected to cut them. But when it came to transport, Ireland's failure was off the scale; without corrective action, its emissions were set to leap 180% in the 20 years from 1990 to 2010 – a rate of increase more than twice that of Spain, which is the second-worst offender (with a projected 75% increase). Even in the face of these bad marks, the FF/PD government insisted that the additional measures it was planning would deliver the Kyoto target. In May 2004 Martin Cullen was still portraying Ireland as the self-proclaimed, if untested, champion sprint-finisher. Asked by Julia Molony of the *Sunday*

Independent if we would meet our Kyoto target, he said: 'I think we will.' And then he qualified his answer: 'Well, at this stage it's difficult, but we're now putting in place the mechanisms that will give us every chance of achieving it.' There was a big problem, however. 'People are selfish too', he said. 'A politician may be in a position of leadership to try and get the debate going, but unless you get the public to buy into the challenges, you are not going to succeed.' The implication was that leaders don't lead any more: they have a new role, 'to try and get the debate going'. The Government certainly failed to get the public to take up the challenge, not least because most of those sitting round the Cabinet table had not bought into it themselves. Cullen concluded his interview with the *Sunday Independent* by repeating 'we are all selfish', adding that 'the biggest problem is our cars'. This was 'a final warning before getting into his black Mercedes' waiting right outside, Molony wrote.

Figures from the EPA, published in August 2004, showed a welcome reduction in greenhouse gas emissions for the second year running, mainly due to the closure of Irish Ispat in Cork Harbour and the IFI fertiliser plants in Arklow and Cork, which saved 940,000 tonnes of CO_2 emissions, and a switch from 'carbon-intensive fuels' such as coal, peat and oil to natural gas. The trend was confirmed by Sustainable Energy Ireland, the statutory agency set up to promote renewables and energy conservation, with figures showing that energy consumption for 2002 remained unchanged year on year, despite an economic growth rate of 7%. 'This marks the first time since 1990 that energy consumption has significantly decoupled from economic activity', it said in a report, *Energy in Ireland 1990-2002*. But Ireland was still overshooting Kyoto. Overall emissions in 2003 were nearly 25% higher than they were in 1990, or nearly double the increase allowed under the EU burden-sharing deal. Most alarmingly of all, emissions from transport had risen by almost 130%, the biggest increase for any sector, with road transport accounting for 93% of the total volume of 11.5 million tonnes of carbon dioxide emissions from transport. Increased vehicle ownership and use were largely to blame: the number of cars on Irish roads increased by nearly 82% in the 12 years after 1990. Transport accounted for 17.7% of total greenhouse gas emissions of almost 67 million tonnes in 2003, with agriculture accounting for 28.9% and energy 24.5%. However, Martin Cullen continued to be upbeat about Ireland's prospects of meeting its Kyoto obligations in an 'economically efficient manner'.

Back in 2002, Cullen told Shane Coleman that achieving the target had to be done 'in an almost non-political way'. Yet there was nothing 'non-political' about keeling over to lobbyists with his housing guidelines on the eve of the local and European Parliament elections in June 2004. Cullen also conceded that the transport sector was Ireland's main bugbear in complying with Kyoto – 'the biggest problem is our cars' – though even he must have known that his housing guidelines would result in ever higher levels of car-dependency. Yet he knew his Sustainable Rural Housing Guidelines would result in ever higher levels of car-dependency. His response to Ireland's slip-shod performance was to scapegoat 'the people'. His Cabinet colleague, Séamus Brennan, was also putting in place a transport policy which is overwhelmingly biased towards private car-use. Yet attempts to highlight the impact of traffic on Ireland's Kyoto target have been repeatedly disallowed at public inquiries into major road schemes.

On energy conservation, the FF/PD coalition delayed the introduction of better energy-efficiency standards for new housing, largely to placate the concrete industry. And when it did act, very late in the day, it brought in a feeble measure. Using the Freedom of Information Act, Gerry McCaughey of timber-frame builders Century Homes unearthed documents on the reform of the Building Regulations. A 1998 Department of the Environment memo acknowledged that the regulations needed to be revised as soon as possible, but warned: 'We don't want to signal this to the outside world just yet because the next leap in building standard insulation will probably involve making it difficult for "hollow block" construction, used widely in Dublin, to survive.' The memo went on to flag the implications for building material manufacturers. In fact, new regulations were not introduced until 2002. Over 200,000 homes had been built during the four years of dithering. And when the new standards were brought in, all planning applications lodged before the end of 2002 were deemed exempt. The Government of the day put the concrete industry ahead of people's welfare, McCaughey told the *Sunday Tribune*.

The cement sector was also looked after in the National Allocation Plan for emissions-trading, although Irish Cement, owned by CRH plc, claimed that the new regime could 'threaten the very existence and development of cement manufacturing in Ireland'. The Government decided to allocate 67.5 million tonnes in free CO_2 credits, which were then distributed by the EPA to more than 100 installations (including 16 power stations), using their emissions in 2002-03 as benchmarks. CRH did particularly well, getting a total of 2.4 million tonnes of CO_2 allowances for its two cement plants and associated operations. The Platin cement works near Drogheda would be allowed to belch out nearly 1.3 million tonnes of CO_2 annually without incurring any penalties. And this generous ceiling, only marginally less than its recent output, will continue at least until 2007. Provision was also made for a planned expansion of CRH's Limerick plant, where almost twice the current level of emissions will be permitted in 2007 – 1.475 million tonnes of CO_2 per annum, as against 813,000 tonnes at present. Irish Cement received an additional allocation of 750,000 tonnes per annum above historical levels, and was the only cement producer to benefit in this way. Figures show that it was treated more generously than either of its main competitors – the Seán Quinn Group and Lagan Cement Ltd – which received allocations of 849,000 tonnes and 374,000 tonnes per annum respectively. In fact, the highly carbon-intensive cement industry, Ireland's second largest industrial source of CO_2 emissions, could be a major beneficiary of the EPA's allocations, even to the extent of selling credits. Cement demand would need to increase to 5.6 million tonnes per annum (from 4.5 million currently) – way above any other European country on a per capita basis – for the industry's CO_2 allocations to be used up. This cannot be justified on competitive grounds, as the Byrne Ó Cleirigh report, on which the EPA's allocations were based, found that the cement industry here is not exposed to any significant foreign competition. Possible reductions that might have been made in the sector will have to be made elsewhere in the economy, inevitably at a cost to taxpayers.

Manufacturers of a new environmentally friendly cement get little credit for not emitting CO_2. Ecocem Ltd, which started production in October 2003 at Ringsend in Dublin, could reduce emissions by up to 300,000 tonnes per annum by replacing ordinary cement in construction with cement made from ground granulated blast-furnace slag, or GGBS as it's known. This would amount to a 7% reduction in emissions from the sector, a saving equivalent to what will be achieved by the tougher insulation standards for housing prescribed by the Building Regulations. The manufacture of every tonne of traditional Portland cement by crushing limestone into powder involves emitting up to one tonne of CO_2 into the atmosphere, in addition to noxious gases such as sulphur dioxide, nitrous oxides and carbon monoxide. Up to 60% of the cement used in Northern Ireland is supplied by the Republic, which is good for exports but leaves us with the CO_2 emissions. Traditional cement manufacturing is also very profitable. According to Donal Ó Riain, Ecocem's managing director, the marginal cost of producing one tonne of cement is €15 for a product that sells for €75 per tonne. 'On that basis, there is no incentive to change the manufacturing process ... If they were to switch over to alternative technologies, they would have to scrap existing plants that are very profitable and sink fresh capital into new plants that are inherently less profitable.' GGBS produces near-white concrete of acknowledged strength and durability, while emitting only a small amount of CO_2 and no noxious gases. It is also 10%-15% cheaper per tonne than ordinary cement, and has been used in such high-profile projects as the William Dargan bridge on the Luas Green Line and the Boyne bridge on the M1 west of Drogheda. The Department of the Environment wants to see more of it used, with a minimum substitution rate of 25% for all public contracts involving the use of concrete. In a 2003 consultation paper, it noted that the public sector is the largest client of the construction industry, financing about one-third of its output by using 1.5 million tonnes of Portland cement annually. 'The manufacture of cement from GGBS generates a small fraction of the greenhouse gas emissions from standard limestone-based Portland cement, as there is no process emissions ... and no energy for heating is required.' Another selling point for GGBS is that it has no impact on the landscape as it requires no quarrying; Ecocem's €10 million Ringsend plant occupies a site of just 1.5 acres. The land area needed for a traditional cement plant is much larger – on average, 50 acres for the plant itself and a further 100 acres for the limestone quarry to supply its raw materials. Irish Cement, which controls about 60% of the market, was not pleased with the initiative. A spokesman said the company would expect to be consulted about any proposal to change cement specification requirements because this would 'raise important issues for the Irish cement industry'.

The nightmare of being located next door to a large cement works has been visited on the main street of Ballyconnell, Co Cavan, which is 'suffering devastating safety and environmental impacts from the high level of truck movements generated by various parts of the Quinn Group', according to An Taisce. Seán Quinn started

↑ *CRH's Platin cement works near Drogheda, Co Louth: allowed to belch out nearly 1.3 million tonnes of CO$_2$ annually without incurring any penalties, under the National Allocation Plan*

out just across the border in Co Fermanagh, but relocated his cement works to a site near the village. Under the Kyoto Protocol, the British government had signed up for a much tougher target than our own on greenhouse gas emissions, so he may have seen some advantage in moving across the border. There is a large Quinn Group warehouse nearby, and just inside Co Fermanagh, on the road to Derrylin, a cement casting works and a glass factory. To this range of operations, the group is adding a foam insulation factory near Ballyconnell, for which planning permission was granted by An Bord Pleanála in March 2004, and two quarries, one of them 11km away. 'None of this should have happened in an area remote from national primary routes and the railway system', a spokesman for An Taisce said, adding that it could undermine the tourism value of the cross-border Shannon-Erne waterway. 'What has happened on the R205 Ballyconnell to Derrylin road ... is that a massive combination of large-scale industrial development has occurred without the land in question ever being zoned for such development.' The R205 is the only road leading from Ballyconnell to the border; the alternative is a much more circuitous route, involving a diversion of 8km (or a new road linking the cement plant with the quarry beyond Slieve Rushden, which is its principal source of limestone). An Taisce appealed against Cavan County Council's decision to grant permission for the quarry complex

↑ *Seán Quinn standing in front of his cement plant outside Ballyconnell, Co Cavan. Quinn relocated his plant from the other side of the border in Co Fermanagh.*

on a 104-hectare (250-acre) site, including retention of an unauthorised development, at Aughrim, Ballyconnell, but to no avail. An Bord Pleanála justified its decision on the basis of the 'established pattern of industrial development' in the area. No planning conditions were specified to mitigate the impact of traffic on Ballyconnell's Main Street, which now faces the increased safety risk of tankers transporting pentane gas to the foam-insulation factory. 'Seven separate environmental mitigation conditions are left to be resolved inappropriately by an internal "approval" procedure between Cavan County Council and the applicant', An Taisce complained, saying this excluded the public. Major issues relating to the operation and reinstatement of the quarry site were also left to be resolved in this way.

However, some industry leaders recognise that global greenhouse gas emissions must be reduced to stave off the catastrophic consequences of climate change. Sir John Browne, chief executive of BP Amoco, Britain's largest company, put forward a menu of options to limit the increase in temperature over the next 45 years to 2° Celsius. Each of his proposals would reduce global emissions by one billion tonnes a year. They included 400 power plants using natural gas rather than coal, each generating 1,000 megawatts; 200 coal-fired power plants using carbon capture and storage; 600 million cars – a third of the world's expected number by 2050 – running on hybrid engines at 60 miles per gallon rather than the current average of 30mpg; the replacement of 200,000 megawatts of coal-generated power with nuclear power; a twentyfold increase in wind-power capacity, together with a 12% rise in solar-power capacity. Browne also pointed to the use of smart local grids where heat generated in factories is used to warm nearby homes. The BP chief took inspiration from the fact that 23 countries had come together after World War II to promote trade and exchange – a process that led to the establishment of the World Trade Organisation. Browne argued that the global challenge presented by climate change requires a similar international response.

Ireland could pursue some of the strategies identified by Browne, or play a part in their implementation. But even taking the Dáil set to be elected in 2007, very few of those TDs would still be around in 2050. The level of foresight needed represents a huge challenge in itself. Irish politicians who could have done something timely include Bertie Ahern, Mary Harney, Charlie McCreevy, Noel Dempsey, Martin Cullen and Séamus Brennan. None has shown any real bottle. Do all of them lack the candour and ability that's needed to give leadership on this vitally important issue? Referring to emissions-trading between countries, Cullen told the *Sunday Independent* that 'it doesn't matter if it's a little bit over here or a little bit over there. It's the overall effect that matters.' Not quite. The Government's failure to move away from generating power using coal and peat, its engendering of car-dependency, and its foot-dragging on energy-efficient homes mean that taxpayers will have to buy Ireland's way out of Kyoto. A burden that might have been entirely avoided is set to fall on society as a whole. In many ways, Ireland's policy on climate change is worse than that of the Bush administration. Underneath, there's the same 'who-gives-a-toss-about-the-next-generation' attitude. Freak weather conditions and rising tides may become more of problem, but as one senior Fianna Fáil adviser put it, 'sure we won't be around then'. The difference between FF/PD ministers and neo-conservatives in the US is that Ireland's leaders lack the honesty of their fellow travellers across the Atlantic. The Irish approach, at least since 1997, has been to parade a concern for the environment while trying to buy, or bulldoze, a way out.

––––––

ENERGY FROM FRESH AIR – THAT WAS THE GREAT PROMISE THAT DREW GEORGE COLLEY, then Minister for Energy, to Denmark in 1980. Clad in a velvet-collared coat on the west coast of Jutland, he inspected the first two experimental wind turbines built by the Danes. By 2002 wind energy accounted for 18% of Denmark's electricity consumption – equivalent to 1.5 million homes. The Danes also became world leaders in the fast-expanding wind-turbine industry, generating €3 billion a year in revenue and employing 20,000 people. And Ireland? By the end of 2002, despite having the most favourable wind conditions in Europe, we had a mere handful of wind farms producing 138 megawatts of electricity, or 1% of our consumption. That's equivalent to 100,000 homes – a fraction of the Danish figure. Despite its undoubted environmental advantages and the worldwide trend towards harnessing it, wind energy is 'treated as an annoying little fly on the back of the elephant', as one industry source put it. And just when wind finally started to make an impact, the national grid pulled down its shutters. In December 2003, at Eirgrid's behest, Electricity Regulator Tom Reeves put an embargo on further wind-power contracts, saying the grid couldn't take more than the 800MW already due to come on-stream. In the same week, the then Minister for Communications, Marine and Natural Resources, Dermot Ahern, was promoting another round of renewable energy contracts, including 140MW of wind, that was meant to contribute to reaching the stated goal of having 500MW up and running in 2005.

It's not a matter of choice, however. Ireland is required by the EU directive on renewable energy to achieve a 13% share for renewable sources – mainly wind – by 2010 as part of the EU's strategy to mitigate climate change by switching from fossil fuels. The national energy bill in 2004 was more than €100 million a week, according to Paul Kellett of Sustainable Energy Ireland. But Eirgrid (also called ESB National Grid; it was hived off from the ESB in 1999) said it couldn't cope with the 'avalanche' of applications from wind-power developers for contracts to connect to the grid, at least until a new code was agreed to regulate the operation of wind farms – for example, how to protect the grid against sudden surges of power in gale-force conditions, especially on the west coast. Wind can't just be switched on or off. As the *Economist* put it, 'too light a breeze means no power; too strong a gale and the turbines shut down to prevent damage. Even the wind-lovers expect that the farms will manage only 30% of their full capacity on average.' Worse still, output can fluctuate rapidly by up to 20% of the total installed wind capacity in the space of a single hour, according to Hugh Sharman, an energy consultant, who has studied Denmark's wind industry. In a typical year like 2002, there were 54 days when the air was so still that virtually no wind power was generated at all. But the Danes manage to cope with this because they can import power from the Norwegian, Swedish and German grids at the flick of a switch. In the Irish context, Simon Grimes, who manages wind power contracts for Eirgrid, cited Co Donegal, where the output of wind farms operating there often exceeds the county's electricity demand. 'This is a situation that no system operator in the world has ever had to contend with', he told the *Irish Times* in February 2004.

But wind-power developers insist that Eirgrid should have known what was coming and prepared the ground for it. 'The PR gloss is that they were ambushed by the sudden rush of renewables, yet they themselves forecast that this would happen and did nothing in the interim to devise a strategy', one said. Following extensive consultations with the industry, a draft wind code was finally agreed in April 2004 and immediately hailed as 'a milestone in establishing technical rules for wind connections to the grid'. Most importantly, Eirgrid needs wind turbine manufacturers to provide true models of their electrical performance so that it can determine how best to rejig the grid to accommodate a fourfold increase in wind generation between 2004 and 2007. Eirgrid continued to maintain, even into 2005, that every 100MW of wind

↑ *A wind farm at Inverin Connemara. An Bord Pleanála has refused permission for similar schemes because of their impact on the landscape.*

→ *Turbines on a new Airtricity wind farm at Meenycat, Co Donegal, one of the largest to be developed in Ireland*
→→ *One of the Airtricity-GE Wind Energy offshore turbines on the Arklow Banks.*
It has a rotor diameter of 104 metres, a hub height of 73.5 metres and a rating of 3.6MW.

power would have to be backed up by an equivalent amount of conventionally generated electricity. But Eddie O'Connor, chief executive of Airtricity, argued in March 2005 that this claim was grossly exaggerated. Writing in the *Irish Times*, he quoted the British energy minister, Patricia Hewitt, as saying that only 600MW of conventional power would be needed to cope with 8,000MW of wind.

Not one of the 255 megawatts in wind contracts awarded by the Department of Energy in 2001 had 'lit up a single light bulb', according to the Green Party's energy spokesman, Eamon Ryan TD. All we had to show at the end of 2003 after six rounds of the alternative energy programme, at least in the wind sector, was 191MW of generating capacity. The rest of them were simply not delivered. Numerous projects failed for one reason or another – some didn't get the required financial backing, others didn't get planning permission, or simply fell apart. The Irish Wind Energy Association did its best to promote the cause, but nearly every round was characterised by recriminations of one sort or another – usually that too many of the con-

tracts were going to the ESB, its subsidiaries or associates. The company denied this, saying it was just 'good at delivering on contracts'. But our reliance on the ESB will reduce over time. The proposed 1,000MW electricity interconnector between Ireland and Britain will 'anchor' us to the wider European grid, making it easier for system operators here to accommodate more wind because of the back-up provided. But the interconnector is good news in another way, too – it will introduce real competition into the Irish market. At present, though there is competition in electricity genera-tion, virtually all of what is produced by other companies is sold to the ESB. And with little competition in supply, additional costs tend to be passed on to consumers. Thus, if the ESB had to buy CO_2 credits to keep its fossil fuel plants going, every household in the state would end up paying the bill. Indeed, the company itself warned in April 2004 that its quota allocation under the National Allocation Plan 'will impose significant costs on electricity consumers'. Moneypoint, for example, was given a quota of 4.4 million tonnes of CO_2 a year, compared with its current 5.9 million tonnes. According to the ESB, the quotas would cause power-generation costs to increase by up to 40%, resulting in an initial 6% increase in domestic prices, ris-ing to 20% when the extra costs are passed on in full. However, as Liam Reid report-ed, 'any rise in consumer electricity prices will be a matter for the Commission for Electricity Regulation (CER), which could decide that the industry must shoulder the additional costs entirely.'

The largest and most impressive wind-energy project in the Republic is the off-shore wind farm being developed by Airtricity and GE Wind Energy on the Arklow Banks, about 10km off the coast of Co Wicklow. Comprising seven massive turbines, each with a rotor diameter of 104 metres, a hub height of 73.5 metres and a rating of 3.6MW, it is expected to generate enough 'green' electricity to serve 16,000 house-holds. Airtricity's founder and chief executive, Eddie O'Connor, billed it as 'the first phase in energy self-sufficiency for this country'. But he also recognised that it was a demonstration project, designed to prove that it is possible to erect such huge struc-tures in the Irish Sea. Though several offshore wind farms have been developed in Denmark, the Arklow Banks project is Ireland's first. Some people objected to the visual impact of the turbines on previously open sea views. Helen Gelletlie of Hunters Hotel near Rathnew, Co Wicklow, described them as 'gigantic', and said the seven under construction were merely the first phase of a wind farm that would see 'up to 200 turbines massed along this magnificent coastline'. New regulations are urgently needed to govern the location of offshore wind farms, she said. 'These should identify coasts suitable for development – surely not coasts designated as sce-nic areas whose beauty is dependent on the seascape – height of turbines, minimum distance from the shore, etc.'

However, others would argue that offshore installations are less obtrusive than wind farms built on the sides of mountains, especially in amenity areas. Such land-based wind farm projects have posed problems for An Bord Pleanála. On the one hand, encouraging alternative energy is declared government policy; on the other, sce-nic areas must be protected from insensitive development. In July 2004 the board confirmed Mayo County Council's decision to refuse permission for a 15-turbine wind farm in the foothills of the Ox Mountains, ruling that it would be 'highly obtrusive' in a sensitive landscape. Kevin Moore, the planning inspector who dealt with the case, noted that an existing 10-turbine wind farm at King's Mountain, south of Templeboy, Co Sligo, was visible from the site, and that the board had already granted permission for a 13-turbine wind farm on Crowagh mountain, west of King's. In his report, Moore concluded that the northern foothills of the Ox mountains were under threat from these type of developments. But such cases have been the exception rather than the rule. Altogether, the board reversed nearly a third (29%) of local authority refusals on appeal in 2003 because of its 'tendency to give greater weight to national policies'; the same was true for often more controversial telecommunications masts.

The landslide at Derrybrien, south Co Galway, in November 2003 was the worst possible advertisement for Ireland's embryonic wind power industry. Certainly, its surreal images of mushy peat and soil flowing downhill like cold lava will not easily be forgotten. The landslide rolled some 1,500 metres through Coillte forestry in the Slieve Aughty mountains before stopping at an unoccupied house. 'Trees were bobbing up and down like corks on water', Thomas Conroy, a Coillte contractor, said at the time. Investigations started straight away, but the cause was clear. As confirmed by a report published in February 2004, site clearance and development works for a 60MW wind farm consisting of 71 turbines had destabilised soft ground beneath the blanket bog. The ESB subsidiary, Hibernian Wind Power, which is developing the €60 million wind farm, accepted the findings of the report by Applied Ground Engineering consultants, which was bound to have implications for other wind farm developments. Some of the 17 recommendations are obvious – for example, a geological consultant should be employed full-time to supervise site development and construction work on relatively unstable blanket bog sites. The Derrybrien case called into question wind farm development on upland blanket bog. Though wind speeds are obviously stronger in elevated locations, the logistics of getting up there, preparing sites, providing access roads and excavating foundations all carry their own risks.

Developers have also drawn flak for choosing sites which are either within, or close to, Special Areas of Conservation under the EU Habitats Directive. And though SACs here still have 'candidate' status, they can't just be ignored. The Irish Peatland Conservation Council successfully appealed against Leitrim County Council's approval of a 25-turbine Airtricity wind farm on upland blanket bog, claiming that it would threaten an internationally important SAC on Boleybrack mountain. Caroline Hurley, the IPCC's conservation officer, described Boleybrack as 'one of the most intact, wild expanses of upland blanket bog left in Ireland', and asked why the National Parks and Wildlife Service was not opposing the Airtricity scheme and a smaller 12-turbine scheme by Stuart Hydro Ltd. In June 2004 An Bord Pleanála overturned the Leitrim decision on the basis that Boleybrack 'hosts extensive priority habitat designated under the EU Habitats Directive, namely upland blanket bog', and that the proposed wind farms 'would have a significant adverse environmental impact

↑ *'Turf lava' outside an uninhabited house after the landslide at Derrybrien, Co Galway, in November 2003. The construction of an ESB wind farm was to blame.*

on the natural habitats of the area'. What concerned the IPCC was that the National Parks and Wildlife Service had consented to these developments and that the apparent disregard for this SAC would have implications for others if the two wind farms went ahead. 'The development of wind farms to provide renewable energy for Ireland is obviously a step in the right direction, but we have to be sure that they are not damaging to our environment', Hurley said. 'Active upland blanket bogs are a threatened habitat within Europe, and Ireland has a huge responsibility to conserve our remaining intact examples of this habitat.'

Wind power has also attracted unprecedented criticism in Britain. The *Economist* carried a jaundiced piece in July 2004, under the heading 'Wind farms disfigure the countryside and threaten to cost £1 billion a year. Apart from that, they're great.' It noted that 'Tories, toffs and country-lovers' as well as 'veteran greens' were involved in a campaign to prevent the installation of 27 wind turbines next to Romney Marsh in Kent, a bird sanctuary and 'beauty spot'. The article also queried whether wind energy was something of a white elephant. 'Although the British Wind Energy Association puts the cost of electricity from onshore wind farms at 2.5p per kilowatt-hour, only slightly more costly than other power sources, the Royal Academy of Engineering claims that on a more realistic view of construction costs it is much dearer: 3.7p when generated onshore and 5.5p offshore.' Bridging the gap between this and the cost of conventional power was estimated at £500 million sterling in 2004, rising to £1 billion a year by 2020. The Conservative Party, tapping into a groundswell of opposition to wind farms, said they would oppose the introduction of new planning guidelines making it easier for developers to get approval. In Ireland, however, fewer people appear to be overly concerned about the visual impact of wind farms – other than in particularly scenic locations. Neither have fears been confirmed that the noise they make is 'like the moans from a mass crucifixion', as a local critic memorably said of a 120-turbine farm in mid-Wales. A survey published by Sustainable Energy Ireland in November 2003 found that people living in the vicinity of wind farms do not, in general, consider that they have any adverse impact on the scenic beauty and wildlife of the area, while more than 60% would favour further schemes.

With advances in technology, wind-energy developers are becoming more and more adventurous. Average turbine size in Germany, which has taken to wind energy in a big way, went from 470 kilowatts in 1995 to 1.4 megawatts in 2002. Enercon, its leading wind power company, is testing a 4.5MW turbine which could produce electricity for 15,000 people. GE Wind Energy, Airtricity's partner in the Arklow Banks project, has developed a turbine for particularly windy sites with a rotor blade diameter of 104 metres (343 ft) and a tower height of between 98m and 140m. To put that in perspective, the latter would be taller than Dublin's Spire. Offshore is increasingly seen as the way to go, even though the development costs are much higher – some €2.5 million per megawatt installed compared to €1.1 million on land. But they offer the advantages of higher wind speeds, fewer environmental restrictions, and, of course, economies of scale. The real danger is that developers will 'ratchet up' the hub height and rotor blade diameter of land-based turbines, with incalculable effects in terms of industrialising Ireland's landscapes.

Martin Cullen was determined to introduce a more liberal planning regime on wind energy, to usher in a bold new era. Draft planning guidelines published in August 2004 favour a 'plan-led' approach which would require local authorities to 'proactively identify' areas of significant wind-energy potential and map these areas in county development plans. Under the guidelines, prepared in conjunction with Sustainable Energy Ireland, planners are told to be 'favourably disposed' towards granting permission in such areas, subject to siting and design criteria. Photomontages of wind farms in various types of landscapes should be included to show how factors such as siting and location, spatial extent and scale, cumulative effect, spacing, layout and height of turbines can best be applied in different landscape types. Hub heights of 50 metres, 75 metres and even 100 metres are to be permitted, reflecting current and near-future technology. 'Consideration of lower ground where feasible may be necessary in sensitive landscapes, but otherwise location on ridges and hilltops may be visually acceptable', the guidelines say. In view of what happened at Derrybrien, the underlying geology of any site is identified as a critical factor requiring detailed assessment at the planning stage, including the risk of 'bogbursts' or landslides, and geotechnical monitoring during construction. Developers are advised to avoid construction on deep (50cm+) peat, and not to dig huge drains. Also, heavy work should be undertaken in drier months. But even SACs and SPAs were not to stand in the way of developments that would, as Cullen said, 'bolster the Government's National Climate Change Strategy and reduce our dependency on dirty fossil fuels'. Indeed, the guidelines explicitly state that the 'designation for protection of natural or built heritage or as an amenity area does not preclude wind farm development'. Neither will visibility of a proposed wind farm from designated views or prospects automatically preclude an area from future development. And in telling planners what they should take into account in considering applications, the guidelines underline 'national policy on wind farms' as an overriding issue. Friends of the Irish Environment immediately warned that an open season on habitat areas would contravene EU directives in what it saw as 'a further attempt by the present Government to systematically undermine what little environmental protection there is in Ireland'. It noted that the omission of potentially extensive and invasive transmission lines from planning applications for wind farms had not been addressed, leaving people unable to assess the full impact of a proposed development on their property. Green Party spokesman Ciarán Cuffe TD also said the right balance needed to be struck between encouraging renewable energy and protecting scenic areas.

The new guidelines were welcomed by Meitheal na Gaoithe, the Irish Wind Farmers Co-operative, as 'a positive move in the right direction', especially if they gave more confidence to rural communities to become directly involved in locally owned wind farms. But it complained that the wind industry in Ireland is now dominated by very large developers, such as Airtricity, the ESB and Treasury Holdings, saying this was virtually eliminating small and medium-sized enterprises and local involvement in the area of alternative energy. 'Unfortunately, the good news on the planning front is not matched by similar advances on the issue of grid connections and power purchase agreements for wind energy', said Meitheal's secretary, Ronnie Owens. 'The failure to develop the national grid in line with government policy and a deep institutional resistance to the development of the independent energy sector have all but stopped new developments in wind energy.' This was a reference to the ESB, Eirgrid, the CER, and even the Department of Communications, Marine and Natural Resources. Though the Department is supposedly encouraging competition in the energy sector, it has never lost sight of the fact that its Minister is the ESB's sole shareholder – and the ESB, a monopoly since Ardnacrusha, isn't much given to rolling out the red carpet for competitors. In February 2004 Dermot Ahern announced that he was setting up the Renewable Energy Development Group, involving 'key players in the renewable energy sector'. It was to be a permanent forum where 'the renewables industry, the CER, SEI and the network operators will … share expertise, and to solve potential constraints to the development of this key sector'. However, when the group was actually set up in May, renewable energy interests such as Meitheal and the Irish Wind Energy Association found themselves excluded. Those on the inside included all the usual suspects – the Department (in the chair, naturally), Eirgrid, the CER and SEI as well as the Northern Ireland Department of

Enterprise, Trade and Investment. Those in the front line were confined to a 'sub-group of industry and sectoral interests' with a role in nominating a couple of representatives to the forum; IBEC, which could hardly be regarded as a 'key player in the renewable energy sector', was also brought in through this door. 'It is not clear why it was felt necessary to exclude us up to now, especially given the Minister's original statement, which put the renewables industry first', Meitheal said. 'Once again, the Minister's efforts are being frustrated by a bureaucratic machine that systematically defends the ESB and its own interests, while resisting change. The Minister's fine talk of "mainstreaming renewables" has fallen at the first fence.'

―――

THE MOST POLITICALLY SENSITIVE DECISION MADE BY AN BORD PLEANÁLA IN THE ENERGY sector did not involve wind farms at all, but something much more important to a fossil fuel-dependent economy – the bringing ashore of more natural gas from the Atlantic. Enterprise Oil had started drilling for gas 50 miles off the Mayo coast in 1996 and announced four years later that it would proceed with developing the Corrib gas field in collaboration with Statoil and Marathon Petroleum. A 1998 report by international oil and gas consultants Wood MacKenzie estimated there was seven trillion cubic feet of gas in the Corrib field. By September 2000, the company was promising 50 full-time jobs at its proposed terminal at Bellanaboy in north-west Mayo and saying, quite confidently, that it planned to have the gas on the commercial market in Dublin by January 2003. For Shell and its partners, the terms being offered by the State could not have been better –full ownership of all of the gas they extracted from the Corrib field and not a cent in royalties to pay on any of it. This highly lucrative arrangement for offshore exploration had been introduced in 1992 by none other than Ray Burke, then Minister for Energy. Under his amending legislation, the State abandoned royalties and earlier claims to a 50% shareholding in oil or natural gas found off the Irish coast in favour of a nominal 25% tax rate on a company's profits. This was widely seen as a sell-out, particularly by SIPTU, the country's principal trade union. After Enterprise Oil was taken over by Royal Dutch Shell in 2002, in a deal which valued the company's assets at €5.5 billion, SIPTU intensified its campaign for the State to look for more royalties. The Mayo West independent TD Dr Jerry Cowley described the terms of the lease granted in November 2001 by Frank Fahey, then Minister for the Marine and Natural Resources, as 'a disgrace'. But a spokesman for Enterprise Energy Ireland – as Shell's new subsidiary was called – said a more recent Wood MacKenzie study from February 2002 had put the Corrib gas field's reserves at 0.875 trillion cubic feet, a fraction of the figure being quoted by SIPTU. Mike Cunningham, a Mayo-based exploration expert, countered this claim saying that Irish people were being 'kept in the dark' about the true extent of gas reserves in the Corrib basin. Of the roughly 150 wells sunk off the Irish coast over the last 30 years, only three have proved commercial – Kinsale, Seven Heads and Corrib – with the Seven Heads regarded as being marginal. (Contrast this with Norway, where, for every 150 wells drilled, 50 are economic.) Indeed, in early 2004, the Department of the Marine, Communications and Natural Resources offered exploration licences for 15,800 sq km in the Rockall basin. Just 10% of this area was taken up, with only two companies showing any interest – Island Oil & Gas, and Shell E&P (Ireland). Paul Griffiths, chief executive of Island Oil & Gas, told John Mulligan of the *Sunday Tribune* that Ireland's fiscal terms are probably 'top of the tree'; at the same time, 'the chance of making a commercial discovery is low.' But if there were national reasons behind the development of Ireland's offshore resources, how were local concerns being addressed?

In February 2001 a report commissioned by Pat O'Donnell, a director of the Mayo-based company Porturlin Shellfish Ltd, warned that discharges of mercury and other heavy metals could contaminate marine life and affect the livelihoods of fishermen and tourism interests in the area. Dr Alex Rogers, of the School of Ocean and Earth Science at the University of Southampton, said the development would have a 'strongly negative effect' on the environment while offering 'very little to the local community'. Rogers also found that little attention had been paid to habitats in the area, including SACs and SPAs with high populations of over-wintering wild birds. O'Donnell told Dermot Ahern: 'We are employing 12 people here in crab processing, and have done since 1992 ... I come from a family of 11, and we made it through the hard times here. Enterprise Oil wasn't around then, and we don't need it now.' The Bellanaboy/Lenamore Concerned Citizens Group appealed against Mayo County Council's decision to approve the gas terminal, where the gas would be processed before being piped to Galway, claiming that it would pose a 'constant danger' to local people. There were legitimate fears about the very idea of pumping gas at high pressure in a pipeline just one metre below ground level, running for a distance of 9km from landfall at Dooncarton to the terminal. Accidents had happened before. In 1989 400 people were burned to death in Russia when a pipeline fractured and the natural gas it was carrying ignited, exploding beside two trains. In 1998 an estimated 1,000 people were incinerated in Nigeria by another gas pipeline explosion. Even in the US, 12 people who had been camping unwittingly near a gas pipeline in Carlsbad, New Mexico, were killed when it exploded in 2000. And as recently as July 2004 a pipeline in Belgium run by Shell itself ruptured 40km south of Brussels, killing 15 people – several of them firefighters. Apart from this grave risk of explosion, some 21 objections by the Bellanaboy/Lenamore Concerned Citizens Group took issue with the proposed removal of more than 600,000 tonnes of peat from the site of the terminal, to be 'stored' in repositories on sloping ground nearby.

But the €900 million project had powerful political support. Frank Fahey complained at the Humbert Summer School in August 2001 that objectors were 'holding up progress in the west'. He subsequently denied a claim by Michael Ring TD (FG, Mayo West) that he was interfering in the planning process to facilitate the project. Fahey had already granted Enterprise Energy a lease for the Corrib gas field, and later issued a foreshore licence for the terminal, pipeline and associated works, in one of his last acts as Minister for the Marine. Extraordinarily, this was the only official

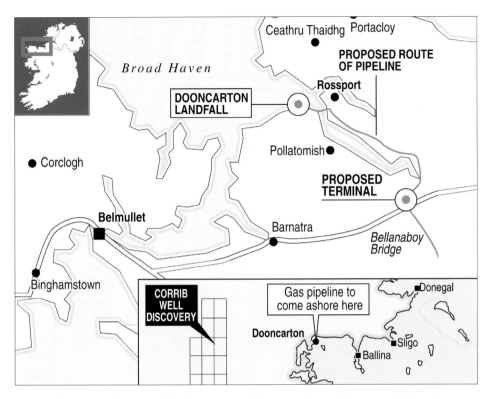

↑ *Map showing the location of Shell's controversial gas terminal and the route of the onshore pipeline in north-west Co Mayo*

consent that the pipeline needed, as it was not just exempt from planning control, but also outside the remit of the Health and Safety Authority. And when An Bord Pleanála stunned the political establishment by refusing permission on the single ground of public safety on 30th April 2003, Fahey warned that if the project didn't go ahead, it would have a 'severe, negative impact' on the west. However, the appeals board said the removal of so much peat from the site and its storage in two 'repositories' would constitute an 'unacceptable risk to the health and safety of the local community and of the general public'. This was a mere 'technicality', according to Fahey, who was now Minister of State for Labour Affairs. Two days later, he wrote to fellow western members of the Oireachtas saying he had asked Andy Pyle, Enterprise Energy's managing director, to meet with those who wanted to see the project proceed 'so that we can demonstrate the widespread support that exists in the west of Ireland for Corrib gas'. Fahey told Lorna Siggins that his aim was 'to get a political consensus in support of the project'. Dermot Ahern had already expressed the Government's regret that the development of the Corrib gas field would be 'further delayed' as a result of An Bord Pleanála's ruling, and said he hoped it would 'not end efforts to tap into this rich vein of energy off our coast, and the jobs, investment and infrastructure which it has the potential to deliver'. The board fireproofed itself against the political fallout by pointing out that its decision to refuse planning permission was unanimous; indeed, it is understood that all 10 board members had visited the Bellanaboy site and then spent two days considering the planning inspector's report before making their decision. The case had also been the subject of two oral hearings lasting a total of 22 days, at which all the arguments were thrashed out. An Taisce hailed the decision as 'one of the most significant and progressive in the board's history', while FIE called it a 'brave defence of basic science'. The local objectors were jubilant. Maura Harrington, their spokeswoman, said it was Enterprise Energy's 'disdain for the communities who lived on and beside that bog at Bellanaboy [which] led to its downfall'.

Less than five months later, in September 2003, there was a devastating landslide on Dooncarton Mountain, just two miles from the proposed terminal; suddenly, it seemed foolish to suggest that the reason given by An Bord Pleanála for refusing permission was merely a 'technicality'. People in the area saw roads severed, bridges damaged and even a graveyard churned up by the slippage of a blanket bog. 'It's been certainly proved that peat can move and this will have to be looked at if there's a new planning application', the Mayo county secretary, John Condon, told the *Irish Times*. A detailed report prepared by Kevin Moore, the planning inspector who conducted the oral hearing, and a specialist consultant, David Ball, had suggested a range of reasons for refusing permission, including the relative remoteness of the terminal from where the pipeline would come ashore, and the danger that it would detract from the area's scenic amenity and degrade its fragile ecology. Their report bluntly said that the development of a large gas-processing terminal 'at this rural, scenic and unserviced area on a bogland hill ... defies any rational understanding of the term "sustainability"'. Given the high level of rainfall experienced in north-west Mayo, the report specifically warned that there was a 'real risk' the storage repositories would become unstable, with 'massive amounts of peat' potentially 'washed off the slope', destroying the drainage system as well as public roads and houses in the vicinity. In its 2003 ruling, the appeals board zeroed in on the peat stability issue, discounting all of the other arguments. Meanwhile, having cancelled contracts worth €360 million, Enterprise Energy Ireland was forced to recast its plans and submit a fresh planning application in December 2003. This time, the 600,000 tonnes of peat requiring relocation to make way for a solid foundation for the terminal was to be transported with the aid of Bord na Mona and spread on a 150-acre cutaway bog near Bangor Erris, 12km from the site; Mayo County Council even pledged to improve the road from Bellanaboy so that it could accommodate heavy trucks. While the council's decision to approve the revised scheme in April 2004 was appealed by local residents, Shell was apparently so confident about getting approval from An Bord Pleanála second time around it began work on the route of the gas pipeline that August, 10 weeks before the decision was issued.

In March 2005 the Green Party welcomed a decision by Minister for the Marine Noel Dempsey to order a safety audit of the project, saying there were serious issues to be addressed in putting a high-pressure gas pipeline in 9km of soft peatland. Dempsey himself admitted that such an onshore pipeline, designed to carry unprocessed natural gas at a pressure of up to 345 bar, was 'unusual and unique both within Ireland and also within Europe'. In fact, there was no precedent for it at all. Natural gas excavated from the bed of an ocean is normally processed offshore before being piped inland at much lower pressure; Bord Gáis Éireann's pipelines carrying gas from the Kinsale Head field to Dublin and other locations have a maximum pressure of 100 bar. But whatever confidence residents in the vicinity of Shell's pipeline had in the 'independent' safety audit was shaken by Lorna Siggins' revelation in May 2005 that the engineering consultancy undertaking it, British Pipeline Agency Ltd, was jointly owned by BP and Shell. After five local men blocked access to their land, obstructing preliminary work for the pipeline, Shell obtained a High Court injunction and then applied to have them committed to prison for defying it. The 'Rossport Five' – Willie Corduff, brothers Vincent and Philip McGrath, Brendan Philbin and Micheál Ó Seighin – were jailed for contempt of court on 29th June 2005, even though Shell's Andy Pyle, who was gung-ho to have them all committed, had been advised that this was 'not the best course of action ... from a public relations point of view'. As Siggins reported, Shell E&P Ireland – in which Statoil has a 36% stake – even discussed suing the State if it failed to have opponents of the project jailed indefinitely. 'It is easy to dismiss the Rossport Five as just another bunch of NIMBYs, standing in the way of necessary development', wrote Fintan O'Toole, 'but in this case ... their imprisonment exposes the hypocrisy of the law, which holds that property rights are sacred except when vast public resources are being given away to powerful corporations, and unimportant people object to having explosive materials pumped through their lands ... If Michael Davitt were to be resurrected, he would find it all too eerily familiar.' Dempsey's response was to order a third 'quantified risk assessment' report, but the five men in Clover Hill prison remained defiant. 'Pipelines rupture: no pipeline engineer intends this to happen, but it does, with sickening frequency. The outlandish pipeline here proposed, to be forced in close proximity past our houses, is the stuff of nightmares', they said in a statement, issued on 14th July. 'The solution we are proposing – a shallow offshore platform – is the only positive one.' Relatives of the Rossport Five called for a boycott of Shell and Statoil service stations to put pressure on the two oil companies to build the terminal offshore, a proposition that also had the Labour Party's support. After it emerged that nearly 3km of onshore pipeline had already been welded together, in breach of ministerial consent for 'preparatory' works only, Noel Dempsey requested the developers to stop, at least until a third safety review of the project was completed.

But even as a 'Shell to Sea' campaign gathered momentum, the Minister gave his consent to proceed with laying the offshore section of the gas pipeline. Michael Ring TD described this as 'an insensitive decision at an insensitive time', while Jerry Cowley TD called for Dempsey's resignation, accusing him of being 'totally spineless' in dealing with Shell. In truth, the Minister was constrained by the 'plan of development' for the Corrib gas field approved in April 2002 by his predecessor Frank Fahey, who had no reservations about the project. *Solitaire*, the world's largest pipe-laying vessel, had been booked to lay the offshore pipeline, but the Erris Inshore Fishermen's Association said they were considering a blockade in Broadhaven Bay in protest over the imprisonment of the Rossport Five. Despite securing three of the seven 'consents' needed to proceed with various elements of it, Shell E&P Ireland announced in August 2005 that it would defer further development until 2006 to 'allow for a period of discussion and dialogue'. A statement from the company said it would 'use this time to address remaining public concerns' about the project, which had been designed to 'address Ireland's urgent need for an alternative indigenous natural gas supply'. Dr Mark Garavan, spokesman for the five men in jail, called on Shell to 'use this pause to reconfigure the entire project, make it safer and better with an offshore terminal, and listen to the people of Mayo'. But the men spent a total of 94 days in Clover Hill Prison before the company lifted its injunction and then began to dismantle sections of the onshore pipeline welded without authorisation. The imprisoned men suffered another setback when Mayo County Council, by 13 votes to 9, rejected a motion calling on Shell to locate its gas terminal offshore, after being warned that this could expose the council to an expensive law suit by the developers.

Whatever its price, the problem is that we need the Corrib gas field because of our staggeringly high dependence on fossil fuels. Oil makes up 56% of Ireland's primary energy consumption, significantly above the EU average of 43%. Gas imports bring the total for imported fossil fuels to 76%, according to figures published by SEI in August 2004. Gerard O'Neill, head of Amárach Consulting, has pointed out that Ireland is the ninth most oil-reliant economy in the world – even more dependent on 'black gold' than the US. In his contribution to *Before The Wells Run Dry*, published in 2003, O'Neill examined the impact of economic growth on oil consumption and discovered that for every 1% of growth, Ireland's use of oil goes up by almost 2%. Contrast that with the economy of the EU before the May 2004 accession: a 1% increase in GDP results in a rise in oil consumption of just 0.6%. 'It wasn't always that way', O'Neill observed. 'Up until the mid-1990s, Irish oil consumption per capita was below the EU average.' But that was before the explosion in car numbers as well as home heating and, to a lesser extent, electricity generation. The price of oil is rising, and is predicted to experience ever-greater price pressure over the next decade, not least because of burgeoning demand from China. In the short term, some of the price increases may be attributed to global instability. But over the medium term the simple fact is that oil is becoming increasingly hard to find in large quantities, or in quantities that make its exploitation economic. This fact alone makes a high level of car-dependency unwise. More importantly, vehicle emissions are a key contributor to global warming. Unless oil is used more sparingly, there is no chance of slowing – never mind halting – the effects of climate change.

Breaking the link between economic growth and environmental degradation is the real challenge facing Ireland, according to the Environmental Protection Agency. The buzz phrase in its report, *Environment in Focus 2002*, was 'eco-efficiency' – in other words, finding cleaner and more efficient methods of production to reduce the use of natural resources. Two years earlier, the agency found that record economic growth had accelerated pressures on the environment – pollution of inland waters, growing waste mountains, traffic in urban areas and soaring greenhouse gas emissions. In confronting these challenges, the EPA's 2002 report used 50 indicators to evaluate Ireland's progress. The overall trend gave 'cause for concern'. In particular, the challenge of 'decoupling' waste generation from economic growth was seen as 'formidable'. Only in the case of sulphur dioxide, where there was a decrease in emissions, had there been 'absolute decoupling', largely due to a switch by industry to sulphur-free and low-sulphur fuels. Greenhouse gas emissions from power plants had also not risen quite so fast because of an increased use of more efficient natural gas for electricity generation. But the positive stuff pretty well ended there. The rising number of households, suburban sprawl, changing agricultural practices and increased waste generation were all significantly adding to the pressures on the environment. The residential sector was identified as the one that shows least eco-efficiency, with waste generation and private vehicle numbers rising considerably faster than the rate of increase in population, mainly because of a trend towards smaller household size. Intensive agriculture also remains a major source of pressure on the environment, and, according to the EPA, it is 'the sector where the need to balance the three dimensions of sustainable development – economy, environment and society – is most evident'. Overall, the pressures on Ireland's environment are increasing at significantly faster rates than in most other European countries, due to rapid economic growth since 1995, and this presents us with problems in terms of meeting our international obligations. 'Ireland urgently requires a modern waste management infrastructure and an integrated, efficient public transport system to address the crisis situations both in the transport sector and in waste management', the EPA said.

In its May 2004 review of the environment, the Agency said pollution from rapidly increasing road traffic has become 'the primary threat to the quality of air in Ireland', hindering the prospects of meeting our commitment to curtail greenhouse gas emissions. The pollutants of most concern in this area are nitrogen dioxide (NO_2) and fine dust particles, or PM_{10}, which are emitted by diesel-fuelled buses and heavy goods vehicles – chemicals known to inflame respiratory illnesses. The results of monitoring, which showed high levels of nitrogen dioxide levels in some parts of central Dublin, indicated that compliance with the stringent new NO_2 and PM_{10} standards 'may present problems in some urban areas'. Abatement of PM_{10} pollution would be 'much more difficult' than the measures used to eradicate winter smog in Irish cities in the early 1990s. To cut PM_{10} might even involve short-term traffic bans, which would represent a major new challenge for local authorities. 'The rate of private car ownership and the volume of road traffic have already reached the levels predicted for 2010, contributing to traffic congestion in cities and huge increases in energy consumption and greenhouse gas emissions', the EPA said. 'The State cannot expect to comply with its emissions ceilings for nitrous oxides and greenhouse gases if their contributions from road traffic are not soon brought under control.' Energy consumption in the transport sector more than doubled in the decade to 2002, with unprecedented increases in the consumption of petrol and diesel – with the figure bloated by 'fuel tourists' from across the border. Most startlingly of all, the EPA found that the use of primary energy in road transport 'now exceeds that in all other major economic sectors, including electricity generation'. That's a real measure of the extent to which we are wedded to our cars. Nationally, 64% of all commuters travel to work by car, as drivers or passengers. As the review acknowledged, little progress had been made in encouraging people to switch to public transport. It blamed the delays in providing Dublin with an integrated transport network on the multiplicity of bodies involved, and said a single authority, responsible for land use and transport, 'should be established without delay'.

––––––

THE MOST CONTENTIOUS ENVIRONMENTAL ISSUE BY A LONG SHOT IS WASTE DISPOSAL. Incinerators and landfills are top of the list. However, recycling facilities, such as a composting plant in St Anne's Park in Dublin, have also drawn fire. But nobody can ignore the growing waste mountain. Household and commercial waste in Ireland increased by over 60% during the boom, with a volume equivalent to 600 kilograms per person each year. In terms of waste, that's the same as 600 bags of sugar. A report by Peter Bacon & Associates, commissioned by Greenstar, one of the Republic's largest waste management companies, estimated the total volume of household, commercial and non-hazardous industrial waste in 2002 at nearly 2.8 million tonnes – way ahead of earlier projections. Indeed, regional waste management plans finally being implemented in 2005 were drawn up on assumptions that such a volume of waste would not be reached until 2013. Bacon also warned that landfill capacity was running out, not just because of rising volumes, but also because, for years, so much of it had been used up unnecessarily by the dumping of construction and demolition waste. This waste, most of which can be recycled, was taking up to 50% of Fingal County Council's Balleally landfill site, for example, until it was finally banned in 2002; it is only used now to cover real rubbish. The report found that charges across Ireland rose steeply after the closure of older dumps that didn't comply with the new EU Landfill Directive. In some cases, notably the controversial landfill sites planned for Kilbarry, Co Waterford, and Carrowbrowne, Co Galway, the EPA granted licences against the recommendation of its inspectors simply because there was nowhere else to put the waste. The escalating cost of operating licensed landfills in the Republic was reflected in gate fees exceeding €200 per tonne, compared to only €50 per tonne in the North. These hefty charges for commercial waste disposal, now topped by a €15 per tonne landfill levy, led to a massive increase in illegal dumping. According to Steve Cowman, Greenstar's chief executive, more than 10% of all commercial, domestic and construction waste generated in 2003 was disposed of illegally, earning as much as €100 million for unscrupulous operators. Even the National Waste Database showed a difference of more than 400,000 tonnes between the amount of commercial and household waste generated in 2001 and the amount landfilled or recycled. No wonder the Bacon report called for the implementation of a fully audited UK-style system of waste tracking, with an emphasis on duty of care, as well as effective punishment for waste contractors involved in illegal dumping.

The discovery in November 2001 of hazardous hospital waste illegally dumped at Coolnamadra and Whitestown, in west Wicklow, dramatically highlighted the scale of Ireland's illegal waste trade. At one stage, more than 100 suspected illegal dumps were being investigated by Wicklow County Council, with an estimated 630,000 tonnes of waste unearthed at five major sites. In the case of Coolnamadra, the council estimated that the clean-up cost would be at least €3 million – or up to €20 million, if the material had to be incinerated. In July 2002 the High Court granted an order requiring Dublin Waste (trading as Swalcliffe Ltd) and its directors, Louis and Eileen Moriarty, to remove hospital and other wastes, and remediate the two-acre site. Evidence was given that the landowner, Clifford Fenton, had received £90 (€114) for every 25 tonne-load illegally dumped by Dublin Waste. If the hospital waste had been properly treated, it would have cost £450 (€571) per tonne – amounting to £11,250 (€14,285) for an average 25-tonne load.

Penalties for illegal waste activity, often less than €10,000 on summary conviction in the District Court, are paltry, though not all judges take a soft line. In one case before the District Court in Naas, involving Nephin Trading, the judge felt the operation of an illegal landfill site was so serious that it should be referred to the DPP for prosecution. But how could all the illegal dumping in Co Wicklow have happened unless the county council turned a blind eye? 'The council's exact "historical record" in relation to the dumps is unclear', wrote Tim O'Brien in March 2003. 'But we do know that, from about 1990 to 2000, hundreds of thousands of tons of rubbish were taken in fleets of lorries down country lanes around the village of Blessington, Co Wicklow, and dumped in holes in the ground, in disused gravel pits and covered over in fields ... From about 1997, the lorries switched much of the activity from Blessington further south, to the area around the Glen of Imaal. Residents of both areas made complaints about lorries damaging roads and, in the case of Whitestown, forwarded details of the lorries to Wicklow County Council. The file was subsequently lost.' In early 2003, extensive illegal dumping was discovered on land owned by Roadstone, the CRH subsidiary, at Dillonsdown, near Blessington – something the company at first denied and later said happened without its knowledge or consent. Dick Roche TD, a former member of Wicklow County Council, who became Minister for the Environment in September 2004, commented that Roadstone's 'see no evil, hear no evil defence means the fairies must have done it'. The company finally admitted in August 2003 that there could be about 60,000 tonnes of illegally dumped waste on its landholding, which – rather alarmingly – abuts Blessington reservoir, the main source of Dublin's drinking water. Roadstone said it was 'shocked and embarrassed' by the discovery of the waste and was working with the EPA on a remediation programme. Embarrassingly for the county council, there was said to be photographic evidence that it had availed of the 'facility' at Dillonsdown. In September 2004 An Taisce revealed that the EPA was now considering 'rewarding the landowners with lucrative licences' to turn illegal dumps into legal ones. Its presi-

↑ *An illegal dump found on Roadstone land at Dillonsdown near Blessington. The company at first denied the illegal dumping , and later said it happened without its knowledge or consent.*

dent, Frank Corcoran, pointed out to the EPA that any movement of hazardous waste must be recorded on what's known as a 'C1' form, which must be submitted to the Agency by 28th February each year. The form contains three key pieces of information – where the waste originated, where it is going, and who is taking it. In other words, the document is vital for checking on suspicious movements. However, according to Corcoran, an EPA official had told him: 'We don't read C1 returns.' In July 2005, however, the EPA surprised its critics by refusing Roadstone's application for a waste licence aimed at legitimising the illegal dump at Dillonstown. One of the things it took into account was a policy direction made by Dick Roche under Section 60 of the Waste Management Act specifying that illegal waste sites adjacent to housing must be 'remediated'. Welcoming the agency's decision, Roche urged Roadstone to 'do whatever is necessary to remove the waste, protect the groundwater and the integrity of the residential properties in the vicinity', even though this would cost the company millions of euro.

Ireland's illegal waste trade has also found a global dimension. Treacy Hogan revealed in the *Irish Independent* that hundreds of tonnes of illegal recycling waste, all originating here, had been seized at the ports of Antwerp and Rotterdam, bound for China and India. Altogether, some 100 containers were sent back home. This is

↑ *Killegar dump is located within sight of the dramatic Great Sugar Loaf mountain, also in Co Wicklow*

'waste tourism', and it's a dirty business. The Basel Convention was signed in 1987 with the aim of preventing unscrupulous companies in the EU and US using countries in west Africa as convenient dumps for hazardous waste. The EU's 'proximity princi-ple' also attempts to ensure that waste is recycled or dealt with as close as possible to its origin. (That is Indaver Ireland's main argument for locating its hazardous waste incinerator at Ringaskiddy in Cork Harbour.) In March 2004 Liam Reid reported that a criminal investigation was under way into illegal dumping of waste from the Republic in Northern Ireland. More than 2,000 tonnes of waste from as far away as Cork had been found in a boggy field just a few hundred yards across the border in Co Fermanagh, while a composting plant in Cookstown, Co Tyrone, contained at least 10,000 tonnes of waste from 13 counties. The North's Environment and Heritage Service suspected that a large volume of waste was passing through from the South on forged documents – much of it destined for landfills in Scotland and England, where disposal charges are a fifth of those in the Republic. The rest was being dumped at some 20 illegal sites in the North. Pressure from the European Commission to put an end to illegal dumping encouraged Martin Cullen to establish an Office of Environmental Enforcement within the EPA, with funding from the plas-tic bag levy. One of the first things the new Office did was commission a major study of illegal waste activity in Ireland. Ministerial orders under the 2003 Protection of the Environment Act reversed the burden of proof so that landowners are required to demonstrate they did not permit illegal dumping on their property. Cullen described it as a 'watchdog with teeth', but the Office is denied the power to prosecute local authorities when they flout environmental legislation.

Local authorities dragged their feet over the adoption of regional waste management plans first drafted in 1998. Councillors in several areas, feeling the heat of NIMBY pressure, baulked at anything that included incinerators, even after participating in junkets to inspect similar facilities abroad, notably in Copenhagen and Vienna. Some of the 'regions' made no sense. Kildare and Wicklow, for example, each opted to become a 'region' in its own right rather than do the logical thing of combining with Dublin. And Meath opted to join a north-east grouping, seemingly forgetting that it is also part of the Greater Dublin Area for the purposes of regional planning. Continued opposition by councillors led Noel Dempsey to rush through amendments to the Waste Management Act in 2002 so that regional waste plans could be adopted by county managers, and this temporary measure was made permanent by Martin Cullen in the Protection of the Environment Act. Yet there has been a reluctance to set up any structure at national level, other than purely advisory bodies, despite a call from Forfás, the industrial policy advisory board, for the establishment of a national waste management agency with 'step-in' powers to implement regional waste plans. Reflecting the frustration felt by industry over the worsening waste crisis, Forfás also proposed in December 2001 that fast-track planning procedures needed to be put in place to speed up the provision of disposal and treatment facilities, by designating their sites as strategic development zones. Under Part 9 of the 2000 Planning Act, an SDZ may be designated if its development is deemed to be of economic or social importance to the State, and this device limits the public to objecting to the principle of what is proposed, rather than the detail. As things stand, the Bacon report for Greenstar said intense opposition to incineration meant that the introduction of thermal treatment would come much later than envisaged by regional waste plans, placing yet more pressure on landfill. 'This is the key finding from our analysis', the economic consultant told the *Irish Times*. Bacon was also very dubious that recycling targets of up to 45% would actually be achieved. In the unlikely event that this unprecedented level of recycling is realised, Ireland would also have to find marketable uses for some 1.7 million tonnes of recycled materials annually – otherwise, as he warned, 'they immediately become waste again'. Even if we achieved a more modest 25% recycling rate – well in excess of the EU average of 14% – and put in place all the thermal treatment facilities proposed, the growth in waste volumes means that the landfill capacity required in 2012 would be similar to that needed in 2005. The performance of local authorities is also highly variable: Mayo County Council, for example, managed to divert less than 3% of household waste from dumps, compared with the exceptional 49.5% record achieved by Galway City Council.

After he took office as Minister for the Environment in June 2002, Martin Cullen quite shamelessly espoused a pro-incineration agenda, favouring a 'limited number of state-of-the-art thermal treatment facilities ... licensed to the most up-to-date and stringent standards'. Incineration had been on the Department of the Environment's agenda for years – justified on the basis that burning waste (with energy recovery) makes more sense than finding new holes in the ground for landfill. Moreover, it occupies a higher place than landfill in the EU's waste management 'hierarchy'. Thermal treatment, as it is officially known, forms part of regional waste management plans for Dublin, Connacht, the north-east and the south-east, which includes Waterford, Cullen's own constituency. Though the Fianna Fáil-Progressive Democrat programme for Government described mass-burn incineration as 'not an acceptable practice today', it left the way open for thermal treatment based on energy recovery from waste. Fianna Fáil, which hadn't a single word to say about incineration in its 2002 election manifesto, went along with the PD line that thermal treatment using the best available technology 'must be based on prior extraction from the waste stream of recyclables and problematic materials' like metals and batteries. The PD formula was seen as an endorsement of the German Herhof process, being promoted here by Treasury Holdings, under which recyclables are extracted from the waste stream and what's left is turned into relatively clean RDF (refuse-derived fuel) for cement kilns and the like. Herhof boasts a recycling rate of up to 50% by separating things like ceramics, water, glass, ferrous and non-ferrous metals from the waste stream before composting or incinerating the residue. Given that all waste is supposed to be treated as close to source as possible, Herhof's idea for Dublin was to have three small-scale plants on the city's periphery, something that would avoid having all the waste trucks converging on Poolbeg. According to John Singleton, the senior engineer in charge of the Poolbeg project, there was 'no objection in principle [to such an approach]. It depends on the volume of waste available.' However, the requirement for on-site incineration at Poolbeg effectively ruled out the Herhof approach. Plans for a Herhof plant in Waterford also foundered. In early 2005 the company ran into financial difficulties, but hoped to resolve these with the conclusion of a joint venture agreement later in the year.

More than 20 waste management companies, many of them from overseas, lodged 'expressions of interest' in building the Poolbeg incinerator as a public-private partnership project when it was advertised in mid-2002. Given the involvement of Danish consulting engineers COWI from the outset, when the first Waste Management Plan for Dublin was drafted in 1997, it was no surprise that a Danish power company, Elsam, finally emerged as the 'preferred bidder' in April 2005. (It is involved in operating nine incinerators in Denmark.) Though the capital cost of the Poolbeg incinerator will be at least €200 million, the value of burning up to 400,000 tonnes of municipal waste annually has been estimated at €600 million over the 25-year contract period. However, it will be 2010 before any waste is incinerated at Poolbeg because Elsam Ireland Ltd must go through the hoops of the planning process in parallel with seeking a licence from the EPA. Neither passage will be easy, given the level of opposition in Ringsend to incineration. Among those who will feel the heat is the Minister for Justice, Michael McDowell, the PD deputy for Dublin

↑ *Vienna's Spittelau incinerator, designed by Hundertwasser, should not be passed off as 'a sort of eco-friendly Disneyland', according to Green Party TD John Gormley*

South East, especially as one of his constituency colleagues, the Green Party's John Gormley, is an articulate opponent of incineration. Which is why McDowell put up strong resistance to the inclusion of waste disposal facilities in the remit of the once-mooted Critical Infrastructure Board.

Apart from dioxins, one of the most frequently expressed concerns is about the traffic impact locally. Based on the average capacity of municipal refuse trucks, this is likely to amount to 182 vehicle movements per day in and out of the Poolbeg site. Writing in the *Irish Times* in June 2000, Gormley disputed attempts to depict Vienna's Spittelau incinerator, designed by artist Friedensreich Hundertwasser, as 'a sort of eco-friendly Disneyland, complete with cartoon "green monsters" to instill civic pride in younger generations'. He also noted that Vienna's other municipal incinerator at Floetzersteig was now required to analyse soil samples from the area to determine the real level of pollutants. 'Consequently, local residents have been warned not to eat certain produce grown in their gardens', he said. More tellingly, Gormley quoted Ludwig Krämer, then head of the EU Waste Management Directorate, as saying that Europe was moving to phase out mass-burn incineration. 'In France, Belgium, Holland, Italy, Germany and Portugal, no more new incinerators are being built because the public will not stand for them', Krämer said. 'They are treated in the same way as nuclear power.'

The biggest battle in Ireland so far has been fought over Indaver's hazardous waste incinerator at Ringaskiddy, Co Cork. More than 23,000 people signed form letters objecting to the plan after it was lodged with Cork County Council in April 2001. 'No incinerator – enough is enough', the car-bumper stickers said. It was a reference to Cork Harbour. First it was Irish Steel, whose Third World-style plant and slag heap represent a slap-in-the-face to Cobh; later it was the Whitegate oil refinery, then the IFI fertiliser factory and a rake of pharmaceutical plants. The tall chimney of Aghada power station can be seen from miles around. Pylons carrying electricity lines march across the landscape – and more would follow if the ESB had its way; a sign at Gobby strand, near the Indaver site, warns anglers that there are live 110kV lines directly overhead. In and around Ringaskiddy, huge box-like structures house big names in

↑ *A child protests against Indaver Ireland's hazardous waste incinerator which is planned for Ringaskiddy in Cork Harbour*

the pharmaceutical sector, such as Pfizer, Novartis, Johnson & Johnson and GlaxoSmithKline. All of them generate hazardous waste requiring treatment or disposal – usually by exporting it to other European countries, or by treating it on-site – though the volume of waste has been reduced in recent years due to more stringent EPA licences. But John Ahern, Indaver Ireland's managing director, pointed out that Ireland was still exporting 24,000 tonnes of hazardous waste a year to Britain, Germany, Denmark or Finland, and that 60% of it arises in and around Cork Harbour. 'We should be big boys and deal with our own problems here at home', he told the *Irish Times* in October 2003. Thus, Indaver's argument for its €95 million plant was based squarely on the proximity principle. But what if something went wrong? 'Nobody can guarantee that something won't go wrong, not even ourselves', Ahern frankly conceded at An Bord Pleanála's oral hearing on the proposed development. 'But we've built every safety precaution into the design of the plant, including its own fire-fighting facilities.'

A lot of people in Cork are not so sanguine about the safety of incinerating toxic waste. When Linda Fitzpatrick, a mother of four young children, first heard the news that Ringaskiddy was being targeted as the site for a national hazardous waste incinerator, she could have cried. Her daughter Zoe has asthma, and she was partic-

↑ *Actor Jeremy Irons outside the Neptune Stadium after appearing at the Bord Pleanála oral hearing to the incinerator plan*

ularly concerned about emissions from the plant as the family's bungalow in the Hilltown countryside is two miles from Indaver's site as the crow flies. So when residents' associations around the harbour banded together to form CHASE (Cork Harbour Alliance for a Safe Environment) in September 2001, with the aim fighting off Indaver, Fitzpatrick became its spokeswoman. By holding coffee mornings and other fund-raising events, CHASE raised enough money to run a vigorous campaign and hire experts to present its case at the oral hearing. It also received discreet support from local business people fearful of the potential fall-out from an incinerator. 'We've kept this going by taking time out of our lives', said CHASE's chair, Mary O'Leary, who also has four children, three of them teenagers. 'The kids understand what we're at and they support us' – which is why so many of them turned up with placards at the opening of the oral hearing at Cork's Neptune Stadium in September 2003. British actor Jeremy Irons, who has a castle near Skibbereen, and renowned chefs Darina and Myrtle Allen of Ballymaloe House in east Cork, also appeared at the hearing and pleaded for the Indaver plan to be refused permission, arguing that it represented the wrong way for Ireland to go.

The omens for a successful outcome to the CHASE campaign were not good, however. An Bord Pleanála had already granted permission to Indaver Ireland in March 2003 for the State's first municipal waste incinerator at Carranstown, Co Meath, between Duleek and Drogheda. The board's ruling upheld the equally controversial decision by Meath County Council to permit the €80 million plant, which would generate electricity by burning 150,000 tonnes of waste per year. More than 26,000 people signed petitions against the project, and 4,500 individual objections were lodged with the council. Among those who appealed the council's decision were former Taoiseach John Bruton and former Attorney General John Rogers SC. Fears about health risks were intensified by the revelation that Indaver's Belgian-owned parent company had been forced to close a plant in Antwerp twice in the previous six months after breaching dioxin limits. The Carranstown decision drew an angry reaction, especially after it emerged that An Bord Pleanála had voted, by seven to two, to reject a recommendation for refusal from the planning inspector who dealt with the case and conducted an oral hearing. 'We will now have an incinerator on our doorstep when the Health Research Board says Ireland does not have the resources to monitor and review the health aspects of it', said Fine Gael TD Fergus O'Dowd. In making its decision, An Bord Pleanála had regard to the regional waste management plan for the north-east, which includes provision for thermal treatment, and the national waste management strategy. While precluded at the time from considering environmental risks, the board said the development of a 'necessary public utility' in an area with established industrial uses would not seriously injure local amenities.

In the case of Ringaskiddy, the appeals board also put government policy ahead of local concerns and granted permission for the second Indaver incinerator in January 2004. In this case, the board also rejected the recommendation of senior planning inspector Philip Jones, who conducted the lengthy oral hearing. Jones had produced a 300-page report which unequivocally rejected the Indaver scheme on 14 counts – in effect, endorsing the case made by its opponents. He argued, with some justification, that the EPA's National Hazardous Waste Management Plan's emphasis on minimising and reducing waste should be given priority over disposal facilities, in line with the EU's established waste management hierarchy. But the appeals board fundamentally disagreed with his interpretation. By a majority of nine members to one, it granted permission after considering the matter over the course of three meetings. The board said it had regard to the national waste management framework as set out in government policy statements, particularly their preference for incineration over landfill, and to the EPA's National Hazardous Waste Management Plan, published in 2001. It also took into account the geographical spread of hazardous waste in the State, with a concentration of large-scale chemical and pharmaceutical industries in the Cork Harbour area, and the fact that Indaver's site is adjacent to the N28 national primary route. Though precluded at the time by the 1996 Waste Management Act and the 1992 Environmental Protection Agency Act from considering issues relating to environmental pollution, the board said it had regard to the Health and Safety Authority's advice on hazards involving dangerous substances. Accordingly, it ruled that the site was 'an appropriate location for a necessary public facility', that Indaver's plan to develop it would not seriously injure the amenities of the area, and that the plant would be 'acceptable in terms of traffic safety'. In an attempt to assuage local fears, the board's 27 conditions included a requirement that bulk storage tanks on the site must have a 'double-skin' construction and be surrounded by an embankment, while those containing hydrochloric acid and aqueous ammonia are to be located in an enclosed building. Doubtless this will come as a great relief to staff and students at the €51 million National Maritime College, which was developed on a site directly opposite Indaver; the storage compound for drums of toxic waste would be located just 25 metres from its entrance. Ironically, the foundation stone for the college, beside the naval base at Haulbowline, was laid just five days after the oral hearing on Indaver's plan opened at the Neptune Stadium.

It seemed to CHASE and many other environmental campaigners that incineration was forced through, irrespective of the cogent arguments made against it – either

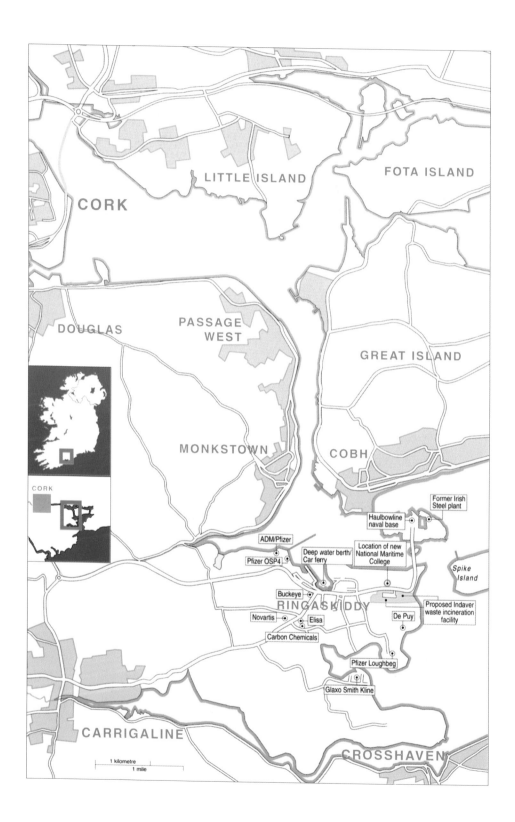

Map labels:

LITTLE ISLAND

FOTA ISLAND

CORK

PASSAGE WEST

DOUGLAS

GREAT ISLAND

MONKSTOWN

COBH

CORK

Former Irish Steel plant

Haulbowline naval base

ADM/Pfizer

Deep water berth/ Car ferry

Location of new National Maritime College

Pfizer OSP4

Spike Island

Buckeye

RINGASKIDDY

Novartis

Elisa

De Puy

Proposed Indaver waste incineration facility

Carbon Chemicals

Pfizer Loughbeg

Glaxo Smith Kline

CARRIGALINE

CROSSHAVEN

1 kilometre
1 mile

↑ *John Ahern, managing director of Indaver Ireland, with a model of its Ringaskiddy incinerator. 'We should be big boys and deal with our own problems here at home', he said.*
← *Map of Cork Harbour, showing Ringaskiddy and nearby towns*

to An Bord Pleanála or to the EPA. Dr Mary Kelly, director-general of the EPA since May 2002, was criticised by the anti-incineration lobby for stating openly that she had no fears about municipal waste incineration. 'Personally, I would prefer to live beside an incinerator than a landfill site', she told the *Irish Times* in December 2002. The credibility of the EPA had also been challenged by the Green Party. Pointing out that Kelly had previously headed IBEC's environment unit, the Greens questioned her credibility and claimed that the 'sustainability agenda' would not be advanced with her at the helm. Though some environmentalists see her as a poacher-turned-game-keeper, few could deny that she played a significant role in changing the mindset of industry while at IBEC. 'When I joined IBEC first, the environment was very rarely discussed at its national executive council, but by the time I left, it was almost con-stantly on the agenda', she told the *Irish Times*. 'There's been a huge change since IPC [integrated pollution control] licensing came in, and it's now very much part of the way they do business. Some have had to invest millions in very sophisticated new technology to ensure that they're not causing environmental pollution.'

Asked where the EPA stands on waste incineration, Kelly said one of its diffi-culties in entering the public debate was that the agency must adjudicate on licence

↑ *Dr Mary Kelly, director general of the Environmental Protection Agency*

applications for thermal treatment facilities, so 'taking a stand may compromise our ability to say yes or no'. Acknowledging that incineration had become an emotive issue and that scientific evidence alone would not dispel public fears, she said: 'Really, what needs to happen for people to believe in it is to have a fully functioning incinerator that isn't causing any problems ... we have got to make sure if we do licence them that they work without a glitch.' Then, bizarrely, the EPA appeared to bias its own consent process. While examining Indaver's application to license Carranstown, Kelly told the *Irish Examiner* that 'we will get domestic waste incinerators, beginning with the Indaver project in Meath where planning approval has been secured'. Dan Boyle, Green Party TD for Cork South Central, the constituency that includes Ringaskiddy, called on her to resign, saying the remark undermined the EPA's impartial role. CHASE also called for her resignation, as did the No Incineration Alliance, which led the campaign at Carranstown. 'What is the point of a community group going through the very expensive process of taking part in an oral hearing if the powers at the head of the EPA believe such a thing should happen?' asked Pat O'Brien, of the NIA. 'Most community groups are left fighting multinationals with bottomless pockets, and we spend 75% of our time worrying about fund-raising.' The EPA would only say that Dr Kelly's remark reflected her 'personal opinion' and was not its policy. In July 2004 campaigners and even a few industry insiders were dumbstruck when Laura Burke, Indaver's project manager for the Carranstown and Ringaskiddy incinerators, was appointed a director of the EPA, particularly as it coincided with the Agency's consideration of the company's licence applications.

In her December 2002 interview with the *Irish Times*, Mary Kelly pointed out that the EPA had already licensed nine or ten incinerators for industry. These were 'all working away quietly in the background under very strict regulation from us. So that in itself is an endorsement of incineration as a valid technology', she said. These incinerators are at Eli Lilly in Kinsale, Novartis and SmithKline Beecham in Ringaskiddy, Swords Laboratories in Cruisrath and Yamanouchi in Mulhuddart, both in north Dublin; Lawter Chemical in Grannagh, Co Kilkenny; and Roche in Clarecastle, Co Clare. Kelly, who holds a PhD in chemistry from TCD, believes the EPA has been very effective, particularly in performing its regulatory role. 'It's done a great job of licensing. Well over 500 IPC licences have been granted across all sectors of industry as well as 120 waste licences, in what is a pretty problematic area.' She agreed that some environmental NGOs perceive it as merely an 'industry-mind-ing' agency, 'but if you talk to people on the industry side, they complain that it's being swayed by the NGOs, so we must be half-way down the middle.' Asked whether the agency is too lenient in ensuring prompt compliance, she said: 'You have to be reasonable and give them a certain amount to time to install new technology, but you also have to be certain environmental pollution is not happening.'

In October 2004 the EPA issued a draft licence for the Ringaskiddy incinerator project, claiming that its 'stringent' conditions met the highest standards set by the European Commission's directive on waste incineration. The draft licence was signed by Dr Jonathan Derham, a senior EPA inspector, who then presided at a two-week oral hearing on appeals made by CHASE and others – including Indaver Ireland Ltd, which objected to its terms because they would limit what the company could burn. Derham ruled that it would be 'inappropriate' for the agency's directors to be called to give evidence on the issues involved, as CHASE had sought. He said the primary purpose of an oral hearing is to gather information and evidence that might support an objection in more detail. 'It is not a forum for the cross-examination of the directors. If that is what some were expecting, you are mistaken.' According to environmental consultant Dr Brian Motherway, who has worked for the EPA, oral hearings 'are being asked to do many things they were not designed to do, and are not capable of doing' – such as debating the merits or otherwise of national policies on waste. Neither could they address planning, social or developmental issues. 'But people want to talk about these issues. They want a wide debate on the merits of this proposal both in itself and in the wider context of Ireland's environmental and economic values.' However, the fact that the EPA decided to postpone its final ruling on Ringaskiddy until the end of 2005 was seen by Dan Boyle and other objectors as a sign that the Agency might be wavering on Indaver's controversial project.

In July 2002, six weeks after taking office as Minister for the Environment, Martin Cullen conceded that progress towards sustainable development in Ireland, as in the rest of the world, was 'slower than had been hoped'. The urgent need to put Europe on the path of sustainable development was underlined by an assessment of climate-change risks by the European Environment Agency, published in August 2004. It forecast more frequent and more economically costly storms, floods, droughts and other extreme weather; wetter conditions in northern Europe but drier weather in the south could threaten agriculture in some areas; more frequent and more intense heatwaves, posing a lethal threat to the elderly and frail; melting glaciers, with three-quarters of those in the Swiss Alps likely to disappear by 2050; and rising sea levels for centuries to come. As well as causing 20,000 additional deaths, the summer heatwave of 2003 resulted in crop harvests in many southern EU countries plunging by as much as 30%. As climate change gathers pace, these calamities will seem minor. According to Prof Jacqueline McGlade, the EEA's executive director, there is now 'a wealth of evidence that climate change is already happening and having widespread impacts, many of them with substantial economic costs, on people and ecosystems across Europe'.

———

7. Transport

THERE WERE SMILES ALL ROUND ON THE PENTHOUSE FLOOR OF THE DEPARTMENT OF Transport on Kildare Street when the chairman and senior officials of the National Roads Authority came to collect a big fat cheque. It was 5th February 2004, and Séamus Brennan had just announced the largest single financial commitment yet made by the Exchequer – €6.8 billion in State funding for motorways and other national road projects over five years. With a further €1.2 billion expected to come from the private sector, to be paid back from tolls, it amounted to an '€8 billion plan'. This sort of multi-annual funding package was exactly what the NRA said it needed to roll out roads. 'Our biggest crib was that we didn't know from year to year where we were going, but now we can run it more like a business – a huge business', said its beaming chairman, Peter Malone. Brennan described the agreement he had reached with Charlie McCreevy and the Department of Finance on multi-annual programmes as a 'very exciting breakthrough' that would avoid the 'slow-downs and restarts' that used to happen when roads were funded year by year. And he set 2007 as his target for the completion of full motorways running north, south and west from Dublin under the programme. 'I'm not saying that every last inch will be done by the end of 2007, but I believe in setting targets.'

After Brennan had put his eggs in the NRA's basket, Green Party transport spokesman Eamon Ryan TD said 'they've pushed aside all criticism because they just want to pour concrete.' He complained in particular about the NRA's plans to proceed with upgrades of the M50 interchanges, saying these were 'low down the list of transport priorities for Dublin' and were only meant to be carried out after major public transport improvements. Pointing to the high level of scrutiny now being applied to proposals for rail and bus, he asked: 'Where is the M50 business plan?' No wonder the Taoiseach sat impassively at an EU Presidency symposium in Dublin Castle, four days before the €8 billion plan was unveiled, as Ton Sleddens, a

→ *Traffic congestion on the roads leading to Dublin has become an endemic feature of commuter life in the capital's hinterland*

↑ *Eamon Ryan, TD: they've pushed aside all criticism of the motorway programme because they just want to pour concrete*

European expert on transport, made a compelling argument that the Irish roads programme failed every single one of 27 indicators of good transport policy. As for the M50, even after an investment of more than €800 million in new interchanges and extra traffic lanes, it will remain as congested as ever, as an environmental impact statement on the 'upgrade' concedes. Traffic levels will soar from around 80,000 vehicles a day in 2004 to between 194,100 and 203,700 a day on different sections of the route after the scheme is completed in 2008. These projections took no account of any increased demand arising from new motorways, such as the M3, feeding into the M50, and they also assumed that major public transport projects, such as the Dublin metro, will help to relieve the growing congestion. And if an IKEA store materialises on a site adjoining the Ballymun interchange, as the Government hopes, congestion on the M50 will be even greater. According to a report commissioned by the Irish Hardware and Building Materials Association, IKEA at this location could generate between 7,000 and 10,000 extra car trips on the motorway, bringing forward the day when 'demand management measures' will be needed to deal with worsening congestion. And when An Bord Pleanála approved the M50 upgrades in May 2005, subject to eight conditions, it specified that such measures must be drawn up by the relevant authorites not later than three years after the project's completion.

Meanwhile, the roads programme trundles blindly along. Among the major schemes finished in 2005 was the Sligo Inner Relief Road, which involved driving the N4 through the middle of the town, effectively cutting off its bus and rail station from the main shopping area. No fewer than 52 houses – most still lived in until they were compulsorily acquired and blocked up by Sligo Borough Council – were demolished to make room for this destructive four-lane dual carriageway. It was approved by Noel Dempsey in August 2000, at an estimated cost of £18 million (€23 million), but the final bill came to €74 million. It is also far from being the 'urban street' that was promised. Houses facing onto the highway and those backing onto it are all fronted by reinforced concrete walls, faced in sandstone panels and limestone-clad pillars for the sake of appearances. Along much of its length, there simply isn't room for new buildings to provide proper street frontages; just like the West Link in Belfast, surviving parts of the urban fabric on either side visibly testify to the damage it has caused. What's more, it won't even solve Sligo's notorious gridlock – a western bypass is already on the drawing boards. Asked if he could name any town in Europe where a similarly disastrous scheme was planned, Peter Malone, formerly chief executive of Jurys Hotels, shrugged his shoulders and smiled.

Though a multi-annual funding package was announced in March 2004 for public transport, there was just €1.9 billion in State money. The private sector was expected to stump up a further €575 million – amounting to nearly one-quarter of the total investment between 2004 and 2008 – but there was no detail on how this would be raised. In terms of State money for new transport projects, nearly 80% was being earmarked for roads. But even €8 billion wasn't enough. Less than two months after Séamus Brennan's announcement, the NRA said it would need an extra €2 billion if there was to be any chance of completing motorways from Dublin to Cork and Galway by 2008. Launching the Authority's annual report, Peter Malone said it wanted 'an answer yesterday' on the additional funding, which was to be raised from mortgaging tolls; otherwise these roads would not be completed until 2010, three years beyond Brennan's target. It was also lobbying for a change in its role from a 'funding agency' to a 'delivery agency', replacing local authorities. But even if the Government coughed up, would €2 billion really be enough? The Minister made no immediate commitment, but he announced just two months later that the NRA would be assuming full responsibility for road contracts from the local authorities. This had been recommended by PriceWaterhouseCoopers in the wake of an investigation by the Comptroller & Auditor General, John Purcell, after the Dáil Public Accounts Committee was told that the cost of building a kilometre of road, as well as acquiring the land for it, had doubled since 1999. Figures provided by the NRA showed a series of spectacular cost overruns – the Cavan bypass from €17 million to €32.7 million, the Nenagh bypass from €21.6 million to €42.9 million, the Youghal bypass from €10.7 million to €43.5 million, the Drogheda bypass from €112.5 million to €244 million, and so on. As a result, the estimated cost of the NDP roads programme had risen from €9 billion to nearly €16 billion in just a few years. In November 2002 the Department of Finance had been warned that the roads programme could cost €22 billion or more unless 'immediate and, if necessary, radical measures' were taken to recast it – a caution issued by Fitzpatrick & Associates in their mid-term review of the NDP. Michael Scanlan, assistant secretary at the Department, implicitly criticised the NRA when he identified a failure to follow 'a prudent approach to expenditure planning'. A central point emerging from the Comptroller's report is that, given the sheer scale of this 'initial' cost revision, it is nearly impossible to contain any subsequent figure. Inflation undermines the calculation of every holding estimate. Allied to this are the NRA's 'problem cases', such as the Dublin Port Tunnel, which more than cancel out projects that stay on target. The cost of the port tunnel first more than doubled – from €220 million in 2000 to €580 million in 2002 – and by July 2004 had increased again, this time by approximately

↑ *Aerial view of the N4 sweeping into Sligo. The recently completed Sligo Inner Relief Road involved driving the N4 through the middle of the town, with the demolition of 52 houses.*

the price of the original estimate. Thus, there is a real possibility of passing the €22 billion figure predicted by Fitzpatrick & Associates.

If the cost of all the motorways is one issue, their capacity is another. Motorways can take 55,000 vehicles a day, but we are actually building motorways to cater for fewer than 3,500 vehicles a day. In fact, about 300km of low-flow motorway is planned. Take the traffic levels on the existing Dublin-Cork road between Portlaoise and Mitchelstown, a distance of some 120km. According to 2002 traffic data, this section is used by about 10,000 vehicles a day. It wasn't all that different back in 1999 when the roads programme was in gestation; at different survey points between the two towns, there was a volume range of 5,400 to 13,500 vehicles. A few fields away from the existing road, the Minister for Transport plans to fund a new motorway using taxpayers' money. About a quarter of vehicles on the existing N8 will migrate to it, a total of 2,500. Only 25% of traffic using the existing road is long-distance, a figure found in a string of reports to government. The rest is local. Roads may account for 96% of all passenger traffic in the State, but the overwhelming majority of these trips are short hops, typically for commuting. Even with freight, close to half of all journeys involve less than 24km (15 miles), according to the Department of the Environment. Then there's the problem of tolling. The proposed

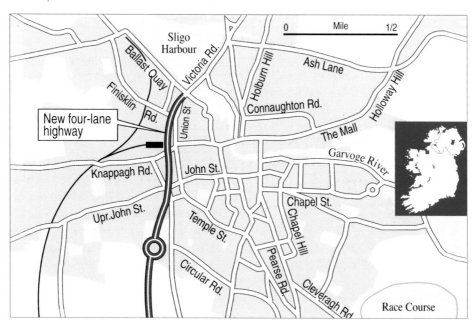

↑ *A view of the recently completed Sligo Inner Relief Road*
↓ *Begun in 2004, the map shows the route of the Sligo Inner Relief Road running through the centre of the town*

motorways between Portlaoise and Cork and Portlaoise and Limerick will have toll booths, but neither the NRA nor the Department of Transport has given any figures for the number of drivers expected to pay. In fact the notion that all long-distance drivers will be happy to forego the existing N8 in favour of a tolled M8 is optimistic. Hauliers have already said they will continue to use the existing road – and trucks account for one-fifth of the traffic it carries. So the tolled motorway will be lucky to see about 2,500 vehicles a day. Going from Portlaoise to Limerick, it's a similar story, at least as far as Nenagh. The planned motorway running parallel to the N7 can expect to see about 2,500 vehicles per day for about 70km. On the proposed M9, north from Waterford city, the traffic flow never exceeds 8,000 vehicles a day for about 40km – and for half this section the figure is below 3,500. The proposed Waterford to Kilcullen motorway is unlikely to average more than 2,500 vehicles per day over its length. Adding up these three routes – 70km on the M7, 120km on the M8 and 115km on the M9 – gives a total of 305km. Multiply this by the cost of building motorways – nearly €11 million per kilometre in 2003 figures – and it becomes clear that the taxpayer is facing a bill of €3.3 billion for three roads set to operate at less than 10% of their capacity.

The NRA's *National Road Needs Study*, published in 1998, included survey data compiled by Scetauroute, a French toll consulting company, of how many vehicles were travelling the full distance between Cork/Limerick/Galway and Dublin. The numbers were low. The Dublin to Cork route came in first with 1,700 vehicles per day. Then came Dublin-Galway at 1,600, with Dublin-Limerick third on 1,450. It was not until two years after the NRA's study was published that an official report was commissioned to examine rail patronage. The report, by Goodbody Consulting, put rail's share of the Dublin-Cork passenger market at 30%. However, it also acknowledged an earlier Iarnród Éireann study which put rail's share of the same market at 50%. There is a huge discrepancy here, but with no research to ground the National Development Plan, the Government never bothered – then, or since – to figure out the number of people making intercity journeys by road and rail. It also never bothered to ask people how they want to travel.

In itself, the 1998 *National Road Needs Study* was a modest document. Existing roads were to be upgraded to motorways, dual carriageways or high-quality single carriageways, with bypasses built to relieve congestion in towns along the way. Working with Scetauroute, the NRA came up with a price-tag of €5.6 billion for these proposals. Noel Dempsey launched the study in July 1998, but less than 12 months later he was thinking much bigger. He wrote to the NRA asking it to consider building five motorways and substantially improving 90% of other national routes. He was informed by the Authority that an additional €850 million would be needed to deliver the five motorways, while a further €550 million would take care of the other routes – a total of €1.4 billion. The NRA would later admit to the Comptroller & Auditor General that it didn't have the expertise in 1999 to make reliable cost calculations, so it guessed. Or, as Séamus Brennan put it, the 1999 estimates were 'rough, ballpark, back of the envelope' figures. But the Comptroller's message, which

Brennan sought to downplay with his casual approach on RTÉ's *Morning Ireland* on 30th June 2004, was completely the opposite: the NRA weren't anywhere near the ballpark.

Why did Dempsey ask the NRA to ditch a year-old study – the costings for which at least had the stamp of French experience – and go for five motorways instead? He told the *Irish Times* in May 2002 that governments had been criticised in the past for not investing adequately in roads, which was why the M50 and its roundabout interchanges were so congested. 'Having made that mistake once, we don't want to do it again', he said. Dempsey was responding to a report by

↑ *Noel Dempsey asked the NRA to ditch a year-old study in favour of the motorway programme*

the Campaign for Sensible Transport (CaST), which said the Government could make an immediate capital saving of €3 billion by scaling down the roads programme envisaged under the NDP. In a 53-page report entitled *The €12 Billion NDP Road Spend Frenzy*, CaST said the priority should be to proceed with bypass schemes for towns on existing national routes, identified in the 1998 Road Needs Study. But come 1999 there was a determination that the days of major routes with roundabouts and traffic lights would come to an end. Instead, whenever roads crossed, traffic would keep moving, with each flow carried on a different level – fully grade-separated interchanges, in engineering jargon. Forfás, the industrial policy advisory board linked to the Department of Enterprise, Trade and Employment, had produced a report in which the amount of motorway per square kilometre in Ireland was compared to a number of other countries. But motorway density is not a particularly useful yardstick. It does not follow, for example, that having a low density of motorways means that it is time to start building big roads. If this was the case, the Scottish uplands, the Lapland area of Finland and the Massif Central in France would be criss-crossed with motorways. But the NRA, oddly for a professional body, also bought into the network density shibboleth; its chairman, Peter Malone, told Lloyd Gorman that Ireland ranked last of 27 selected countries in terms of motorway density.

Even in 1999 it was clear that large-scale motorway building was going to cost a fortune. But when Dempsey sought the additional €1.4 billion the NRA said was needed for a ramped-up programme, Charlie McCreevy refused to increase the roads allocation in the NDP above €5.6 billion. He suggested that 'main arteries' should be completed by 2006, with a looser timescale for other projects. So a schedule of projects was included in the NDP with a fictional price-tag. The research was equally bogus. Asked what the NDP roads programme was based on, the Department of the Environment pointed to a Forfás report *Infrastructure Priorities for Enterprise*

↑ *Séamus Brennan: NRA cost estimates for the motorways were 'rough, ballpark, back of the envelope' figures*

Development in the Regions, compiled in early 1999. But this report is a jumble of contradictions. On the one hand, it advocated an 'immediate focus' on completing 'all town bypasses', while putting forward a strong case for 'motorway standard road links between urban centres'. Forfás apparently didn't realise that building motorways would render the town bypasses redundant. In a very short bibliography, the policy advisory board cited a handful of papers with a macro-economic focus; literature on road network design appears to have been ignored or missed. As a result, Forfás failed to spot that there might be much more efficient ways of making new intercity road connections than mimicking the old road network. For example, it didn't examine the possibility that a motorway from Cork could have first been routed north to cater for Cork-Limerick traffic and then continue north-eastwards to Dublin – something Joe Rea was later to advocate. Alternatively, a Cork-Dublin motorway could have been routed east via Waterford – as suggested in a 1988 study commissioned by the European Committee of the Regions. In the case of the Mid-West, Forfás earmarked the Limerick-Galway road as the major priority, not the Limerick-Portlaoise one. Its report specifically did not put forward what emerged with the NDP – five motorways converging on Dublin – so in no sense could the Forfás work be said to provide any basis for what the Department of the Environment claims it

↑ *Four lanes of morning peak-time traffic bound for Dublin, heading towards the N4 junction with the M50*

supports. Yet documents later released under the Freedom of Information Act showed that the report was supposedly relied on by the Cabinet sub-committee on infrastructure, consisting of Bertie Ahern, Mary Harney, Charlie McCreevy, Noel Dempsey, Mary O'Rourke and John O'Donoghue. The upshot is that the Government had no material before it on which to ground its 1999 decision to go for five motorways.

Prior to the adoption of the NDP, Ireland's 2,800km national route network was treated the same. Routes were upgraded or bypasses built when long streams of slow-moving traffic snarled things up. Tailbacks were objectively measured with 'level of service' standards applied to determine the extent of the work to be undertaken. There's an analogy here with supermarkets; when queues build to a certain point, extra checkouts are opened up. At the heart of the 1998 Road Needs Study was the idea that the same level of service should be maintained on every national route, so if the Sligo-Galway road was experiencing convoy-style traffic, with too few opportunities to overtake, then the level of service yardstick would catapult the Sligo-Galway road to the top of the 'to do' list. However, as documents from mid-1999 show, a uniform national standard was under threat during the formation of the NDP. And on the day the NDP was published – 15th November 1999 – the equal treatment of Ireland's national route network effectively died. Instead, following a process with no accountability, four corridors were picked out for motorway treatment and a fifth was marked 'maybe'. As the NDP itself said, 'the development strategy for national primary roads will include the development by 2006 of the following routes in their entirety to motorway / high-quality dual-carriageway standard: Dublin to Border (M1), Galway to Dublin (N4/N6), Cork to Dublin (N8), Limerick to Dublin (N7), Waterford to Dublin (road type and route to be further evaluated).' While the plan also pledged to improve other national routes, the Department of Finance had declined to increase the funding package above €5.6 billion. According to the Comptroller & Auditor General, the NRA viewed the NDP as a Government direction to build five motorways and do 'as much as possible' for other national routes.

With a motorway between Kilcullen and Waterford approved later at the insistence of Martin Cullen, there would now be five motorways to Dublin. And they would all be greenfield motorways. Taking its cue from the NDP, the NRA is sticking to a design strategy whereby new motorways will run in parallel with all of the old roads they supplement. Back in 1965, in his seminal work *Traffic in Towns*, the late Colin Buchanan wrote that motorways should not follow the inherited road system of a country. Instead, he recommended streaming traffic onto a new network which would be relatively 'skeletal' compared to its predecessor. The point is that, freed from national route alignments, the road-builder no longer has to parallel old roads. Yet 35 years after Buchanan's report, the NRA was proposing to relieve a problematic section of the Cork-Killarney road between Ballincollig and Ballyvourney with a new dual carriageway running alongside it. The Save the Lee Valley campaign, affiliated to CaST, queried the blueprint, saying 'one of the central criticisms of the NRA is that it proceeds directly to draw up a particular road plan ... without first producing an overall concept to justify the proposal.' The N22 caters for about 7,000 vehicles per day, and this was going to be supplemented by a dual carriageway with a capacity for 55,000. However, after picking a preferred alignment in April 2002, the NRA later decided to discard its proposals in favour of a new wide two-lane road. The reason? Mid-2002 was a time of fiscal retrenchment, and not being one of 'the five major inter-urbans', the dual carriageway plan got the chop. If the Nenagh bypass experience is anything to go by, the current plan to relieve the N22 by building a wide two-lane road alongside it isn't particularly smart. Assessment work for the NDP showed that adding two lanes to Nenagh's bypass would cause its bridges to fail the motorway height requirement by 20cm. As a result, the road will have to be reconstructed in the event it is brought up to motorway standard. Here, the NRA had ignored basic research, including the advice of experts like Mateu Turró, a senior official of the European Investment Bank. As he pointed out in his 1999 book, *Going trans-European*, 'new road sections should be designed with parameters and reserves allowing for easy expansion into motorways.'

Without any rigorous research to guide it, road-building in Ireland seems to have become an end in itself, divorced from regional and industrial policy. Regional imbalance was identified by the NDP as Ireland's critical weakness, but then the plan for five motorways feeding into Dublin was plucked out as 'the solution'. In short, the plan was drafted on the dubious assumption that the best way to develop regional cities at a faster rate than Dublin is to ensure better access to and from Dublin. Though 'parity of access to infrastructure' was promised for all of Ireland's regions, Dublin will be the only place where drivers can leave one motorway and go onto another. The NRA's *Review of 2001 and Programme for 2002* states that five radial motorways will 'facilitate access to the regions'. But the grand assumption that a radial network would redress regional imbalance was never secure. For example, will regionally based companies have easier access to neighbouring regions? And are cities in the south or west well located to take advantage of a radial network? It's impossible to answer yes to either question. A radial network only facilitates 'access to the regions' if the enterprise is Dublin-based in the first place; locating in Sligo or Galway wouldn't give anything like the same access. The NRA, incidentally, is based in Ballsbridge.

There is no suggestion that the choice of a hub-and-spoke network focused on the M50 was deliberately made to enhance Dublin as a location for new enterprise. In all probability, the greater 'enhancement value' placed on the M50 was completely unrealised by the designers of the new network. Subconscious or unconscious, the point is that a multi-billion euro motorway programme designed to spread development west will further concentrate it in the east. This 'gold plating' of greater Dublin through the NDP's roads programme can be shown in a very practical sense by the example of an inter-regional journey from Rosslare to Galway. A transport company is likely to use the M11/N11 route to Dublin and then take the M4/M6 to Galway. In other words, the NDP network will alter journey patterns with an increased number of vehicles seeking to use the M50 en route. This goes to highlight the competitive advantages of locating near the M50 in the first place. Of course, the motorway ring is notoriously congested at times, but there's a plan to spend millions more on an outer ring road – or M50 bypass – again eating into the funding for road projects that would help regional cities. By enhancing the M50's strategic value to a much greater extent than the regional centres, the NDP has always been a plan at odds with itself. Mateu Turró also realised that a radial motorway network would reinforce Ireland's existing imbalance. In Germany, he pointed out, road planners prevent the development of a hub-and-spoke motorway network because they realise that the centralising effects of such a network would be virtually impossible to counter. Those in charge of routing new roads in Portugal, who undertook a similar process to us in 1999, were also aware of the importance of accessibility between regions.

In that sense, the NDP roads programme is not a plan at all, and never was. As Julie O'Neill, secretary-general of the Department of Transport, told the Dáil Public Accounts Committee in July 2004: 'It is very clear that we are not talking about the same programme that was published in the National Development Plan.' The programme was so unclear and open-ended that to attack it in 1999 was to box shadows; even today it remains a moving target. We now know that the five motorways proposed by the NDP are to be routed through open countryside, not on the bed of pre-existing roads. All are planned to run within 7.5km of their 'ancestor' route, with

↑ *Julie O'Neill, secretary general of the Department of Transport*

↑ *Michael Tobin, chief executive of the NRA, and* ↓ *Joe Rea, ex-IFA leader*

some new sections of motorway criss-crossing older roads to achieve this. Or put another way, a series of national roads, denoted by the letter N, are to gain a neighbouring M. Yet it was impossible to say this in 1999: even the key paragraph of the roads chapter is framed in terms of 'developing' roads to motorways, and the notation of the national route network was used. For 12 to 18 months after the NDP was published, politicians in the thick of it still thought that greenfield road-building would be the exception. A number of Kilkenny councillors campaigned for a motorway in their county, thinking it would be built on the existing roadbed – a belief which turned out to be mistaken, as Chris Dooley reported.

During 2000 and 2001, it became clear that a significant amount of greenfield road construction was under consideration. On the August bank holiday weekend of 2001, the NRA's chief executive, Michael Tobin, wrote a newspaper article to explain that 'upgrading existing roads is likely to entail very serious implications for houses along the route'. He drew attention to the Cashel to Cullahill section of the Cork-Dublin N8 route where 63 houses would have to be demolished if the existing road was widened; only three houses would have to be knocked if an entirely new road was built. In May 2002 Noel Dempsey warned that up to 1,500 homes would have to be demolished to improve existing national routes along the lines proposed by the Road Needs Study. 'What we're trying to do is to get value for money by long-term planning', he told the *Irish Times*. But if one-off housing was forcing the NRA into virgin agricultural land for new roads, surely there was a case to minimise the spread of houses along the existing road network? After all, if the number of houses is kept to a minimum, then additional space for slow-moving vehicles in the form of passing lanes can always be added. The NRA was well aware of the situation. The 1998 Road Needs Study warned that one-off housing had compromised, and was continuing to compromise, significant stretches of Ireland's network of main roads. Widening national routes was being thrown into jeopardy – a caution set out on page 79 of the study, and repeated again 10 pages later. Under the 1993 Roads Act, the NRA falls under a duty to maintain the operational efficiency of Ireland's national roads. But since its establishment in 1994, the Authority has been loathe to use its position as a pre-scribed body to appeal against new housing, even where it would compromise road-widening options. It was not until March 2004 that the NRA lodged its first-ever appeal to An Bord Pleanála against permission for yet another one-off house fronting the N22 at Glenflesk, near

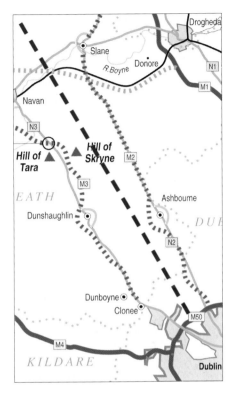

↑ *Representation of the Ballinter Residents Association proposal for a single motorway instead of the proposed M2 and M3*

Killarney. And the NRA only did this after being warned by An Taisce that failure to observe its legislative duty could leave it open to claims from road accident victims. Asked why no other appeal had been made over the previous decade, a spokesman for this organisation, with its annual billion-euro budget, said: 'We're a small body and we wouldn't have the resources.'

Well-informed public consultation was not much of a priority either, so it was impossible to get a handle on the future shape of Ireland's motorway network. But even with low-quality, piecemeal information, some commentators spotted that a monumental mistake was in the making. In a series of articles in the *Farmers' Journal* during July and August 2001, Joe Rea pointed to the mismatch between the extent of proposed motorway and the low traffic flows. 'Value for money must always be the main criterion', he wrote. 'Surely now it is time that we paused and examined our road building programme. Let's not proceed on a basis of a rush of blood to the head – motorways, we must have them! Transport decisions must be made on the basis of factual measurement and independent assessment ... Why not clarify the issues now under debate on the basis of fact, transparency, accountability and information before proceeding further?' Rea suggested that both Limerick and Cork could be served by one motorway routed via north Tipperary; traffic going between Cork and Limerick would be combined with traffic travelling between Cork and Dublin. 'Can a saving of £1 billion be ignored by Mary Harney and Charlie McCreevy, the Government's guardians of financial correctness?' he asked. 'Both Ministers have already caused a rethink on the Bertie Bowl. Why not do the same for roads?' The NRA wasn't listening. It didn't need to because late 2001 also saw a stand-off with farmers who were denying access to land earmarked for road-building. For every newspaper article weighing up NRA plans there were perhaps three or four opinion pieces hitting out at farmers. 'A million pounds a week' farmers were costing the tax-payer read the headline on an Emer O'Kelly piece of August 2001. That now seems a pittance to pay for a little scrutiny to avoid the waste of billions.

Those who privately urged the NRA to recast its plans also got short shrift, mainly because the Authority managed to escape with answers that were, in the words of one airline chief executive, 'bollocks'. The proposed M3 between Clonee and Kells, steered through the planning process by Meath County Council and the NRA, mimics the path of the existing road. In early 2000, an alternative was put forward by the Ballinter Residents Association, with the involvement of retired civil engineer Alan Park. They wrote to the NRA proposing that, since the N2 and N3 were so close, a new motorway should be built between them instead of two motorways, each beside the old national route. Having sat on the proposal for 10 months, the NRA responded saying that the idea was 'not in accord' with the NDP. But the NDP merely talked of 'upgrading' the N2 and N3, not of replacing them with new greenfield motorways. The proposal by the Ballinter Residents Association fulfilled the NDP as validly as the NRA's own plans. Instead of grappling with the substance of the issue, the Authority criticised the idea of an intermediate motorway on the grounds that it would 'run through a landscape currently undisturbed by major road infrastructure, with potentially serious implications for communities, the environment and farm severance'. This was a preposterous response, because the NRA's proposals involve precisely the same action and have precisely the same adverse effects. The difference, as the Ballinter Residents Association noted, was that one intermediate motorway would cause about half as much damage. The real reason their idea was rejected, according to one member of the group, was that it fell into the category of NIH – 'not invented here'. Tagged with this label, the alternative simply could not be entertained by Meath County Council or the NRA.

In August 2003, just after An Bord Pleanála had rubber-stamped the M3, the authors of this book met with the Minister for Transport, Séamus Brennan, while working on an RTÉ radio series *Transport in Crisis* with producer Richard Hannaford. Inevitably, the board's decision to approve the M3 came up. 'Sure, that'll never happen', Brennan said of the road scheme. Indeed, he could see the logic of routing an M3 into the Drogheda bypass to direct traffic onto the M1, which is currently operating at about half of its capacity. It could easily take traffic diverted from the N2 and N3. The best option would be a motorway link between the outskirts of Navan to the Drogheda bypass on the M1, following the route of the railway line that carries ore from Tara Mines. The rationale is simple. Minimal severance would be caused by such a plan, while the archaeological risks are likely to be a lot less serious than on the proposed route of the M3. In addition, the proposal would take the traffic burden away from Navan and Slane. The suggested link road would also be much shorter (at 26km) than the two motorways and, therefore, much cheaper to build (at around €260 million). Even allowing for the extra cost of bypassing Dunshaughlin, Ashbourne and Slane, with its notoriously dangerous bridge, it is obvious that the overall bill would be considerably lower. Another beneficiary would be Drogheda Port.

Indeed, the possibility of linking the N2 and N3 with the M1 was examined in a 2001 study on the viability of an 'outer orbital route' around Dublin. Though it found merit in the proposal, implementing it had to take into account 'the limited availability of funding and the competing demands for this funding'. The NRA's response to the specific proposal to link Navan with Drogheda was given by Michael Egan, its head of corporate affairs. Interviewed by LMFM (Louth-Meath FM) in mid-December 2004, he called it 'child-like'. His comment sits uneasily with best practice in countries like France, Germany and the Netherlands. All three have located road and rail lines beside each other to minimise severance. For a considerable period of time, the NRA had declined to follow European practice on the provision of crash barriers and motorway service areas. It did a U-turn in both cases, and on the outer orbital route, too. In February 2005, during the Meath and North Kildare by-election campaigns, Transport Minister Martin Cullen announced that the NRA was now 'priotitising' another feasibility study of the proposal, which the Taoiseach himself already said he favoured. Experts were to provide detailed costings for Cullen on a route from Drogheda to Navan and around to Naas. And this was in addition to the planned outer ring road, just a couple of miles west of the M50. Conceding that the more far-flung outer orbital route, 'will not happen overnight', Cullen said: 'Now is the time to explore how it could work, the difference it could make and how much it would cost.' The ballpark estimate was 'over €1 billion'. Asked about the coincidence with the by-elections, then just 10 days away, in two constituencies plagued by traffic congestion, the Minister said: 'I never put it in that context at all.'

Doubtless, it is only a matter of time before the NRA embraces European practice and looks at existing severances before routing new roads. Like Séamus Brennan seeing the logic of an east-west link between Drogheda and Navan, a major road running north of Waterford to New Ross could be built more economically along a defunct railway line instead of cutting a swathe through the countryside. Reducing the land acquisition bill would save a lot of money, but this doesn't seem to rank high on the NRA's priorities. The Comptroller & Auditor General found that the cost of acquiring land for new roads had 'increased disproportionately in recent years' to 14% of programme costs. Working with a figure of €8.32 million for one kilometre of motorway back in 2000, the NRA thought the land acquisition element would come to just over €330,000. Two years later, it recalculated the cost of motorway at €10.32 million per kilometre, and 14% of this comes to almost €1.5 million. In other words, the cost of land is five times what the NRA originally reckoned. But

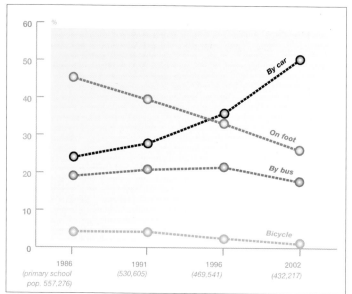

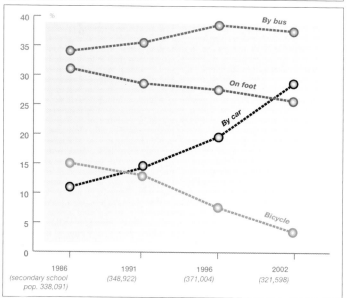

← In a relatively short period there has been a dramatic decline in the number of students walking or cycling to school; instead they go by car

[source: CSO]

this huge leap doesn't seem to have prompted it to wonder whether its objectives could be achieved with substantially less land acquisition. As Gene Kerrigan observed when the Comptroller's report was published, 'it's only public money'.

As well as establishing the NRA, the 1993 Roads Act put an onus on the Authority to deliver a 'safe and efficient' road network. It was also required by Section 18 of the Act to 'prepare a draft plan for the construction and maintenance of national roads' every five years. The plan was to be the subject of detailed public consultation as well as an 'independent assessment' before being submitted to the Minister for approval. However, no such plan has ever been prepared. Instead, we got the NDP.

The failure of the Authority to produce a coherent long-term plan has had an untold impact, especially in highly sensitive areas like the Tara-Skryne Valley. When An Bord Pleanála approved the M3 in August 2003, it apparently did so under the mistaken impression that proposals for a motorway alongside the N2, about 12km to the east, had been dropped, and it came as a surprise to board members to learn that proposals for an M2 were still being advanced. The appeals board also approved plans for the M7/M8 interchange south of Portlaoise, despite being urged to reject this scheme by Danny O'Connor, the former Fingal county engineer, who dealt with it as a planning inspector. As designed by the NRA and Laois County Council, the interchange would only cater for Dublin-Limerick and Dublin-Cork traffic; it would be completely useless to Cork-Limerick traffic. This made nonsense of the Government's declared policy of promoting 'balanced regional development'. Yet the scheme passed through the entire process of consideration, design and approval before anyone seriously questioned it. Indeed, of the 16 major road projects processed by the appeals board in the two years since assuming appellate jurisdiction for them in January 2003, not one was refused. However, the board's cave-in on the motorway programme can't be blamed entirely on the fact that the NRA has never produced a roads plan. At the time, An Bord Pleanála was under the dire threat of being replaced by a Critical Infrastructure Board which would steamroll major roads and other 'essential' projects; that's why it acquired the nickname 'An Bord Stampála'. The last thing it could be seen to do was stop and think. Without ever producing legislation to set up the new board, it had apparently been cowed by Martin Cullen into making hasty decisions. The true costs were never considered.

A key reason for the growth in traffic congestion is the 'school run'. In 1986 close to half of all primary school children in Ireland walked to school. By 2002 this was down to just over a quarter. Walking to secondary school is also down, though the drop is not as steep. Almost one-third of 13 to 19-year-olds walked in 1986; in 2002, just one-quarter did. Cycling to school has seen fivefold decreases at both pri-

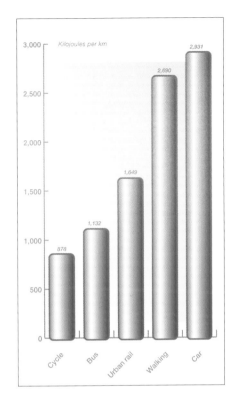

↑ *Energy used by each mode of transport*

[*source: Timoney, 'A Future for Motoring' paper to Institution of Engineers of Ireland conference, 2003*]

mary and secondary level in the period 1986 to 2002. In both streams, the car is gaining ground, and fast. Half of all primary school students were taken by car in 2002, double the 1986 level. Nearly 30% (28.6) went to secondary school by car in 2002 as against 11% in 1986.

A municipal bus service goes hand-in-hand with walking and cycling. Public transport offers independent mobility; a 15-year-old may live within walking distance of schools and sports fields, but the cinema could be in the middle of town, and his or her bus journey unlocks opportunities for social interaction. Unless bus routes are designed to integrate with new housing, the result, as US commentators have noted, is children 'grounded' in suburbia for want of transport. The term 'conscript chauffeurs' has emerged to describe parents, usually mothers, who end up ferrying children here, there and everywhere. Public transport is also indispensable for older people: without a readily accessible service, a disproportionate number of the elderly become prisoners in their own homes.

A planning report prepared for the National Spatial Strategy concluded that towns need to have a population of 20,000 or more to support bus services, and suggested that future growth should be focused on these towns. Buses would cater for journeys where walking or cycling is difficult or, for personal reasons, impossible, so the town centres would not be clogged by cars. However, it is self-evident that housing needs to be closely knit to support public transport. That's why attempts to provide a bus service in Mullingar, for example, have failed. Though the town has seen its population double over the past 15 years, it is so spread out that nearly everyone has to rely on cars to get around. To have a bus service with 10-minute frequencies, at least 35 homes per hectare are required, according to the 1999 report of Britain's Urban Task Force chaired by architect Richard Rogers. So even good-sized towns need to be relatively compact, preferably kept to within a 5km radius of the town centre. By focusing on walking, cycling and short-hop public transport in larger towns, congestion and the amount of energy used in getting around would be kept as low as possible. The alternative is oil-dependence, sedentary lifestyles and social exclusion – all of which are caused, at least in part, by excessive car-use.

Motorways are the sinews of sprawl, encouraging the creation of new 'suburbs', which are more low-density and car-dependent than anything built before. Even though it involves spending more than €20 billion, the roads programme currently being pursued has no research basis. As Gary Fitzgerald of the Campaign for Sensible Transport put it, the stated justification for the motorways became a moveable feast: 'First, there was an attempt to defend it on the basis of necessity, but that was debunked on capacity grounds. After that, they said it was good for balanced regional development, but the 2002 census exposed that. Then they started using the safety argument.' We all hear reports of serious road accidents week in, week out. One of the most horrific, in January 2004, was a six-vehicle crash on the N8 near Mitchelstown. Claiming the lives of four members of the same family, it occurred on a 'wide, flat and largely straight stretch of road with good sightlines in each direction', Tim O'Brien reported. However, a spokesman for the NRA confirmed that roads like this were 'a cause of concern' – precisely because their 'good' characteristics might encourage motorists to feel over-confident and resort to speeding. It was precisely because of these accidents that the existing road network was being replicated by motorways, according to the NRA. But Irish motorways aren't particularly safe, as Ferdia O'Dowd noted in July 2001. 'When a priest from North County Dublin was killed earlier this year by a car which crossed the central median of the M50, it underlined the fact that Ireland is one of the few remaining countries in the European Union where such a fatal accident could have happened', he wrote. Throughout Europe, the typical motorway crash barrier is made from precast concrete 'heavy enough and strong enough to deflect a fully laden articulated lorry back onto its own side of a dual carriageway or motorway, never mind a car'. O'Dowd contrasted Ireland and Sweden, which had installed nearly 650km of barrier-protected three-lane roads, rearranged as 'two up and one down', or vice versa. Even the Swedish Roads Authority was taken aback by the results of its 2+1 programme; the accident rate turned out to be only one-seventh of what it had predicted in advance.

After articles by commentators like O'Dowd, the NRA set up a working group to look at installing barriers on existing roads. Its report, published in April 2004, set out a plan for 2+1 roads capable of handling flows of 11,600 to 17,250 vehicles per day. The key advantage of this type of road, as the report noted, is the 'reduction in driver frustration by the provision of overtaking opportunities every 2km'. No matter how slow the driver in front is going, there'll soon be a chance to overtake, and, crucially, an overtaking lane dedicated to you. And because it is barrier-protected, unlike a wide two-lane road, there is no threat of another driver hurtling towards you in the wrong lane. Cross-over accidents in Ireland are almost double the rate of Sweden or the UK, thus highlighting the need for a barrier system, the working group said. So the adoption of 2+1 would help to eliminate head-on collisions, the single largest fatal accident type (at 37%) on national primary routes.

Even within the NRA, the case for retro-fitting one recently built wide two-lane road – the Portlaoise-Limerick section of the N7 – as a 2+1 road is seen as 'massive', one of its officials told us. A similar case could be made for the proposed road from Gowran Park, in north Kilkenny, to Waterford, instead of building it as a greenfield motorway, and, indeed, for the N3, as an alternative to the controversial M3 – as transport researcher Brian Guckian proposed in April 2005 – to provide one element of an integrated 'transport corridor' for Co Meath involving bus, road and rail. As it is, 41km of 2+1 road is to be built under the first four projects, which the NRA has termed 'pilot' schemes. But even before announcing them, it had already decided that another 809km of 2+1 road would be built, bringing its complement up to 850km – almost as much as the proposed motorways. What this shows is that when the NRA got the time and space to do some real research, it seized on 2+1 as a particularly suitable road type for Ireland. The big difference, of course, is that the 2+1 programme takes safety as the supreme law – not road-building for its own sake. But the NRA is riding two horses – motorway building and safety. And there is an inherent conflict between bringing Ireland's existing 2,800km national route network up to

↑ *Views of 2+1 roads showing how the central barrier is used to allocate the second lane in both directions*

a proper safety standard and going off building a whole lot of motorways. Sure, the elimination of uncontrolled right-turning movements will inconvenience property owners along each route selected for retro-fitting because they may be required to drive longer distances to access their properties. Some people with driveways exiting onto national routes will not be happy. But this merely serves to highlight an area where the NRA has been seriously remiss, at least in the 10 years up to 2004 – defending Ireland's national route network from one-off housing. To do that, however, it would need more political support.

As well as being a good match in safety terms, the NRA discovered that 2+1 is practically tailor-made for Ireland's traffic volumes. To build anew, it would cost €3.6 million per kilometre (2004 figures) – marginally cheaper than a wide two-lane road, and about a third the cost of a motorway, freeing up significant sums to put safety first. On any reading, the Authority's 2+1 report demolishes the case for proceeding with the National Development Plan's motorway programme – particularly as the roads replaced by greenfield motorways would have to be retro-fitted with barriers anyway, for safety reasons. As we have seen, the process that produced 900km of motorway was arbitrary. The 1999 pro-motorway submission from Forfás was an extremely weak document. Having missed all the road design literature, it failed to realise that safety was the first priority. The advisory body never made the distinction between reducing the accident rate on the existing network and coming up with a coherent plan for motorways in the long term – for example, Joe Rea's idea of routing a Cork-Dublin motorway to serve Limerick on the way. Just look at the figures. About 120km of motorway is earmarked for Mitchelstown to Portlaoise, another 100km is planned between Limerick and Portlaoise, and a further 100km between Limerick and Cork. That makes up a triangle of motorway 320km in length, costing about €3.3 billion at 2002 costs. Now, instead of a triangular arrangement of motorways, consider a tripod – a motorway running from Cork meets a motorway from Portlaoise south-east of Limerick: the result in monetary terms is €1 billion less. For politicians who care about the way public money is spent there is still an opportunity to recast the 1999 plan, but such politicians, if they exist, would need to act quickly.

The problem in Ireland is that road designers don't seem to give much thought to the function of roads; they just want to build them. A classic example is access to

↓ *The four routes approved by the National Roads Authority for Swedish-style 2+1 treatment*
[source: NRA, April 2004]

Project	County	Length	Build type
Ballybofey to Stranorlar (N15)	Donegal	16km	greenfield
Castleblaney to Clontibret (N2)	Monaghan	8km	greenfield
Dromod / Roosky bypass (N4)	Leitrim	8km	greenfield
Mallow to Rathduff (N20)	Cork	9km	retrofit

Rosslare from the midlands, Connacht and west Ulster. Plans for the new motorway between Kilcullen and Waterford might have been routed via New Ross, with the result that exporters serving counties like Kildare or Longford, when going to Rosslare, would enjoy a high quality road for at least half their journey. But the NRA overlooked this opportunity and the southern leg of the proposed M9 mimics the existing N9. Ports like Rosslare have been the main victim of this unthinking attitude. But then, ports are the 'hind tit of Irish transport policy', as a managing director of one of Ireland's leading logistics companies put it. True, they play a decreasing role in passenger traffic – a by-product of low-cost air travel. But the Celtic Tiger grew up on international trade. Some 95% of Ireland's GDP is attributable to exporting, up from 37% when we joined the EEC in 1973. Measured by volume, 99% of Ireland's overseas trade passes through its ports. By 2007, traffic through the ports will have increased 50% above 2002 levels, according to figures published by the Department of Communications, Marine and Natural Resources in April 2003. While multinational companies account for a staggering 84% of Ireland's exports – a figure cited by the Irish Exporters Association – those firms rate the country's ports policy as 'poor', according to a Government task force on cargo traffic. In a 2002 report the task force recommended that a Department of Transport be set up with full responsibility for the development and implementation of policy across all transport modes. But in June of that year, when Séamus Brennan was appointed to head such a department, the port sector, which had cogently articulated the case for more joined-up decision-making, was excluded. Seven members of the task force, including its chairman Dr John Mangan, wrote to the *Irish Times* saying they were 'utterly dismayed' that the Government had ignored maritime transport by leaving it outside the remit of the new Department. That Ireland could at least try to learn from other countries was a central thread of the letter. 'A key element of successful transport policy is the effective integration of all forms of transport (witness, for example, the ultra efficiency and competitiveness of all aspects of the Dutch transport network). Roads, rail lines, airports and ports should all be developed as part of a coherent framework. Choosing to ignore one mode of transport is a recipe for both fragmentation and inefficiency, and renders the transport chain only as strong as its weakest link.' And, according to the signatories, there would be long-term consequences for divvying up ministerial portfolios in such an arbitrary manner. 'Sadly, then, it is likely that the development of Irish road, rail and air transport will not be co-ordinated with the development of ports and maritime transport. It is nonsense to suggest that the appointment of a Minister of State or the establishment of inter-departmental co-ordinating committees will remedy this shortcoming. The effects of this policy fiasco, while not immediately obvious, will significantly restrict our economy.'

While the recommendations of one report were being ignored, the compilation of another was under way. Soon its recommendations would, like the first report, be sat on, dithered over, ignored or otherwise not implemented. The latest report had an impressive title: *The High Level Review of the State Commercial Ports*. Commissioned before the 2002 election, it was compiled by Raymond Burke, Farrell

Grant Sparks, and Posford Haskoning, who found a 'lack of ports policy and no clear guidance of what the ports should do'. The purpose of their report, published in April 2003, was to advise the Government on how to modernise Ireland's port sector, with particular emphasis on institutional reform, including possible mergers. 'Vessels will become larger and deeper, and become more sophisticated from a handling perspective. Economies of scale will force them to visit less ports than heretofore, and only to those ports which can offer fast turnaround, efficient loading and discharge, flexible working arrangements and safe and easy access at all times of the day or night.' Ports unable or unwilling to keep pace with shippers' requirements would be left behind, it warned.

Even though business increased quite spectacularly in the Celtic Tiger years, there are more goods handled in Grimsby, one of the largest ports in Britain, than all Irish ports put together. Nonetheless, as the high-level review found, 'many ports have extensive investment aspirations in infrastructure which they believe will generate new business.' In light of global trends, the consultants were sceptical: 'Port companies should be consolidated on a regional basis to reduce overheads ... and to rationalise investment.' Dublin Port is as large as all the other ports combined, but despite its robust financial position, it has continued to receive considerable State funding, including a grant of €4.6m in January 2003. The other ports were just about ticking over. 'Most ports other than Dublin could not afford significant new investment', according to the review. It recommended that the Government should no longer finance port expansion, a proposal the Department of Communications, Marine and Natural Resources essentially endorsed in January 2005. But the Government has failed to prepare the ground for other key recommendations. Dublin is the only port big enough to fund investment. So unless there are port mergers along the south and west coast, as the review recommended, Dublin will continue to gain market share, particularly across Munster and south Leinster. The task force saw a way out of this conundrum by using the rail system to serve a network of western freight depots, known as 'dry ports'. 'The development of these dry ports on a regional basis can contribute greatly to the strengthening of regional development policy', effectively by providing a similar level of shipping services to the west and the midlands as is available in the east. They would also facilitate the movement of freight by rail at night directly to the Continent, instead of having to rely on Britain as a 'landbridge'.

More Munster-based companies are sending goods destined for the Continent through Dublin, even though it's a longer journey. Freight forwarders such as DHL have increased their dependence on British roads since 1999; another company, DFDS, with bases in Cork, Dublin, Naas and Shannon, now sends 70% of goods destined for the Continent via Britain. The policy vacuum means that firms across the south of Ireland are finding themselves increasingly locked into Dublin Port, and, in the process, are becoming needlessly reliant on British roads. But the Government hasn't even taken the first step towards filling the policy vacuum by making a decision on the future catchment of Dublin Port. The task force found that 53% of goods landed in Dublin are destined for the city and county, 21% are delivered in the rest of

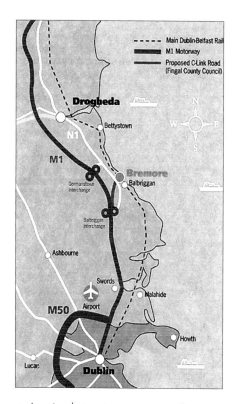

A map showing:
- - - Main Dublin-Belfast Rail
M1 Motorway
Proposed C-Link Road (Fingal County Council)

Drogheda
Bettystown
N1
M1
Gormanstown Interchange
Bremore
Balbriggan
Balbriggan Interchange
Ashbourne
Swords
Airport
Malahide
M50
Howth
Lucan
Dublin

↑ *A major deepwater cargo port at Bremore, Co Dublin, is being promoted by Drogheda Port Company [see www.portofdrogheda.com]*

Leinster, and 26% go to destinations outside the province. Positioned smack in the middle of Dublin Bay, any plan to relocate the port would push delivery distances up. Such a plan was put forward in 1989 in a feasibility study by ESB International for a site at Loughshinny, in north Co Dublin. In 2000 ESBI and the Irish National Petroleum Corporation identified the possibility of running a pipeline between an inland terminal on the M50 and Dublin Port. After working up the proposal, they realised there would be a 50% shortfall in capital costs, and the idea was not pursued further. Dublin Port, with its sizeable footprint, has great scope to maximise the use of its land with new technologies. Capacity has been greatly boosted since 2000 with more modern crane equipment and automation, and both these initiatives have allowed the port to increase its throughput to 20 million tonnes.

But the controversial plan to infill 50 acres of the inner bay opposite Clontarf appears to have stalled on environmental grounds. Even more questionable was the clandestine deal Dublin Port struck with the Anna Livia consortium – a group comprising Bennett Construction, Kilsaran Concrete and the Gallagher developer family – so that they could bid for the National Conference Centre. If the port was so short of land, why was it prepared to sign away property worth millions of euro per acre in such a secretive fashion? The 50-acre infill may no longer be necessary because, in early 2005, proposals for a large port in north county Dublin resurfaced at Bremore, about 12km from Loughshinny. This wasn't a bid by Dublin Port to move north. Instead, it was the Port of Drogheda seeking to relocate 15km south. Consultants retained by the port company studied 11 possible sites. Bremore came out on top and the company secured rights to develop 150 acres in an initial phase of development. The facility being planned would be capable of handling five million tonnes of freight annually, and even more in the future, because the port company also has the option of buying an additional 250 acres. According to Paul Fleming, its chief executive, 2009 is the targeted opening date. During 2005, the priority was to work on a Local Area Plan, a focused blueprint to ensure that a new port campus complies with the broad objectives of the Fingal County Development Plan. Whether Bremore can take business from Dublin Port – or even replace it – remains to be seen.

But given its strategic location adjoining the Dublin-Belfast rail and road corridors, and with links to both being 'designed in', the project has every prospect of success.

Ireland's major ports are on the east or south coasts because almost all of our exports not being delivered to Britain or western Europe go to feeder ports like Rotterdam or Hamburg, and, from there, around the world. Handling 17 million tonnes in 2003, Dublin Port is overwhelmingly dominant in catering for high-value goods. Shannon Foynes handled 10 million tonnes in the same year, and is Ireland's second largest port company in terms of tonnage, with bauxite for Aughinish Alumina and coal for Moneypoint the staples of the port's business. According to the high-level review, the Shannon Estuary is 'Ireland's greatest maritime national asset due to its naturally occurring depth and sheltered waters'. But the estuary faces west, so if it did try and cater for higher-value goods, the ships carrying them would have a few hundred kilometres added to their journeys. Another downside of the Shannon estuary is that good transport links go only as far as Foynes, while the deeper water is further west.

Cork's facilities are also scattered throughout its harbour. As the high-level review pointed out, the container terminal at Tivoli, just east of the city centre, is running short of capacity. Even if the existing site could be better used it doesn't have the depth of water needed for the new generation of ships. The Port of Cork wants to relocate the container terminal nearer Ringaskiddy, where there is already a roll-on, roll-off facility, but this investment could 'not be covered by operating expenditure'. Also, such a move would take the container terminal away from the Cork-Cobh line, ruling out the prospect of ever railing containers to a new port.

Waterford's container port at Belview faces similar problems and couldn't take the new generation of ships, even if expanded. Waterford also spends about €1 million a year on dredging. To provide one metre of additional clearance, the port would have to more than double its dredging efforts, and the annual cost could surpass €3 million. Currently, it is the only port in Ireland where containers are moved directly between train and ship. Before the collapse of the Cahir viaduct on the Waterford-Limerick line in October 2003, Belview was increasing rail traffic between Cork and Waterford, with a depot at North Esk acting as a small 'dry port' for Cork. About 80km (50 miles) east of Waterford, the port of Rosslare is still grossly underused despite being well-located to serve traffic bound for Britain as well as the Continent. It also offers the fastest possible turnaround times largely because there's no estuary to navigate. The Europort, as Rosslare calls itself, saw €40 million invested in the 10 years between 1992 and 2002, putting it 'in a position to provide a first class service', according to the high-level review. However, although Rosslare is rail-connected, the vacuum in ports policy means that it doesn't handle containers. And as this vacuum continues, uncertainty pervades the future of ports along the south and west coasts. The reason is simple. As the high-level review starkly put it, there are 'too many commercial port companies, many of them operating in close proximity to each other'. Even if they merged, Shannon Foynes, Cork, Waterford and Rosslare would have no more than the 40% share of the national market held by Dublin Port.

↑ *Rosslare Europort in Co Wexford is still grossly underused even though it has had €40 million invested in it in the 12 years since 1992*

Dublin's ability to offer one sailing after another got it where it is – a dominance secured by critical mass, in other words.

Eoin Gavin, former secretary of the Irish Road Haulage Association, has noted that widening the M25 around London gave rise to an increase in demand much greater than the extra capacity provided. While the National Spatial Strategy acknowledged the need to avoid a similar zero-sum gain around Dublin, 'our National Development Plan seems to be only active in the Greater Dublin Area', Gavin told the Association of Irish Regions in Tralee in October 2003. The most traffic-choked intersections in the country were along the M50, something that pointed to the need to promote a major alternative to Dublin Port, he said. Two of the world's largest ferries – the Stena *Adventure* and Irish Ferries' *Ulysses* – were introduced on the Dublin-Holyhead route in 2003 but, according to Gavin, 'one has to question the arrangement whereby the 9am and 9pm sailing times favour both manufactures and exporters in the GDA.' In order to make the evening sailing, an 'export from the west of Ireland has to be on a truck by lunchtime'. A later sailing time would suit companies based in the regions better, but speed and capacity on the Dublin-Holyhead route has forced regionally based companies to grin and bear awkward sailing times. Though 'the shortest landbridge route to UK and mainland Europe is through

Rosslare', the port remains relatively underused. Gavin pointed out that efforts to increase capacity at Dublin Port would widen 'the prosperity gap between the regions and the Greater Dublin Area', while also exacerbating 'problems of traffic congestion, environmental pollution and uneven distribution'. Road-building was set to produce results contrary to declared policies; however, no one in the Government seemed to care.

Port-related traffic is centrally important to the future of Iarnród Éireann's freight business. Yet a report by Arup Consulting for the Department of the Marine in October 2000 said it was 'remarkable how poor the rail connections are to major ports such as Dublin and Cork. In each case, the rail freight depot is located one to two miles away from the ports' container terminals.' And, in the case of Dublin, the port's container business has become increasingly concentrated on the south bank of the Liffey, and the cost of building a new rail link across the river is seen as too high to even contemplate. Nonetheless, Arup found that 'rail has the potential to greatly increase its share of port traffic'. And the National Climate Change Strategy, also published in October 2000, specifically pledged that 'any remaining barriers to the transport of freight by rail will be identified and removed'. Nothing has happened.

Iarnród Éireann has not publicly made the case to develop one full-service port with proper rail access, nor did this feature in any of the official reports done for the company. In fact, Iarnród Éireann has consistently played down the potential of its freight operations. As Mary Canniffe reported in 2001, a study by its own freight division said the Irish market for rail freight was hampered by 'relatively short, therefore uneconomic transport distances' and a 'restricted network which necessitates the addition of road haulage to give a door-to-door service'. But as short-hop airlines have long-realised, turnaround time is much more important than distance. The rail freight division has a fairly unorthodox way of doing business, according to Irish Railway News (IRN), an Internet lobby group. In November 2001 one of Iarnród Éireann's biggest customers, Coillte Teoranta, was hit by a 60% increase in tariffs. It refused to pay and timber traffic ceased until an intensive lobbying campaign managed to have it resume two years later. Late 2001 also saw Iarnród Éireann demand a 50% price increase from CRH to continue carrying gypsum. CRH declined to pay and this traffic has not returned. In 2002 the company said it wanted to withdraw from all container traffic, not long after completing the purchase of 24 state-of-the-art container wagons for €4 million, raising all bridges on the Dublin-Belfast line to accommodate high-clearance containers, and erecting six new cargo cranes at freight depots, each costing somewhere in the region of £1.5 million (€1.9 million).

IRN drew attention to the semi-state's accounting policy, under which revenue and expenditure for rail freight is lumped together with passenger traffic. Fixed costs (such as track wear) are not apportioned between freight and passenger services so it is impossible to gauge the financial implications of ceasing freight on a particular line. Detailed figures are only press-released selectively, usually in an attempt to close a line. For example, an annual revenue figure of €100,000 was released when the company sought to close the line from Rosslare to Limerick Junction. The closure proposal was actively supported by Martin Cullen. He told a meeting of Waterford

Container depot	new £1.5m crane 1995-99	Average no. lifts per day in 1999	Containers handled 2004
Dublin	√	86	yes
Cork	√	37	yes
Waterford		17	yes
Ballina		16	yes
Limerick	√	10	yes
Mallow		6	no
Dundalk	√	4	no
Longford		2	no
Belfast	√	2	no
Sligo	√	1	no
Galway		1	no
Tralee		0	no

← *Iarnród Éireann invested heavily in new rail freight facilities, but failed to win the customers needed to justify the outlay*

[source: Arup Consulting Engineers / Iarnród Éireann]

City Council in November 2002: 'We simply don't have the resources to develop everything and choices must be made.' According to a report in the *Munster Express*, he even suggested that the viability of the city's proposed western bypass and new bridge over the River Suir could hang on the termination of the Rosslare line. 'To be viable, the bypass will need a critical mass of traffic – of every kind', he said; more juggernauts on the roads, in other words. Cullen had simply taken it at face value that the line was no longer viable.

The Strategic Rail Review, published in April 2003, pointed out that some 20% of Iarnród Éireann's freight trains were either cancelled or delayed, compared to just 4% for a Scottish rail company of similar size. Booz Allen Hamilton, the consultants who carried out the review, found that there was a litany of lost opportunities. The case of Lisheen Mines in Co Tipperary was detailed under a heading that ran: 'Bulk traffic on the roads due to lack of a policy framework'. Lisheen produces around 400,000 tonnes of ore concentrate a year from reserves estimated at more than four million tonnes. Even though the 1997 Programme for Government strongly advocated rail transport for mines, there was no support or framework for this. As a result, the Lisheen transport contract was awarded in mid-1999 to a road haulage company. Instead of two trains, 80-90 trucks make round trips of 260km to transport 1,350 tonnes of ore each day. If the authorities had been willing to part-finance the £6.7 million needed to get the ore to Foynes by improving the rail link, it could have saved on external costs in terms of pollution, accidents and noise, as well as road mainte-nance – a combined bill of €4 million a year, according to the consultants.

Booz Allen Hamilton identified the fact that CIÉ receives lump-sum grants as a problem. The money is not tied to the number of passengers or freight carried. This means there is no incentive for Iarnród Éireann to go from carrying one container to taking five. The consultants bluntly warned that rail freight was 'at risk of irreversible decline if the current policy vacuum continues', and calculated that its meltdown would cost €63 million annually – €27 million in additional operational and road maintenance costs together with €36 million due to pollution and road accidents. In

July 2003 Brian Ranalow, president of the Irish Exporters Association, called for the introduction of a properly structured rail freight allowance. He pointed out that rail freight rebates aimed at reducing road congestion are available across the EU, but not in Ireland. The Government isn't interested, however. Responding to a question from the Labour Party's transport spokeswoman, Róisín Shortall TD, on 25th March 2004, Séamus Brennan said there were 'no plans' for a rail freight allowance. Blithely ignoring statistics showing that rail's market share plummeted from 5% in the late 1980s to about 1% by the end of the millennium, Brennan disingenuously told the Dáil that the current way of doing things would 'serve to reduce the impact of freight on the road network'. A year later, his own party colleague, John Ellis TD, complained that Iarnród Éireann was 'using their monopoly position to dump everything on the roads'.

The Government appears to be stewarding a policy which will ultimately see all freight go by road, even though this has the potential to raise costs for Irish exporters in the longer term. Countries across northern Europe – Britain, Denmark and Sweden in particular – are pressing companies to consider rail or at least adopt an approach that leaves the rail option open. The reason is simple: their governments know that labour costs, energy efficiency and environmental compliance – or any combination of these – may soon make it cheaper to rail goods across Europe. For Ireland to skew its exporting options by only being able to deliver goods within driving distance would be foolhardy. We may not be far from the day when the cheapest way to get a container full of Coca-Cola concentrate from Ballina to Barcelona is to bring it to the local rail depot and have it travel unaccompanied to Spain. The problem is that Irish transport policy doesn't have anything to say on this. In fact, Ireland is back in the starting blocks. A major full-service port aside from Dublin, served by rail and road, has yet to be chosen.

The grand plan to make Ireland's chief port more accessible by road is the Dublin Port Tunnel. Way back in 1992, National Toll Roads plc proposed an east-west tunnel. Broadly parallelling the path of the River Liffey, this option would have split truck traffic north and south along the M50. The idea made a lot of sense. Instead, it wilted and died because the preferred north-south tunnel had the support of those who saw it as the first leg of a motorway route running all the way from Lissenhall to Leopardstown – the so-called Eastern Bypass. (How this remains on the drawing board without proof of the journey demand to justify it is something of a mystery. As Tim Brick, Dublin City Council's deputy city engineer, frankly put it in March 1999: 'Anyone who thinks that it will remove a solitary vehicle from St Stephen's Green is living in cloud-cuckoo-land.') But Bertie Ahern threw his weight behind a north-south route because it might offer some relief from through-traffic to his constituents in Drumcondra. Facing northward, the reality is that the Dublin Port Tunnel is best suited to catering for traffic from that direction. If Dublin Port draws in more business from Munster and south Leinster, it will inevitably result in greater traffic congestion between the M50's Red Cow and M1 interchanges – as if there isn't enough already.

The saga of the Port Tunnel's height shows that its designers were not keeping abreast of the latest developments. A 1997 study by the School of Management at Edinburgh's Heriot-Watt University noticed a steady growth in lightweight goods, as plastic and other synthetic materials increasingly replaced heavier traditional ones. The authors of the study, Alan McKinnon and James Campbell, found that light products tend to fill the available floor area of a truck very quickly, leaving it well below its weight limit. Inserting an upper deck into lorry trailers not only made better use of space, it also reduced total truck numbers. 'In the UK, where most roads have five-metre height clearances, double-decking of articulated vehicles carrying low density products could cut haulage costs by around £340 million per year and carbon dioxide emissions by 0.5 million tonnes per year', the study found. That larger vehicles result in fewer trucks on the road has been borne out by British figures: the number of heavy goods vehicles there dropped from a peak of 593,000 in 1967 to 422,000 in 2001. A similar drop in vehicle numbers would happen in Ireland, if larger trucks were permitted here. The potential saving in carbon dioxide emissions would amount to 34,000 tonnes, or 3% of the country's total transport emissions in 2003. Given that transport is the sector where Ireland faces its greatest Kyoto challenge, this is not to be sniffed at. In 1998, a year after McKinnon and Campbell published their study, the British Department for Transport began to promote double-deck trucks – a strategy underpinned by a new policy document, *Towards Sustainable Distribution*. This was followed in August 1999 by new rules for motorway bridges and tunnels, requiring them to be built to a height of 5.3 metres with a clearance of 5.03 metres.

Throughout the 1990s, Ireland was experiencing the same truck trends as Britain, and the NRA was already applying British standards in the design of motorway bridges. On East Wall Road, one of the main arteries into Dublin Port, a 4.6 metre railway bridge was replaced with a 5.3 metre structure in 2002. Before being dismantled it was the most collided-with bridge in Ireland, taking 104 hits from trucks between 1985 and 2002 – and, critically, 51 of these were recorded before 1998; the Dublin Port Tunnel got the go-ahead in December 1999. At the time, the opening date was given as 2003 and the cost was put at £204 million (€259 million). The plans

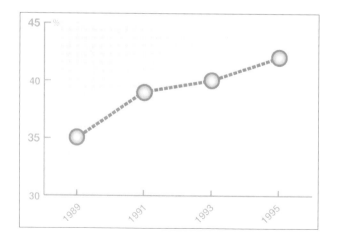

← *Low-density products account for an increasing share of transport movements in the UK.*

[*source: CSRGT, reproduced by McKinnon and Campbell, 1997*] *Note: The market is measured in tonne per kilometre and is confined to goods taken by road.*

provided that the tunnel would be built to a height of 4.9 metres, with an operational clearance of 4.65 metres.

In September 2001, after discovering that the motorway standard was not being applied, the Irish Road Haulage Association asked Dublin City Council for a review. In response to criticism that it should have raised this issue sooner, Seán Murtagh wrote a letter to the *Irish Times* saying hauliers assumed the clearance would be 'similar to bridges on all national roads and motorways'. The authorities still had plenty of time. Of the 5.6km route, some 1.1km is surface road. This leaves 4.5km of tunnel, of which 2.4km was excavated by massive battery-shaped tunnel-boring machines, and the other 2.1km by 'cut and cover' tunnelling. It was later to emerge that the boring machines were more than large enough to deliver an operational clearance of 5.03 metres; it was the plans for the cut-and-cover section that really needed to be tweaked. Even though tunnelling would not begin until spring 2002, the hauliers got a frosty reception at their initial meetings with the project team. The senior engineer then in charge, Seán Wynne, insisted there was 'no design flaw'. However, he did acknowledge in a letter to the *Irish Times* that the kilometre-long Conwy tunnel on the approach to Holyhead had a clearance of 5.1 metres – meaning that some trucks travelling through a tunnel on the eastern side of the Irish Sea would slam into the roof of what Dublin City Council and the NRA were planning on its western shore. Wynne also told Tim O'Brien that Ireland's legal limit for the height of trucks was 4.25 metres. The Department of the Environment, then overseeing road construction, had no choice but to contradict him: the limit of 4.25 metres was never valid because there had been no consultation with our EU partners when it was proposed back in 1996. In July 2000 the 1996 regulations were officially revoked, making the height of the Dublin Port Tunnel a matter for ongoing design review. Originally, the hauliers sought motorway/dual carriageway standards for the tunnel – i.e. an operational clearance height of 5.03 metres. However, at a meeting with city officials in December 2002, it was agreed an operational height of 4.9m would be satisfactory. Afterwards, deputy city engineer Tim Brick, who had taken charge of the project following Seán Wynne's untimely death in July 2002, wrote to the hauliers telling them the council was 'conducting a review of the feasibility and cost of adjusting the finished road levels and overhead equipment fittings in the tunnel, to see if the overall operating clearance height could be increased by 20-25cm'. For the next six months, figures of €20-€120 million were bandied about as the likely cost of raising the height. The lead contractor on the project was Nishimatsu Mowlem Irishenco, but no-one with the authority to ask them to cost a full-height tunnel actually did so. Instead, a host of widely differing estimates were given to journalists as if confusion itself was a virtue.

Séamus Brennan's answer was to propose banning trucks too high to fit in the Dublin Port Tunnel. But Austin Gilligan, general manager of Gwynedd Shipping, said banning double-deck (or 'super-cube') trucks would have economic as well as environmental drawbacks. 'Hauling paper tissue once accounted for 100 journeys a month: now, with high-clearance trucks we carry the same volume in 56 trips.' His experience tallies with the '40% increase in usable volume that double-decking typically permits', a finding by McKinnon and Campbell back in 1997. IRHA spokesman Jimmy Quinn noted that the Dublin Port Tunnel had a projected life of 100 years, and said we 'should be looking forward to the future, not to the past'. The *Irish Times* also wondered if those in charge of the project had noticed the growing use of double-deck trucks. 'How confident can they be that the tunnel will still cater for the vast bulk of port-related traffic in, say, 50 years time?' it asked in an editorial. A plethora of companies would be affected by the lower limit, among them An Post, Marks & Spencer, C&C, Bulmers and Tayto. Some 60% of car transporters would be banned if the cut-off was set at 4.65 metres. Ireland would also be in trouble at European level: any truck ban would be open to challenge for breaching EU rules on the free movement of goods. In June 2003 the president of the IRHA, Eamonn Morrissey, recalled a telling vignette of Irish engineering history at a meeting of the Oireachtas Joint Committee on Transport: 'It has been said that the port tunnel has a lifespan of 100 years. A great piece of engineering carried out in my area in 1923 was the Ardnacrusha power plant, which was designed by Siemens in Germany. The recommendation at the time was to put dual-carriageway bridges over the river. The authorities replied: "No, we have only ass and carts in Ireland. We will never go over with anything else." If we had taken on board the plans at the time, there would be no need to bypass Limerick city because we would have dual-carriageway bridges over the river. However, we took the easy and cheap option. If the same option is taken with the port tunnel, what will people say in 100 years' time?'

For Morrissey, the debate soon moved much closer to home, with Limerick County Council and the NRA unveiling plans for a 900-metre tunnel across the Shannon estuary with the same operational clearance as the Dublin Port Tunnel – 4.65 metres. 'Was nobody listening?' wondered Jerry Kiersey, of the Transport Umbrella Group, which had been campaigning for the Dublin clearance height to be raised. The €100 million tunnel would be the last link in a €350 million southern ring road sweeping around Limerick to connect all the main roads leading into the city. In April 2004, at the oral hearing into the tunnel plan, An Taisce joined hauliers in emphasising that five-metre motorway bridges were pointless if major bypasses weren't going to follow the same standard. As Tim O'Brien reported, the NRA's response was to claim that 300 railway bridges in the State were no higher than 4.65 metres. But this didn't tally with Iarnród Éireann's website (www.irishrail.ie), notifying drivers of just 31 bridges with low clearances, some of which are higher than 4.65 metres. Childers Road bridge in Limerick has a clearance of 5.03 metres, for example. In Dublin, rail bridges across Pearse Street, Westland Row, Clontarf Road, Gardiner Street, Beresford Place, Talbot Street and Store Street all provide 5.03 metres clearance, or more. Curiously, from an NRA point of view, all new railway overbridges must provide a clearance of at least 5.03 metres – merely to comply with the Authority's own standards; the bridge on East Wall Road is a case in point. As the IRHA's Jimmy Quinn told Gordon Deegan in August 2004, the costs of providing such a clearance under the Shannon are 'very, very small'. Talking to the authors of this book, Michael Egan, the NRA's corporate affairs manager, expressed a similar view. He said the NRA would be happy to revisit this issue when the Department of Transport introduced standards for vehicle heights, redressing a lacuna that has existed since the 1996 regulations were revoked.

Politically speaking, the Minister for Transport had an easy exit strategy. He could have decided – as the British government did in August 1999 – that all new tunnels would have an operational clearance of 5.03 metres. In July 2004 the NRA and Dublin City Council told the Department of Transport that a higher clearance on the Dublin Port Tunnel could be gained by moving the lanes away from the sides of the tunnel, slightly reducing their width. However, they said the Department would have to take responsibility for this course of action. In August 2004, then junior minister Jim McDaid again raised the issue of banning trucks higher than 4.65 metres. The Department's reasoning was based on allowable vehicle heights across all the EU member states. But Britain remains our single largest trading partner, and the British Department for Transport had been promoting 'supertrucks' since 1998. McDaid even ventured that double-deck trucks 'must' be more dangerous, although double-deck buses are less than a foot (30cm) lower than these trucks. But maybe McDaid didn't know that the EU had acknowledged the benefits of 'supertrucks' in 1997. Evidence-based policy was something for other countries.

———

AIRPORTS POLICY HAS BEEN MORE INFORMED, BUT NOT GREATLY SO. IN DECEMBER 2002 Senator Shane Ross candidly recalled being on the receiving end of great generosity from Aer Rianta, the State agency then responsible for Cork, Dublin and Shannon airports. It was 1991 and Aer Rianta had invited an entire Oireachtas committee to Russia for a look around their duty-free shops there. They were treated to a week to remember. 'We visited the Hermitage and the Winter Palace. Vodka for the drinkers was plentiful.' Ross, being a teetotaller, couldn't take advantage of the free booze, but he didn't have to put his hand in his pocket all week. 'I do not believe I fondled a single rouble', he confessed. The trip served a useful purpose. The TDs and Senators witnessed excellent work by the semi-state company, but for Ross it also highlighted the close relationship between politicians and Aer Rianta. 'We were culpable, cosying up to the state sector. It would have been wiser to spend just two days there. Five was a trifle generous. The cost to the taxpayer was £7,000.' In return for its generosity, the airports authority was 'indulged, allowed to build its empire'. What's more, 'Aer Rianta is a Fianna Fáil fiefdom', wrote Ross. 'Meetings of the board of Aer Rianta must resemble FF cumann affairs. In the chair sits the crusty FF stalwart Noel Hanlon, an old-style soldier of destiny. Beside him perches Tadhg O'Donoghue, not so long ago the FF director of elections for Dún Laoghaire-Rathdown. On his left sits Freda Hayes, a woman with long-time FF associations, and beside her you might find party activist and FF national executive member Dermot O'Leary, the veteran of many semi-state controversies. The poor worker directors must feel hopelessly out of place.'

↑ *Senator Shane Ross, who confessed that he hadn't 'fondled a single rouble' on a week-long Aer Rianta junket to Russia*

By attempting to restructure Aer Rianta, Séamus Brennan was attacking a Fianna Fáil bastion. Not long after he began considering plans to break it up, the *Sunday Independent* published a scurrilous story, by its political editor Jody Corcoran, alleging that an unnamed Cabinet minister, soon revealed as Brennan, had failed to pay a bill of €5,000 for a pre-Christmas consignment of cognac and cigars from the duty free shop in Dublin Airport back in 1992. When weight was given to the story by crane-hire agent and Aer Rianta board member Dermot O'Leary, who said he had been aware of the alleged debt since 1993, it seemed as if the Minister would have to go. But a thorough inquiry by the Department of Transport came up with nothing to substantiate it, and neither did Aer Rianta. There was 'no smoking cigar', as Mark Brennock reported. The idealism had been sapped out of semi-state enterprise long before the cognac and cigars tale broke; jobs for the boys had overtaken the aims set out in the late 1920s by Cumann na nGael. From Shane Ross's account of the 1991 Russian junket, it is clear that a back-slapping relationship had developed between Aer Rianta and the political establishment. Leaving office, chairman Noel Hanlon's decision to dole out €9,000 Cartier watches shouldn't have caused any surprise. The beneficiaries of this last hurrah were selected departing and former Aer Rianta board members, some of whom sent them back after a public furore. Without critical oversight or scrutiny, semi-state flab and organisational gold-plating were inevitable. But ultimately, it was the public's experience at the hands of the semi-state companies – particularly in the transport sector – that paved the way for their restructuring.

Despite opening a €130 million extension to its main terminal building in June 2002, incipient or actual chaos still characterises Dublin Airport. Architect and frequent flyer John Meagher, who acts for Ryanair, is scathing about the layout, circulation pattern and facilities of the main terminal building, which dates from 1972. 'People are nearly hysterical by the time they get out. Pedro Almodóvar should make a movie about it, something like *Women on the Verge of a Nervous Breakdown*', because the airport evolved 'as a series of add-ons, like a tinker's yard', as his colleague Adrian Buckley put it. Meagher continued: 'Going out through Dublin it's not so bad. The new shopping mall in departures is better than most, there's a bit of light and air, and at least you're going off somewhere. But visitors coming into Dublin Airport for the first time, especially through Pier B, must wonder what kind of country they've landed in, and ask themselves, "is it all like this?".' Problems are all put down to the fact that it is 'bursting at the seams', but Kevin Myers exploded the myth that the total number of passengers in 2000 – 14 million – was fantastically high. On busy days that summer, about 60,000 people went through the airport. 'An All-Ireland every day', said an Aer Rianta spokesman. Not so, according to Myers. Allowing for a 6am to midnight working day, the figure equated to 3,300 people an hour, or under 60 a minute – 'about as many who enter Brown Thomas or Clery's in the same period'.

Paradoxically, the opposite problem faced Shannon Airport. As global liberal-isation of air travel loomed, the big issue was how Shannon would fare with 'open skies'. Calls to end the Shannon stopover came to head in the early 1990s. In late October 1992, on the eve of a general election, the then Minister for Transport, Fianna Fáil's Máire Geoghegan Quinn, pledged that 'there will be no change in the Shannon stopover'. The following July saw her successor, Brian Cowen, replace it with an agreement requiring an equal number of flights to stop at Dublin and Shannon – the 'dual gateway' arrangement, as it became known. Síle de Valera TD and Tony Killeen TD resigned the Fianna Fáil party whip over the deal. Business at Shannon took a nosedive; the number of year-on-year transatlantic passengers going through the airport fell from 707,993 to 465,627. But ever since the dual gateway agreement took effect, public representatives have known about the airport's vulner-ability, but they had little to offer in new ideas. Then came September 11th, 2001. Air travel in general took a sudden dip and transatlantic traffic plummeted. In April 2002, with the effects on the tourist season apparent, Maurice Pratt, then chairman of the Dublin Chamber of Commerce Transport Committee, was reported as labelling the maintenance of the 1993 bi-lateral agreement with the US an 'act of national sabo-tage'. Pratt's comments were actually a little more nuanced. 'I don't believe that any Irish government could engage in an act of national sabotage indefinitely and the proper way to react now to the inevitable abolition of the stopover should be to plan for change.' What Shannon needed was a strategy to develop flights, together with marketing supports, improved land-side access, and the development of airport-relat-ed services, Pratt said. But the use of the word 'sabotage', as an editorial in the *Limerick Leader* pointed out, connotes a deliberate act. The paper acknowledged that maintaining the 1993 deal might be misguided, but it was not done in bad faith. However, in saying 'the proper way to react now to the inevitable abolition of the stopover should be to plan for change', Maurice Pratt had made a valid point.

What exactly open skies might herald has been a matter of much head-scratch-ing. Relying on a report prepared by Brattle Consulting for the European Commission, the Irish Hotels Federation suggested US tourism to Ireland would grow 10% when the dual gateway goes. John Power, its chief executive, told the fed-eration's annual conference in 2004 that cities like Dallas, Orlando and San Francisco have large catchments of potential visitors that cannot easily reach Ireland. 'Between 1989 and 2002, over half of all US visitors flew directly to Ireland, while 46% came via Britain and mainland Europe.' In the six years after 1994, US visitors increased by 114% thanks to the dual gateway agreement, something that pointed to a definite correlation between direct air access to Ireland and increased travel. 'We know that American travellers are high-spend individuals, with the average US visitor spending

€840 in 2002 compared to €470 for all other overseas visitors.' Relying on evidence that American tourists travel extensively throughout the country, the Federation also believed that open skies can deliver a good regional spread. In 2003, with Aer Lingus carrying one million passengers on services to five US cities – New York, Boston, Chicago, Los Angeles and Baltimore – chief executive Willie Walsh said the airline would fly to two more airports as soon as the bilateral agreement was changed. 'Within six months we would open a further two gateways almost doubling the number of US cities we serve.' Competition and low fares had led to huge growth in travel within Europe, and Walsh saw no reason why the same wouldn't happen on transatlantic routes. Tourism expert Carmel Needham pointed out in 2003 that Dublin's share of Ireland's tourist cake expanded from 29% to 36% between 1995 and 2002. Judging from figures reported by Fiona Tyrrell, it looks set to surpass 40% in 2005. More visitors are coming to Dublin and staying there longer. A survey by accountants Horwath Bastow Charleton showed profit per room in hotels along the west coast was €5,743 in 2003, compared to €12,687 in Dublin, where the increased number of visitors coming through the airport was 'having a positive ripple effect on the hotel industry in the area'.

But the abolition of the dual gateway could mean losses of up to €10 million at Shannon, according to internal Aer Rianta documents, the *Sunday Business Post* reported. Shannon Airport lost €5.4 million in 2002, despite earning €4.5 million from the 50% of all US flights landing there. Aer Rianta estimated that 3.5 million low-cost passengers would be required to replace the transatlantic throughput, which stood at just over one million in 2002. The reason nearly four times as many low-fare passengers would be needed to replace lost US tourists is simple enough: Americans travelling into Shannon spend an average of €46.65 in the airport, which is four times what a low-fare passenger spends. However, when Shannon's operating costs are factored into this scenario, Aviation Regulator Bill Pfasfika found that the cost per passenger ran to €30 at Shannon in 2002 – more that double Cork or Dublin. According to Pfasfika's calculations, Shannon was over-staffed, with personnel costs at the airport exceeding €14 per passenger, compared to €6 at Cork and €5 at Dublin. However, Aer Rianta queried the Regulator's assessment, saying it was based on six-month projections and failed to take account of the fact that catering, retailing and fuel supply are provided in-house at Shannon. Since Pfasfika's report, Shannon has reduced its workforce, with the number of full-time staff falling from 528 in January 2002 to 446 by July 2004. Over the same period, the complement of temporary employees stayed in or about 160.

In 2002 Aer Rianta cross-subsidised losses at Shannon (€5.4 million) and Cork (€1.1 million) with a €22 million profit at Dublin Airport. Its 2002 accounts also showed accumulated debts at Shannon and Cork of €70 million and €40 million respectively. Borrowings for the redevelopment of Cork Airport are expected to come to €150 million. Even before September 11th, there was a realisation that Shannon and Cork were slipping behind. In 1999 throughput at Dublin Airport reached 13 million passengers, but the total for all three airports in the same year was just 16.5 million. As Tim O'Brien wrote, this 'reveals a familiar pattern: a massive over-concentration of facilities and growth in the Dublin area where the infrastructure is severely hampered'. For Shannon, the warning signs were all there. It has traditionally been much more reliant on transatlantic routes. In 2000, over a third (36%) of its custom was transatlantic compared to just 7% at Dublin, so it was hardly surprising that Shannon was worst affected by September 11th. But Aer Rianta was never given any real leadership by political figures in the Mid-West; the most prominent politician in the region at the time reacted by burying her head in the sand. According to Síle de Valera, it was all down to 'Dublin interests who are trying to use any opportunity to undermine the stopover'. And she added: 'We do not want to entertain the possibility of change.'

In response to the slump in tourism bookings for 2002, the Government set up an interdepartmental working group which recommended, among other measures, the development of a new low-cost pier at Dublin Airport. Aer Rianta responded by playing the regional development card. It told the Government that building a new pier at Dublin raised 'many financial, competition and security issues'. Shannon, on the other hand, had excess capacity and had also been most adversely affected by the events of September 11th, and Aer Rianta put forward the idea of turning it into a low-cost hub – an apparent effort to head off the pressure for a new pier at Dublin. The Government regarded this response as 'unbelievably brazen', Shane Coleman reported, and, as Brian Carey noted in the *Sunday Tribune*, there was some logic behind Aer Rianta's stance: 'Which part of the country is suffering most from the drop off in transatlantic traffic? The West. Which part of the country would benefit from a new "low cost airport" at Shannon? The West. And which airport will be wiped off the map if the EU finally declares open skies across the Atlantic and hence desperately needs to develop new routes? Shannon ... Aer Rianta should have developed Shannon as a low-cost hub years ago. It didn't; it was far more interested in over-spending on facilities in Dublin, engaging in retail development rather than airport management.'

A key reason Aer Rianta was against a low-cost facility at Dublin Airport was that any cut-price deal offered to Ryanair would have to be made available to all airlines at the airport and this would decimate the company's revenues. For Carey the future of airports policy could be summed up with two questions: 'Does the Government want [Michael] O'Leary to become the most powerful man in Irish tourism? Equally can it rely on Aer Rianta to provide a service that will really tempt tourists and really develop Shannon as a stand-on-its-own-two-feet airport?' In September 2001 O'Leary had told the *Sunday Tribune* that he wouldn't stand for any other operator coming into Ireland 'trying to eat our lunch', a reference to Ryanair's use of cut-throat pricing to see off Virgin Express at Shannon and Go from Dublin. 'Are these the actions of a man who has the interests of Irish tourism at heart, or of Ryanair?' Carey wondered. In December 2004, less than six months after the passage of the State Airports Act (designed to break up Aer Rianta), Ryanair announced nine new routes from Shannon to Britain and the Continent. From May 2005, Shannon was to become one of the airline's European hubs.

Aer Rianta was eventually cajoled into a plan for a new low-cost facility at Dublin in early 2002. Pier D was approved in February 2002 by the then Minister for Public Enterprise, Mary O'Rourke, but found few fans. If built, the proposed pier would partly occupy the site viewed by Ryanair as the best location for a second terminal at the airport. Aer Lingus also expressed opposition to the design and siting of Pier D. It was to be located north of the airport's original 1944 terminal building – a protected structure. Pier D, designed by international architects Skidmore Owings & Merrill, was to be linked to the main terminal by an elevated glazed walkway looping around the old terminal building. It would provide 12 new aircraft stands at a cost of €50 million. Construction of the elevated walkway brought the total estimate to €70 million. However, four existing stands would have to be demolished to make way for Pier D, so the net addition would be just eight, giving a cost per stand of €8.75 million. And because the pier would be reliant on the main terminal building, the closest gate would be 600 metres from check-in and the furthest would be more than one kilometre – a long walk by any measure. Aer Rianta's master plan also envisaged that both Pier A and Pier B would ultimately be rebuilt.

Ryanair was one of 13 bidders who responded to an invitation for expressions of interest in building a second terminal in 2002. Ryanair's proposed terminal, designed by de Blacam & Meagher Architects and priced at €114 million, would provide 24 aircraft stands in the first phase – representing an 80% increase on the airport's current capacity – and 12 further stands in the second phase. The capital cost worked out at €4.75 million per stand, just over half of Aer Rianta's unit cost for Pier D. And because it would be a full terminal rather than an additional pier, the nearest gate would be just 63 metres from check-in. Check-in islands would be widely spread to make more room for queues in an airy Stansted-like environment, with all services located at ground level. It would require the demolition of the old North Terminal, the more recent VIP suite, an aircraft hangar and the Aer Lingus technical services building, but Ryanair said all these facilities would be replaced. And since it could be plugged in to the existing road layout at the airport, it would make a lot more sense than the rival scheme by brothers Des and Ulick McEvaddy for a second terminal on the remote western side of the airport – a plan akin to Terminal 4 at Heathrow.

The Department of Transport was to decide by 17th January 2003 whether the 13 expressions of interest to build a second terminal warranted a full tender process. That target date was missed, and what happened in the succeeding 18 months? 'Nothing', according to Michael O'Leary's full-page ads in national newspapers, first run on the eve of the local and European elections in June 2004. Writing in the *Sunday Tribune* under the headline 'What part of five million tourists does Bertie Ahern not understand?' Ryanair's shoot-from-the-hip chief executive acknowledged that Séamus Brennan had 'hit the ground running' by inviting offers of interest in developing a second terminal at Dublin Airport. But the subsequent two years were 'marked by delay, dither and fudge', and, at the root of this, was 'the inability of Bertie Ahern to make a decision which (though opposed by a small number of trade

unions) would be great for ordinary consumers. When will he keep his election
promises? When will he make a decision?'
O'Leary asked. Ryanair's chief was 'acting
honourably in putting forward his arguments publicly', Brian Carey later wrote in
the same paper. And Carey added some
criticism of Bertie Ahern to boot. Irish aviation policy should 'not become a bargain-
ing chip in national pay talks'. Yet the
Taoiseach 'seems to believe that trade
unions – who, remember, represent just
20% of the people working in Ireland –
have a right to hijack large chunks of government policy and threaten industrial
action to derail them.'

↑ *Michael O'Leary shows Ryanair's tax
contribution for the year. He claimed the
new terminal at Dublin Airport had been
marked by delay, dither and fudge.*

All the while, Brennan was pushing
his Aer Rianta Bill along. Eoghan Williams
reported in the *Sunday Independent* that he 'ignored protocol and declined to address
the parliamentary party', holding talks with Fianna Fáil TDs on a one-to-one basis
only. But Brennan got it through just before the Dáil shut down for the 2004 summer
break. The new legislation would 'give Shannon and Cork their commercial freedom', he told RTÉ's *Morning Ireland*. But thanks to a late change secured by Charlie
McCreevy, the final break-up depends on government being satisfied with business
plans produced by the newly formed boards of the three airports. Under the State
Airports Act 2004, all three airports remain government-owned. For Matt Cooper it
was 'the lesser of two evils that the monopoly should reside with the State instead of
with private operators'. He characterised Aer Rianta's 1999 scheme to sell 50% of its
share capital to the private sector as a plan under which directors, managers and
employees all 'saw free shares coming their way'. He also backed the idea of an independent second terminal at Dublin Airport. Despite 'angry and disingenuous
denials', Aer Rianta 'presided over dangerous conditions at Dublin airport for years',
according to Cooper. And lax security arrangements, too. In mid-April 2005 the new
Dublin Airport Authority had to order an immediate review after officials carrying
out an EU security audit managed to get knives and a fake bomb through the scan-
ners. This review led to long queues in the main terminal, exacerbating an already
difficult situation for passengers using the airport.

Martin Cullen's attempt to grapple with the issue of Dublin Airport's future
after he took over as Minister for Transport in September 2004 envisaged that the
Dublin Airport Authority would build the second terminal, and, as a sop to Mary
Harney's commitment to competition, Aer Lingus would be partially privatised.
Cullen claimed this decision was based on 'what's best for Irish aviation, best for the
customers and best for the employees'. However, as Shane Coleman shrewdly

observed in March 2005, 'history shows us that when it comes to key decisions at the State's airports, what's best for Irish aviation and customers has been largely irrelevant. However good Minister Cullen's intentions may be, in any Government headed by Bertie Ahern there will be one key factor determining what happens with the second terminal – keeping the unions happy. For a movement supposedly in serious decline, it is staggering to behold the enormous influence trade unions hold over government policy. In the last 12 months alone, the unions have successfully ensured that proposals to break up CIÉ and deregulate the Dublin bus market have been sidelined. They forced the shifting of a transport minister who did not share their ideology to a different department. They effectively drove the most successful chief executive in Aer Lingus's history [Willie Walsh] into the arms of rival airline BA, and diluted proposals to break up Aer Rianta into three independent State companies. Now it would seem they have put the kibosh on the plan for a privately owned terminal at Dublin Airport. That is some record ... It's true that the break-up of Aer Rianta went ahead after the Tánaiste threatened to pull out of government if it did not happen. But it was surely no coincidence that just a few months later the unions' *bête noir* Séamus Brennan was shifted from the Department of Transport ... The harsh reality is that if what was best for Irish aviation and best for customers really counted, a decision would have been made on Aer Lingus's funding needs several years ago and the second terminal would already be in place.'

Week after week, a Cabinet decision was supposed to be 'imminent' on what became known as 'the aviation package'. But sharp divisions between Fianna Fáil and the Progressive Democrats over how a second terminal at Dublin Airport should be procured, and who should run it, turned into an unseemly public row. The issue was deeply political, as Mark Brennock wrote. 'On one side are the Progressive Democrats, arguing that competition is almost always the best means to efficiency and to providing the best service for the consumer ... On the other side you have Fianna Fáil with a pragmatic rather than an ideological view of competition. They listen more sympathetically to trade unions who argue that competition will lead to a deterioration of workers' pay and conditions. The party also holds marginal seats in several north Dublin constituencies, inhabited by thousands of voters who either work at the airport or with Aer Lingus.' Incredibly, a third terminal was put into the pot, as a sweetener to the PDs, even though this would clearly be a long-term project. The final deal, unveiled on 18th May 2005, had something for everyone – the sale of a majority stake in Aer Lingus; the construction of a new pier at Dublin Airport by 2007; the development of a second terminal by the airport authority two years later, subject to a competitive tender for its operation; and a third terminal, to be built at some stage in the future when passenger numbers nudged towards 30 million. According to Martin Cullen, the package 'gives Irish aviation a clear strategic direction and an unambiguous mandate for growth'. However, the airport authority was left to decide where the new facilities would be located, and it endorsed Aer Rianta's dog-eared plan for Pier D, opting to build the second terminal to the south, rather than to the north, of the existing main terminal. As for the planned second runway, UPROAR

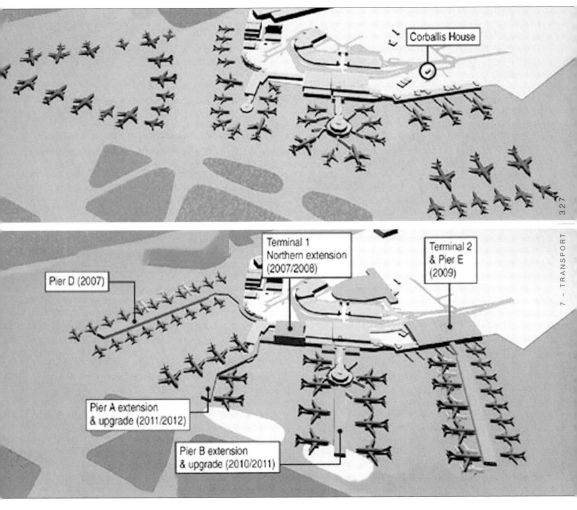

Labels within image (top): Corballis House

Labels within image (bottom): Pier D (2007); Terminal 1 Northern extension (2007/2008); Terminal 2 & Pier E (2009); Pier A extension & upgrade (2011/2012); Pier B extension & upgrade (2010/2011)

↑ *Aerial perspectives showing the existing terminal buildings at Dublin Airport (top) and the developments planned over the next seven years*

(United Portmarnock Residents Opposed to Airport Runway) tried to persuade Cullen to commission a cost-benefit analysis of the plan, which would also look at alternative locations for building airport capacity, but he declined to do so.

The delays and capacity problems at Dublin surely give Shannon and Cork every opportunity. When the State Airports Bill was passed, a *Sunday Tribune* editorial said the change in how they are run would allow Shannon aggressively chase new business, something 'that was not happening while it was under the control of Aer Rianta'. The number of transatlantic passengers getting on or off at the airport has risen in recent years, reaching 685,000 in 2003, a significant portion of which will be lost. Views vary on how far this figure will fall – a drop to 500,000 is seen as optimistic, but in a worst case scenario it could drop as low as 250,000. Some airlines could well redirect all transatlantic flights to Dublin because this would allow them to close their Shannon base. The number of transatlantic transit passengers is likely to become very small, relying mainly on volatile military custom. Increasing European business is vital, such as for city breaks in Galway or Limerick, but even if this blossomed it wouldn't make up for the lack of connection to the US. Most foreign direct investment along the west coast, be it biopharmacy in Cork, computers in Limerick, or health science in Galway, has come from the US; if airlines consolidate in Dublin, these companies would lose out. At the moment, Cork Airport is restricted in the type of transatlantic aircraft it can handle. There's a lobby to extend the airport's runway, but that would increase the danger of Cork and Shannon competing with each other for US business. One solution would be for Cork and Shannon to specialise in catering for different destinations, and both airports to put real effort into marketing each other, as a means of increasing their combined patronage, aided by good surface connections between them. Whatever form of support is put in place to maximise US flights, be it Aircoach-style services from Cork and Galway or inducements to airlines to retain a Shannon base, it is bound to be seen as a handout. But these types of subsidies could prove cost-effective, and might not be needed in the long-term if Shannon bounces back. And that's an awful lot more than can be said for the air travel subsidies handed out at the moment.

Regional air services are run under Public Service Obligation contracts with the Department of Transport. PSOs were first signed for two routes, Galway-Dublin and Kerry-Dublin, in 1995. Donegal was added in 1996, Sligo in 1997 and both Derry and Knock in 2001. A review by DKM economic consultants, published in March 2004, found that the cost of these contracts had soared from €1.1 million in 1995 to €20 million in 2003 – not including a shared 'marketing grant' of €2 million for the five regional airports. Over the same period, the average load factor on the air services fell from 65% to below 50%; in other words, most planes flying the six routes were less than half full. Some routes are subsidised more than others. DKM found that a Dublin-Knock return fare of €110 (or less) required taxpayers to chip in €557 per passenger, or nearly five times as much as the ticket price. It would be cheaper, and possibly faster door-to-door, to get a cab. As Shane Coleman noted, the total cost to fly return between Dublin and Knock Airport 'is 50% more than the taxi fare for the 250-mile return journey'. DKM was 'unable' to establish that the benefits of regional air services exceeded their costs. 'The issue for public policy is whether the benefits are commensurate with the now very substantial costs, and we are not aware of any studies or analyses which establish that this is so.'

DKM found the subsidy levels per passenger on regional air services 'far higher than those available on other public transport modes'. Bus Éireann carried 46 million passengers in 2002 and received a subvention of €21.77 million – minuscule per passenger journey, as the graph shows. Iarnród Éireann carried 11.2 million passengers on its intercity routes in 2002. If half the company's €155 million subvention was attributable to intercity services – a figure DKM felt was a 'reasonable guess' – the subsidy per rail passenger-trip was small compared to the PSO contracts for

→ *Total government spending on regional flights, 1995-2003*

[source: DKM Economic Consultants, 2004]

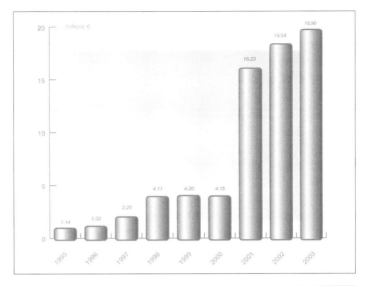

→ *Breakdown between air fare and State subsidy for each ticket (2003 figures)*

[source: DKM Economic Consultants, 2004]
Note: Subsidy figures for Donegal and Sligo from 2002, all other data from 2003; ticket price is maximum return fare.

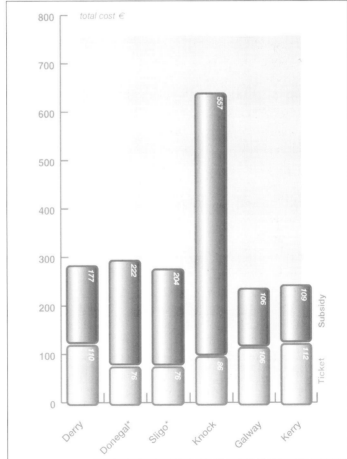

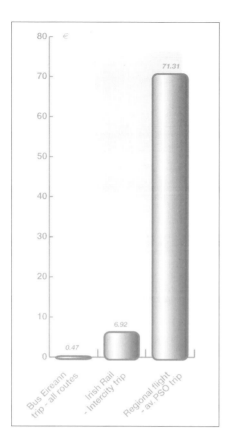

↑ Amount paid by the taxpayer in subsidies for bus, rail and regional air travel per passenger trip in 2002 [source: DKM, 2004]

regional air services. In 2002 these services carried 260,000 passengers and received a subvention of €18.54 million. With the average flight subsidised to the tune of €71 per passenger, this works out at more than 10 times the subvention for rail and 152 times that for bus. The DKM report also pointed to a regional policy at odds with itself. An airport needs to serve around 500,000 passengers annually to break even, but 'none of the Irish regional airports has any prospect of achieving traffic volumes which would bring them close to operating break-even for the foreseeable future.' However, the report suggested that both Cork and Shannon should be capable of breaking even because airports handling around two million passengers 'are known to achieve this elsewhere'.

The Sligo service was found to be third most expensive to maintain, with the Exchequer paying roughly €200 for each €100 return fare. Yet Sligo is only 57km north of Knock Airport and, even with the roads the way they are, the journey takes less than 50 minutes, according to the AA's web planner. DKM pointed out that while Knock is the busiest regional airport with close to 400,000 passengers per annum, it was unable to draw on a significant urban centre for custom. In terms of the Sligo to Dublin journey, time savings offered by air travel would be close to zero if planned rail improvements were implemented. In this regard, Sligo was one of two routes – the other being Galway – where future rail journey times would be as low as 2¹/₂ hours. However, as DKM acknowledged, Government approval for the phasing of rail improvements was still outstanding. Galway city is also close to Shannon and will become more so in the coming years with the bypassing of Ennis and Gort. As well as being vulnerable to the loss of the dual gateway, Shannon was suffering because Galway-Dublin flights were 'attracting passengers from the immediate Shannon Airport hinterland', while Kerry was also taking business away. 'Looked at objectively, Shannon is the natural commercial airport for the Limerick-Clare-Galway region, in a way that Galway cannot be because of infrastructural limitations', according to DKM. Planned road improvements would also make Shannon more accessible. And in the case of Kerry, proposed rail improvements – if implemented – would cut the train journey times from Tralee to Dublin to just under 3¹/₂ hours, and the Killarney to Dublin journey to three hours. Cork and Shannon airports are also less than two hours by road from either Tralee or Killarney.

The DKM report is important because it substantiates two points. First, the only way of accessing Knock, Shannon or Cork from a catchment area now served by a lightly used (and heavily subsidised) regional airport is by road. However, the national roads budget is almost monopolised by routes to Dublin. Second, in terms of getting to Dublin, the fastest land option would be rail, but either the money hasn't been committed to the planned rail improvements, or there is an attempt to bring road journey times on a par with rail, with rail plans being long-fingered. DKM showed that over 60% (93% on the Dublin-Derry route) of subsidised flights were used simply to get to or from Dublin. For the 40% of passengers connecting with foreign flights, faster access to airports like Knock, Shannon and Cork would avoid having to fly to Dublin. The key point is the availability of direct flights from Cork, Shannon and Knock to London, Brussels and Frankfurt, together with a variety of tourist destinations. It is true that frequencies from Knock may not be as high, and Shannon may be the sole provider of transatlantic flights, but this just underscores the need for better roads linking Cork to Sligo, via Limerick, Shannon and Galway rather than motorways converging on Dublin. And for the 60% who just want to get to or from Dublin quickly, there's a strong case for bringing forward investment in rail, given that it's capable of providing the fastest journey times. But the ability of inter-regional synergy to offset ridiculously high levels of subsidy would require joined-up thinking – and that is in short supply. The reality is that about 20 million passengers use Dublin, Cork and Shannon airports, or nearly 100 times the number availing of heavily subsidised regional air services – a mere handful, at 266,000, for the annual €22.6 million subsidy. And, as the Fáilte Ireland figures show, the existing system is doing next to nothing for regional balance. Yet in July 2004, Séamus Brennan told members of the board of Kerry Airport that he was committed to maintaining the current levels of subvention – to facilitate access to Dublin.

———

ALTHOUGH IRISH INTERCITY RAIL SPEEDS ARE AMONG THE SLOWEST IN WESTERN EUROPE, the lack of fast trains is not a dominant theme in media coverage here. There are much more basic things to be sorted out, such as overcrowding, outdated ticket-selling, and poor time-keeping. Seats on Iarnród Éireann trains are available on a 'first-come, first-served' basis, which seems fair, but the company doesn't appear to be aware when it is selling more tickets than it has seats. When Gene Kerrigan and his family took a 10.50 train from Dublin to Killarney in December 2002, they got seats only because they arrived at Heuston 35 minutes before it was due to depart. 'Other families were not so lucky. In the gaps between the carriages, and around the doors, and in the spaces where luggage is stored, and in some of the aisles, people stood, leaned, sat and sprawled. People were crushed into tiny spaces, and there they tried to amuse their small children. Dublin to Killarney is a three-and-half hour train journey. Some of those who got seats had people standing almost on top of them. You could go to the jacks, if you could find one that didn't have someone using it as a compartment to accommodate a whole family. You could buy coffee or tea, but only the reckless did, as it meant stepping over prone people and bored, agitated kids, trying not to scald anyone.' The explanation for this sorry state of affairs was simple enough, according to Kerrigan: 'Politicians made no effort at dismantling the patchwork, dysfunctional set-up built in the bad times. Public service is a foreign concept to these people. Much more fun to dream up mad diversions such as Mr McCreevy's Free Money Scheme or find ways to squander millions on unbuilt stadiums and other pet projects.' The *Sunday Independent* columnist was fatalistic. 'Hundreds of people had a bad time on trains last week. Ho hum. This has been happening for years, and it will not change.'

With unpunctual trains there's a whole spectrum of delay, from being a 'small bit late' to the comically late train, where the engine has to be replaced or a faulty carriage decoupled and shunted to sidings. At the heart of the matter, as Rachel Andrews wrote, is the question of consumer confidence. After telling of a $2^{1}/_{2}$ hour delay, Andrews reasoned: 'With the price of a train ticket in Ireland often costing more than a Ryanair flight to London, is this really any way to run a country, or, come to think of it, a supposedly buoyant economy? How many hours of economic time are lost by unreliable trains and services? Why would a Cork-based business person, under pressure to make an early morning engagement in Dublin, put any trust in the train?' In August 2004 the company was to start an internet reservation system for premium-priced seats. But one month later, when the authors of this book took a Dublin-Cork trip, the conductor told us there wasn't much point in travelling club class because there was no dining service anyway. It was the same on the way back, apparently because the company can't get staff to do it in either direction. So what is the point of rolling out an Internet reservation system for club class seats when there often isn't a club class service to go with them? Yet figures show that Iarnród Éireann is grossly over-staffed compared to similar-sized railway companies in Britain. Indeed, consultants Booz Allen Hamilton ranked its journey-per-employee ratio as the lowest in these islands. But it hardly needed an official report to confirm the 'stand around' culture in Iarnród Éireann. At any of the main railway stations, you'll find groups of uniformed men – and it's usually men – standing around chatting. By contrast, in well-run train companies across Europe, one employee inspects tickets, attends to passengers, and prepares a train for turnaround. There is a distinction between these managerial failings and complaints which can be traced to lack of State investment – rickety 40-year-old carriages and heating and ventilation systems that either don't work or don't exist. For the most part, Iarnród Éireann meets complaints with the response that it has been starved of funds for years. The problem is that investment in new trains and stations won't amount to much if the benefits are lost because of poor maintenance or management. These failings could all be addressed without leaning on the taxpayer.

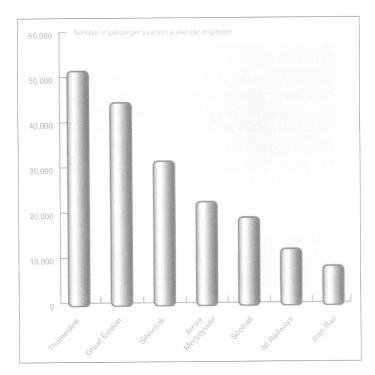

→ *Passenger journeys per annum per employee on selected northern European railways*

[source: Booz Allen Hamilton, 2004]

After a Westport-bound train derailed at Knockcroghery, Co Roscommon, in November 1997 – fortunately with no fatalities among its 150 passengers – a draft accident report was particularly critical of Iarnród Éireann's safety standards, saying that parts of the rail network 'pose unacceptable risks to passengers'. While the final version concluded that no line sections 'exceeded the intolerable risk benchmark', a stark choice still faced the Government: close significant sections of the network or rebuild them. Since it could not preside over an unsafe railway or risk political opprobrium by closing down lines, the Knockcroghery accident led to the 1999-2003 Railway Safety Programme approved in March 1999 and later repackaged for inclusion in the National Development Plan. This €635 million programme provided for 490km of track renewal, 20 new mainline carriages, safety improvements to over 530 level crossings, and works to around 100 bridges or structures. Speed targets were left vague: 'The investment will permit a maximum speed of 160kph (100mph) on the Cork and Belfast lines and 110-145kph (70-90mph) on the other passenger lines.' With speed targets framed in this way, there has been no onus on Iarnród Éireann to make journeys faster; the main idea was to keep the trains on the tracks.

Now and again, Iarnród Éireann claims journey times are improving. Track re-laying was 'yielding improved journey times as well as safety benefits', it said in a promotional supplement at the start of 2003. And Bertie Ahern told that year's Fianna Fáil ardfhéis: 'Journey times are being cut ... Ireland is building a better transport system.' But faster rail journeys are still the exception. In late 2002, Chris Ashmore found a host of rail trips to be slower than they were 20 years previously. 'The quickest train journey times from Tralee, Waterford, Westport and Galway to Dublin, are now all slower that they were for the timetable of 1978', he wrote. A trip from Tralee to Dublin was 21 minutes longer, while the Waterford to Dublin journey took 10 minutes more. The Westport-Dublin and Galway-Dublin routes were both marginally slower. At 2 hours 27 minutes, the fastest Dublin-Cork train took seven minutes longer than it did in the in 1980s. Indeed, the Limerick-Waterford line had faster journey times when it opened back in the 1850s, according to Hassard Stacpoole, editor of Irish Railway News. There's a host of reasons why journey times aren't any faster, he said, but the main ones are the lack of passing places on single-track lines – known as passing loops – or the failure to use technology to make better use of these loops.

Investment under the 1999-2003 Railway Safety Programme was confined to the radial routes converging on Dublin. This left any other line hanging by a thread. The last train from Limerick to Galway ran in November 2001, and since then Iarnród Éireann only allow the odd weed-sprayer along the track between Ennis and Athenry. A year later, the CIÉ board proposed closing the line from Limerick to Ballybrophy Junction – known as the Nenagh-Roscrea branch – as well as the Rosslare-Limerick Junction line. Irish Railway News tore into CIÉ's proposals, saying the soon-to-be published National Spatial Strategy wouldn't be 'worth a penny candle' if most of the track between Waterford and Limerick became 'a trail of weeds'. Bizarrely, in November 2002, Iarnród Éireann was investing in the very same lines that the CIÉ board was canvassing for closure. The Nenagh-Roscrea branch saw level crossings upgraded and passing loops rebuilt. At Tipperary station, between Rosslare and Limerick Junction, Irish Railway News estimated that €1 million worth of civil engineering works were carried out in the second half of 2002. An Taisce pointed out that if CIÉ prevailed with its closure bids, it would succeed in shutting down some 40% of the network inherited by Iarnród Éireann on its inception in 1987. As one Irish Railway News member put it, Irish Rail could soon rebrand itself 'Pale Rail'. The lobby group complained that strategic planning at the rail company seemed to be founded on a belief that commuter trains bound for Dublin pay better than, say, an intercity train between Galway and Cork. Sure, the long-distance inbound commuter train may be full at 8.15 am, but what about outbound services, or the time between the morning and evening peaks? IRN's point was graphically illustrated when Iarnród Éireann went that extra mile – in fact, 38.5 miles (60km) from Dublin – and opened a commuter rail station in Monasterevin, at a cost of €3.5 million, that caters for just 60 people a day.

The closures canvassed by CIÉ were put off in November 2002 when Séamus Brennan asked its board not to make any decisions until the Strategic Rail Review was completed. But when it did come out in April 2003, the SRR seemed to reflect current thinking within Iarnród Éireann rather than help the company fulfil the priorities set out in the National Spatial Strategy. Booz Allen Hamilton, the consultants who compiled the review, did consider three new schemes in their 'Going for Growth' scenario – Cork Suburban, Galway-Cork (via Limerick), and Limerick-Shannon-Ennis – commenting that they 'fit particularly well with the NSS'. However, only

Cork Suburban made it onto the investment list. The consultants were also sceptical about reopening the Western Rail Corridor, saying the projected cost of €572 million made it unviable. Séamus Brennan told the Council for the West in April 2003 that he would like the local authorities along the corridor to show how a rail service might be viable, and he later set up a working group chaired by Pat McCann, chief executive of the Jurys Doyle hotel group, to look into it. North of Galway, unfortunately, the railway line was 'lightly built', with few enough bridges and a lot of level crossings. Between Tuam and Collooney, there are 60 level crossings – about one a mile. Bends are sharp, visibility is poor, and speeds always had to be kept down; no wonder train drivers nicknamed it 'the Burma Road'. One option that should be examined would involve realigning the route to serve the two major destination points between Galway and Sligo – Knock Shrine, which attracts 1.5 million visitors annually, and Knock Airport, which caters for 400,000 passengers a year. But virtually all of the €8.5 billion spending package recommended by the rail review was earmarked for radial lines converging on Dublin. As An Taisce pointed out, this would simply exacerbate the 'suction effect' of the capital, a view shared by Opposition parties. Even the Chambers of Commerce of Ireland said it was concerned about the compatibility of the review with the NSS. Like Iarnród Éireann's 'Monasterevin experiment', the consultants presented no figures suggesting that a train running between Portarlington and Dublin would have a higher load factor over the course of the day than a regular-interval Cork-Galway service. Evidence-based policy-making took another hit. When a €262 million investment in new trains was eventually announced in January 2005, it was clear that the radial pattern of Ireland's rail network would be reinforced. The contract with Mitsui/Tokyu of Japan and Rotem of South Korea was for 120 air-conditioned carriages to replace clapped-out rolling stock on the Dublin-Westport, Dublin-Galway, Dublin-Tralee and Dublin-Waterford routes. Due for delivery in 2007, the new carriages would be added to 67 others scheduled to enter service in 2005 to enable Iarnród Éireann to offer hourly departures between Dublin and Cork and Dublin and Limerick, as well as Dublin and Galway, at least at peak times. Their arrival will also allow more modern rolling stock to be diverted to the Dublin-Sligo route. A further €83 million is also being invested in more carriages for commuter services running into Dublin from Drogheda, Kildare and Maynooth.

———

What was intended as the grand plan for transport in the Greater Dublin Area had been launched with some fanfare in October 2000. Covering the event for the *Irish Times*, Frank McNally was struck by the 'all-star chorus line including the Taoiseach, Tánaiste and Minister for Public Enterprise'. They 'tapped their feet in unison with the National Roads Authority, the Dublin Transportation Office and CIÉ'. According to McNally, 'clever choreography combined the upgrading of the rail network, the revamp of the Dublin Bus fleet and the transformation of city and suburban rail into one breathtaking spectacle. The Government's programme notes somehow summarised the action in a single page. And in the space of a few short paragraphs it mentioned that the elements of the plan were "moving ahead rapidly", "rapidly progressing", "ahead of schedule" and "moving ahead rapidly" (again)'. The DTO's *Platform for Change* plan was based largely on figures for 1997 when 72% of all morning peak-hour trips in Dublin were made by car. Rather optimistically, it envisaged that by 2016, nearly two-thirds (63%) of all trips would be made by public transport – 49% by rail and just 14% by bus. Construction industry economist Jerome Casey had no faith in the DTO's approach, because no comparable low-density city had 'ever attempted to implement a strategy based on car demand suppression and the massive switch to rail for commuting'.

Owen Keegan, Dublin City Council's traffic supremo and an economist by training, also challenged the DTO's strategy. In April 2003 he told the Statistical and Social Inquiry Society of Ireland that it had been finalised 'when the country was in a euphoric mood and there was boundless optimism about ... the availability of public funding'. Under the DTO strategy the role of the bus is seen as changing from being a primary public transport mode in its own right to become a feeder service for rail. But Keegan didn't think this held water: 'It isn't clear that passengers enjoying a good level of service on the bus will want to change to rail-based systems.' Because of the massive amounts of money required to build railways, 'it is hard to justify significant public expenditure to achieve a switch between different transport modes', he said. Keegan also had statistics on his side. Between 1997 and 2001, the bus share of morning peak-hour trips in Dublin climbed from 19% to 23%. Over the same period, the car share slipped from 72% to 70%, while the rail share also went down by 2% to 7%. As Keegan said, 'it seems clear that investment in the bus service offers by far the best option in terms of achieving desired modal change', concluding that the priority should be to bring bus to its full potential, develop rail by maximising the use of existing lines, and exploit information technology with integrated ticketing based on smart cards. The other point that Keegan stressed is that quality bus corridors (QBCs) can be built and new buses bought reasonably quickly. The era of the belching bus is also becoming a distant memory with the development of hybrid electric buses, producing very low emissions compared to the 1980s. In February 2004 the *Irish Times* reported that a hybrid electric bus now costs only 25% more than a diesel-only one, and, critically, is 30% cheaper to run.

By contrast, the enormous cost of Luas and the delays in delivering it have hardly been a good advertisement for rail investment. In August 2002 the Rail Procurement Agency, the body charged with building the Luas lines serving Sandyford and Tallaght, told Martin Fitzpatrick it was standing by its opening date of December 2003, then just 17 months away, and the completion cost of the system would be €560 million, the RPA assured him. Barely 20 months later, the RPA conceded that it would cost €790 million to complete the two lines. For the Sandyford line, another six months had to be added to the opening date. Another nine months was needed for the Tallaght line because its dog-legged route is overwhelmingly on-street. The RPA seemed to have a problem with figures. For the proposed 11.5km metro line between St Stephen's Green and Dublin Airport, it first estimated the cost at €4.8 billion – or just over €420 million per kilometre. Then, after this estimate was greeted with gasps of incredulity in Leinster House and elsewhere, the RPA lopped €1.5 billion off the bill, saying 'changes in scope' had been made. Pádraic White, the RPA's chairman and a former chief executive of the IDA, went on Today FM to explain the markedly different figures. Presenter Matt Cooper put three points to him: first, the downward revision was enormous; second, as Tom Morrissey, the PDs' transport spokesman, put it, this showed the RPA was 'not up to the job'; and third, the credibility of the RPA was in tatters. White said he wouldn't accept Cooper's charge regarding the agency's competence. Turning to the revised cost estimate, he gave an answer later printed verbatim in the *Sunday Tribune*: 'When you add on insurance and allow for inflation, which is a very important matter for public figures when they come later to question how products escalated, we have built in the inflation fact, and when you add on VAT you get a figure of €2.8 billion; then if you take a construction period of four years and the construction costs have to be financed by the private sector, you add on a financing interest cost which takes you to €3.4 billion, right, so that is an escalated cost into future money prices but come back then to as somebody said lets take the total capital cost and discount it with present day value, you get a figure of roughly €2 billion so what I would suggest the relevant figures are the core construction cost of €1.5 billion and the discounted present day value of all the other basic cost excluding the financing for [the] private sector and that gives you €2 billion.'

Documents released under the Freedom of Information Act showed that Charlie McCreevy, with the airport metro line very much in mind, had upbraided Séamus Brennan for 'sponsoring proposals in the area of public transport ... which are totally unrealistic' in the context of budgetary constraints. But Brennan threw caution to the wind and, throughout 2003 and 2004, continually set himself deadlines to bring the RPA's metro plan to Cabinet – only to set a new date as each deadline became imminent. With an expected annual cost of €250 million a year for 20 years, the Department of Finance remained resolutely opposed to the project. Its scepticism was reinforced in February 2003 when it was revealed that Madrid had built its latest metro line for less than €50 million per kilometre – a fraction of any of the RPA's 'moving target' estimates. The Oireachtas Joint Committee on Transport wasn't able to get the RPA to detail the benchmark projects it had used to compile estimates for building the airport metro line. It took direct contact with Prof Manuel Maynar Melis, head of metro construction in Madrid, to get some proper figures. In June 2004, four days after Brennan told journalists he was taking a 'finalised' metro plan to Cabinet, the Oireachtas committee recommended that a body other than the RPA – one with 'demonstrable experience of delivering a project of this nature' – should oversee any metro project. But despite these damning conclusions, Brennan floated the agency's plan again in August 2004. He was going to ask his colleagues to approve a €2 billion-plus plan at the first Cabinet meeting after the summer break, Alison O'Connor reported in the *Irish Independent*. When RTÉ radio, among others, went

M.C.W. =
Mugret Cement Works

Line types in Ireland

- • Placenames
- —•— Double Line
- —•— Single Line
- —•— Freight only (ROI)/Redirect passenger trains for operational reasons (NI)
- —— Closed line (High density [>5 per 12km] of level crossings)
- —•— Closed line (Low density [<5 per 12km] of level crossings)
- —— ROI / NI border

↑ *Queuing for the bus: there were fewer buses serving Dublin in November 2003 than a year earlier. The Dept of Transport has no accurate records for Cork, Limerick, Galway or Waterford.*
← *Map of Ireland's railway network*

to follow up the story they found out that the Minister had gone on holidays that morning. For one rail industry insider, this was Brennan's way of keeping in touch with his constituents while he was away: 'Just look where his metro line would end up – Dundrum, his home base.'

The Minister had so identified himself with the metro that he appeared unable to consider alternative ways of serving the airport, such as a spur running west from the DART line between Baldoyle and Portmarnock, or from the Maynooth line. Either of these would make even more sense in the context of Iarnród Éireann's plan for an underground rail interconnector between Spencer Dock and Heuston Station. This would run via Pearse Station (where it would interchange with the DART), St Stephen's Green (Sandyford Luas line), the Liberties and Heuston (Tallaght Luas line and Kildare Arrow service). The cost of the 5.3km of tunnel required for this strategically crucial link was estimated at €1.3 billion in February 2004, or €245 million a kilometre. According to Dick Fearn, Iarnród Éireann's chief operations manager, the interconnector would come at the end of a series of building-block projects, all substantial in themselves and none mutually exclusive. These 'building blocks' include the Kildare Route project, a plan to increase the number of tracks on the approach to Heuston Station, and, in the process, serve developing areas such as Adamstown, Balgaddy and Clondalkin. Then, east of Glasnevin along the Maynooth line, new stations would be built and signalling upgraded, again with the aim of serving high-density development under way at Ashtown, Pelletstown and the former Phoenix

Park racecourse. The opening of a new station at Spencer Dock near the IFSC would also relieve the capacity constraints at Connolly Station, creating room not just for more Enterprise services to and from Belfast, but also for commuter trains from the north, south and west. The advantage of Iarnród Éireann's proposals is that they allow the Government to approve rail investment on a step-by-step basis.

But whatever decisions are made on rail, some figures cannot be ignored. In 2005 Dublin Bus was carrying 490,000 passengers on a typical weekday; factor in private buses and this rises almost to 600,000, compared to 120,000 using the DART and other commuter rail services. Turning to trams, the number of Luas passengers on a typical weekday rose to 60,000 in 2005. It is not an exact measure, but of those taking public transport in Dublin, 77% travel by bus, 15% by train, and 8% by Luas. And that's why, even though its report was commissioned to pressure-cook the RPA's metro costings, the Oireachtas Joint Committee on Transport found that a 'bus-based public transport system must for the foreseeable future remain at the heart of the greater Dublin public transport system'. Bizarrely though, of the €41 million allocated for QBC construction in 2002, €10 million had to be given back because it wasn't spent due to difficulties such as hiring qualified staff to implement the programme. There was no excuse for this. In 2000 average bus speeds were tabulated for 100 cities around the world and Dublin came a pathetic 94th, mainly because buses are still not given priority at most traffic lights. In 2002 peak-hour bus speeds in the city were no more than 13.5kph, compared to the European average of 20kph.

However, instead of pressing for a better product, Séamus Brennan was more concerned with process. Soon after taking office he turned his attention to the bus service in Dublin, and in November 2002 announced a plan to franchise bus routes. 'From the beginning of 2004', Tim O'Brien reported, 'up to 25% of an expanded bus network in the capital should be in the hands of private operators.' But it was never clear exactly what the Minister had in mind. Were a quarter of the routes currently operated by Dublin Bus to be farmed out to private operators, or would 25% more routes routes be created and these offered to new operators? As Arthur Beesley understood it, the Minister wanted to see 'the opening of 25% of bus routes in Dublin to competition'. There was also uncertainty about who would oversee a franchising system and make sure new operators were providing the bus services they were contracted to provide. All Brennan did was create a hiatus, according to Declan Martin, of the Dublin Chamber of Commerce; when questioned on the newly launched initiative, neither he nor his officials 'had the answers to those questions'. Pressed by Opposition deputies, the Minister belatedly acknowledged that a regulator or some form of transport authority would have to accompany the franchising scheme. According to a report by Niamh Connolly in the *Sunday Business Post*, Dublin Bus estimated the annual cost of a transport regulatory authority at €14 million – and this would oversee just 25% of the market.

Uncertainty also surrounded the reasons behind Brennan's move. In an interview for RTÉ's *Transport in Crisis* series, he suggested that competition would cut costs and improve services. He compared bus franchising to the competition that exists between Aer Lingus and Ryanair, asking radio listeners to imagine a situation where there was no choice between airlines. This analogy is misplaced. The Minister's bus plan was based on franchising, i.e. routes are put out to tender, and would-be operators submit bids stating the level of subsidy they would require to operate them, usually over a five-year period. In other words, it is competition *for* a market rather than competition *in* the market. Airlines, on the other hand, compete head-to-head on the same routes every day. Brennan was comparing chalk and cheese. Yet over the course of 2003 and 2004, the Minister essentially restated the position he had outlined in November 2002, in the teeth of bitter opposition from trade unions. There were talks, refusals to talk, talks about talks and even some work stoppages. There was no increase in services. In fact, there were fewer private bus operators serving the capital in November 2003 than there were a year earlier, with Dublin City Council's canal cordon recording a 4% fall. The Dublin Bus fleet remained static over the same period. It was also unclear why Brennan did not run with a 2002 plan by Dublin Bus, which had been agreed with the unions, that 200 new buses would be provided by private sub-contractors. This agreement offered considerable leverage. The Minister could insist, for example, that the operation of 'in-house' buses be benchmarked against the 200 new ones using standard criteria – punctuality, unit cost, employee absenteeism, and so on. Instead, he proceeded with patchy franchising proposals, which, if extended across the network, would have phased out Dublin Bus. And this was being planned at a time when the company was 'showing real improvements' in the service it provides, as Fintan O'Toole noted. He cited a 1999 World Bank report on bus services in Britain which showed that reductions in the levels of public subsidy in the mid-1980s were largely offset by a substantial fall in the number of passengers, making each journey actually more expensive to the taxpayer. Bus fares increased in real terms, investment in the industry declined significantly, and, as a result, the average age of buses rose by 30%. 'Even the promise of competition was not really fulfilled, as smaller operators sold out to big conglomerates and ownership was gradually concentrated in the hands of just three companies', O'Toole noted. 'Why should we hop off a public transport system that is at last going somewhere and climb on to a decrepit ideological bandwagon on the road to nowhere?'

Painstakingly slowly, the penny dropped. In July 2004 Chris Dooley reported that Séamus Brennan 'has now conceded that whatever new arrangements are agreed, Dublin Bus must not be diminished in size and must be allowed to grow'. The minister also sanctioned parallel discussions to ensure standards of employment are maintained under any new arrangements, setting a deadline of September 2004 for agreement between unions and Government. Not for the first time, Brennan's deadline came and went. The Cabinet reshuffle that month saw him moved to Social and Family Affairs, with Martin Cullen installed as the new Minister for Transport. Cullen dropped the aim of carving out a 25% share of all bus routes in Dublin for private operators, replacing it with a plan where they would serve '15% of new routes' – a much more modest target.

Brennan (and Cullen) appeared to accept that head-to-head competition along the same city routes usually turns into a complete shambles. Bus argy-bargy, cut-throat competition, too many buses on some routes, under-busing of others, topped off by reduced bus-use were all seen in British cities where such competition was introduced. Yet a licence was granted in January 2004 to Donal Joyce, owner of City Direct buses, to run a service between Salthill and Eyre Square in Galway in head-to-head competition with Bus Éireann. And so Joyce's claim that the State company (sole shareholder: the Minister for Transport) obstructed his service by parking some of their vehicles at stops used by City Direct didn't come as a bolt out of the blue. Little surprise too that the Bus Éireann service on the west side of Galway – Joyce's catchment area – has increased immeasurably. Now, with two operators, one bus can cut in front of another, leaving the second bus with just a handful of passengers because most people just get on the first bus that comes along. City Direct grew out of providing bus services for the unserved population of 14,000 in Knocknacarra, a suburb hurriedly built in the Celtic Tiger years with few facilities. Now, with Bus Éireann directing a lot of its energies to counter the competition, it is the east side of Galway city that's suffering.

It was a similar story 100km down the road in Limerick. Here, in November 2003, the Department of Transport granted a licence to Pat Curtin to run buses from the suburb of Annacotty to the city centre, via the University of Limerick. In response, Bus Éireann improved its UL-to-city-centre service 100%, according to Curtin. As in Galway, there is jockeying at bus stops and over-concentration on certain routes while others go under-bused. Occasionally, races develop between competing buses. Like his fellow entrepreneur in Galway, Curtin was drawn into the business after spotting a neglected market; he began with a school run in Castletroy, busing children to and from the city centre. For any number of reasons, their parents needed the service. 'Maybe there was just one car and it was taking the breadwinner in the opposite direction, or maybe there was no-one to bring them home at half-three', he recalls. Over time, the children passed through secondary school and Curtin turned his attention to Annacotty. To get his licence, he went door-to-door across the new suburb, interviewing 300 people. Some 95% were in favour of a bus service. John O'Sullivan, Aircoach's get-up-and-go founder, had also spotted an untapped market for an executive-style bus service between Dublin Airport and the capital's southside, calling to major hotels along the way. In Limerick and Galway, however, the buses run by Curtin and Joyce do much more to provide mobility and combat social exclusion. But whatever the focus, Séamus Brennan – and, by extension, Ireland – has failed to come up with a rational regulatory framework that taps the energy of public transport entrepreneurs.

Yet good public transport works. Among major cities in Ireland and Britain, Dublin is the only one able to prove that an increase in bus-use resulted in a drop in car commuting. Over the seven years from 1997 to 2003, car traffic crossing the canals in the morning peak period declined by nearly 14%. QBC-served routes saw a 23% drop in the number of cars, while non-QBC routes only went down by 6%. According to planning consultant Malcolm Buchanan, Dublin has shown how good

QBCs can attract custom right across income groups – something borne out by the opening of laptops and the sounds of 'DORT-speak' aboard the 46A. The arrival of Luas, even at enormous expense, gave public transport in Dublin a smart new image and raised customer expectations, giving every reason to modernise the bus system rather than neglect it. The National Development Plan 2000-2006 promised to build on the success of QBCs by providing an extra 275 buses for Dublin's fleet. But figures released in February 2005 to the Labour Party's transport spokeswoman, Roisín Shortall TD, showed that the net addition acutally amounted to just 93 buses. In effect, 'the size of the Dublin Bus fleet has remained static since 2001, despite promises to expand the fleet in the NDP and in the face of a growing population on the east coast', she said. Claims that the Government had rebuffed the company's plans to buy more buses were dismissed by Bertie Ahern as 'gobbledegook'. In fact, since 2002, Dublin Bus had been denied the funds to buy 150 more buses until agreement was reached on the privatisation of new routes in the capital. As Fine Gael transport spokeswoman Olivia Mitchell pointed out in July 2005, the Government's own progress report on the implementation of its policy programme said: 'Exchequer funding for new buses in Dublin is being withheld at the present time pending the outcome of the discussions on the future regulation of the bus market.' Yet, in terms of capacity, investment in new buses makes sense. Luas came in at a cost of just under €800 million, with the trams providing a total of 9,600 passenger spaces at an average of 240 per tram. The same amount of money would buy 3,000 buses at an average cost of €240,000 per bus, and provide 180,000 passenger spaces – enough to double the number of buses operating in each of Ireland's cities. Only this scale of capacity can really counter our growing car-dependence. Five-minute frequencies could

↓ *More people travel across Dublin's canal bridges in buses than cars during the morning peak*
[sources: Dublin City Council and Dublin Bus, November 2003, inbound traffic]

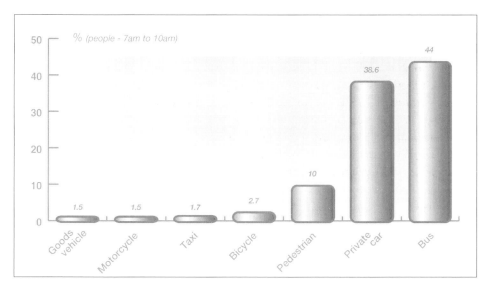

become the norm on many existing routes, and communities left without public transport would finally get a proper service. But there doesn't appear to be the political will or administrative energy to do this, so the long wait at bus stops goes on and on. Tired of this paralysis, many commuters feel there's little for it but take their car, or if they don't already have a car, to buy one; car sales in January 2005 were 19% up compared to the same month the previous year. Even with the price of crude oil at an historic high and showing little sign of dropping, those at the helm of the Department of Transport appeared to be looking the other way – towards more motorways.

By boasting, as he did in July 2004, that we were then spending a record €150 million a month on roads, Séamus Brennan conjured up Digby Parkhurst, the demented Thatcher-era transport minister in Ben Elton's hilarious 1991 novel *Gridlock*. Parkhurst throws caution to the wind at a Tory party conference in a desperate attempt to ingratiate himself with his frustrated, car-driving audience: 'I shall tell you what we are going to do', the minister declares. 'We are going to build roads! We are going to build roads, roads and then more roads! We are going to build roads to tunnel under roads, roads to fly over roads, roads to fly over roads flying over roads. Roads, roads, roads, roads, roads!'

———

NOVEMBER 1ST, 2005, SAW THE LAUNCH OF THE GOVERNMENT'S LONG-HERALDED 10-year national transport plan in front of an invited audience at St Patrick's Hall in Dublin Castle, with a press briefing afterwards in the Throne Room – the grander the plan, the grander the setting. Dubbed 'Transport 21', because of its 21st-century focus, it had been cobbled together after almost a year of often-difficult negotiations between the Department of Transport and the Department of Finance, and came with a staggering price-tag – €34.4 billion. This allowed the Taoiseach to say that nearly €9.5 million would now be spent 'every day' up to 2015 to give Ireland the transport services needed by a modern economy and expected by foreign investors in a prosperous country. 'It is not an aspirational plan', Bertie Ahern insisted, adding that all of the projects included in it had been 'fully evaluated and built into budgetary planning over the next 10 years'. Tánaiste Mary Harney hailed Transport 21 as 'very ambitious and very radical', while Minister for Finance Brian Cowen said it would involve a 'massive and necessary commitment of resources for a key sector of our economy'. Martin Cullen, who had been working on the plan since he took over from Séamus Brennan as Minister for Transport, declared that it would deliver an integrated transport system for Dublin as well as completing, albeit four years late, the inter-urban motorway network envisaged in the National Development Plan. Altogether, the Exchequer was expected to invest €26.4 billion in the programme, with €6 billion being raised through PPPs and a further €2 billion from road tolls. The breakdown between roads and public transport was also more favourable this time, with €16 million (46%) earmarked for public transport projects.

Outlining details of his package, Cullen told the overwhelmingly male audience in Dublin Castle – 'the boys with toys', as one jaded hack observed – that the emphasis in the first five years of Transport 21 would be on finishing the inter-urban roads linking Dublin with the other main cities. After 2010, some 150km of dual-carriageway, 400km of 2+1 roads and 300km of single-carriageway roads would be developed under the programme. These would include an Atlantic Road Corridor linking Letterkenny with Waterford, via Sligo, Galway, Limerick and Cork, to counterbalance the dominance of Dublin – at least partly delivering on a project long-canvassed by Dr Ed Walsh. The Western Rail Corridor would also be reopened on a phased basis, starting with reinstating the line from Ennis to Athenry, and moving on at least as far as Claremorris, though probably not to Sligo – much to the regret of Lisa McAllister, chief executive of the Western Development Commission, who said the entire

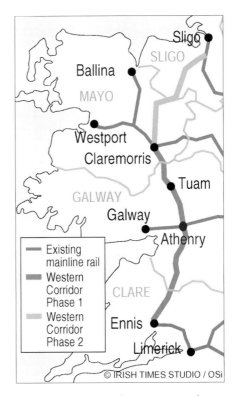

↑ *The Transport 21 plan to reinstate the Western Rail Corridor*

route would only cost 1% of the total spend envisaged for Transport 21. Existing mainline rail services were to be upgraded with new rolling stock and much-improved train services running every hour on the Dublin-Cork route and on the Dublin-Galway and Dublin-Limerick routes, at least at peak periods. Less heavily patronised services on the Sligo, Tralee, Rosslare, Waterford and Westport routes would inevitably be less frequent. There was also a promise to upgrade bus services and develop QBCs in Cork, Limerick, Galway and Waterford, as well as a firm commitment to extend rail commuter services in Cork along the existing Mallow line and a reinstated Midleton line, as well as between Athenry and Galway.

But much of the focus of Transport 21 was on the Greater Dublin Area, where Martin Cullen foresaw a 'huge increase' in public transport capacity over the 10-year period. Indeed, the plan anticipates the number of public transport passengers will almost double, from 200 million to 375 million a year by 2015, when all the elements of the programme are in place. These include a metro line from St Stephen's Green to Swords, via Glasnevin, Dublin City University, Ballymun and Dublin Airport, enabling airport users to reach the city centre in 17 minutes; a second orbital metro line linking Tallaght, Clondalkin and Blanchardstown, though it's hard to see how it can be justified; a new Luas line from Lucan to the city centre, running via Liffey

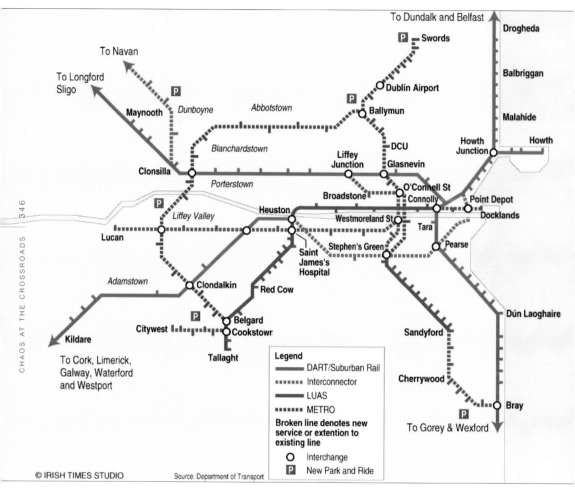

To Dundalk and Belfast

Drogheda

Balbriggan

Malahide

Howth

To Navan

To Longford
Sligo

Swords

Dublin Airport

Ballymun

Abbotstown

Maynooth

Dunboyne

DCU

Blanchardstown

Liffey
Junction

Glasnevin

Howth
Junction

Clonsilla

Porterstown

O'Connell St

Broadstone

Connolly

Point Depot

Liffey Valley

Heuston

Westmoreland St

Docklands

Lucan

Tara

Stephen's Green

Pearse

Adamstown

Clondalkin

Saint
James's
Hospital

Red Cow

Citywest

Belgard
Cookstown

Dún Laoghaire

Kildare

Sandyford

To Cork, Limerick,
Galway, Waterford
and Westport

Tallaght

Cherrywood

Bray

To Gorey & Wexford

Legend

— DART/Suburban Rail
••••••• Interconnector
— LUAS
••••••• METRO

Broken line denotes new service or extention to existing line

○ Interchange
P New Park and Ride

© IRISH TIMES STUDIO   Source: Department of Transport

The Government's Transport 21 programme, launched in November 2005
↑ *Full integration between DART, suburban rail services, new Luas lines and two metro lines*
→ *How Ireland should look after the Government rolls out its roads programme*
↓ *The Government's plan for commuter rail services in Cork*

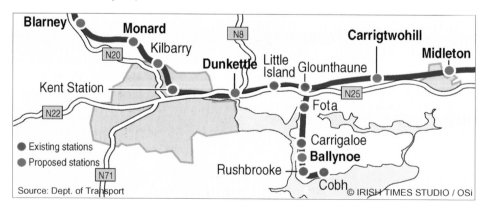

Blarney

Monard

Kilbarry

N8

Carrigtwohill

Midleton

N20

Dunkettle

Little
Island

Glounthaune

Kent Station

Fota

N25

N22

Carrigaloe

Ballynoe

Rushbrooke

N71

Cobh

● Existing stations
● Proposed stations

Source: Dept. of Transport

© IRISH TIMES STUDIO / OSi

Motorway / Dual Carriageway

Routes to Border / North West / West

Atlantic Corridor - Letterkenny to Waterford

Other key National Primary Routes

National Secondary routes targeted for upgrade works. Upgrade work will primarily consist of renewal work on selected sections of corridor

Valley, where it would connect with the orbital metro; joining up the two existing Luas lines in the city centre, as originally planned; extending the Sandyford line northwards via Broadstone to connect with the Maynooth line at Liffey Junction, and southwards to Cherrywood, and later to Bray, to connect with DART; extending the Tallaght Luas line to Docklands and building a spur to serve Citywest; re-signalling to relieve congestion on the city-centre rail network, principally around Connolly Station, to increase the number of trains in each direction from 12 to 16; upgrading the Heuston-Kildare line, as planned by Iarnród Éireann, to separate mainline and commuter trains and provide a service to places like Parkwest and Adamstown; electrification of the Northern, Kildare and Maynooth commuter lines as far as Balbriggan, Hazelhatch and Maynooth (respectively); reopening the railway line to Navan on a phased basis, initially with a spur off the Maynooth line as far as Dunboyne; and opening the rail interconnector running underground from Heuston Station to Spencer Dock, which many see as the most strategic element of the package even though it is not scheduled for completion until 2015. Under the plan, St Stephen's Green would become be a key transport hub, enabling transfer between Luas, metro and suburban rail; in effect, Cullen said, 'it will be to Dublin what Grand Central is to New York'.

Journalists arriving at Dublin Castle on that sunny autumn afternoon expected to be given comprehensive briefing material on the various elements of Transport 21, but were presented instead with a folder of ministerial scripts, a few maps and diagrams, and an indicative timetable for the completion of major projects. 'Never in the history of public transport has so much been promised by so many ministers backed up by so little paperwork', wrote Mark Hennessy in the *Irish Times*. 'There is no detailed plan', said a highly sceptical editorial in the same paper. 'Providing a gross figure of €34 billion for the entire programme, without a breakdown of the cost of specific projects, is something of a confidence trick.' The *Irish Daily Star* went even further, banner-headlining it as 'Bertie's Con Job'. And indeed, much of the content of Transport 21 had been seen before. As Fine Gael deputy leader Richard Bruton TD pointed out, the Dublin Airport metro was included in the Fianna Fáil-PD Programme for Government, with 2007 set for its completion; the extensions to Luas and the city-centre rail interconnector featured in the Dublin Transportation Office's *Platform for Change* policy document, which had been launched with similar fanfare in October 2000, and the NDP's inter-urban motorways were all supposed to be finished by the end of 2006. But then, as former Taoiseach Garret FitzGerald commented on RTÉ radio's *Morning Ireland*: 'It is a curious feature of Irish political and media life that measures largely announced previously can be relaunched as new.'

It seemed to him, and to many other commentators, that the Government had begun to prepare the ground for a general election that must be held by June 2007 at the latest. In this context, Martin Cullen deserves some credit for attaching completion dates to major projects in Transport 21. Because if it becomes clear to people at the time of the election that nothing much is happening to deliver, say, the reopening of the Cork-Midleton line or the Ennis-Athenry section of the Western Rail Corridor

– both scheduled for completion in 2008 – then Fianna Fáil and the PDs risk an electoral scalding. Other measures promised which will need to be delivered if Transport 21 is to have any credibility include enactment of the Critical Infrastructure Bill to fast-track major projects, and the establishment of a new transport and land-use planning authority for the Greater Dublin Area 'with real powers to ensure joined-up thinking and delivery across all the transport modes', as Cullen himself put it. But that, too, had been proposed before, in 2002, and nothing was done about it. There was also a belated commitment to transfer responsibility for the major commercial ports from the Department of Communications, Marine and Natural Resources to the Department of Transport, as proposed in 2002 but again not acted on, even though such a move is clearly in the interest of better integration of transport investment strategies. The lesson for the Government seemed to be that, instead of repackaging projects and reforms previously heralded, it would win more brownie points with the public by actually delivering them. Yet, despite the elapse of time – five years, in some cases – there was no evidence of any research to support the schemes included in Transport 21, even though Brian Cowen had earlier made it clear that all public capital projects costing €30 million or more would henceforth be subjected to cost-benefit analysis.

Perhaps most disappointing of all, neither the Taoiseach nor the ministers who made speeches at the Dublin Castle launch mentioned the words 'walking' or 'cycling', and there were no references to them in the accompanying press pack. Clearly, the Government had ignored census data stretching back to 1986 showing that school runs account for a significant proportion of traffic congestion – explaining why, when schools are off, tailbacks trail off and complaints are few. With all the emphasis on expensive projects, there was nothing about 'walking bus' programmes to bring children to their classrooms – the first step in recognising that a more physically fit society is needed to curb the habits of an increasingly sedentary age. Dublin Bus got short shrift too. Transport 21 only foresees a 16.5% increase in bus patronage in the city – 80,000 on top of the 480,000 daily passengers in 2005 – even though Martin Cullen pledged to build an additional nine QBCs, doubling the current number. And despite an assessment by Dublin Bus that the city needed an extra 400 buses, primarily to support the QBC programme, Cullen promised just 20 – the only measure in the entire programme that was to happen immediately. Liam Tobin, general secretary of the National Bus & Railworkers' Union, described it as inadequate and 'incredibly short-sighted, especially given the fact that all the experts agree that buses provide the quickest and cheapest solution to the current traffic congestion in the capital'.

Transport 21, with its Luas extensions, metro lines and rail interconnector, is a blueprint for a consolidated city – bizarrely put forward by the same Government which did nothing to prevent the sprawl of Dublin. As a direct result of its laissez-faire planning policies, the plan will be of little or no use to the thousands of long-distance commuters now living in dormitory towns throughout Leinster and even parts of Ulster.

8. Conclusion

So what is to be done? Will the tentacles of Irish cities and towns reach into the far corners of our countryside, with headlamps illuminating every boreen before sunrise? Or will we confront the central challenge of consolidating urban areas and, in the words of Dick Gleeson, Dublin City Council's chief planning officer, 'create good places for people to live and work'? Martin Cullen presented his rural housing guidelines in March 2004 as if there were only two options: suburbanising the countryside or developing 'urban jungles' – clearly a false choice. Jack Fitzsimons, author of *Bungalow Bliss*, has acknowledged that the popularity of his best-seller owes much to formless urban design. And Ireland's experience of 'rapid and inept urbanisation in the 20th century suggests we will have to re-learn how to make towns and cities well', according to architect Colm Murray. The prevailing development pattern still involves the rapid creation of new residential areas without adequate infrastructure or social facilities – repeating mistakes we've been making since the 1960s, as Brendan Williams and Patrick Shiels of the Dublin Institute of Technology have pointed out. More than 30 years on, we still have no urban structure plans to regulate the ad-hoc addition of new housing. Part of the reason for this is that planners find it difficult to make the leap from coloured maps and diagrams to the more refined level of creating places. What they should be doing, Gleeson said, is to 'break the mould of featureless suburban housing crawling across the landscape' by offering new models to the public.

Back in 1976, research by An Foras Forbartha found that 71% of people living in one-off houses in the countryside had grown up in villages, towns or cities. The desire to have more living space is there in most of us, and, as the AFF study showed, a rural or urban upbringing isn't determinative one way or the other. But romantic attachment to 19th-century patterns of development is no more than that. Dispersed housing in rural areas not only diffuses civic energy, it locks householders into high-

→ *Where the buck stops! The imposing façade of Government Buildings on Upper Merrion Street, Dublin, designed by Sir Aston Webb in 1904*

cost living. Public investment needs to be aligned with a long-term vision of land use and transport. There is little point in employing the language of sustainability if the net result of governmental action is to clog roads with urban-focused development that is ever more distant from its target centre. A laissez-faire policy favouring rural housing will not only destroy the landscape – and with it, the raw material of Irish tourism – but cities and towns will suffer too by failing to achieve the desired critical mass. Yet, even after recognising the problem of one-off housing in the countryside, the Department of the Environment produced no measures to redirect growth to help create dynamic urban centres. With projections that the State's population could reach five million by 2020, the key issue we have to address is how to accommodate as many of the additional people as possible in well-served cities and towns. It stands to reason that this cannot be done by permitting unrestricted development of housing in the countryside.

At present, most towns are developing outwards along arterial routes (on each side of the Tulla, Kilrush and Galway roads, taking Ennis as an example). As development stretches further and further away from the urban centre, car-dependency increases. John O'Connor, chairman of An Bord Pleanála, complained in November 2004 about the 'astonishing number' of poorly designed 1970s-style suburban housing estates – most of them without the involvement of architects – being 'tacked on' to towns and villages throughout the State, with no regard for their setting. The sensible alternative would be to fill out a grid street pattern from the town centre outwards. This would unlock lands close to the middle of towns – in the case of Ennis, within walking distance of the railway station. Residents living close to a station are more likely to take the train for inter-regional journeys. In other countries, the promotion of satellite towns has been quietly shelved in favour of the 'network city' – an area where the home, work and recreation are sometimes interspersed, but always linked with each other. In that context, the consolidation of existing 'edge city' areas is the optimum choice from a public transport perspective. Examples include Swords, Blanchardstown, Clondalkin, Tallaght/Citywest, Sandyford, Bray/Greystones in Dublin; Rochestown and Mahon in Cork; Dooradoyle/Raheen and UL in Limerick.

Planning consultant Fergal MacCabe, who contributed to the Bacon reports on house prices and also the 1999 Residential Density Guidelines, suggested in August 2001 that local authorities should draw up plans for the development of villages with falling populations because of the drift of housing into the countryside. The biggest obstacle he saw was that Irish people 'don't yet have an appreciation of urban values which might convince us that more beautiful houses could be built in towns and villages'. The appeal of the main street of an attractive town, such as Kenmare, is obvious, but there must be factors deterring people from living in such places. Is it because too much traffic trundles past? Or is it the lack of access to safe play areas for children? One measure that might help tilt the balance is a change in capital taxes to favour land directly adjacent to cities and towns. A radius of development would need to be drawn for every large urban centre. For villages, a standard cut-off might apply, say 500 metres from the defined village centre. The definition of a village must contemplate some critical mass. Arguably, a primary school should be a mandatory requirement, complemented perhaps by four facilities from a list of eight: a shop, resident GP, place of worship, pub, civic centre, sports centre, long-established sports club.

Any introduction of a definition for 'village', together with a limitation on one-off housing outside the development zone, would need to be tempered by making exceptions for houses in the countryside used to exploit rural resources. However, it would make sense to insist on a business plan for, say, agri-tourism; otherwise the spirit of the exemption may be contravened by attempts to build holiday homes, pushing the price of land beyond those who actually want to work on it. The tax code should also be used to curb the demand by urban dwellers for second homes in rural areas, as the ESRI has proposed. At present, owners of holiday homes pay no tax on such properties; if they were to be levied for a percentage of the value on an annual basis, it might make them think twice about adding yet another rarely lived-in house to the countryside. Instead, they might take their breaks in B&Bs and local hotels, thereby making a real contribution to the economic and social fabric of the locality. Another, perhaps simpler, measure would be to use existing legislation. Under Section 48 of the 2000 Planning Act, local authorities are empowered to demand a financial contribution from all applicants for planning permission to improve roads and other services. In order to focus developers' interest on the existing urban footprint, they could set this levy so that it increases with distance from a town centre. To be effective, however, a carrot-and-stick approach would need to be evenly applied by all 88 local authorities, many of whom currently apply an identical policy in completely different ways.

To stem the demand for houses in rural areas, several local authorities have tried to restrict planning permission to people from the locality. In 2003 Kerry County Council denied that planning restrictions favouring locals were unconstitutional. But having sought advice on the matter, the council only published a summary version of the legal opinion; the full text was withheld. In the Blasket Islands case, the Supreme Court struck down a law differentiating between owners of land before 17th November 1953 and those who held it after that date. To draw a distinction on the basis of when land came to be owned was, according to the court, 'based on a principle – that of pedigree – which appears to have no place (outside the law of succession) in a democratic society committed to the principle of equality'. Finding that Ireland's Constitution 'should be pedigree blind just as it should be colour blind or gender blind', it struck down the 1953 distinction as unconstitutional. The Supreme Court's judgment may have stark implications for councils that restrict house-building to local people. In the light of the Great Blasket Island case, Irish courts would be unlikely to find that favouring those with links to or roots in an area – whatever this means – outweighs the guarantees of equality under Irish and European law.

One of the problems in Ireland is that we have turned the constitutional right to private property into a presumptive right to develop land, whatever the public interest may require. Anyone who owns a piece of land feels that they have an almost

↑ *Surely the appeal of living on the main street of an attractive town such as Kenmare, Co Kerry, should be obvious*

God-given right over it. 'These are my effin' thistles, and I can do what I like with them' is the phrase used by Leo Hallissey of the Connemara Environmental Education Centre to sum up this psychosis. Allied to this, land prices have rocketed in recent years. As Labour's environment spokesman Eamon Gilmore TD has repeatedly pointed out, the site cost of a house rose from about 15% of the purchase price in the early 1990s to almost 50% in 2004, though a 2003 *Building Industry Bulletin* report by construction economist Jerome Casey found no evidence of a price cartel. However, in a *Business and Finance* special report, Fearghal O'Connor maintained that 'developers often worked together and a "quasi-club" exists'. Those identified as having become 'fabulously wealthy' as a result of land deals and house-building over the past decade include the Bailey brothers (Bovale Developments), Seán Dunne (Mountbrook Homes), Richard Barrett and Johnny Ronan (Treasury Holdings), David Daly (Albany and Trident), Joe, Michael and Peter Cosgrave (Cosgrave Group), Joseph O'Reilly and Liam Maye (Castlethorn Construction), Gerry Gannon (Gannon Homes), Joe Moran (Manor Park Homes), Michael Whelan (Maplewood Developments), Séamus Ross (Menolly Homes), Michael Cotter (Park Developments) and Seán Mulryan (Ballymore Properties). Quite a club. But in the end, O'Connor did not conclude that developers were hoarding land. It remains the

↑ *Children play on the wide balcony of a social and affordable apartment block at Coin Street, on the south bank of the Thames, with London's Eye turning in the background*

case that rezoning – changing the classification of farmland to building land – means little more than the land can be built on at a future date. It doesn't mean that a local authority is in a position to serve the area with water mains, sewerage and so on. For example, in April 2004 the *Irish Times* revealed that more than 1,400 hectares (3,360 acres) of land in Fingal which was zoned for development in 1999 was still undeveloped five years later. At the higher residential densities now permitted, this would be sufficient to provide 50,000 new homes.

These hold-ups have contributed to the price spiral. 'Based on a 1991 index of 100 points, in 1995 the average earnings of adult workers stood at 116, house-building costs stood at 114, consumer prices stood at 111 and the price of a new house stood at 116. By the fourth quarter of 2003, house-building costs were 176, consumer prices were 144 but the price of houses had rocketed to 352', as Fearghal O'Connor noted. 'Critics of developers put this dramatic change between house prices and the cost of building them down to the slow drip-feed of land onto the market.' As long ago as 1973, the Kenny Report on Building Land recommended a way out, by proposing that all land required for urban development should be compulsorily acquired by local authorities for 25% more than its agricultural value. And that's exactly what we should do, according to the All-Party Oireachtas Committee on the Constitution in April 2004. The report compiled 31 years earlier by Judge John Kenny, a noted constitutional lawyer, had not been acted on by any government because of untested fears that its central recommendation could be unconstitutional. The very core of what the Planning Tribunal is inquiring into – corrupt payments to politicians to secure the rezoning of land – stems from the abject failure of successive governments to implement Kenny. But the All-Party Committee noted that the Supreme Court had upheld Part V of the 2000 Planning Act, and it concluded that implementing a 'Kenny-type mechanism' was also likely to be upheld by the court.

There has also been a spectacular failure to realise a key objective touted by all political parties in the late 1990s – to counteract the tendency of the private sector to deliver socially segregated housing. A much-trumpeted scheme, ushered in by Part V of the 2000 Planning Act, was meant to provide homes for first-time purchasers who found themselves priced out of the property market. Its constitutionality had also been upheld by the Supreme Court. But as Carl O'Brien reported in September 2004, it produced a derisory 163 new homes in 2003, out of a record output of 68,819 units. Internal projections by the Department of the Environment estimated that around 500 'social and affordable' homes would be built in 2004, 1,000 in 2005, and 2,000 in 2006. The figures came almost two years after the Government watered down a provision that up to 20% of all private developments must contain social and affordable housing. That was in November 2002 when Martin Cullen, under intense pressure from the building industry, allowed developers to swap land or pay financial compensation to a local authority instead of having to provide a batch of 'social and affordable' homes on any given site. O'Brien quoted a construction industry source, who said one factor was that private home-buyers simply did not want to live in a scheme with a 'social and affordable' component. 'People are very fussy over who they live next door to', the source said. 'Ninety per cent of punters don't want to be near social housing, and builders are faced with that problem. Everyone's putting their heads in the sand on this issue.' When Fingal County Council sought to build 24 'social and affordable' homes in an overgrown field in Sutton, it was vigorously opposed by local residents. 'In more than 150 letters to the council, residents raised issues of security, safety, fears of "anti-social behaviour" and the arrival of "undesirables" in their midst', Tim O'Brien reported in April 2004. Specific issues mentioned by one couple were 'under-age drinking, burglary, damage to property and general criminal activity'. Another said this was 'just not on and will be resisted utterly'. They were backed by Martin Brady TD (FF) – who asked the council 'to look favourably' at the objections 'as I fully support the residents' views' – and former minister Dr Michael Woods TD (FF). It didn't seem to occur to any of them that their own children might happily settle for one of these affordable homes.

Less than 8% of the new homes in 2003 – 5,000 out of 68,819 – were built by local authorities, even as the waiting lists lengthened to 48,000-plus. As for the 10,000 new 'affordable' homes promised by the Government on State-owned land as part of the 'Sustaining Progress' social partnership agreement, 'not a brick has been laid', as the *Irish Times* said in September 2004. 'Protests by the Taoiseach, Mr Ahern, that his Government is "socially caring" will carry little weight with a growing number of families that are waiting to be housed by local authorities and homeless agencies. While builders and developers make enormous profits from a record number of house completions and prices continue to rise, the least well-off are losing hope.' Meanwhile, Dublin City Council announced in August 2004 that it would offer its stock of almost 16,500 flats, valued at about €3 billion, for sale to tenants at discounts of up to 30% on their market value; officials had overcome an earlier legal difficulty by agreeing to maintain common areas. Six years earlier, the housing department was buying back houses at full market value years after selling them to former tenants 'for buttons' in one or other of the earlier 'sales of the century'. Only in Docklands was the 20% 'social and affordable' rule being applied on a site-by-site basis. The most successful scheme is Clarion Quay, by Urban Projects – except that no children are allowed to play on its green space by order of the management committee representing residents.

Thanks to Martin Cullen's change to Part V of the 2000 Planning Act – which removed the requirement to provide site-specific social and affordable housing – the development of mixed-income neighbourhoods was dealt a severe blow, and the opportunity to dislodge long-held prejudice through workable examples is passed on to another generation. The sad thing is that Cullen never tested other approaches that would foster mixed-income housing. He could, for example, have proposed reducing the corporate tax rate for developers who rent or sell a percentage of what they build to people below the average income, which is part of housing law in many US states. Granted, Noel Dempsey's Part V scheme was fairly rough and ready. For example, it never even applied to about half of all housing output; schemes of four homes or less were exempt – something that gave further impetus to small-scale projects, particularly one-off housing. Moreover, Section 96 of the 2000 Act makes it clear that Part V applies only to 'land zoned solely for residential use, or for a mixture of residential and other uses'. Thus, any developer who manages to get planning permission for a housing estate on unzoned land can evade it altogether. And since much of the land in predominantly rural counties remains unzoned, this is a significant loophole. As originally enacted, the legislation left plenty of scope for equivocation and even graft: the price paid by councils for homes, serviced sites or land transferred to them came out of a process of horse-trading between local authority officials and developers. Martin Cullen's introduction of the 'buy-out' option in 2002 has magnified this horse-trading: instead of transferring homes, serviced sites or land at less than market value, the developer can pay to do nothing – and there's no surefooted way to calculate the amount of compensation. Still, because it involves a little bit less uncertainty, most developers pitch for the buy-out option as their first port of call. Part V was bad law-making from the start, and Cullen had the opportunity to address its fundamental weaknesses. Instead, he threw his hands in the air, turning the aim of achieving more social integration into a tool to lever cash for councils.

The horse-trading inaugurated by Cullen's change to Part V looked set to be intensified by the Government's latest initiative on affordable housing. Announced by

↑ *A new housing estate backing onto fields at the edge of Balla, Co Mayo. Because it was built on unzoned land, none of the houses needed to be 'social and affordable'.*

↓ *Unique selling point on an estate agent's sign in Camden Street, Dublin 2: 'No Social And Affordable Housing Provision' in this apartments scheme*

the Taoiseach himself at the ICTU annual conference in Belfast in June 2005, it involves the State bartering sites in public ownership for X number of homes on newly built housing estates, more often than not on the urban edge. The pilot land-swap deal involved trading a prime site at Harcourt Terrace in Dublin city centre with Durkan Homes for 193 units in three locations – two in Clondalkin and one just south of the Citywest business park. Speed was the only plus. Though the Harcourt Terrace site is more than likely to be developed for another 'exclusive' block of apartments, the deal meant that South Dublin County Council was able to lay its hands almost immediately on nearly 200 new homes in a state of virtual completion, to be allocated to lower-income people who would qualify for them. But who's to decide on the value of publicly owned sites and how this can be measured by the number of homes being swapped for them? Surely it would be cleaner if the State sold surplus sites at full market price and used the cash to buy new homes directly. It was difficult not to conclude that the Government was desperate to be seen to do something, even at the eleventh hour, to fulfill its pledge made in 'Sustaining Progess' to increase the supply of affordable housing by 10,000 units, which was meant to be met by the end of 2005. Certainly, its initiative gave no indication of the clear focus which the British government now has of developing sustainable communities that are 'active, inclusive and safe, well-run, environmentally sensitive, well-designed and built, well-connected and thriving', for the most part on brownfield sites.

———

FEATURELESS SUBURBS WILL CONTINUE TO CRAWL ACROSS THE LANDSCAPE AS LONG THE vast bulk of Ireland's housing output is made up of houses of one or two storeys, reflecting the fact that most Irish people still aspire to that quintessentially English ambition of owning a detached or semi-detached house with a front and back garden. There is a reluctance to bring up a family in an apartment – typical on the Continent – although this is entirely understandable. Basic issues such as where children can play safely must be addressed first, particularly in urban areas where, for example, space could be provided for five-a-side football pitches, but this will only

↓ *Young people playing hockey in Vancouver, against the downtown skyline. Basic issues such as where children can play safely must be addressed in inner-urban areas.*

happen with good planning. And in the suburbs, instead of having lifeless strips of open space and small rear gardens enclosed by breeze-block walls, why not group houses around a shared space which would have a children's playground as well as areas where people could relax? At present, however, poorly focused planning results in the most banal solutions to maximise the commercial potential of any site, according to architect Paul Keogh. 'Estates lack any structured pattern of open spaces ... The design of the public realm is neglected: spaces between buildings are left-over spaces rather than places with their own identity and character.' He branded the failure of policy and development plans to 'give priority to design and the creation of communities' as one of the greatest indictments of planning in Ireland. By seeking merely to mediate in real estate development, these plans have produced a form of settlement which is unsustainable in environmental and urban-design terms. Keogh also queried whether the numbers-driven agenda of the construction industry would go on to deliver housing estate after housing estate. Or could we make the political choice between the dynamism of urban culture instead of the endless expansion of suburbia?

It's not as if there are no models. Examples of sustainable housing that's successful by any social or environmental yardstick can be found throughout Europe, particularly in Denmark, Finland, Sweden and the Netherlands. So why do we always seem to think that we must reinvent the wheel? Even the message about increasing residential densities is garbled and misinterpreted as a move towards high-rise housing, perhaps even on the Ballymun model, when the truth is that Ballymun was actually a low-density housing scheme. With all the formless open space between its towers and 'spine blocks', there were only 10 homes per acre. Now high-rise buildings seem about to erupt all over Dublin, not just in Docklands and around Heuston Station, but in Sandyford, Stillorgan and other improbable places – all justified on the basis that the city needs a crop of contemporary 'gateways' and 'landmarks'. Plans for 'focal point' towers of 12 to 24 storeys, flanked by apartment blocks of six to eight storeys, have raised the hackles of suburbanites who fear that the low-rise character of their areas is being turned into 'something like Hong Kong'. In the city, An Bord Pleanála's approval for a 32-storey tower opposite Heuston, based on the quality of its design by Paul Keogh Architects, was seen by several developers as a green light for similar schemes. It almost seemed as if 32 had become the magic number. Treasury Holdings had plans for another 32-storey tower at Barrow Street, in the Grand Canal Docks, but they were withdrawn after the planners requested a raft of further information, including a 'microclimatic assessment', studies showing its impact on the skyline, and a 'shadow analysis' to gauge its effects on nearby houses. Also in Docklands, Harry Crosbie unveiled plans for yet another 32-storey tower beside the Point Theatre. Scott Tallon Walker's design seemed to underline a point made by one of the contributors to a lively online debate (www.archeire.com) that 'many high rises are just one floor multiplied by X'. The architects claimed that this 'signature building' would mirror U2's much-publicised 'twisting' tower on Britain Quay, directly across the River Liffey, also set to soar to a height of 100 metres, and thus provide a

↑ *A sketch perspective by Scott Tallon Walker Architects showing the proposed 32-storey tower and Point Village scheme for the North Wall in Dublin's Docklands*

'maritime gateway to Dublin'. And when developer Seán Dunne agreed to pay €50 million per acre for the Jurys Hotel site in Ballsbridge, he mooted the prospect of building another 32-storey tower there. 'What we need to avoid is "plonk architecture", with high-rise buildings arbitrarily placed without regard for their context', one senior planner said, off the record. But even if a cluster of landmark towers emerges in Docklands, it will be small compensation for the wasted opportunity represented by phase two of the IFSC where, as City Architect Jim Barrett once famously remarked, most of the buildings on the riverfront look as if they had been 'given a crew-cut'; the real problem is that the general height of buildings along the Liffey in Docklands is disproportionately low in relation to the breadth of the river.

The 1999 Residential Density Guidelines had nothing to say about high-rise housing. All they did was set out to achieve a modest increase in the number of homes per acre, particularly in the vicinity of public transport nodes – something that could be achieved by reconfiguring shared public spaces. Although there is now general agreement on the underlying principles – notably the importance of mixed land use linked to good public transport – getting down to detail about how new development areas are going to work has been more difficult. 'Creating urban form is one of the most challenging things around', planner Dick Gleeson conceded. 'Sometimes you

←↑ A model and montage of the 32-storey tower and associated development, approved by An Bord Pleanála for a site opposite Heuston Station

→ The competition-winning U2 Tower for Britain Quay, by Burdon Craig Dunne Henry Architects; it is currently being redesigned to rise to a height of 100 metres

have to work ridiculously hard at it.' The Irish model has yet to be created.

Strategic Development Zones, brought in under the 2000 Planning Act, promised much but have delivered little. Apart from facilitating industrial development, SDZs were intended to speed up the delivery of housing and tackle backlogs in providing roads, schools and sports facilities. Yet even getting the master plan for Adamstown, in west Dublin, from its first unveiling to final approval took nearly 2½ years. Progress on Pelletstown, a site with a much smaller acreage near Finglas, earmarked to cater for a population of up to 10,000, was equally tortuous. With an SDZ, the local authority still steers the project, but the fact is that none of them has the money or clout to lay on bus services or ensure that schools are built.

Adamstown has been put forward as 'a realistic high-density, mixed-use, public-transport-based alternative to the low-density, mono-use, roads-based development' of South Dublin's earlier suburbs, in the words of its planner, Paul Hogan. Roads designed as streets rather than traffic conduits, and urban parks instead of 'the usual formless prairies' – as Eddie Conroy, South Dublin's deputy county architect, calls them – are among the key elements of the planning blueprint for this 550-acre swathe of land adjoining the Dublin-Cork railway line. Produced in May 2001 by a team that included both architects and planners, the blueprint envisages that most buildings in Adamstown will be three to five storeys high. 'The use of varied building heights is a useful device to create urban enclosure, forge a strong sense of place, and highlight the individual identity of locations throughout the new district', the plan says. In general, taller buildings will be located at important corners, focal points, and at the end of vistas. The objective is to provide 'a lively and interconnecting network of streets, squares and public gardens with a wide range of public spaces and interesting buildings'. The plan emphasises the importance of mixed use. In addition to some 10,000 homes, there are to be shopping, leisure and community facilities, as well as offices and light industry, making it possible for people to live and work in the same area. The range of homes will be diverse – apartments, duplex units and townhouses – laid out on squares, along avenues, or in courtyard or mews settings, while all public open spaces will be overlooked to ensure 'passive surveillance' as a deterrent to vandalism and other forms of anti-social behaviour – 'eyes on the street', as American architecture critic Jane Jacobs called them. At the same time, gated housing estates surrounded by walls or railings are to be avoided in the interests of promoting 'physical and social connectivity'. That in itself would mark a welcome departure from the corral-type arrangement that now characterises far too many 'exclusive' suburban enclaves. Clearly what the planners have in mind is more like Stockholm than Stillorgan.

But without first-rate public transport, Adamstown would turn into a 'planning nightmare', as Paul Gogarty, the local Green Party TD, warned in May 2003. Putting the plan in perspective, he said a new town the size of Drogheda (pop. 25,000) would be 'spliced into Lucan', which already had the fastest growing population in the State. Gogarty was reflecting the fact that ordinary people are naturally sceptical about higher-density residential development, especially in established suburbs.

'Densification' may be encouraged by official policies, but there has been quite a negative reaction on the ground to what are sometimes seen as ravenous schemes for multi-storey apartment blocks in areas with a predominantly low-rise character. Yet without higher densities and a more compact urban form, Dublin and other cities cannot support a high-quality public transport system. If the promised public transport did not materialise to serve Adamstown, particularly a new station and more frequent services on the Arrow line, the fear locally is that 10,000 new homes will translate into at least 12,000 cars, inevitably generating yet more traffic congestion throughout the area. When it approved the Adamstown SDZ in September 2003, An Bord Pleanála effectively tied the construction of new homes to Iarnród Éireann's timetable – in particular, the provision of a new railway station on the Kildare line and the building of two extra tracks. All the appeals board can do is force developers to stop and wait until these are provided – the opposite of what should be done, which is making sure that water, housing, schools, transport and so on all come on stream together.

What this really shows is that, however good they might be at producing plans, local authorities have no direct role in securing the public transport services needed to support them. The Government did produce a consultation paper in April 2001 proposing the establishment of a new regional authority for the Greater Dublin Area, with a likely annual budget in excess of £500 million and wide-ranging powers for strategic planning, land use and transport provision. At the time, Bertie Ahern said this was 'the only way' of reconciling 'too many different agendas' among the vari-

↓ *Gated housing estates such as this one at Ardilea Wood, in Clonskeagh, Dublin 14, are to be avoided in the development of Adamstown, according to its master plan*

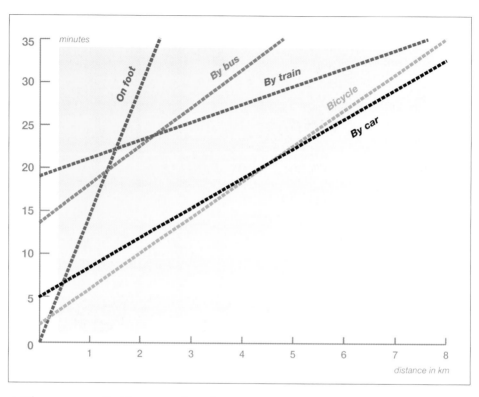

↑ *Bikes compete well with cars on urban trips* [source: Brachter, 1988]
↓ *The population of Leinster has grown dramatically compared to other provinces since the 1920s, with the pace increasing rapidly over time* [source: Central Statistics Office]

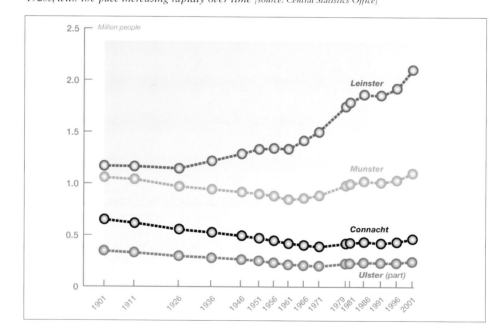

Computer-generated images of some of the housing proposed for Adamstown, south of Lucan
↑ Streetscape of four-storey duplex buildings
↓ Central amenity area, with a landmark building in the foreground

← Cycle lanes do more harm than good if they are badly designed. In this picture, taken near Dundrum, cars exit from the left at speed and go straight into the path of cyclists. Cycle paths should be continuous, not partly on the road, partly on the footpath.

← Here, at the busy junction under the Luas bridge in Dundrum, cyclists are forced into the path of pedestrians waiting to cross to road. All the engineers have done here is facilitate the faster movement of cars.

← The addition of slip roads to the M50 junctions has discouraged cycling. On the approach to the Ballymount interchange, a cyclist going straight on would be vulnerable to fast-moving vehicles veering left onto the slip road. This design flaw needs to be addressed.

ous agencies, but the idea was quietly pigeonholed because the mandarins – and, on reflection, the politicians themselves – didn't like it. The danger was that a Greater Dublin Authority would become too powerful. Having rejected joined-up thinking for Dublin, the Government didn't facilitate it anywhere else either. For example, Limerick City Council's development plan reads: 'It is the policy of the City Council to co-operate with the bus service providers to provide a quality bus service to the community of Limerick.' Its aim is laudable but would read more realistically as: 'We are 100% behind the idea of quality bus corridors. But we can't actually deliver them.'

A four-part television series, *The Changing Face of Dublin*, broadcast by RTÉ in May 2002, suggested that Ireland's commitment to sustainable development could be measured, first and foremost, by examining its housing and land-use policies. The documentary showed that Dublin's footprint is twice to three times that of some European cities with similar-sized populations, such as Amsterdam, Brussels, Cologne and Turin. The 2002 census recorded 42 people per hectare in Dublin compared to 31 in Cork, 26 in Limerick, 13 in Galway and 11 in Waterford. If Dublin city and county are taken together, the figure drops to 13 people per hectare, revealing a lot about the way the capital developed in the latter half of the 20th century. But even with this very modest urban density, a report in 2000 by Goodbody Economic Consultants found that 22% of all trips in Dublin were by public transport. All the figures 'argue for an enhancement of bus services in Cork, Limerick, Galway and Waterford', Goodbody said – something that hasn't been delivered on since. Curiously, Cork had a lower level of bus-use than Limerick, at 8.5% of trips compared to 9.3%, even though it has more than double the population. Bus-use in Galway clocked in at 7%, which was still ahead of Waterford at 4%; a spread-out pattern of development was blamed for its poor performance.

Excessive car-dependency and the traffic congestion it generates are the almost inevitable consequences of sprawl. The questioning of 'car culture' comes at a time when congestion is beginning to hurt Ireland economically as well as well as socially. In an international comparison of urban journey times (based on the delivery of a 5kg package over 5km), Dublin fared worst in Europe and was ranked second-last in the world. Until the gremlin of congestion manifested itself, there was little recognition of the 'the human ecosystem' – the linkages in our own way of life – in Ireland. Now, it is increasingly realised, even in North America, that the development of areas distant from an urban core increases travel times while reducing leisure time and inter-personal contact. For more than half a century, millions of Americans have 'acted as if moving out to the suburbs is the same as moving up in life', Parris Glendening, governor of Maryland, wrote in 2001. 'Rather than stopping to think about how to make our communities better places to live, many of us rushed headlong into the countryside. Gradually, we are beginning to realise that our growth patterns are destroying our cherished landscapes. On top of its impact on farm and forest lands, low-density sprawling growth has destroyed the beauty of our communities, made congestion worse and forced our citizens to pay higher and higher taxes to

← *The deadening effect of a multi-storey car park on Limerick's Thomas Street. What developer is going to take on restoring the warehouse opposite?*

← *TDs and senators were shamelessly parking their cars, for free, on what used to be a lawn at the Merrion Square frontage of Leinster House*

meet the demand for sprawl.' According to Glendening, Americans are 'beginning to realise that we need to rethink the way we grow' through the Smart Growth Movement. As governor of Maryland, he has been a leading proponent of 'smart growth' – an approach to development that promises to create more liveable communities while preserving open space and other environmental amenities. Under a blueprint called New Community Design, new houses and shops are arranged so that the easiest way to get from one to the other is on foot or by bicycle. The aim is to reintroduce walkable communities, with well laid-out public parks, streets and squares.

Achieving sustainable development in Ireland, it seems to us, involves a three-step process. First, there is the issue of better cities. Second, we need to be able to get around these cities. And third, efficient travel between cities is vital. Taking those three steps must involve improving public transport as a major priority, because only it offers the prospect of sustainable accessibility. At present, because of our very high level of car-dependency, much of the urban fabric must be hewn out just to store cars. As the authors of *Suburban Sprawl* put it: 'Engineering standards that respond to automobile dependence create environments in which walking is even less viable. Parking lots built to contain all the cars necessitated by an automotive environment cause buildings to be located increasingly further apart, again making walking less likely.' All the techniques developed in response to car-dominated land-use patterns 'end up perpetuating those very patterns', they conclude. One by-product of car-dependence – parking – saps life out of streets. Look at the Thomas Street multi-storey car park in Limerick and observe the deadening effect it has on the immediate area. What developer is going to take on restoring the warehouse opposite? Who wants to wake up every morning and stare into a lifeless zone?

One of the contributory factors to our high car-use is that so many employees are provided with free parking at their workplaces – something that encourages them to drive to work as long as it remains an untaxed perk. If we really want to ease congestion, let's start taxing company parking spaces. As things stand, a city parking space is worth more than a typical company car, and providing spaces is a tax-efficient way to give perks to employees, as a 1999 report by DKM Economic Consultants concluded. It suggested that parking cordons should be mapped out for Dublin, Cork, Limerick, Galway and Waterford. Inside the cordons, private non-residential parking spaces would each be valued at €3,000 a year and taxed as a benefit-in-kind. A tax on workplace car-parking has proven effective in Australia in influencing the locations chosen for new development. If replicated in Ireland, employers would begin to eye buses and bikes with more enthusiasm. Charlie McCreevy appeared to commit the Government to doing something about this in his 2000 Budget, but an interdepartmental tax-strategy group could find no 'practical, straightforward and equitable' way to implement the measure. This was hardly surprising, since so many civil servants – especially in the upper echelons – enjoy free parking, even within the historic precincts of Dublin Castle, while TDs and senators quite shamelessly parked their cars for six years on the tarmac-covered lawn in front of Leinster House. So nothing was done.

Cities, according to David Engwicht, developed to 'maximise exchange and minimise movement'. Some movement is necessary, of course, but the aim is to keep distances down while enjoying everyday human interaction as we move about. Concern over our increasingly sedentary way of life is coming to influence transport policy more and more. According to the 2002 National Health and Lifestyle Study, Ireland's growing levels of obesity have more to do with reduced physical activity than with changes in diet. Increasingly, planning applications for office developments must be accompanied by mobility-management plans, to cut the time employees spend getting to work and encourage them to consider other means of travel, such as bike, bus or train. One of the root causes of traffic congestion in Dublin is poor planning, as Conor Faughnan, of AA Ireland, has cogently argued. 'The city is spreading outwards at a ridiculously disproportionate rate. There's an awful lot of idle land within Dublin that could be used for housing. We need some economic incentives to make sure it's used rather than using greenfield sites ever further from the city ... Places like Edenderry, Dundalk and Carlow are becoming suburbs of Dublin, which is absurd. There is no way we can adequately serve people who come to work in Dublin from outlying counties with public transport. The car becomes their only option to get to work. When they reach the M50, they become part of Dublin's problem. We need better public transport and a higher density of housing.' But in terms of urban journey time, bike is actually the closest competitor to the car, as shown by the graph of door-to-door travel times. Cycling is also the most energy-efficient transport mode. However, poor road design has a lot to do with the collapse of cycling in Ireland.

———

IN THE MEANTIME, WE ARE HEADING WILLY-NILLY TOWARDS THE LEAST DESIRABLE OF outcomes – a Dublin so dominant that Ireland becomes a city-state. Projections by the Central Statistics Office in May 2005 confirmed this general trend. They suggested that the GDA's population would reach 2.1 million in 2021, accounting for 40.7% of the population of five million forecast for the State as a whole. If Dublin's outlying dormitories all over Leinster were included, its share would obviously be even higher. It is true that the increase in the GDA's proportion of the total population will be relatively marginal – up from 39.2% to 40.7%. But even a net increase of 1.5% is in the wrong direction, and will only serve to intensify congestion in and around Dublin. As CSO figures show, the number of people living in Leinster began to part company with the population of other provinces in the late 1920s. Regional disparity, whether manifest in population statistics or airport use, will widen until Munster and Connacht develop robust cities, and support them with good connections. 'Any plan for a counterpole to Dublin must be tested by whether or not it will halt or reverse the drift to Dublin', as Dr Edward Walsh, UL's former president, wrote in June 2003. 'The only regional development initiative of consequence in the history of the State emerged from a different process. Seán Lemass, in the late 1950s, with minimal consultation and much vision, provided Brendan O'Regan with funds and discretion

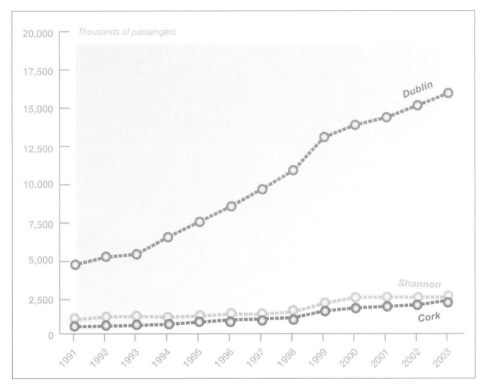

↑ *Since the early 1990s Dublin Airport has experienced runaway growth, while traffic in Cork and Shannon remained relatively static* [*sources: Central Statistics Office, Aer Rianta*]

to establish Shannon Development ... Two generations later something similar is called for to stem the drift to Dublin, while addressing Ireland's declining reputation as a good place in which to live. Malaysia attracted much international attention with the 1998 launch of its grand vision for the Multimedia Super Corridor. It stretches 50km south from Kuala Lumpur and provides for the most advanced knowledge infrastructure, including the development of two "smart cities": Putrajaya and Cyberjaya. Ireland should have no reason to lack the confidence to do something at least as adventurous. Or put another way: can the Atlantic Technopolis offer a better lifestyle, communications, transport and housing infrastructure than Dublin?' Walsh's vision has three elements: a Galway-Limerick-Cork-Waterford alliance; a major road axis between Cork and Galway linked to the south east; and direct air services from Shannon to continental Europe.

Real political impetus to develop Cork, Galway, Limerick and Waterford would save a lot of foot-stomping about CIÉ's reluctance to run trains between them. And there's the rub. The mini-Cabinet assembled in late 2003 to decide on decentralisation didn't want to know about cities. They just wanted to 'grow everywhere'. Unfortunately, to 'grow everywhere', half-thinking this might limit Dublin, is to grow nowhere in particular. Even though an industry cluster in Cork accounts for close to

30% of our exports, the city is grossly undervalued. This can no longer be excused, as the role that cities, particularly Dublin, played in the second half of the 1990s is well-documented, and because the National Spatial Strategy spelled out what is need-ed to counter the capital, even if it failed to make sensible choices. As Peter Clinch, Professor of Urban and Regional Planning at UCD, pointed out, the decentralisation programme does nothing to create a counterweight, and Dublin would regain the loss in population within two to three years – a figure he put at 40,000. What happened was totally at odds with the way public policy should be made. As outlined as long ago as 1953 by Prof Patrick Lynch, a former civil servant: 'Public confidence in the administrative machinery of the State and in the capacity and judgment of its per-sonnel would be immeasurably strengthened if the facts and considerations on which policy decisions are based were frankly and fully disclosed to the public.' The fact is that the decentralisation programme is grounded in nothing more than hot air. Its cost has been continually revised upwards; at the time of writing it was put at €900 million – a €700 million hike in just 20 months. As Eamon Gilmore TD pointed out, 'not a single new job will be created in the public sector' as a result of this shameless squandering of public resources. 'The only "benefit" will be a political dividend which the Government parties hope to reap in the towns and districts to which civil servants are being sent' – towns and districts that mostly fall outside NSS designations.

Actually developing the gateway cities of the south and west would require a much more focused approach. In Switzerland, the function of the railway system isn't just to make one or two cities accessible; it's about getting to all cities, and the Swiss have designed an integrated national timetable, the *Taktfahrplan*, to make this possi-ble. For an Ireland tilting more and more towards the east, the prospect of rail-con-necting its five cities by smart timetabling should at least be examined. As the illus-tration shows, it would not be too difficult to serve the twin objectives of catering for journeys between regional cities as well as to and from Dublin. With this kind of timetable, 'developing Cork, Galway, Limerick-Shannon and Waterford as an increas-

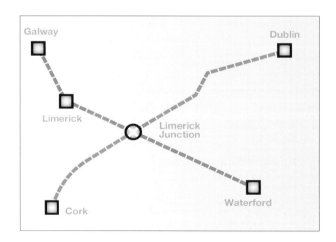

← *Limerick Junction could become the hub for faster rail services connecting all of Ireland's cities*

Concept: trains converge on Limerick Junction at hourly intervals; passengers change trains, if necessary, and continue their journey

ingly interconnected and developed network of co-operating and complementary cities', as the NSS put it, is much more achievable. What's needed is a sea-change in timekeeping. Limerick Junction is the obvious crossing point on such an integrated network, though it would need to be reconfigured to cater for Galway-Waterford trains as well as those running between Cork and Dublin. If double track is needed to cope with all the rail traffic it could easily be provided. Between Galway and Limerick, a 57km section of line would have to be reopened from Athenry to Ennis, which could be done for not much more than €100 million.

———

WHAT WE HAVE IN DUBLIN NOW AND IN OTHER IRISH CITIES IS AN INCREASINGLY European-style core, peppered with apartment buildings and cappuccino bars, surrounded by an expanding American-style edge of suburban housing, business parks, shopping malls and retail warehouses. Dublin's Temple Bar can lay claim to be the most photographed project in Irish architectural history, but, as architecture critic Raymund Ryan has written, it is the M50 with its flyovers, roundabouts and car parks that 'may prove to be a far more significant artefact in the Irish environment, greatly increasing Dublin's urban scale'. Whatever about Temple Bar's fine-grained urban renewal, Ryan said other paradigms may be needed to put some shape on our prosperous little patch of 'the 24-hour global village'. If architects were to make their mark, they would have to 'invest at least as much energy in suburbia and in infrastructure as in single figurative objects'. Writing in the *Irish Architectural Review 2001*, Ryan voiced concern that Architecture (with a capital A) is being left behind by Ireland's unprecedented rate of change.

Inevitably, globalisation has played a role. As Saskia Sassen, one of its leading querists, has pointed out, a city that strives for inward investment must provide the 'state-of-the-art' urban infrastructure demanded by global capital – hence, the impact of flagship projects such as the Guggenheim in Bilbao, which was all about a 'shock-and-awe' rebranding of a tired industrial Basque city. Cities have to go for the 'big fix' to put themselves on the global map, many 'imagineers' maintained. As Ryan wrote, international architects are being parachuted in to design 'signature' buildings as part of a repackaging of urban identity, such as Daniel Libeskind with his '*Close Encounters*' plan for a Centre for the Performing Arts in the Grand Canal Docks, or the commissioning of the world's best-known bridge-builder, Santiago Calatrava, to design two new bridges across the Liffey. According to Ryan, the two squares in Temple Bar and the reorganisation of both Smithfield and O'Connell Street have all been consciously designed to create 'unique destinations in a metropolitan mix of heritage and fashion'. For in the new international weave of money and media, urban design has too often become 'little more than a fancy theming strategy'. Lessons could be drawn from the Temple Bar experience in terms of striking a balance between potentially conflicting uses in the urban core. In a 2004 postgraduate thesis at UCD, titled 'The responsibility of planners for the "Ibiza culture" in city centres',

↑ Graffiti defaces the Irish Film Centre in Dublin's Temple Bar

John Sheehan investigated how planners could help 'decouple' city regeneration projects from drunken and anti-social behaviour, instead of leaving drink-fuelled delinquency to be dealt with under public order laws. 'There is virtually no planning policy relating to the problem and very little consciousness among planners, even in the Department of the Environment, of a need for any such policy', he found. Even if they recognised delinquency as a problem, planners would be 'handicapped by several statutory anomalies between the licensing and planning codes'. According to Sheehan, any policy would also need to address pub size – something that was forgotten in Temple Bar and other urban-regeneration initiatives.

More fundamentally, we as a people have a problem with the public realm – we just don't think of it as ours, something we all share collectively. Thus, when the Cow Parade went on show in July 2003, many of the colourful fibreglass models were vandalised within days. 'One had its wings snapped off, another was decapitated. All had graffiti on them within hours of going on show', Shane Hegarty wrote. 'What is our relationship with art? Are these incidents a result of a deep-rooted distrust of it or simply a by-product of an aggressive drink culture?' He quoted Ciarán Benson, professor of psychology at UCD and former chairman of the Arts Council, as saying that a lack of respect for public spaces was at the root of it. 'There is a primitive, profound ignorance. It's not just about art. We could equally be talking about why it is that people destroy trees.' Dublin City Manager John Fitzgerald agreed. 'As a society we have a problem, there's no doubt, and it extends to the whole realm of public behaviour. We have to sit down and examine our conscience', he told Hegarty. In Fitzgerald's view, the problem was one of high tolerance of low behaviour, from drug-dealing, begging and littering, to the drink culture that now tarnishes St Patrick's Day.

The opening of the Dublin Port Tunnel in 2006 is intended to relieve the Liffey Quays from being pummelled by juggernauts. But what plans are being made for the river banks? Will more cars be allowed to fill up the space vacated by all the trucks, or will the footpaths be widened, cycle lanes provided and more trees planted? And even if there are such plans, who will pay for their implementation? It was fine at the height of the boom to plan the Spire, the remaking of O'Connell Street and

Smithfield, and the restoration of City Hall because there seemed to be an unlimited supply of funds. Other local authorities who availed of the boom to provide themselves with award-winning new headquarters are counting their blessings because they know they couldn't do it today. The truth is that few of them have much discretionary money left for civic-improvement projects. They would have money, of course, if local government was funded by domestic rates, or some sort of local property tax, but the old system was abolished by Fianna Fáil in 1978, and no politician – not even Noel Dempsey – has the guts to propose publicly that we should bring it back, whatever they may say in private.

What's really disheartening, as architect Seán Ó Laoire told the National Sculpture Factory's 'Designing Cities' symposium in Cork in June 2001, is the absence of discourse and leadership on the one hand and, on the other, our ability to speak out of both sides of the mouth at the same time. The greatest failing in this area is the approval of aspirational plans followed by a refusal to implement them. In the words of Ian Lumley: 'It's at the heart of Irish culture to have a whole set of guidelines, policies and regulations to protect the environment, water quality, the landscape, our architectural and archaeological heritage, regional planning and so on, without ever having any intention to comply with them.' Ó Laoire squarely blamed the dynamics of a governmental system suffused by bureaucratic in-fighting and political clientilism for having 'strangled' the adoption of workable solutions.

Any commitment to implement the State's high-minded policy on architecture also seems to have withered on the vine since the death of Rachel MacRory in June 2002 at the tragically early age of 35. The publication of *Action on Architecture* a few months before she died was the culmination of her seven years' work in the heritage policy unit of the Department of Arts, Heritage, Gaeltacht and the Islands. As a memorial to her, the Government might show some interest in this area. For, as Séamus Heaney once reminded architects, every time they design or build a new building they are, 'in a profound metaphorical sense, recreating the world'. The same goes for those who commission new buildings, including the State. But there is no three-dimensional vision of what should be built. The fine words of *Action on Architecture* do not translate into bricks and mortar, or glass and steel, mainly because there are few qualified staff at senior level in most local authorities to insist on higher standards. What talks in the end is money. After all, plans to provide up to 20 new secondary schools are contingent on a failed British type of public-private partnership (PPP) model, in which architecture is very much a secondary consideration. The debacle over the National Aquatic Centre at Abbotstown dramatically highlighted the risks of using such a procurement method. Fast-tracked to open in time for the Special Olympics in June 2003, the €62 million facility had part of its roof ripped off in a storm on New Year's Day 2005. Amid a welter of recrimination over how this relatively new building could have suffered such damage, a High Court judge, Mr Justice Peter Kelly, said it was 'nothing short of astonishing' that a valuable State property had been leased to a company with a share capital of €127 and no fixed assets. He also found it difficult to understand how Dublin Waterworld Ltd, as operators of the Aquatic Centre, could have paid €4.5 million to a subsidiary company for unspecified services at a time when it owed €1 million in rent to the State. Despite this, Minister for Sport John O'Donoghue was still pursuing the development of a 'necklace' of facilities at Abbotstown, including an indoor sports centre and all-weather pitches for Gaelic games, rugby and soccer, to rescue elements of what Minister for Justice Michael McDowell had dismissed as Bertie Ahern's 'Ceausescu-era Olympic project'. The price-tag for the 'first phase' was put at €120 million, and all of the new facilities were to be built on a 500-acre site at the city's edge.

––––––

THE NATIONAL ECONOMIC AND SOCIAL COUNCIL, IN *HOUSING IN IRELAND: Performance and Policy*, published in December 2004, spelled out the need for 'a clear vision of the kind of high-quality, integrated, sustainable neighbourhoods that are worth building'. It likened the magnitude of this task to other great challenges Ireland faced and met over the past half-century – the Lemass-Whitaker 'opening up' of the Irish economy in the 1960s, and the creation of a dynamic 'new economy', through social partnership, from the mid-1980s onwards. According to NESC, misguided 'self-perceptions' are the root of the problem. 'The recasting of policies and approaches in the 1980s challenged the self-perception that the Irish are a creative and convivial people, but not capable of high-grade manufacture of sophisticated objects.' Twenty years on, the challenge is similar: 'Achievement of the new principles of urban development and social integration seem to be blocked, more than anything else, by the self-perception that Ireland is so attached to extensive development that … we cannot make quality, sustainable, socially cohesive cities and towns.' NESC disagreed with this fatalistic view. 'Since the earlier perceptions were confounded by the emergence of a prosperous society and a world centre of engineering and information technology, there is no reason why we cannot prove ourselves wrong again.'

The challenge of logically extending cities and towns isn't made any easier by corruption. The Planning Tribunal's interim report, published in September 2002 by Mr Justice Flood, nailed former Fianna Fáil minister Ray Burke for having received 'corrupt payments' from builders, developers, and at least one radio promoter in the late 1980s. In April 2003 Rachel Kenny, then president of the Irish Planning Institute, said abuses of the planning system would continue to happen unless zoning legislation was changed. Addressing the institute's annual conference in Limerick, she said wrongdoings 'could occur again tomorrow, notwithstanding the introduction of public office and anti-corruption legislation', because the mechanism for rezoning land by a simple majority vote remained the same as it was in the Burke era. In amending development plans that primarily focused on what can and can't be done inside particular zones, some councillors were 'seemingly unperturbed by the threat of public shame or less still the threat of legal consequences for their actions … The primary consideration appears to be "whose turn it is to become a millionaire?", with decisions being made based on individual constituents interests over the common good.'

↑ *A pavilion café in the central open space of Brindley Place, an award-winning mixed-use scheme in the once derided centre of Birmingham*

Such land rezoning was not a 'victimless crime', she said. 'It is the general community that has to pay the bill, whether in direct monetary terms or in the poor quality of development and lack of community that has characterised many of our suburban areas.'

Until this system is changed, all the dubious decision-making of the Burke-Lawlor era will go on. Throughout the chronicle of sprawl, so many politicians were clearly acting with an eye to their own interests, and even as we write, there are reports of jiggery-pokery in a number of local authorities. The whole thing stinks, but only some of it slips out. Rachel Kenny cited two examples of highly questionable decisions – one in Loughrea and the other in Kenmare. In the case of Loughrea, a majority of Galway county councillors voted to rezone one landowner's property for industrial development 'in the full knowledge that the land was earmarked for building the town's long-awaited bypass'. Making way for one constituent to become a millionaire, at public expense, was clearly more important than the advice they received. 'The fact that they eventually backed down, in the face of threats by the National Roads Authority to shelve the bypass project, is little credit to them', she said. In the case of Kenmare, Kerry county councillors decided to rezone nine acres outside the town for development. Two successive applications for housing on the land were then granted by the council, only to be turned down on appeal. As a result, the landowner was entitled to €381,000 in planning compensation, which the council had to fund by cutting back on key public services. It should have been a warning to councillors to heed planning advice. But instead they went on to indulge in a spree of Section 140 motions, changing the development plan for the whole area typically for the benefit of individual voters, or what might be described as client groups. Kenny suggested that it may be time to consider diluting or removing the responsibility of councillors for land rezoning, just as their role in deciding on regional waste management plans had been circumscribed. The institute recommended that all draft development plans providing for the zoning of land should be subject to public inquiry by an independent, external planning inspector from the Department of the Environment or An Bord Pleanála.

But should reform go even further? Politicians in Catalonia effectively collaborated to take themselves out of property development. There, a land use and transport authority buys a swathe of land, works up a master plan, and then sells on chunks of it to developers at a margin that covers the cost of providing community facilities – schools, libraries, parks and swimming pools. Critically, by maintaining control over where things are built, the Catalonian authorities are able to make sure that housing is not only provided, but properly served. New quarters are linked up, so there is opportunity to walk and cycle. Neither Berlin nor Boston, this is Barcelona. In Ireland, however, there's often no money for schools, not to mention swimming pools or parks. New residents tend to crowd in on existing small schools, and narrow roads try to cope with all the extra traffic. The same disjointed approach gives us cul-de-sac after cul-de-sac, with each developer building in isolation without the benefit of an overall street plan. More than 200 years ago, we made every effort to facilitate short distances on foot, whether in planning Georgian Limerick, Waterford or Dublin. Today, we let a 'chicken scratch' street pattern prevail, the inevitable result being tailbacks at every major junction. Taken together, the list of problems for which Ireland's planning system is responsible reads like a schedule of dilapidations – wink-and-nod zoning, windfall gains for the few, master-planning with little more than colour felt pens, no logical extension of urban areas, no finance for shared services, and an inordinately high level of car-dependence.

The political system needs root-and-branch reform. In January 1997, before he became Minister for the Environment, Noel Dempsey floated the idea of replacing multi-seat constituencies with single-seaters for roughly half of the Dáil's membership and a German-style list system to fill the rest. Unlike previous Fianna Fáil attempts to change the system, proportional representation and the single transferable vote would be retained so that each single-seat constituency would be fought like by-elections are now. Former Taoiseach Garret FitzGerald commended Dempsey on his initiative because it would allow TDs to concentrate on their role as legislators instead of spending a 'disproportionate amount of their time and energy nursing their constituencies'. But FitzGerald's former colleagues in Fine Gael and Opposition parties, other than the Greens, saw the proposal as 'Fianna Fáil kite-flying', and there was no serious debate. Undeterred, Dempsey returned to the fray in July 1999 with a revised proposal which would see the Dáil reduced from 166 members to no more than 120 – a figure that would still meet the constitutional requirement of at least one TD for every 30,000 people. As Kevin Rafter noted, a study by Prof Michael Laver of TCD found that such a system, giving list seats to parties winning above 2% of the first-preference vote, 'would produce a parliament with a membership composition almost identical to that of the present Dáil'. There would be significant salary increases for the reduced number of TDs, in the hope that this – as well as being freed from the tyranny of running errands for constituents – might attract better people to run for the Dáil.

In August 2001 Dempsey was congratulated again by Garret FitzGerald for another 'courageous' and 'refreshing' speech in which he had excoriated clientilism, with specific reference to the failure to adopt the Buchanan report on regional development in the late 1960s. The Fianna Fáil minister had even queried whether politics in Ireland could survive if politicians continued to be dominated by the parish pump at the expense of the national interest, saying it was no wonder that political life and the standing of politicians here were at such a low ebb. However, as FitzGerald noted, Dempsey 'ruefully recognises that, by using such a word as "vision", he is taking his life in his hands. You're always safer in this country not talking about the vision thing, [which] leads to people thinking that you're losing the run of yourself.' But without a wider vision, politicians become 'so immersed in local delivery and local services' that eventually they're no good, not even to their own communities. FitzGerald felt Dempsey's broadside against clientilism was so passionately and cogently argued that it 'demands ... a reaction from the leadership not just of his own party, but also of all the other political parties represented in Dáil Éireann'. There was no response, of course. The folks in Leinster House seem to be immune from even scenting that it reeks of systemic decay as well as moral and intellectual bankruptcy.

Dempsey's proposal for directly elected mayors with real power also died a shameful death. Although his successor, Martin Cullen, managed to get through legislation to abolish the dual mandate, the idea of having powerful mayors was dropped – precisely because they would be powerful; the last thing the Government, or most TDs on all sides, wanted was to have to compete with high-profile Ken Livingstone types. Yet if they are to be successful, cities need a share of political power. Importantly in the case of Barcelona, the impetus for its spectacular regeneration was politically driven by its Socialist former mayor, the inspirational Pasqual Maragall, who has since become President of Catalonia. 'The trick in Barcelona was quality first and quantity second', he once said. 'A commitment to develop networks of new plazas, parks and buildings was the cause of our success.' There is no equivalent of Maragall in Ireland, no-one with political power who might articulate a vision for the future of any of our cities. How else can one account for the Government's outrageous decision to overlook Cork, the State's second largest city, in its decentralisation programme?

*← Parc Bercy in Paris: inner-
city areas need places like
this in which people can
relax*

Paul Keogh

One of Noel Dempsey's arguments has been that electoral reform would increase the quality of political decision-making. Yet, ironically, it was the Meath deputy himself who made the greatest wrong call of the last decade by recommending the motorway programme, subsequently approved by Bertie Ahern, Mary Harney, Charlie McCreevy, Mary O'Rourke and John O'Donoghue. But making the right call depends on the quality of the research you carry out. And in that context, the failure to lead change since signing the Kyoto Protocol on Climate Change in 1997 is off the scale. Work done by the ESRI that year showed transport emissions had the potential to gallop out of control. Before McCreevy was dispatched to Brussels, the authors asked the Department of Finance if it had estimated the consequences for Kyoto compliance of pursuing a motorway programme. Furnished under the EU's Freedom of Information Directive, this was the reply: 'The Department has no records dealing with ... the impact of road-building on the observance of the Kyoto Protocol.' Charlie ('when I have it, I spend it') McCreevy just didn't want to know.

↑ *The Ateneu Fort Pienc civic centre in one of Barcelona's new development areas*
↓ *Barcelona's success is attributed to the way it has developed a network of new public spaces, such as this one in the old city*

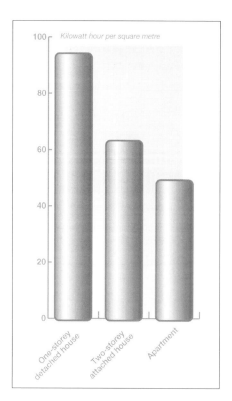

100 ┌ *Kilowatt hour per square metre*

80

60

40

20

0

One-storey detached house

Two-storey attached house

Apartment

↑ *The amount of energy needed to heat a 120m² home depends on the type of housing*

[source: Norwegian Ministry of Oil and Energy – see Journal of European Planning Studies, *9, 4, 2001]*

But then, in September 2004, the Government took the easy option: not alone did it ditch proposals for a carbon tax, it didn't bother to put anything in place that might help to reduce carbon emissions from transport over the longer term. As Pat Finnegan of GRIAN said, this was a 'shameful and cowardly' sell-out on the most serious environmental threat facing humanity.

Ireland's education system must bear some responsibility for the apparent disregard for the environment. The main initiative to boost eco-awareness among students is run by a voluntary body. Green Schools, a programme managed by An Taisce in co-operation with local authorities, attracted 1,811 primary and secondary schools in 2005 – nearly half of the total. The idea is that students examine their own environmental performance on issues from litter to energy, and devise solutions to minimise these impacts. Participating schools tend to reduce their waste going to landfill by half, and achieve high levels of energy conservation. Surely this work should also find expression in the primary school curriculum? From what we remember, 'nature class' was something that largely concerned itself with tadpoles. The teacher put a bunch of them in a wide jar. Their growth into frogs was observed and, well, that was about it. Nature class could be broadened considerably to encompass eco-awareness as well as a rudimentary knowledge of the built environment. It could illustrate how examples of reckless human behaviour – like illicit dumping of hazardous waste – can kill small creatures like tadpoles. There might be case studies outlining what happened in places where profligate water use turned into a water shortage. Students might be shown examples of areas which became so overwhelmed by littering or graffiti that people just couldn't put up with it anymore and stamped out the problem by dint of collective effort. Ireland's lackadaisical approach to land use and transport, and its very real consequences for almost everyone, might also be outlined. Even if we are slow to admit the facts to ourselves, we have a duty to put them before the next generation. The further away we live from one other, and from the facilities we use, the greater the burden on the environment. The more outer wall each home has, the more it costs to heat, and so on. All of these issues, and more, need to be spelled out.

'ALL THINGS ARE CONNECTED', CHIEF SEATTLE OF THE SUQUAMISH TRIBE IN WASHINGTON State is reputed to have told its first governor in 1854, in response to an offer from the US government to purchase their lands. 'Whatever befalls the earth befalls the sons of the earth. The white man, too, shall pass – perhaps sooner than other tribes. Continue to contaminate your bed and you will one day suffocate in your own waste. When the buffalo are all slaughtered, the wild horses tamed, the secret corners of the forest heavy with the scent of many men, and the view of ripe hills blotted by talking wires, where is the thicket? Gone. Where is the eagle? Gone. And what is it to say goodbye to the swift pony and the hunt? It is the end of living and the beginning of survival.' Whether Chief Seattle actually delivered these lines is neither here nor there; what's important is the message. Change a few words and you have Ireland 150 years later.

Yet who will shout stop? Who in the black hole that is our political system will admit that what's going on in this country is profoundly unsustainable? Calls for sensible policy-making go unheeded month after month. Dr Ed Walsh's effort to breathe real life into the National Spatial Strategy has been treated with little more than contempt by Dáil Éireann. The case to consolidate our cities, cogently made by Colm McCarthy and others, has been completely ignored, at least since 1997. Diarmuid Ó Gráda's work on the financial consequences of urban-generated rural housing is left unread on the shelf. All we have is the occasional reminder from commentators that there are fundamental conflicts involved. What Eoghan Harris wrote in August 2002 is just one example: 'For every single farmer who wants to sell a site for a holiday home, and liquidate a historic landscape, there are tens of thousands of city workers who want to hold that heritage for their children, and their children's children.' But with farm incomes falling further behind average earnings, selling sites makes up the difference. In effect, one-off housing is the flipside of not rewarding farmers properly for protecting the landscape. As in so many areas, joined-up thinking at government level is needed to find a solution. All too often, we allow 'the culture of the time' to be raised as a defence for blatant failures. As James Wrynn suggested in the *Irish Times*: 'When a future enlightened commission examines the desolation of our physical environment ... will those responsible say, "That's the way things were done then"?' In this book, we've charted not simply where things are going wrong, but also how and why, so those in power can no longer plead ignorance. If they choose to stick with the current programme, the destruction of Ireland will surely be wilful.

———

References

SOURCES

■ 1 – INTRODUCTION

Banister, David; Berechman, Joseph, *Transport Investment and Economic Development* (University College London Press, 2000)

De Rossa, Proinsias, letter to the *Irish Times*, 15th July 2004

Goodbody Economic Consultants, *Transport Demand*, November 2000

Hennessy, Mark, 'Taoiseach indicates incinerator route must be taken', *Irish Times*, 21st January 2005

Holland, Kitty, 'New president of An Taisce wants it to lose its "elitist" image', *Irish Times*, 7th July 2004

Holmquist, Kate, 'Go, go, go', *Irish Times*, 30th April 2005

Leyden, Kevin, 'Urban sprawl not the social way', *Irish Times*, 8th May 2001

Lynas, Mark, 'The Concrete Isle', *Guardian*, 4th December 2004

McDonough, Terence, 'Some basic economic principles in the roads debate', Campaign for Sensible Transport website, September 2001

O'Leary, Jim, *Sunday Times*, 8th July 2001

O'Toole, Fintan, 'Bulldozing history and landscape', *Irish Times*, 16th March 2004

Putnam, Robert, *Bowling Alone: The Collapse and Revival of American Community* (Simon & Schuster, New York, 2000).

Staunton, Denis, 'EU censures Ireland over illegal dumping', *Irish Times*, 27th April 2005

■ 2 – SPRAWL

McDonald, Frank, 'Turning town plans into profit', *Irish Times*, 28th April 2003

—— 'Growth in all the wrong places', *Irish Times*, 2nd May 2003

—— 'The big picture with room for local colour', interview with Martin Cullen, *Irish Times*, 6th May 2003

O'Brien, Tim, '29 Laois towns set for expansion', *Irish Times*, 5th February 2005

Reid, Liam, 'Council relaxes rules for new Wicklow homes', *Irish Times*, 11th August 2004
—— 'Wicklow land rezoning was based on wrong information', *Irish Times*, 17th August 2004
Sheridan, Kathy, 'Getting the balance right', *Irish Times*, 26th April 2003
—— 'New life in an old town', *Irish Times*, 28th April 2003
—— 'Stretching the new commuter belt to fit', *Irish Times*, 29th April 2003
—— 'All zoned out with no place to go', *Irish Times*, 2nd May 2003
—— 'A slice of lakeside life', *Irish Times*, 5th May 2003
—— 'Making the great escape', *Irish Times*, 6th May 2003
—— 'Bigger, better, cheaper and friendlier', *Irish Times*, 7th May 2003
—— 'Commuting Life: Carlow to Dublin', *Irish Times*, 7th May 2003

■ 3 – BALANCED DEVELOPMENT

Beesley, Arthur, 'Parlon raises fears for future of landmark buildings', *Irish Times*, 6th December 2003
—— 'Decentralisation about as voluntary as the press gang', *Irish Times*, 17th April 2004
—— 'Low level of interest shown in public jobs transfers', 9th July 2004
Brennock, Mark, 'Tax break strategy could mean seven more hospitals', *Irish Times*, 7th March 2003
—— '"Trust us. We're right" is not good enough', *Irish Times* 1st May 2004
—— 'Unpopular policies blamed for drop in FF support', *Irish Times*, 14th June 2004
—— 'Decentralisation U-turn a response to arrogant image', *Irish Times*, 25th November 2004
Buchanan & Partners, *Regional Studies in Ireland*, An Foras Forbartha, 1968
Dooley, Chris, 'State bodies concerned over plans for decentralisation', *Irish Times*, 17th July 2004
FitzGerald, Garret, 'Most flagrant example of stroke politics', *Irish Times*, 10th March 2003
Fitzgerald Report, *Outline of the Future Hospital System*, Stationery Office, 1968
Hennessy, Mark, 'Requests under FoI are halved under new limits', *Irish Times*, 8th October 2003
—— 'Behind closed doors', *Irish Times*, 1st March 2003
—— 'Government rules out hearing on decentralisation', *Irish Times*, 27th May 2004
—— 'Civil Service boycott to be addressed', *Irish Times*, 10th July 2004
Irish Times, 'Information closure', editorial, 14th October 2003
—— 'Planning for decentralisation', editorial, 28th May 2004
McDonald, Frank, 'Ideas and cost of a "Stadium for the New Century" have grown' (Abbotstown chronology), *Irish Times*, 21st April 2001
—— 'The big picture with room for local colour', interview with Martin Cullen, 6th May 2003
Mansergh, Martin, 'Rising to the challenge of decentralisation', *Irish Times*, 28th February 2004
—— 'Prosperity of regions is key to decentralisation debate', *Irish Times*, 10th July 2004
Western Development Commission, *The State the West: Recent Trends and Future Prospects*, July 2001

■ 4 – RURAL HOUSING

An Foras Forbartha, *Urban Generated Housing in Rural Areas*, June 1976

Coleman, Shane, 'One-off housing is a political joke', *Sunday Tribune*, 7th March 2003

Cullen, Paul, 'An Taisce accuses owners of sites of fraud', *Irish Times*, 11th November 2002

Deegan, Rory, 'Protester wants end to ban on "outsiders" building homes', *Irish Times*, 2nd July 2002

Irish Letter, 'Goodbye to the Countryside', March 2004

Irish Rural Dwellers Association, *Positive Planning for Rural Houses*, 2004

Irish Times, 'Open season for bungalow blitz', editorial, 5th March 2004

Lucey, Anne, 'Survey shows tourist concerns on transport and prices', *Irish Times*, 31st October 2003

MacCabe, Fergal, 'How we wrecked rural Ireland', *Pleanáil*, August 2001

Mansergh, Martin, 'What ordinary people want still counts for something', *Irish Times*, 13th March 2004

McDonald, Frank, 'Rural housing advocate advises tourists to go to Scotland', *Irish Times*, 13th March 2004

—— 'Planners paint a bleak picture', *Irish Times*, 24th April 2004

Myers, Kevin, 'An Irishman's Diary', *Irish Times*, 9th March 2004

Nix, James, 'Urban Sprawl, One-Off Housing and Planning Policy: More to do, but how?', *Irish Student Law Review*, vol. 10 (Dublin 2002)

—— 'Group may challenge legality of local rules on planning', *Irish Times*, 4th September 2003

—— 'Downside of one-off rural housing', *Irish Times*, 17th September 2003

O'Toole, Fintan, 'A classic Fianna Fáil scheme', *Irish Times*, 18th May 2004

Slattery, Laura, 'Bungalow bliss is easily gained', *Irish Times*, 12th March 2004

Smith, Michael, 'One-off housing is bad for society and the environment', *Irish Times*, 6th June 2002

Smyth, Jamie, 'An Post plans outdoor letter boxes to cut delivery costs', *Irish Times*, 7th January 2003

Waters, John, 'Snobbery over rural housing', *Irish Times*, 8th March 2004

Western People, 'Easing rules for one-off houses', 14th January 2004

Wexford Echo, 'Can't eat scenery? Well, you sure can't eat bungalows!', 7th November 2003

www.castlebar.ie, 'No justification for preventing people building one-off houses', 12th October 2003

■ 5 – HERITAGE

Boland, Rosita, 'No homes to go to', *Irish Times*, 21st February 2004

Buckley, Ciarán, 'Shopping Centre Developer Owns Motorway Lands', *Sunday Business Post*, 27th February 2005

Carolan, Mary, 'Judgment in Desmond's planning case reserved', *Irish Times*, 22nd July 2004

Crosbie, Judith, 'Kildare road prompts EC environment warning', *Irish Times*, 15th February 2001

Cullen, Paul, 'Angered by a culture of greed and ineptitude', *Irish Times*, 11th November 2003

Deegan, Rory, 'Aer Rianta knew about toxic waste at airport', *Irish Times*, 24th October 2003

—— 'West Clare golf club offsets global warming', *Irish Times*, 5th December 2003

—— 'Time to shout stop?', *Irish Times*, 13th December 2003

—— 'Aer Rianta fined for pollution', *Irish Times*, 27th March 2004

—— '€1,500 fine for destruction of habitat', *Irish Times*, 4th June 2004

Hogan, Dick, 'Golfers and public at loggerheads in Kinsale', *Irish Times*, 4th September 2001

Irish Times, 'Enforcing the planning laws', editorial, 25th April 2003

—— 'A National Trust', editorial, 9th September 2003

Judge, Theresa, 'Development fears on Leitrim's small coastline', *Irish Times*, 6th October 2000

Keena, Colm, 'Up to €380 million in lost taxes spent on 'holiday' homes', *Irish Times*, 25th August 2003

Kelly, Olivia, 'Campaign to protect round tower', *Irish Times*, 21st June 2004

Lee, John, 'Tara Tycoons', *Ireland on Sunday*, 13th March 2005

Letter from academics re. Tara, *Irish Times*, 5th April 2004

McDonald, Frank, 'The golf course of Irish history', *Irish Times*, 30th August 2000

—— 'Tide of development swamping coast', *Irish Times*, 30th October 2001

—— 'Mansfield expects council to lose court challenge', *Irish Times*, 4th November 2002

—— 'Ruling could upset plans of developers', *Irish Times*, 25th February 2003

—— 'House at Yeats tower refused', *Irish Times*, 25th March 2003

—— 'National trust to be set up to protect great Irish houses', *Irish Times*, 8th September 2003

—— 'Council members to visit Killiney gallery', *Irish Times*, 27th October 2003

—— 'Withdrawal of appeal against hotel in Trim to be challenged', *Irish Times*, 7th November 2003

—— 'Planning laws no obstacle for man in a hurry to get things built', *Irish Times*, 6th January 2004

—— 'Cullen rejects advice on nine developments', *Irish Times*, 7th January 2004

—— 'Tara alternative outlined in 2000 study', *Irish Times*, 6th December 2004

—— 'Minister to press ahead with Tara route for motorway', *Irish Times*, 31st March 2005

Myers, Kevin, 'An Irishman's Diary', *Irish Times*, 5th April 1996

O'Brien, Tim, 'Conservationists take legal route to halt South Eastern Motorway', *Irish Times*, 21st September 2002

—— 'Lethal pollution linked to Offaly sawmill', *Irish Times*, 16th January 2003

—— 'Crucial week for castle site as dig end on road route', *Irish Times*, 25th January 2003

—— 'Residents urged to stop using contaminated water in wells', *Irish Times*, 24th February 2003

—— 'No action taken months after retention permission refused', *Irish Times*, 21st November 2003

—— 'Offaly sawmills again warned by EPA for breach of pollution control licence', *Irish Times*, 12th March 2004

—— 'Will law be a licence to bypass our heritage?', *Irish Times*, 19th June 2004

O'Faoláin, Nuala 'No Moher visitor centres', *Irish Times*, 2nd February 2002

O'Rourke, Daire, 'Archaeology offers complicated and tantalising route', *Irish Times*, 4th September 2004

O'Toole, Fintan, 'Bulldozing history and landscape', *Irish Times*, 16th March 2004

O'Toole, Shane, 'Back from the Dead', *Sunday Times*, 13th June 2004

Reid, Liam, 'Council proposes to rezone controvesial Citywest site', *Irish Times*, 25th August 2004

RTÉ Radio 1, *Today with Leo Enright*, April 2003

—— *News at One*, 7th January 2004

RTÉ TV, 'The Planning Game', *Prime Time* special, 19th April 2004

Salafia, Vincent, 'An act designed to facilitate roads and real estate', *Irish Times*, 17th August 2004

Siggins, Lorna, 'Yeats scholars object to house plan', *Irish Times*, 2nd December 2002

Tyrrell, Fiona, 'New Academy for Heritage aims to protect historical environment', *Irish Times*, 23rd April 2004

Viney, Michael, 'Republic lags behind a greener North', *Irish Times*, 28th September 2002

—— 'Pollardstown snail now miner's canary', *Irish Times*, 26th February 2005

■ 6 – KYOTO AND WASTE

Ahlstrom, Dick, 'UN warns insurers to pay attention to the weather', *Irish Times*, 9th October 2002

Brown, Paul, 'CO_2 levels highest for 55m years', *Irish Times*, 14th July 2004

Browne, Sir John, 'Small steps to limit climate change', *Financial Times*, 30th June 2004; *Foreign Affairs*, July-August 2004

Buckley, Donal, 'Shedding light on emission debate', *Irish Times*, 19th March 2004

Coleman, Shane, 'State facing multi-billion euro fine, over emissions', *Sunday Tribune*, 14th March 2004

Economic and Social Research Institute (ESRI), *The Cost to Ireland of Greenhouse Gas Abatement*, 1997

Economist, 'Wind farms disfigure the countryside and threaten to cost £1 billion a year. Apart from that, they're great', 29th July 2004

Environmental Resources Management, *Irish Times*, 19th May 1998

European Environment Agency, *Greenhouse gas emission trends and projections in Europe 2003*, August 2004

Fitzgerald, Kyran, 'Agency turns up the heat', *Irish Examiner*, 26th July 2003

Fortune magazine, 'Pentagon says global warming is a critical national security issue', 26th January 2004

Gormley, John, 'Incineration is no answer to waste management', *Irish Times*, 9th June 2000

Hogan, Treacy, 'Tonnes of illegal India-bound waste shipped back to Ireland', *Irish Independent*, 10th February 2004

Fitzgerald, Kyran, 'Agency turns up the heat' (interview with EPA director-general Mary Kelly), *Irish Examiner*, 26th July 2003

King, Sir David, *Science*, January 2004

MacConnell, Seán, 'Bumper grain harvest in danger', *Irish Times*, 20th August 2004

McDonald, Frank, 'Global warming may bankrupt world, says insurance expert', *Irish Times*, 24th November 2000
—— 'Ireland at risk of "dirty man" tag', *Irish Times*, 21st August 2001
—— 'Ireland "facing most severe test of its resolve"', *Irish Times*, 5th July 2002
—— 'Incineration part of waste control, says Cullen', *Irish Times*, 26th July 2002
—— 'Waste crisis is worse than had been thought', *Irish Times*, 12th August 2002
—— 'Cleaning up our act', *Irish Times*, 7th December 2002
—— 'Carbon tax to meet Kyoto to mean dearer fuel', *Irish Times*, 10th January 2003
—— 'ESB's €200m will not cut gas emission', *Irish Times*, 10th April 2003
—— 'Devastation vindicates rejection of gas terminal', *Irish Times*, 23rd September 2003
—— 'An Taisce appeals against new quarry', *Irish Times*, 14th April 2004
—— 'Toxic incinerator plan generates controversy', *Irish Times*, 13th October 2003
Molony, Julia, 'Colour of money ain't Green', *Sunday Independent*, 30th May 2004
Mulligan, John, 'Deep sea prospects in Rockall are not rocking the oil world, *Sunday Tribune*, 21st August 2005
O'Brien, Tim, 'What a load of rubbish', *Irish Times*, 11th March 2003
O'Sullivan, Kevin, 'Forestry holds the key to tackling global warming', *Irish Times*, 19th June 2000
O'Toole, Fintan, 'Let's get the facts straight Mr Cullen', *Irish Times*, 14th January 2003
—— 'Supine State bows to Shell', *Irish Times*, 5th July 2005
Pocock, Iva, 'The sky high cost of flying', *Irish Times*, 4th April 2004
Reid, Liam, 'Cabinet is split over plans to bring in carbon tax', *Irish Times*, 25th July 2003
—— 'A dirty business', *Irish Times*, 27th March 2004.
—— 'Electricity prices may rise 6% due to rules on emissions', *Irish Times*, 17th April 2004
Siggins, Lorna, 'Fahey denies acting for Shell subsidiary on developing gas field', *Irish Times*, 6th May 2003
—— 'Shell link to "independent" consultants for gas pipeline', *Irish Times*, 28th May 2005
—— 'Memos show Shell talked of suing State', *Irish Times*, 5th July 2005
Townsend, Mark; Harris, Paul, 'Now the Pentagon tells Bush: climate change will destroy us', *Observer*, 22nd February 2004
Weston, Charlie, 'We are burning money when we use peat for electricity', *Irish Independent*, 11th August 2005

■ 7 – TRANSPORT

Ashmore, Chris, 'Train journey times getting slower', *Sunday Tribune*, 6th October 2002
Atkins McCarthy Consulting, 'Transport Corridors in Europe' (2000), available at www.irishspatialstrategy.ie
Beesley, Arthur, 'Government to push ahead with CIÉ break-up', *Irish Times*, 10th January 2003
Brennock, Mark, 'No evidence uncovered to tarnish Brennan', *Irish Times*, 30th November 2002
Canniffe, Mary, 'Iarnród Éireann plan may transform deficit into a surplus', *Irish Times*, 20th October 2001
Carey, Brian, 'Better value, but for whom?', *Sunday Tribune*, 25th November 2001

—— 'Shannon: alone it may stand', *Sunday Tribune*, 8th September 2002

Coleman, Shane, 'Report gives go-ahead for new pier at Dublin Airport', *Sunday Tribune*, 27th January 2002

—— 'It's not rocket science – so why is the metro so costly?', *Sunday Tribune*, 7th September 2003

—— 'State pays €557 for every Knock-Dublin passenger', *Sunday Tribune*, 18th April 2004

—— 'For government and the trade unions, breaking up is the hardest thing to do', *Sunday Tribune*, 27th March 2005

Coleman, Shane; Nix, James, 'Dublin's first plan for an underground', *Sunday Tribune*, 28th November 2003

Connolly, Niamh, 'Aer Rianta axes controversial Dublin airport Pier D plan', *Sunday Business Post*, 14th April 2002

—— 'Creation of new transport authority could cost taxpayers €13.6 million', *Sunday Business Post*, 6th June 2004

Corcoran, Jody, *Sunday Independent*, 24th November 2002

DKM Economic Consultants, *Taxation and Demand Management in the Transport Sector*, December 1999

FitzGerald, Garret; Nix, James, 'Exclusively overground rail link to Dublin Airport is way off track', *Irish Times*, 27th August 2002

Fitzpatrick, Martin, 'The Luas: a puffing silly', *Sunday Indepentent*, 11th August 2002

Hennessy, Mark, 'New vision for an embattled Cabinet', *Irish Times*, 2nd November 2005

Hennessy, Mark; McDonald, Frank, 'Ahern says €34bn transport plan will meet its targets', *Irish Times*, 2nd November 2005

Horwath Bastow Charleton, *Ireland and Northern Ireland Hotel Industry Survey*, June 2004

Irish Daily Star, 'Bertie's Con Job', front-page headline, 2nd November 2005

Irish Hotels Federation, 'New air agreement to increase US visitors by over 1 million', IHF Press Office, 29th February 2004

Irish Times, 'Wish-list on transport', editorial, 2nd November 2005

Kerrigan, Gene, 'Head of steam on a service badly off track', *Sunday Independent*, 5th January 2003

Mangan et al, *Final Report of the Task Force on Transport Logistics in connection with Ports* (Dept of the Marine and Natural Resources, February 2002)

McDonald, Frank, 'Scaling down of road projects advised', *Irish Times*, 14th May 2002

—— 'Blueprint for a consolidated city', *Irish Times*, 2nd November 2005

—— 'St Stephen's Green to be a key transport hub', *Irish Times*, 2nd November 2005

National Roads Authority, *National Road Needs Study* (Dublin, 1998)

Nix, James, 'When it comes to developing a truly national motorway programme, less is more', *Irish Times*, 27th December 2002

—— 'All change here for a one-change rail plan', *Irish Times*, 28th February 2003

—— 'Tunnel needs extra height', *Irish Times*, 2nd April 2003

—— 'High-tech charging systems are needed', *Irish Times*, 2nd July 2003

—— 'Use Shannon for 5 million passengers', *Irish Times*, 7th October 2003

—— 'A better way to pay for transport links', *Irish Times*, 8th October 2003

—— 'All roads lead to Dublin, unfortunately', *Irish Times*, 15th October 2003

—— 'If we really want to ease congestion, let's tax company parking spaces', *Irish Times*, 2nd February 2004

—— 'Sick of jams? Take the bus', *Irish Times*, 2nd February 2004

O'Brien, Tim, 'CIÉ abolished, Dublin Bus monopoly to end', *Irish Times*, 8th November 2002

O'Connor, Alison, 'Back on rails: Brennan still pressing for airport metro', *Irish Independent*, 3rd August 2004

O'Toole, Fintan, 'Transport of delight, in part', *Irish Times*, 1st July 2003

Raymond Burke Consulting et al, *High Level Review of the State Commercial Ports operating under the Harbours Acts 1996 and 2000* (Dept of Communications, Marine and Natural Resources, April 2003)

Ross, Shane, 'Brennan set to slay dinosaurs', Sunday Independent, 1st December 2002

Smyth, Jamie, 'Esat BT to pay CIÉ €2m to end network fee row', *Irish Times*, 30th July 2004

Sustainable Energy Ireland, *Energy in Ireland 1990-2002* (2004)

Williams, Eoghan, 'Fianna Fáil TDs angry at rush on Aer Rianta Bill, *Sunday Independent*, 27th June 2004

■ 8 – CONCLUSION

Benfield, F Kaid; Terris, Jutka; Vorsanger, Nancy, *Solving Sprawl: Models of Smart Growth in Communities Across America* (Natural Resources Defence Council, 2001)

Engwicht, David, *Street Reclaiming: Creating Livable Streets and Vibrant Communities* (New Society Publishing, 1999)

FitzGerald, 'Garret, Electoral reform could ease local pressures on TDs', *Irish Times*, 18th January 1997

—— 'Dempsey's courageous stance challenges all parties', *Irish Times*, 1st September 2001

Guckian, Brian, 'National Transportation Corridors: the NEXT Programme and the NTC'', delivered at the symposium 'Transport in Ireland – The Emerging Crisis', 12th April 2005

Harris, Eoghan, *Sunday Independent*, 25th August 2002

Hegarty, Shane, 'What do we have against art?', *Irish Times*, 7th October 2003

Irish Times, 'Still waiting for affordable homes', editorial, 3rd September 2004

McDonald, Frank, 'Quality' planning is the only antidote to urban sprawl', *Irish Times*, 13th March 2001

National Economic and Social Council, *Housing in Ireland: Performance and Policy* (Dublin, 2004)

O'Brien, Carl, 'Only 163 "affordable" houses were built last year', *Irish Times*, 3rd September 2004

O'Brien, Tim, 'Adamstown development zone approved', *Irish Times*, 27th September 2003

—— 'Residents oppose plan for social and affordable homes', *Irish Times*, 1st April 2004

—— 'Fingal adds to development land bank', *Irish Times*, 7th April 2004

O'Connor, Fearghal, 'Is Dublin's Land being Hoarded?, *Business and Finance*, 12th August 2004

Rafter, Kevin, 'Dempsey's calls for electoral reform raise instant suspicion from Opposition', *Irish Times*, 6th August 1999

Ryan, Raymund, 'Effecting Architecture Today' in John O'Regan (ed.), *Irish Architectural Review*, 3 (RIAI, Dublin; Gandon Editions, Kinsale, 2001)

Walsh, Edward, 'An Atlantic Technopolis needed to counter the drift towards Dublin', *Irish Times*, 6th June 2003

Wrynn, James, 'No one but us to blame for the state of things', *Irish Times*, 9th August 2004

■ FURTHER REFERENCES

2002 Census of Population – Principal Socio-Economic Results (Central Statistics Office, 2003)

An Foras Forbartha, *Urban-generated Housing in Rural Areas* (Dublin, 1976)

Association of Higher Civil and Public Servants, *Public Service Relocation Programme: an opportunity missed and a challenge to meet* (2004)

Bacon, Peter & Associates; MacCabe, Fergal, *The Housing Market: an Economic Review and Assessment* (Dept of the Environment, 1999)

Brady Shipman Martin; Kirk McClure Morton; Fitzpatrick Associates; Colin Buchanan & Partners, *Strategic Planning Guidelines for the Greater Dublin Area* (Dublin, 1999)

Brady Shipman Martin; Kirk McClure Morton, *Strategic Planning Guidelines for the Greater Dublin Area: Review and Update* (Dublin, 2000)

Brueckner, Jan K, *Urban Sprawl: Diagnosis and Remedies* (Institute of Government and Public Affairs, University of Illinois, 1999)

Clinch, Peter; Convery, Frank; Walsh, Brendan, *After the Celtic Tiger* (O'Brien Press, Dublin, 2002)

Cork County Council, *Building a New House in the Countryside: Cork Rural Design Guide* (2004)

Darley, Mary (in association with the DTO, Fitzpatrick Associates and Dublin Corporation) *Strategic Planning Guidelines for the Greater Dublin Area: Review and Update* (Dublin, 2001)

Dept of the Environment, *Sustainable Development: A Strategy for Ireland*, 1997

—— *Residential Density: Guidelines for Panning Authorities* (1999)

—— *Implementation of the National Climate Change Strategy: progress report* (2002)

—— *Making Ireland's Development Sustainable: review, assessment and future action* (2002)

—— *Sustainable Rural Housing: Guidelines for Planning Authorities* (2005)

Dept of the Environment / Dept of Public Enterprise, *New institutional arrangements for land use and transport in the Greater Dublin Area*, consultation paper, 2001

Douthwaite, Richard (ed), *Before the Wells Run Dry: Ireland's Transition to Renewable Energy* (Lilliput Press, Dublin, 2003)

Dublin Chamber of Commerce, *Dublin Port 2000: Gateway to the World* (2000)

Environmental Protection Agency, *Environment in Focus 2002* (2002)

—— *Ireland's Environment 2004* (2004)

European Commission, *Reclaiming city streets for people: Chaos or quality of life?* (2004)

Fianna Fáil, *Our Environment – Our Future* (Dublin, 1997)

—— *Protecting Our Environment: A Blueprint for a Cleaner, Greener Ireland* (2002)

Fianna Fáil / Progressive Democrats, *An Agreed Programme for Government* (2002)

Fitzpatrick & Associates, *Evaluation of Investment in the Road Network* (Dublin, 2002)

Fitzsimons, Jack, *Bungalow Bliss* (Kells Art Studio, 1971 et seq)

Graby, John; Meghen, Kathryn (eds), *The New Housing* (RIAI, Dublin, 2002)

Hughes, Brian, *Population, Migration and Housing Issues: the Strategic Planning Guidelines for the Greater Dublin Area* (Dublin Institute of Technology, 2000)

MacCabe, Fergal; O'Rourke, Bryan; Fleming, Margaret, *Planning Issues Relating to Residential Density in Urban and Suburban Locations* (Dept of the Environment, 1999)

Naess, Peter, 'Urban Planning and Sustainable Development', *European Planning Studies*, vol. 9, no. 4 (2001)

National Children's Office, *Ready, Steady, Play! A National Play Policy* (2004)

National Development Plan 2000-2006 (Stationery Office, 1999)

National Spatial Strategy 2002-2020 (Stationery Office, 2002

Nix, James, 'Time to Re-develop: the Burden of Part V of the Planning and Development Act, 2000', *Irish Student Law Review*, vol. 9 (Dublin, 2001)

Private Property, Report of the All-Party Committee on the Constitution, April 2004

Progressive Democrats, *The Environment: our greatest asset* (Dublin, 1997)

OECD, *Environmental Performance Reviews: Ireland* (2000)

O'Malley, Eoin; Scott, Sue; Sorrell, Steve, *Barriers to Energy Efficiency: evidence from selected sectors* (ESRI, 2003)

Ratcliffe, John S, *Competitive Cities: Five Keys to Success* (Dublin Institute of Technology, 2003)

Roads Act, 1993 (Stationery Office, 1993)

UK Dept for Transport, *Sustainable Distribution: A Strategy*

Williams, Brendan; Shiels, Patrick, *Twenty-First-Century Dublin: the Edge City and Commuterland* (Dublin Institute of Technology, 1998)

—— 'Acceleration into Sprawl: Causes and Potential Policy Responses', *Quarterly Economic Commentary* (ESRI, 2000)

Worldwatch Institute / Earthscan, *Vital Signs: the trends that are shaping our future 2002-2003* (2002)

Index